AUTISM SPECTRUM DISORDERS
from **A** *to* **Z**

ASSESSMENT, DIAGNOSIS...& MORE!

Barbara T. Doyle, M.S.   Emily Doyle Iland, B.A.

AUTISM SPECTRUM DISORDERS from A to Z

All marketing and publishing rights guaranteed to and reserved by

721 W. Abram Street
Arlington, Texas 76013
800-489-0727
817-277-0727
817-277-2270 (fax)
E-mail: info@futurehorizons-autism.com
www.FutureHorizons-autism.com

Printed in the United States of America

Cataloging in Publications Data is available from the Library of Congress.

ISBN   1-932565-07-8

DEDICATION

To Tom, whose presence in our lives has enriched us, inspiring us to help him and all the other "Toms" we can; to our husbands, Edward Kenney and Stephen Iland, for their support and encouragement; to Danny and Lisa Iland, who inspired us to remember the needs of all family members; and to our parents, Patrick and Catherine Doyle, whose lives demonstrated work and caring at their finest.

DISCLAIMER

The material in this book is intended to help parents and professionals work together for the best possible outcomes for individuals with an Autism Spectrum Disorder (ASD). The authors make no claim as to the suitability of any particular practice or idea contained in this book for any specific individual. Diagnosis, treatment, action plans and medications are the domain of medical, health, educational and other professionals who should be consulted in assessing and treating each individual. The authors disclaim any direct, indirect, consequential, special, exemplary or other damages arising from any person following information contained in this book or referred to in this book.

TABLE OF CONTENTS

Chapter Five
Types of Assessments and What They Measure 145

Chapter Six
Differences in Opinion and Diagnosis 235

Chapter Ten
Cause and Cure

INTRODUCTION

About the Authors

Barbara Thompson Doyle, M.S., is a special education professional with 32 years of experience in developmental disability services. A consultant in private practice, she is well known and respected for her practical and positive approaches to addressing the needs of children and adults with disabilities. As an enthusiastic lecturer, teacher and trainer, Ms. Doyle travels extensively to bring her holistic, humane and effective approaches to others. Ms. Doyle is "Aunt Barbara" to Tom Iland, who has an autism spectrum disorder (ASD).

Emily Doyle Iland, B.A., is Barbara's sister and mother to Tom, Lisa and Danny. She has helped herself and her family understand Autism Spectrum Disorder and is paving a path to support her son in educational and social settings. She advocates for professionals, families and children, sharing her knowledge and experiences to support and inspire others. Emily is working on a variety of projects and is the California representative for the University of Minnesota's *Yes I Can Program for Social Inclusion*.

Please visit our website at www.asdatoz.com

Introduction from Emily

Dear Parents and Professionals,

I will never forget the shock of hearing that my child had autism. Although I had the benefit of having the diagnosis suggested by my sister, Barbara, I did not accept it. The biggest obstacle to my understanding was the fact that Tom loved his family, had relationships and was connected to us. I had seen his "reciprocity of emotion!" I truly believed that because he was loving and had feelings, he could not have autism.

I held the common misconception that people with ASD "don't relate" or are not capable of loving. I was also confused, because I thought Tom had to have every single characteristic on the "list" to "qualify." These misconceptions (that I did not know were incorrect) were an obstacle to recognition, understanding and progress.

It still took me a great deal of time before I "believed" and accepted that it was true. As I learned more about the disorder so many things in the past began to make sense. I recognized that our family had made many, many adaptations to accommodate Tom's "differences" without realizing that his differences could be explained in terms of sensory, communication and social deficits and the resulting behavior.

Getting help through the school district was a strain, and I was overwhelmed and intimidated by the special education process. I found that first I had to convince the Individualized Educational Program (IEP) team that Tom needed help in spite of his strong academics, many capabilities and excellent behavior. I was met with great skepticism. I expected the school district personnel to be experts at helping students with needs like Tom's. Instead, I found that the leadership was going to come from me. I had to both figure out what Tom needed and educate others about what should be done. I did not have these answers, but was determined to get them.

And I had to learn fast! When I began to do research, I was amazed by the complex and often contradictory views of the experts in the field. Often, the information I found was written in a style that was hard to read or understand. And I was discouraged that while I found ideas about "what to do," it usually did not include "how to do it." It was a blessing that I could rely on the expertise of my sister Barbara who happened to be an autism consultant for the State of Illinois at the time! Her guidance was crucial.

I hired an advocate to help me plan goals based on Tom's needs and attend IEP (Individualized Education Program) meetings with me. I joined the Santa Clarita Valley Autism Support Group, the Autism Society of Los Angeles, and the Autism Society of America. I went to lectures and seminars, surfed the net and read, read, read. I met other parents and learned from their experiences. I went from knowing very little to being a resource to others in a short time. The educational professionals and district staff on the IEP team progressed along with me broadening their understanding of ASD and Tom's unique needs. Our view of what we as a team could do and provide to help Tom make progress continued to evolve.

Initially, Tom was distressed, to say the least, when my husband and I explained to him that he had an ASD. He worried that he was "broken" and couldn't be fixed. At the same time, he was relieved to find that his problems and difficulties had a name. He became comfortable enough to explain to himself or to us, in a matter of fact way, "Oh well, that's an Autism thing!" Understanding the disorder, and the way it affected him helped him make sense of his experiences and accept himself as a unique and wonderful individual. He is now able to identify with famous personalities, past and present, who have similar disorders, but who have created successful lives for themselves.

Tom has made tremendous progress and we are very proud of him. I am not alone in believing that his successes are due to the supports that we have helped to put in place for him. It was a struggle, but well worth it! We are also feeling optimistic about his life after high school and the future.

I often meet parents who are struggling with the possibility of, or just getting a diagnosis of, autism, Asperger Syndrome, or Pervasive Developmental Disorder (PDD) for their child. They are very anxious to hear the advice of parents who are experienced with the complexities involved. My sister Barbara and I realized that, together, we have a unique perspective and could offer practical guidance for parents and professionals about how to help a child or adult with any ASD (such as Asperger Syndrome, PDD, autism, or related disorders). That is how the idea for this book came about.

We believe there is a need for a book like ours that explains the main issues of ASD in easy-to-understand language. We intentionally made the book as complete and comprehensive as possible so that it could be a valuable resource to be read and referred to as needed, over time. We suggest useful resources and strategies from our combined experiences. We want readers to feel confident that you can find balanced and objective information in these pages and guidance to find still more information.

Our work has been divided into two volumes because of the huge amount of material. This book, Volume One, contains the most essential information to know about Autism Spectrum Disorder. We selected topics in response to the hundreds of questions that I had and sought answers for, the hundreds of questions I have personally been asked about Autism Spectrum Disorders, and the ongoing dialogue between Barbara and the families and staff she has met and worked with for over three decades. This volume includes many ideas about what to do and how to do it, particularly in the process of identification, assessment and diagnosis, understanding and sharing information, strengthening the family and finding support, and actively promoting collaberation between families and professional staff.

There is a striking "thirst for knowledge" when parents and staff feel ready and determined to find out what they need to know to take action and helped a loved one, student or client with ASD. Reading this book could feel like "drinking from a firehose," a bit overwhelming! So, I suggest you "take small sips" and absorb as much as you can, as you need it. You can always "come back for more," especially as you make progress and go through the stages of identification, assessment and diagnosis and then move on to coping and action plans!

Emily Doyle Iland

Introduction from Barbara

Dear Professionals and Parents,

After more than 30 years in the field of working with children and adults with special learning needs, I find myself filled with an urgent need to share information and ideas that apply to both families and professional staff. During my career, a whole generation of people with disabilities was born, got diagnosed and treated, completed their educations, became adults and are trying to live successful lives. I have done things, and watched others do things, that have resulted in wonderful outcomes for people with disabilities, their families and staff. I have made mistakes and seen others do the same, and the results have been less than satisfactory outcomes.

Hundreds of families have allowed me to assist them in the process of negotiating the maze of diagnoses, treatment and educational planning. Over the years, a "core" set of skills has crystallized - skills staff and families need to learn if they're to achieve greater success for the individuals they support. In this book, my sister Emily and I will share what we have learned and hope you will use it with your own creativity, ingenuity and love.

Children and adults with ASD can and should constantly improve in skills, communication and relationships. If they do not, we need to change our approach, rethink our programming and learn more ourselves. Autism and related disorders are not progressive, even if there is regression at the time of onset of symptoms. In other words, the person should not get worse and, in fact, should continuously improve.

The person with ASD may experience smooth periods of learning and growth alternating with more difficult cycles over time. Progress may be uneven, and growth spurts may alternate with periods that seem regressive or stalled. Temporary regression or disturbance may occur at times, such as during adolescence, or when sick or injured. Some people with autism may develop seizure disorders that have a negative effect on their performance and participation until the seizures are treated and controlled. In spite of these very real challenges, families and professionals can hope for and work together toward progress and improvement.

Parents and professionals must take responsibility if improvement is not ongoing. We cannot expect the person with autism to suddenly "wake up" one morning and begin to benefit from approaches that have not worked in the past. To help a person with autism change, WE must change first.

The life of the person with ASD may not be the one you imagined before you knew that the person had special needs. However, the child or adult in your care can have a good life full of work, relationships, health, interests and fun. This book can be used to create a vision for the future and design a lifetime plan to reach those dreams and goals.

Some people wonder if individuals with ASD can be successful. Our reaction is to say, "of course!" The Frostig Center, a non-profit organization in Pasadena, CA, dedicated to learning disabilities, discusses the idea of "life success" as follows:

> *"Success is not easy to define. It means different things to different people. In addition, it may mean something different at different times in a person's life. However, although views of success may differ, there appear to be a number of things that most people include when they think of success. These include good friends, positive family relations, being loved, self-approval, job satisfaction, physical and mental health, financial comfort, spiritual commitment and an overall sense of meaning in one's life. Of course, different individuals may place lesser or greater emphasis on these various components of success."*[1]

"Success" is individual and will not look the same for everyone. Success can be viewed as reaching potential, being as independent as possible and having choices. Success can mean a life that is satisfying, rewarding and productive. When we think about our loved one, student or client with ASD, we want to envision and plan for learning, improvement and progress that will affect these quality of life issues. Even when there are limitations in learning or functioning, teams can focus on quality of life issues and success as safety, security, participation and happiness.

Here is one basic principle to achieve greater success: Parents and professionals need to participate together in training and teaching opportunities. The more time that is spent together learning, talking, listening and thinking, the better it will be for all people with ASD. It is true that sometimes it is uncomfortable to hear and discuss difficult things together, but a better understanding and ability to communicate is most often the result. When we know and understand one another, we can create the most successful programs and services. We can really work together.

Guidelines and suggestions are offered to make parent/professional communication more comfortable and effective. It is true that there have been many "bad" experiences that families had with staff and vice versa. However, the only way to create "good," effective teams is to train together in how to teach, learn and communicate both with the person with autism and with one another. We address this need in our book.

My experiences with thousands of very special people over more than 30 years have taught me to value individual differences and appreciate different kinds of communication, learning and personalities. I feel privileged to have developed skills that allow me to access the unique gifts of so many individuals. The opportunities to work with many special people and the people who love and support them have profoundly improved my life. My wish for you is that your contact with individuals with ASD will profoundly improve your own life as they teach us the value of their uniqueness, courage, dedication, hard work, loyalty, relationships and love.

Barbara Thompson Doyle

Purpose of this Book

This book is intended to help parents and professionals who want to learn about the subject of Autism Spectrum Disorders (ASD). It contains "must know" information, the most essential ideas and concepts, from the starting point of suspecting a problem and getting a diagnosis, to understanding the unique needs of a person with ASD and designing effective supports for the individual. Practical ideas are suggested for each stage of the process.

Parents often feel overwhelmed by the whole idea of autism and ask us, "Where do we start?" School personnel and adult service providers often ask, "What are the core knowledge and essential skills that we should be teaching to our staff and families?" The current and upcoming volumes of this book are designed to answer these questions. We hope that schools, agencies, and adult providers will be able to use information found in these pages to plan training opportunities for parents and staff as well as to design performance evaluations for staff and programs.

Several chapters bring together information about current issues and trends in ASD from respected and reputable sources and present it in a "reader-friendly" style. Some scientific and educational terms are presented and explained, without being too technical, to help readers become aware and perhaps more comfortable with them. Without oversimplifying, the goal is to offer "readable" discussions about the nature of ASD, the diagnostic process, the possible causes, and considerations in education, therapies and treatments.

Some sections contain brief descriptions of the theories and work of some of the most outstanding researchers in the field. There are many conflicting opinions regarding autism spectrum disorders, and for informational purposes, we'll present various ideas. Readers are encouraged to go to the source for indepth analysis of complex issues of interest. Our bibliography lists the many sources used to prepare this book. These and many excellent books are available to help families and school/adult services personnel. Throughout the book, we suggest books and internet sites we've found useful.

Terminology

Terms Used In This Book

We/Us	the authors
Individual	a person of any age with autism spectrum disorder or a related disorder
Very young child	a child age 3 or less
Preschooler	a child age 3-5
Student	a person age 5-21
Adult	a person over age 18
Parent	a parent, legal guardian, or a person in the role of parent
Families	parents, foster parents, brothers, sisters, grandparents, step-parents, extended family members and close friends of the family
Staff/professionals	persons paid to work with an individual in education, adult or community services
AS	Asperger Syndrome or High Functioning Autism
HFA	High Functioning Autism- the features of autism with many areas of competence
ASD	Autism Spectrum Disorder
Cognitive Disability	problems learning as easily or at the same rate as others. Sometimes called mental retardation or mental disablities.

Use of the term "Autism Spectrum Disorder" includes the following diagnostic labels:

Pervasive Developmental Disorders (PDD), Pervasive Developmental Disorder Not Otherwise Specified (PDD-NOS), Autism, Atypical Autism, and Asperger Syndrome (AS).

For gender equality, the pronouns "he" and "she" are used alternately. For simplification, the possessive pronouns "his" or "hers" are used.

Who Is This Book Intended to Help

The outcome or goal for anyone with ASD should be a happy, fulfilling life, with work, money, friends, a great place to live, healthy recreation and the ability to contribute to the world at large. This book is designed to help staff and family achieve this goal for every person with autism or a related disorder, to the greatest degree possible, now and in the future. Adults who think that they themselves may have a disorder within the autism spectrum may also find the information contained in these pages useful.

The content may be helpful to teachers, staff and family members who support individuals of any age who:

- Have a disorder within the autism spectrum.

- Display characteristics and behaviors similar to those described as an Autism Spectrum Disorder, but who have no formal ASD diagnosis.

- Display characteristics and behaviors similar to those described as an Autism Spectrum Disorder, but who have one or more different diagnoses, such as:

  — Attention Deficit Disorder, Attention Deficit Hyperactivity Disorder, Obsessive Compulsive Disorder, Tourettes's Syndrome, Self-Regulatory Disorder, Rett's Syndrome, Childhood Disintegrative Disorder, Fragile-X Syndrome, Nonverbal Learning Disability, Semantic-Pragmatic Disorder, or Hyperlexia.

- Have no current diagnosis, but who display some or all of the characteristics of ASD (See the description of ASD in Chapter One).

Who Should Read This Book?

Adults who think that they themselves may have a disorder within the autism spectrum as well as parents, friends, family members, educators, program staff and professionals who support children and adults with these areas of differences:

- Social interaction differences from others of their age and culture.

- Verbal and non-verbal communication/language/comprehension differences.

- Unusual reactions to sensory input.

- Unusual behavior in response to the world around them.

- Unevenness of learning across skill areas and environments.

- Unusual interests and activities.

- "Strange" or mysterious behavior that is difficult to understand and presents problems to others who know the individual.

In the past, autism or related disorders seemed to touch the lives of very few people. Due to the current increase in diagnosis, ASD now touches the lives of many. Many more people now want information to learn if they themselves, a member of their family or a person in their care, has a disorder within the spectrum. Even when the diagnosis is uncertain or undetermined, ideas in this book may be used to help children and adults who have learning problems that affect social skills, communication and behavior. As you proceed through the book you may begin to recognize people with autism or related disorders that you have known all of your life. You are right; people with ASD have always been here!

CHAPTER 1

UNDERSTANDING AUTISM SPECTRUM DISORDERS

Perhaps you have just received a diagnosis of autism for your child and you need to know much more about it. Maybe you suspect that your child, a family member or even yourself may have an autism spectrum disorder, and you want more information. Does a child in your class or an adult in your care have a diagnosis that you feel does not accurately describe the features and behaviors that you are seeing? How do we describe and make sense of the characteristics that we see?

In this chapter you will learn:

- What the term "Autism Spectrum Disorder" (ASD) means.

- The characteristics of ASD.

- Barriers to recognizing ASD.

- Implications of ASD.

Talking About People

It is difficult to open a book and leap right into facts, figures, and complicated terms. There is one crucial reason to focus on the question of diagnostic terms and to develop a good understanding of the meaning behind a diagnosis. Readers need to be able to define important characteristics within the autism spectrum, acquire a diagnosis that ensures eligibility for services, and then get down to the business of teaching the individual to be more successful in life!

We must be able to understand, recognize, and describe the features we see to cope with and contribute to the process of diagnosis. This includes learning to use concepts and terms that are the "jargon" of development and diagnosis. While the words and abbreviations may appear daunting at first, they may soon be part of your everyday vocabulary.

The Diagnostic Process

The process of getting a diagnosis of ASD is similar to going to a doctor when you are ill. When you feel sick, you tell the doctor what the symptoms are, where it hurts, and how long the symptoms have been going on. The doctor attempts to recognize and identify any known pattern of disease by listening carefully and asking questions to ascertain all the necessary facts.

Medical professionals consult reference books that list the symptoms of various diseases and illnesses, and these medical references help doctors recognize patterns of symptoms that indicate an illness. The standards and guidelines professionals use to identify the characteristics of diseases and disorders are called **diagnostic criteria**.

Diagnostic criteria for a disorder establishes accuracy and consistency among doctors so that:

- Each person with particular symptoms should get the correct diagnosis.

- People with the same symptoms should get the same diagnosis.

- Doctors can ensure that all necessary criteria are met.

• No significant symptom is left unaccounted.

The diagnosis of ASD is not made by describing physical symptoms. Diagnosis involves looking at development, learning, behavior and communication. The diagnostic criteria that apply to ASD are found in the Diagnostic and Statistical Manual of Mental Disorders of the American Psychiatric Association. It is commonly referred to as the DSM-IV, or the revised DSM-IV R.

The DSM-IV includes descriptions and criteria for mental, developmental, and psychiatric illnesses. An autism spectrum disorder is not a mental illness or a psychiatric disorder. They are medical and developmental disorders involving physical and/or chemical aspects of the brain. Disorders on the autism spectrum are included in the DSM-IV because they are brain-related and behaviorally diagnosed.

Some professionals use the International Classification of Disease, a diagnostic manual developed by the World Health Organization, known as the ICD-10. The ICD-10 serves the same purpose as the DSM-IV, but varies in some areas from the DSM-IV. Once a diagnostician clearly understands what is involved, the DSM-IV and ICD-10 provide mental health professionals, neurologists and other medical professionals with guidelines and standards to recognize the symptoms and patterns of a disorder and arrive at an accurate diagnosis.

The criteria used in the ICD and the DSM are agreed upon by teams of experts. Their standards reflect both a specialized level of understanding and the shared beliefs of people experienced in a particular area. The criteria are revised as new science changes understanding of a disorder or when the existing criteria do not seem workable, consistent or satisfactory for any reason. Some differences between criteria used in the DSM and the ICD may reflect the variations in scientific understanding and scientific culture in different parts of the world.

Pervasive Developmental Disorders (PDD): The Umbrella Category

Pervasive Developmental Disorders (PDD) is a diagnostic category described in the DSM-IV and ICD-10. Understanding the meaning of PDD helps in understanding the common elements of the disorders grouped within it. The following statements, which are true for PDD, are also true for autism, Asperger's Syndrome and several other disorders:

- "Pervasive" means that it is a disorder that affects many areas of development.

- "Developmental" means that it is something that happened during early development and not as the result of an accident or injury.

- "Developmental" means that the condition is expected to continue to affect the child's development, be present for his entire lifetime and won't be outgrown or cured.

- "Developmental" means that it is not a mental illness or a psychiatric disorder. It is not an emotional disturbance or a behavior disorder even though emotions and behavior are affected. A developmental disorder is not contagious.

- "Developmental" means that part of the process of diagnosis looks at the rate and patterns of the first few years of the development of the individual, no matter what his age is now.

- "Disorder" means that the areas of learning and development are affected (but not completely non-functional) and that learning CAN occur (and does!).

- "Disorder" applies only to the functions affected by the disorder; other areas of learning and ability may be good, or even exceptional.

ASD and PDD Overlap and are Often Used Interchangeably

To simplify discussion in this and many other books and articles, the terms "Autistic Spectrum Disorder" or "Autism Spectrum Disorder" are often abbreviated as "ASD." The idea of a spectrum of disorders in the PDD category reflects the fact that the features of the disorders are similar and overlap in a significant way. While each disorder is "clinically" considered separate from the other, it is practical to identify the common features in order to assist staff and families.

The term ASD usually includes the following diagnostic categories:

- Pervasive Developmental Disorders (PDD)

- Pervasive Developmental Disorder Not Otherwise Specified (PDD-NOS)

- Autism

- Atypical Autism

- Asperger's Syndrome (AS)

- High Functioning Autism (HFA)

[Note: In the DSM-IV, two other diagnoses are listed in the PDD category. These are Rett's Disorder and Childhood Disintegrative Disorder. These two disorders differ from the others listed above in that they tend to have a more progressive course, with the loss of skills and abilities over time. Although we do not include these two disorders as part of ASD, many of the suggestions and information herein will assist staff and families working with individuals with Rett's Disorder and Childhood Disintegrative Disorder.]

Characteristics of ASD

Definitions of the terms categorized as ASD vary greatly, from what you will find in the dictionary to what you will find in the DSM-IV or ICD-10. The federal definition of autism as described in the United States legal code, "Individuals with Disabilities Education Act," says:

> *"A child is classified as having autism when the child has a developmental disability that significantly affects verbal and nonverbal communication and social interaction, that is generally evident before age three, and that adversely affects educational performance."*
>
> *Code of Federal Regulations 1308/ 1308.15*

The following section elaborates on the federal definition and describes ASD (autism, PDD, PDD-NOS, atypical autism, and Asperger's Syndrome) in simple terms.

Autism Spectrum Disorders:

- Are disorders that may have multiple causes, occur early in life and are expected to last the lifetime of the individual.

- Are syndromes, that is, a collection of characteristics, not just one or two differences from typically developing children.

- Occur in both males and females, although more males are diagnosed with ASD than females.

- Are "severe and pervasive," affecting all or most areas of the person's functioning whether the individual is very intelligent or "high functioning," or if the individual has cognitive impairment (sometimes called mental retardation or mental impairment).

- Are neurobiological, that is, affecting the physical brain and brain chemistry.

- Affect the individual's ability to communicate using speech or language; speech may be delayed or the quality of the communication or verbal skills can be affected.

- Affect the individual's ability to communicate using "unspoken language" such as gestures, facial expression, body language or other non-verbal communication.

- Affect the individual's ability to understand and respond to the verbal and non-verbal communication of others.

- May cause the individual to have difficulty in making and keeping friends and sustaining typical social relationships at any age, despite the fact that she may want to do so.

- May cause the individual to be particularly sensitive or unusual in responding to stimulation through touch, smell, taste, hearing or sight (sensory information).

- May cause the individual to have difficulty making sense of, or "processing" sensory information and keeping themselves under control.

- May result in uneven development of learning and skills, so that people with ASD may be very good at some skills while finding other areas very difficult.

- May cause individuals to develop or learn skills in some areas on their own timeline and not necessarily according to the expected calendar of development or milestones.

- Are increasing in incidence, and occur in all races, and in all cultural, social and economic groups in all parts of the world.

- Are apparent by an early age, with unusual differences first noted from several months old to age 3 (In some cases, parents note differences from shortly after birth. In other cases, parents report quite typical development until 18 months to two years when a change occurred and the child "turned within" or "stopped responding.").

- Can occur in conjunction with any other condition, disorder or disability such as deafness, attention deficit disorder, Down syndrome, cognitive disabilities, blindness, cerebral palsy, epilepsy, etc.

- It is important to remember that if a person has an ASD in conjunction with any other disability, the characteristics of the ASD may be presenting the most problems in learning and relationships.

- Include (or included when the individual was a child) some or all of the following features or characteristics:

  — Unusual, focused interests.

  — "Aloneness," more often playing on her own or passively alongside others, rather than actively engaging with them.

  — Repetitive actions, activity or speech.

  — Echoing language or repeating lines from television shows, commercials, videos, etc.

  — Unusual repetitive movements of the body and/or hands.

  — Unusual reactions to the people and events in their lives.

  — Delay in developing physical skills.

  — Need or desire for sameness in everyday life.

  — Naïve, one-sided or childlike approaches to relationships.

  — Clumsiness or lack of coordination.

  — Intensely focused interests or topics.

  — Motoric (movement) problems, such as problems getting started or problems stopping an action or activity after getting started.

  — Difficulty shifting focus or attention when asked.

  — Problems with transitions from one activity to another or one place to another.

  — Apparent lack of interest in "getting to know" others.

— Difficulty coping with unexpected (or sometimes expected) changes in the usual routine.

— "Pickiness" in eating, not enjoying many different varieties of food.

— Difficulty focusing on things, unless it is an area of intensely focused interests.

— Difficulty adjusting to new people or situations.

— Difficulty making and keeping friends, knowing how to play, what to say and not say, how to join into a group activity, etc.

ASD is NOT:

• A mental illness.

• A behavior disorder.

• An emotional disturbance.

• Caused by parents or as the result of parental behavior, before, during or after pregnancy.

• Able to be "cured" completely (See Chapter Ten on "Cause and Cure").

Range of Effects

While individuals with ASD have certain "core" characteristics in common, there is tremendous diversity among people who are affected. This may cause ASD to "look" very different from one individual to the next. This "uniqueness" may contribute to difficulty in diagnosing ASD or in choosing one clinical label to describe a person. It can lead to misconceptions or false beliefs about who has autism and who does not, based on comparing one person with ASD to another person with ASD.

There are five areas to consider when looking at the range of effects:

• **Cognitive or intelligence**: the individual may have cognitive impairment, normal intelligence or superior intelligence.

- **Severity of the effects of ASD**: the results of the characteristics of ASD may affect the individual in a more or less severe way.

- **Ability to communicate**: the individual may or may not be able to speak, may appear to have very limited communication skills, may communicate in what seems a nearly typical way, may seem to talk too much, or may only use language to get his needs met.

- **Age and Experience**: The age of the individual and the learning experiences that the individual has had.

The combination of the *effects* of intelligence added to the *severity* of the effects of autism, the ability to *communicate* and the *age* of the individual results in each individual with this diagnosis manifesting in a unique way. As a result, each person will need a unique array of supports and services. The range of differences is a factor in the use of the terms "Autistic Spectrum Disorder" or "Autism Spectrum Disorder." The term "sub-types of autism" is used to describe the variation among affected individuals.

Table 1.1
The Range of Effects in Autism Spectrum Disorders

Affected			
❏ Intensely	❏ Moderately	❏ Less Intensely	
Intelligence			
❏ Cognitive Impairment	❏ Average Intelligence	❏ Above Average Intelligence	
Verbal			
❏ Non-Verbal	❏ Moderate Verbal Skills	❏ Very Good Verbal Skills	
Age			
❏ Birth	❏ Youth	❏ Midlife	❏ Old Age
Experience			
❏ Few Opportunities to Learn	❏ Some Valuable Learning Experiences	❏ Intensive Learning Experiences Over Time	

Table 1.1 may help in visualizing the variations within ASD. You may wish to mark an "X" in each of the five areas listed to indicate or describe where the person of interest to you "fits in" along each continuum. Other factors such as personality, family and social environment, physical and medical issues contribute to the "individuality" of people with these disorders. And finally, effective educational supports, or the lack of them, will contribute to the person's progress and the unique identity of each person with ASD.

Common Misconceptions that Hinder Recognition of ASD

Many incorrect ideas about autism and Autism Spectrum Disorders persist and cause confusion. Contrary to myth and popular beliefs, many people who have an Autism Spectrum Disorder CAN:

- Use eye contact.

- Be intelligent and obviously able to learn.

- Relate to others and have relationships with others.

- Be different than other people with ASD that someone has met.

- Care about others.

- Be affectionate with family or others.

- Approach others to start a conversation.

- Improve.

- Have some other disability label already.

- Seem to like being around other people.

- Be friendly.

- Want to have social connections and friends.

- Have really good skills in some areas, such as math, science, or art.

Another common misconception is the belief that a person must have every single feature in every diagnostic category or else they do not have the disorder. This is not true. There is probably no person who has every feature in every category. There will always be at least one or two features that just don't fit the person with ASD. If a particular number of the "required" features are present, the diagnosis can be made. The number of characteristics that must be presrent are specified in the DSM-IV and are described in Chapter Two.

Other people "rule out" the possibility of an ASD because a person with ASD may function very well in many areas. This may be a serious mistake. More and more individuals, of all ages, who function well in many ways, are being diagnosed with ASD today. This is because significant deficits in social skills, communication, behavior and sensory issues are being recognized in spite of the presence of other skills and abilities. Identifying the core features of ASD in a high-functioning person often reveals that these features are substantially problematic to him.

The effects of time may be an obstacle to recognizing and understanding the presence of ASD in an adolescent or an adult. It may be helpful to think of the past and present of a person with ASD like "before" and "after" snapshots. Learning, improved behaviors and coping strategies may help the affected person appear more typical. These changes, over time, may make it more difficult to get an accurate picture of the person's characteristics and development. It is important to see the "masking" effects of learning and improvement that can be an obstacle to identifying the true nature of the disorder. The early development and childhood characteristics of an individual are very important and are essential to describe in diagnosing adolescents and adults who have learned and made progress.

Implications of Autism Spectrum Disorders

As individual and unique as each person with ASD may be, people with a disorder on the autism spectrum have particular things in common. Here are some obvious and some subtle generalizations that are often true for people with ASD:

- Individuals with ASD can and should consistently improve IF appropriate educational, adult and in-home services are provided. The diagnosis of ASD is NOT a prognosis for an unhappy life.

- There is no automatic implication for aggression, property destruction or self-injury in the diagnosis of ASD. These are usually learned behaviors and can be replaced with other learned behavior.

- Although they share common diagnostic characteristics, each person with ASD is a unique individual with unique, multiple needs.

- To improve the behavior and learning of individuals with ASD, we need to change both our approach to the individual, and the world around them.

- Even if the individual has a high level of intelligence, the effect of ASD is severe because it affects all aspects of life, especially relationships.

- People with ASD can care about others, although they may not be able to express that caring in a typical way.

The behavior and functioning of the individual and the characteristics of ASD should change over time for the better. This positive change may even happen if a person has not had an "official" diagnosis and support, but has been mentored by caring parents or intuitive teachers. An individual with ASD can learn to interact, relate to others, care about others, be affectionate, and improve. The goal is to help the person function to their greatest potential.

Treatments and supports will need to be modified over time as the individual progresses. Individuals with ASD may be unique and successful, even if they will never be "typical." The disorder is always present. There is no treatment or service currently known to be a true cure for ASD.

Usual Learning Strengths and Difficulties of Individuals with ASD

Each individual with ASD is unique. However, there are often patterns in behavior and learning, both in areas of strengths and difficulty. Here are some areas in which people with ASD often have strong ability to learn:

- **Spatial awareness** (where things and people are, where items are kept, how things fit together) and spatial memory (maps, drawings).

- **Rote memory** (memory for things that they have seen or experienced the same way every time like videos, routines parents or staff have created, ways of doing something that has been taught the same way every time, or facts).

- **Object use** (knowing what objects are for and how to use them).

- **Visual memory** (remembering what they saw) and processing (taking in information through the eyes and being able to use it).

- **Sequential learning** (learning things one step at a time in a way that makes common sense).

- **Logical thinking** (thinking that makes sense from the point of view of the person) and mathematical thinking (numbers, sequence, time, dates, calendars).

Many individuals with ASD may be particularly challenged to:

- **Understand and use spoken language to communicate effectively.**

  — He may find it difficult to effectively send and receive needed messages, whether he cannot speak at all or can talk very well. (Talking is not the same as communicating)

- **Understand and use non-verbal communication in a typical way.**

  — He may find it difficult to use and understand facial expressions, body language, gestures, etc.

- **Understand the point of view and perspectives of others.**

  — A person with an ASD often has limited success in understanding or guessing what another person is thinking or wants, or imagining someone else's feelings or reactions. (This is referred to as "theory of mind")

- **Describe an internal state.**

  — He may not spontaneously tell other people about his level of physical comfort or discomfort, or describe his own emotional states accurately.

- **Process sensory information.**

  — He can become "overloaded" and unable to cope with sensory input, or may ignore and fail to respond to sensory input.

- **Process rapidly changing input.**

  — The individual may have difficulty coping with several things that are all changing at the same time.

- **Learn and remember social rules and behavior.**

  — Even after being told and shown what to do, why to do it, and how to do it many times, this often remains a challenge.

- **Make and keep friends.**

  — He may have no friends or only friends who "use" the individual to their advantage. He may not know the difference between friendly behavior and simply getting the attention of others, or he may count everyone as his friend in a way that is too naive for his age.

- **Use learned material in other settings.**

  — Even if he sometimes does what he learned in one situation, he may not automatically use it when a new situation presents itself.

He may use learned material in a similar situation when it
does not apply.

• **Understand cause and effect.**

— He may get "stuck" at an early stage of cause and effect, such as
wanting to turn lights or water on and off repeatedly, and he may
do some other actions repeatedly to get the same results. He may
not really understand what makes things happen in his world, i.e.,
"if" I do this, "then" that will happen.

• **Predict events or outcomes.**

— An individual with ASD may be unable to predict what others will
do when he is watching them, interacting with them, or reading
about them, and he may be unable to predict or understand what
consequence will arise from his own behavior even if he can say
the rule that applies.

• **Understand safety or danger.**

— He may persist in doing dangerous things even after being told or
shown what else to do. He may not realize why something is
dangerous and may not understand or fear consequences of
dangerous behavior, like running into the street.

• **Engage in imaginative activities.**

— He may not automatically play imaginative games. He may not be
able to imagine situations about other people and may not be able
to imagine things beyond his own experience of reality.

• **Learn to play.**

— He may not imitate others or enjoy "pretend play," like playing
school or pretending an object is something else (drinking straw
becomes a water hose, etc.). He may not use toys such as dolls or
trucks in a way that shows he knows what these items represent, or
may focus on a part of a toy or line toys up instead of playing with

them. What looks like imaginative play is often repetitive activity or the reenactment of a story, video, t.v. show or event.

- **Understand social rules.**

  — He may not know how to join in with others or do what others expect, may spend much playtime engaged in solitary activities, may seem to not want to play or be with others.

  — He may not use toys such as dolls or trucks in a way that shows he knows what these items represent, or may focus on a part of a toy or line toys up instead of playing with them.

- **Be interested in what others want them to be interested in.**

  — He may have limited interests and may have problems shifting focus from what is interesting to him to what others find interesting or want him to pay attention to.

- **Seek out and engage others to increase personal enjoyment.**

  — He may like or have fun in an activity, but may not get pleasure from sharing the activity with others.

As you read the above list of strengths and difficulty, did it begin to sound like a child or adult you know? If so, regardless of the diagnostic label applied to that individual, the information contained in this book may help you understand how the individual learns, how to design needed services and how to teach effectively. So, read on!

For Sources used in this chapter and the next, see the end of Chapter Two.

CHAPTER 1 SUMMARY

- A diagnosis of Autism Spectrum Disorder involves looking at development, socialization, communication, behavior and learning during a person's lifetime. Professionals identify patterns and account for symptoms and features seen in an individual now and in the past.

- Diagnoses in the "umbrella category" of Pervasive Developmental Disorders are apparent by an early age, may have multiple causes and significantly impact all areas of development during a person's entire lifetime.

- PDD and autism are described as "spectrum disorders" because the features of the disorders overlap significantly. The combination of the level of intelligence, how severely the person is affected, the ability to communicate and the age and experience of the person results in each individual with these diagnoses manifesting in a unique way.

- ASD and similar disorders are neurobiological, affecting the physical brain and brain chemistry. Developmental disorders are NOT the same as mental illness, behavior disorders or emotional disturbances.

- ASD is not caused by parents or the result of parental behavior, before, during or after birth.

- ASD occurs in both males and females, but four times as many males are diagnosed with ASD than females. ASD is increasing in incidence throughout the world, occurs in all races, and in all cultural, social and economic groups.

- ASD can occur in conjunction with any other condition or disorder. If a person has ASD with another disability, the characteristics of ASD may be causing the most problems in communication, relationships, behavior, and learning.

- People with ASD may have a pattern of strengths shared with others with ASD.

- People with ASD can have areas of need in common with others with ASD such as:

  — An impaired ability to communicate using speech, language gestures, facial expression, or body language.

  — A naïve or one-sided approach to relationships, or difficulty forming relationships and making and keeping friends.

  — Restrictive and repetitive behaviors, unusual reactions to the people and events in their lives and a need for predictability and sameness.

  — Sensitivity or an unusual way of processing and responding to sensory information such as touch, smell, taste, hearing or sight, or problems of balance or coordination.

  — Uneven development of learning and skills (being good in some areas, finding other areas very difficult).

  — An atypical or unusual timeline for developing or learning skills.

- ASD can be treated with many effective interventions, and people with ASD can learn and make progress, although ASD cannot be "cured" completely. People with ASD can have successful, productive and meaningful lives.

- Barriers to diagnosis may include the passage of time, misconceptions about ASD, and confusion caused by the fact that ASD is a spectrum disorder that affects each person differently. Myths or false beliefs, such as thinking that a person must have every characteristic of the disorder can be a barrier to diagnosis.

CHAPTER 2

"There are no shortcuts to anyplace worth going."
Beverly Sills

CONSIDERATIONS IN THE DIAGNOSIS OF AUTISM SPECTRUM DISORDERS

Perhaps your child, an adult in your care, or a student in your class *has not* been diagnosed with any disorder, but is having significant difficulty at home, school, work, or in social settings. You may have observed unusual characteristics and behaviors that interfere with learning and functioning. Perhaps you are an adult seeing these things in yourself.

In this chapter you will learn:

- The source of some of the confusion in recognizing and describing ASD.

- What a differential diagnosis is and why it is used to identify ASD.

- The current official diagnostic criteria and how it is applied.

- Considerations for distinguishing ASD from other disorders.

- The importance of an accurate diagnosis and the link to eligibility for services.

Making Sense of What We See

Getting a diagnosis helps explain and make sense of the perplexing and confusing characteristics, behaviors and problems that a particular person experiences. An accurate diagnosis helps others understand why an individual behaves and communicates the way he does. Dr. Edward Ritvo, of UCLA, told Emily, " Everybody has an explanation. It's just a question of figuring it out." A diagnosis may make the individual eligible for services from schools and other providers. A diagnosis will also guide professionals in providing the right services for the child or the adult in your care, or for you.

Here is an analogy: If you are going to play a sport, you need to know which sport so that you can bring the right equipment, show up at the right place and know how to play the game. If you think you are going to play tennis, but the game is really baseball, you will not be prepared to participate. You could certainly never win a game if you didn't know which game you were playing!

In order to assist a person with special learning needs, you need to know **what kind** of special learning needs are present so that you will have the **right tools** to help, know **who** is available to help and **how** to achieve the most success.

Recognizing the Need to Get a Professional Opinion

The first steps in the diagnostic process are having reasons to believe that there is a problem and wanting to find out what it is. Sometimes parents or staff have some idea of what the problem or diagnosis might be, and sometimes they have no idea. Adults may be unsure of what the problem may be when they seek a professional opinion about their own symptoms and difficulties.

Making the Connection with ASD

The connection between the individual and the possibility of Autism Spectrum Disorder may be made when parents or staff see information about ASD on television, or in books or magazines. They may meet or hear about a person who already has a diagnosis and feel that "their" individual is very similar. A friend or relative who knows the person well may bring information about ASD to the attention of parents, staff or an adult who may be affected.

Sometimes the school or care agency contacts the family when serious problems arise. Teachers who are aware of the progress and development of each child in the class can see if a particular child is having substantial difficulties compared to other classmates. A teacher or other educational staff might suggest or ask that an assessment be done to determine if there is a disability involved. In this case, the school or agency professionals may or may not recognize or report signs of ASD.

A pediatrician or physician who is tracking the individual's development and characteristics may become aware of differences as the child grows. Pediatricians and medical professionals carefully monitor growth and the age or stage when the child is able to accomplish important mental and physical functions. A medical professional who is familiar with the child and has concerns will sometimes refer the child to a neurologist or psychiatrist for further evaluation. Language or speech delay is a cause for concern and sometimes the reason a referral is given. Sometimes medical personnel will not "see" any problems in social interaction during the course of a typical office visit, or will suggest a "wait and see" approach when parents are worried.

In the case of adults, there may be a suggestion from a family member or friend, or a referral from a medical or educational professional who suggests that ASD may be involved. Sometimes an adult comes across information that causes him to recognize the possibility of ASD in himself and refers himself for diagnosis. In other cases, a parent or adult family member recognizes features of the disorder in himself when a child or another family member is going through the process of being identified.

Difficulty and Differences Using Diagnostic Terms

When parents meet with a medical or mental health professional to discuss their child's situation, it can be hard to predict which diagnosis will be given. The same is true when a staff refers an adult for diagnosis or when an adult who believes he may have ASD begins the diagnostic process. A diagnostician may choose from several choices in the diagnostic manuals that describe features within the autism spectrum. He will determine the diagnosis according to what he thinks most accurately describes the features seen in the individual. He may think that particular features "rule out" some diagnoses. Will the disorder be recognized as part of the autism spectrum at all? Will it be called Autism, PDD, or Asperger Syndrome? Does the professional prefer one term to another? Will the professional choose a very different diagnosis?

Let us say this from the beginning: we do not believe it is helpful to argue over diagnostic terms. All over the world, people are arguing about how to diagnose people who have a common set of characteristics. While parents and professionals may be confused by complicated jargon, it is important to realize that there is some "confusion" among diagnosticians and medical professionals as well. "Labels," while useful, are not precise. However, arguments over labeling can prevent us all from identifying an individual's needs and meeting them.

Part of the problem is the "newness" of the disorders in the autism spectrum. Leo Kanner first published his paper, "Autistic Disturbances of Affective Contact," on autism in 1943. It was based on the cases of eleven children. Autism did not appear as a diagnostic category in the DSM until 1980 (See the section on resources to read Kanner's paper online).

Hans Asperger wrote his paper in 1944 about four representative boys with "autism personality disorders in childhood." Based on his work with about 200 boys, it was not really "noticed" until, Uta Frith, of the United Kingdom, published a translation (from German) and Lorna Wing wrote a review of his work in 1981. The diagnostic labels of "Asperger Disorder" or "Asperger Syndrome" appeared for the first time, years later, in the Fourth Version of the DSM-IV, 1994 and in the ICD-10 in 1990.

Lorna Wing was the "instigator" of the translation of Asperger's work. She brought the work of Asperger to the attention of the medical community. Wing wished to expand the view of what autism included: high-functioning, intelligent people who have pervasive communication and social deficits. These people might have never been thought to have autism before Asperger Syndrome was included in the spectrum of pervasive developmental disorders.[2]

The "newness" of the interpretation of autism as a spectrum disorder helps to explain why many adults are now being diagnosed. Some people had received some type of diagnosis before Asperger Syndrome was included in the DSM-IV. Now that Asperger syndrome is an option, many professionals and individuals are reviewing their cases. They find that Asperger syndrome is a better and more accurate description of the behaviors and characteristics many individuals have.

In other cases of adults, no diagnosis had ever been made because of the confusing coexistence of deficit areas along with areas of ability and competence. Many adults who have struggled to get by are now recognizing features of ASD in themselves as more information is learned and publicized about ASD.

Researchers and professionals, such as psychiatrists, neurologists and educational specialists, disagree about the terms and diagnostic criteria currently in use. One problem is that there is disagreement in interpreting the work of Kanner and Asperger. Asperger himself never wrote any diagnostic criteria for what is now called Asperger syndrome! Some people point out that some of the children seen by Kanner and Asperger might not fit the current diagnostic criteria for autism and Asperger syndrome used today.

Based on varied interpretations, different guidelines for diagnosis have been developed that sometimes conflict with one another. There is no doubt that the diagnostic criteria will be once again discussed at length by those who contribute to revisions for the DSM-V.

Differential Diagnosis

Differential diagnosis is the process of looking at the characteristics an individual displays, finding a pattern and determining which diagnostic label most accurately describes the individual. This includes taking into account how the characteristics of different kinds of disabilities and disorders appear or are manifested. Professionals who diagnose ASD must "rule out" or eliminate other disorders that could be the cause of the characteristics they observe.

The diagnostic professional must rule out physical injury and illness as a cause, such as when a person has had a head injury, a neurological disease, a brain tumor, or hearing loss. They must rule out psychiatric or mental health problems, such as Schizoid Personality Disorder or Obsessive-Compulsive Disorder. Then they look at the criteria for the disorders within the Pervasive Developmental Disorders or autism spectrum arriving at the diagnosis that best fits the characteristics of the individual. They must decide if the individual has more than one disorder present.

If a child or adult has the characteristics of autism or a Pervasive Developmental Disorder, and there is no other reason known for these characteristics (such as a brain tumor or injury to the brain or another disorder), they can be diagnosed as an individual within the autism spectrum. The official diagnostic criteria for these disorders are discussed at the end of this chapter.

Barriers to Accurate Diagnosis: Not Recognizing Autism

Many parents and staff describe the struggle of trying to get a diagnosis for a child or adult family member with ASD. Sometimes this problem is compounded when educators and support professionals in the school setting, adult services, or medical profession, have limited awareness of ASD. They may have misconceptions about ASD. As a result, they may not know that autism could be the cause of a person's problems and may not refer an individual to an appropriate specialist for help.

Some parents face the frustration of being told that there is "nothing wrong" except willfulness and defiance on the part of the child and poor discipline and parenting skills on the part of the parents. Teachers may be accused of being unskilled or overzealous. This is extremely disheartening, and parents and professionals will continue the process of seeking an accurate and objective opinion until the puzzle is solved. Unfortunately, others will give up and go home, or pass the child or adult to the next class or program.

A totally opposite problem can occur: parents go directly to an autism specialist who determines that the child does not have autism, when they actually do. Often this situation arises because a very young child, who is still developing speech and reasoning skills, is very difficult to assess. This starts a painful process of going from specialist to specialist only to end up with an autism diagnosis after all. A growing number of specialists, recognizing both the importance of early diagnosis and the difficulties involved, are asking the parents to bring the child back again in a few months if there is any doubt, particularly when a child is under the age of three. In the meantime, carefully designed services can be initiated that are most likely to benefit the child, regardless of the diagnosis.

Case Example from Barbara

I recently observed a four-year-old child in a pre-kindergarten program, previously diagnosed with "speech and language disorders." The little girl, Sarah, had just been given an official diagnosis of autism. At age 2 ½, Sarah's parents knew that "something was wrong" and brought Sarah to the local provider of early intervention services to be screened and tested. Sarah clearly had difficulties in social interaction that showed up in her play (or lack of play and seeming lack of interest in other children). She was not talking very much and when she did, the speech was "odd" and almost too sophisticated. She sometimes looked at people who were talking to her, was very predictable in terms of activities and toys in which she was interested, sometimes seemed to become very frustrated and cried, and was very loving and affectionate with familiar adults.

Sarah's diagnosticians did not see "enough" of some characteristics to feel comfortable in giving a diagnosis of ASD at that time. However, they identified areas of deficit, areas of need and areas of learning strengths and started providing individualized services under the eligibility of "speech and language delays." By the age of four, Sarah was talking very well, often using functional, original speech mixed in with some echoed phrases. She was able to play with the other children in her pre-kindergarten program who had been coached to play with her. She played with a wider variety of toys. She rarely cried and continued to be loving and affectionate. The diagnosis of autism was confirmed at this time, even though Sarah was progressing with support, because the core deficits were still present and affected her in all aspects of functioning.

The Expert's Point-of-View

Some diagnosticians may not have had recent training in autism and related disorders. Therefore they may not recognize these disorders. Instead, they may give a diagnosis of a similar or overlapping disorder, based on a point of view influenced by their own training, experience and area of expertise. It is not realistic to think that an accurate diagnosis of an ASD can be given by someone who does not have training, knowledge or experience with ASD—no matter how professional and educated a person may be in a different area of expertise.

Diagnosticians are human too. Each "expert" may see the problem from his own point of view and use a label with which they are most familiar. For example, medical and mental health professionals well-versed in Attention Deficit Disorder and Attention Deficit Hyperactivity Disorder may see those features in a person who actually has ASD. A psychiatrist may see Obsessive-Compulsive Disorder with Tourette's Syndrome, when a person actually has ASD. This difficulty can arise because the characteristics of ASD may be manifested in a wide variety of ways and do have some features in common with other disorders.

Sometimes the inaccuracy in diagnosis occurs when a qualified professional does not have enough information. Only limited aspects of a disorder may be observed while an individual is in a clinic for an assessment. Thus, a diagnostician will only see a part of the problem or will not have enough information to draw an appropriate conclusion. A diagnosis that describes only one part of the whole picture may result, unless the diagnostician receives complete and accurate information about the individual's development, socialization, communication skills and behavior.

Parents and staff have a great deal of responsibility in providing the information needed to make a diagnosis, but they may not know how to objectively describe the individual's characteristics to the diagnostician, and an inaccurate or incomplete picture may be presented. Very few programs in teacher and staff training teach how to be accurate and objective in describing people and behavior, and most parents certainly have not been taught how to describe it! Throughout this book, we strive to model the use of accurate, objective, and respectful language to describe the characteristics of ASD, and avoid psychiatric terms or judgmental language.

The ability of parents to objectively report the features and characteristics they see may be affected by other people's opinions. This includes common, well-intended comments like "he'll outgrow that," "I know another child like him, and he's doing fine now," or "don't worry yourself over nothing." When things are explained away, they are often forgotten.

Parents may have difficulty remembering, or may not realize which events in the child's development are significant and relevant to the diagnosis. Many parents have little experience to help them compare a child's typical development to the development and features they see in their own child. This may be especially true when the child thought to have ASD is the only or oldest child in the family.

Chapter Three contains many ideas to help parents and staff organize and present the information about the child's or adult's developmental history, and discusses ways for parents and professionals to notice and describe important features for diagnosticians. This is an essential activity that contributes to the accuracy and success of the diagnostic process.

ASD, By Many Other Names

Often, more than one diagnosis is given to the same person over time. There are several reasons for a diagnosis to change. One of the most important reasons is that the current diagnosis is not "satisfying." It does not accurately and completely describe the characteristics, features and behavior being observed in an individual. So a second, or third, or fourth opinion is sought.

It is common for many children with ASD to first be diagnosed as having mental impairment, mental retardation, Attention Deficit Disorder (ADD), Attention Deficit Hyperactivity Disorder (ADHD), Behavior Disorder (BD), Obsessive-Compulsive Disorder (OCD), Oppositional Defiant Disorder (ODD), a Learning Disability (LD) or Emotional Disturbance (ED) before the collection of characteristics of ASD is fully recognized. This may be due to the fact that many of the characteristics of these disorders are similar to or overlap with Autism Spectrum Disorders.

People with an ASD who are verbal and capable in many areas, are often first diagnosed with ADD, ADHD, LD, OCD, Non-verbal Language Disorder, or Semantic-Pragmatic Disorder. Sometimes they are identified at school as "Gifted but Learning Disabled," or "Hyperlexic." Again, this may be due to the fact that many of the characteristics of these disorders are similar to or overlap with Autism Spectrum Disorders.

Another reason that people with ASD get different diagnoses or labels over time is because people with autism change. Someone who looked typical in the first two years of life may be very different at age four. High-functioning people with ASD often learn to compensate for their deficits and "mask" the nature of their disorder until, at some point, they can no longer cope. They may have many unofficial labels, being called shy, immature, serious, different, depressed, a loner or even a "nerd" or a "geek."

The differences between the "regular kids" and the undiagnosed or incorrectly diagnosed child who has ASD become more and more noticeable over time. As classmates continue to progress socially and academically, it becomes more obvious that the child with ASD does not fit in and is struggling. A child who managed to stay "glued together" during most of elementary school may be in crisis later in elementary school or as junior high begins. When a crisis results, the pattern of difficulty that has always existed may finally be recognized and make sense. Sometimes, individuals manage to somehow get by, and do not recognize or have their symptoms recognized, until adulthood.

Many adults have a diagnosis that was arrived at many years ago and wasn't revisited. Family members and service providers may not recognize features of ASD that have always been present because they assume that another diagnosis is accurate. Staff and family members may need to take a new look. Remember that before 1994, Asperger syndrome was not even a *choice* as a diagnosis! People diagnosed now, or re-diagnosed, may often find a diagnosis in the autism spectrum very fitting.

A last consideration in the recognition of ASD is that some people have *more than one disorder.* An individual may have Down syndrome and ASD or Cerebral Palsy and ASD. A person can be blind and/or deaf and have autism. A person can have ASD with ADHD, Oppositional Defiant Disorder or Bipolar Disorder. *Autism spectrum disorders can coexist with any physical, pschycological, or developmental disorder.* This fact can complicate the recognition of the features of ASD in a person of any age. The diagnosis of ASD may be added when someone finally recognizes that the pattern of the syndrome of ASD is present. The individual has difficulties in social interaction, communication, and unusual responses to the world around them, and these difficulties cannot be explained by the other diagnosis alone.

When it's "Autism Spectrum Disorder," Which Label Will Be Chosen?

When presented to a diagnostician with experience in ASD, a person with the characteristics may be given a diagnosis within the spectrum of the disorder: Autism, Asperger syndrome, Pervasive Developmental Disorder, Pervasive Developmental Disorder Not Otherwise Specified, or Atypical Autism. The term Autism Spectrum Disorder (ASD) is not an "official" term because it is not a diagnostic choice in the current diagnostic manuals. ASD is commonly used by individuals, families, staff and in the literature to emphasize what the disorders have in common and simplify the use of terms and abbreviations. Sometimes autism is described as "mild," or a person is said to have high functioning autism (HFA). These descriptive terms are not "official" categories in the diagnostic manuals, but are added to give a more precise idea of the level of cognitive functioning (intelligence) of the individual.

Some psychiatrists or neurologists may avoid giving a diagnosis of "autism" because they believe it is too harsh a word for the family to hear (Some people call autism the "A" word because it is laden with emotional meaning.). Parents, and the public in general, have specific associations with the word autism (a common one is Dustin Hoffman's character in the movie "Rain Man"), and a negative reaction to the word is quite common, especially in people who have limited understanding or experience of the disorder.

Mental health and medical professionals may feel that Pervasive Developmental Disorder, PDD, is a "kinder" term. Some people use PDD when they think parents are not ready to hear or would be too shocked by the word "autism." PDD is a preferred term in some geographical areas. However, it may not be a useful term if it is too ambiguous or does not help to qualify the individual for services. It may be better to be realistic and "tough" with terminology if it makes a difference to the interests or the outcome for the individual. "PDD" may not be a "kinder" term if it confuses parents.

Case Example

One parent had a very upsetting experience at a school meeting with special educators. He knew that his daughter had "PDD," but no one had explained to him that PDD had anything to do with autism. He found out what the connection was the day his daughter was made eligible for special education services in the category of "autism." He was completely unprepared for the emotional shock and was devastated to get the news in this way. In this case, the label of PDD had "shielded him from the pain," but also shielded him from accurate information and the reality that others understood.

Autistic-Like

It is possible for individuals to display some of the characteristics of ASD and not meet the criteria for the diagnosis. As a result, many individuals have been "labeled" "autistic-like" or are said to have "a tendency towards autism" or "autistic features." Is it possible to get appropriate services if you are considered "autistic-like?"

Individuals described as "autistic-like" may be best served if they receive the positive treatments and services that are known to benefit people with autism even if a formal diagnosis is not obtained. In describing other disorders, no one uses terminology such as "blind-like" or "brain-injured-like" or "a tendency towards cerebral palsy." It may be time to recognize that the term "autistic-like" may be a barrier that confuses, not clarifies. In these cases, it is most helpful if diagnosticians list what characteristics they observed rather than just using the term "autistic-like." Diagnosticians will benefit from observing these children and adults in multiple settings. In settings beyond a clinic or office, other features of the disorder may become more apparent. School psychologists may use the term "autistic like" because they are not allowed to make a clinical diagnosis but want to qualify the student to be eligible for special education classes.

What Difference Does the Diagnosis Make?

Parents and staff involved in the diagnostic process need to be aware of the importance of the correct diagnosis. One purpose of a diagnosis is to identify the areas of need or impairment. This is a key point because the most accurate diagnostic label should lead to the most appropriate services and supports. The diagnosis becomes the first step to helping the individual learn language and communication skills, learn to relate to and interact with others, find and use areas of learning strengths, and be as successful as possible.

The diagnosis given to a person may affect her eligibility and access to services, depending on where she lives and whether the support services are provided by private practitioners, the school district, a government agency or other providers. Even insurance companies may provide coverage for people with one diagnosis, but not another. Staff and families need to find out and inform diagnosticians about the labels that can insure eligibility to services and supports. For example, a diagnostician may be willing to use the term "autism" instead of "PDD" if the diagnostician considers the terms interchangeable and is aware that a diagnosis of autism could make the individual eligible for services, and a diagnosis of PDD might not.

There is sometimes a difference between a clinical diagnosis and a diagnosis for eligibility for services. For example, a child may have a clinical diagnosis of PDD-NOS given by a psychiatrist or neurologist, but the child's school program will not have an eligibility category for PDD-NOS. The educational team can make the child eligible for services under "Other Health Impaired" or "Autism." Parents and staff need to make sure that the label used for service eligibility is the one that results in the child or adult being able to receive all of the services that are needed.

Diagnostic confusion may continue for some time until more is known and understood about the causes of Autism Spectrum Disorder and the effects on the functioning of the individual. Increased public awareness, education, research, funding, and the continued dedication and persistence of families, staff, specialists and researchers holds promise for the future. In the meantime, we can all be as objective, factual and clear as possible in identifying the past and present characteristics and needs of an individual who is going through the diagnostic process.

How Diagnostic Criteria Are Applied

The information in this section is taken from the DSM-IV-R, the *American Psychiatric Association's Diagnostic and Statistical Manual of Mental Disorders, Text Revision, 2000*. Professionals use descriptions of diagnostic features and apply specific criteria to determine whether or not a person has a disorder within the autism spectrum. That judgment is based on understanding the personal history and development of the person and observations of current behavior and functioning.

There are categories of characteristics in the diagnosis of each disorder. A person does not have to have every single characteristic in each category in order to receive that diagnosis. Minimum requirements are bolded in the following text.

299.00 Autistic Disorder

"The essential features of Autistic Disorder are the presence of markedly abnormal or impaired development in social interaction and communication and a markedly restricted repertoire of activity and interests. Manifestations of the disorder vary greatly depending on the developmental level and chronological age of the individual."

Diagnostic Criteria for 299.0 Autistic Disorder

A. A total of six (or more) items from (1), (2), and (3), with at least two from (1), and one each from (2) and (3):

(1) Qualitative impairment in social interaction, as manifested by at least two of the following:

(a) Marked impairment in the use of multiple nonverbal behaviors, such as eye-to-eye gaze, facial expression, body postures, and gestures to regulate social interaction.

(b) Failure to develop peer relationships appropriate to developmental level.

(c) A lack of spontaneous seeking to share enjoyment, interests, or achievements with other people (e.g., by a lack of showing, bringing or pointing out objects of interest).

(d) Lack of social or emotional reciprocity.

(2) Qualitative impairments in communication, as manifested by at least one of the following:

(a) Delay in, or total lack of, the development of spoken language (not accompanied by an attempt to compensate through alternative modes of communication such as gesture or mime).

(b) In individuals with adequate speech, marked impairment in the ability to initiate or sustain a conversation with others.

   (c) Stereotyped and repetitive use of language or idiosyncratic
       language.

   (d) Lack of varied, spontaneous make-believe play or social imitative
       play appropriate to developmental level.

(3)   Restricted, repetitive and stereotyped patterns of behavior, interests,
       and activities as manifested by at least one of the following:

   (a) Encompassing preoccupation with one or more stereotyped and
       restricted patterns of interest that is abnormal either in intensity or
       focus.

   (b) Apparently inflexible adherence to specific, nonfunctional routines
       or rituals.

   (c) Stereotyped and repetitive motor mannerisms (e.g., hand or finger
       flapping or twisting or complex whole-body movements).

   (d) Persistent preoccupation with parts of objects.

B. **Delays or abnormal functioning in at least one of the following areas, with
   onset prior to age 3 years:**

(1)   Social interaction.

(2)   Language as used in social communication.

(3)   Symbolic or imaginative play.

C. **The disturbance is not better accounted for by Rett's disorder or childhood
   disintegrative disorder.**[3]

If a person has a total of at least six features, including at least two from sections A
(1), at least one from section A (2), and at least one from section A (3) and also meets
the criteria of sections B and C, a diagnostician will give a diagnosis of Autistic
Disorder. Autism can be considered when a child that had been developing normally
loses functions and capabilities or regresses. Other instructions in the DSM tell

professionals that if the criteria for autism are indeed met, then no other diagnosis in the Pervasive Developmental Disorder category needs to be considered. Sometimes, when the criteria of autism are applied, the minimum of six criteria is not met. This can be called "sub-threshold symptomology," meaning that while some symptoms are present, there are "not enough" to make the diagnosis of autism.

Autism is considered a developmental disability that occurs in early childhood. An older child or adult can be diagnosed with autism at any age, as long as it is agreed that the symptoms were present before age 3. The symptoms of autism must be evident by age 3, even if they are not recognized as symptoms or considered cause for concern at the time. If the symptoms were not present before age 3, this is called "late age of onset," and the diagnosis of autism may not be given.

What guidance are diagnosticians given when there are not enough symptoms, the onset is late, or the professional considers the symptoms to be different from what is usually seen or generally expected in "typical" autism? That is when the diagnoses of Pervasive Developmental Disorders, Not Otherwise Specified (PDD-NOS) or atypical autism are used. In the DSM-IV, the following description is given:

299.80 Pervasive Developmental Disorder, Not Otherwise Specified

"This category should be used when there is a severe and pervasive impairment in the development of reciprocal social interaction or verbal and nonverbal communication. For example, this category includes "atypical autism" - presentations that do not meet the criteria for autistic disorder because of late age of onset, atypical symptomatology, sub-threshold symptomatology or all of these."[4]

Readers will want to know that many professionals consider the diagnoses of PDD and PDD-NOS as forms of autism or part of the autism spectrum. The strategies and supports contained in this manual and other books about autism, Asperger Syndrome and Autistic Spectrum Disorders may be of benefit to someone diagnosed with PDD or PDD-NOS. In some cases, children or adults, have some features of autism but do not truly meet the criteria for any autism disorder. In this case, the term pervasive developmental disorder may be the best choice. Services can be individualized and selected to meet the identified needs.

What is Asperger Syndrome?

Let's start with the diagnostic criteria that professionals use and then discuss what it means. Again, the required symptoms have been typed in bold for emphasis.

299.80 Asperger's Disorder

A. Qualitative impairment in social interaction as manifested by at least two of the following:

(1)   Marked impairment in the use of multiple nonverbal behaviors, such as eye-to-eye gaze, facial expression, body postures and gestures to regulate social interaction.

(2)   Failure to develop peer relationships appropriate to developmental level.

(3)   A lack of spontaneous seeking to share enjoyment, interests, or achievements with other people (e.g., by a lack of showing, bringing, or pointing out objects of interest to other people).

(4)   Lack of social or emotional reciprocity.

B. Restricted, repetitive and stereotyped patterns of behavior, interests, and activities as manifested by at least one of the following:

(1)   Encompassing preoccupation with one or more stereotyped and restricted patterns of interest that is abnormal either in intensity or focus.

(2)   Apparently inflexible adherence to specific, nonfunctional routines or rituals.

(3)   Stereotyped and repetitive motor mannerisms (e.g., hand or finger flapping or twisting, or complex whole-body movements).

(4)   Persistent preoccupation with parts of objects.

C. **The disturbance causes clinically significant impairment in social, occupational or other important areas of functioning.**

D. **There is no clinically significant general delay in language (e.g., single words used by age 2 years, communicative phrases used by age 3 years).**

E. **There is no clinically significant delay in cognitive development or in the development of age-appropriate self-help skills, adaptive behavior (other than in social interaction) and curiosity about the environment in childhood.**

F. **Criteria are not met for another specific pervasive developmental disorder or schizophrenia.**[5]

In the case of Asperger Disorder, two symptoms from (A), one symptom from (B), plus C, D, E, and F must be satisfied in order to give the diagnosis. There is an instruction to diagnosticians in the DSM-IV that "Asperger Disorder is not diagnosed if criteria are met for Autistic Disorder." Asperger Syndrome is not diagnosed if the person meets the criteria for any other specific Pervasive Developmental Disorder or Schizophrenia. Notice that section A for Asperger syndrome is *identical* to section A1 for autistic disorder and Section B of Asperger syndrome is *identical* to Section A3 of autistic disorder.

In light of the features in common, people often ask, "which criteria diagnostically distinguish a person with autism from a person with Asperger syndrome (AS)?" People ask what is meant by "no clinically significant general delay in language, no clinically significant delay in cognitive development or in the development of age-appropriate self-help skills, adaptive behavior (other than in social interaction) and curiosity about the environment in childhood." There is no in-depth explanation of these features contained in the diagnostic criteria. Many clinicians and diagnosticians have gone back to the work of Asperger and to materials written about ASD to interpret these characteristics.

Here are some interpretations about these features that are commonly held and discussed in lectures and literature on the subject.

1. **Individuals with AS usually have better interpersonal communication skills than do people with autism.**

   People with AS do not generally experience clinically significant language delay, and may speak on time, or even early. Single words are used by age 2, and communicative phrases are used by age 3. It is often noticed that early speech may be very complex, leading families to assume that the child is precocious or gifted. Individuals with AS may still have an unusual way of communicating, such as echoing, repeating lines from commercials or videos, or almost never asking questions. Individuals with AS may have had single words by age two, but may not necessarily have used them in a typical way. They may not use language to share feelings or start a conversation.

2. **Individuals with AS do not have a cognitive delay.**

   This refers to the development of thinking and learning skills. People with AS are usually of average or above average intelligence. This is compared to the range of intelligence in autism that includes gifted and normal I.Q.s, but also the possibility of cognitive impairment.

3. **Individuals with AS often have age-appropriate self-help skills, meaning that they learn some skills like most other children, such as dressing and using the toilet.**

   Their adaptive behavior, how they learn routines and learn new responses to new situations, may be good, except in the area of social interaction. Physical skills, such as running, catching, etc., are usually learned close to the time, or slightly after other children learn them. It is often noticed that children with AS are somewhat uncoordinated or clumsy. The skills are there, but perhaps the quality of performance is not typical. Asperger noted clumsiness as a feature of some of the children he described. Although it is not written into the DSM-IV, many diagnosticians connect the feature of clumsiness to an Asperger diagnosis.

4. **Children with AS are thought to be curious about the world around them, which may be shown by awareness, interest, investigating and exploring.**

    They will be particularly interested in things that are fascinating to them, while other things may be of no interest at all. People with AS may have such intensely focused interests that they often memorize facts and become experts on particular topics. Sometimes the area of interest is "mainstream" or common, like computers and dinosaurs, and other times the area of interest is more unusual or obscure, like insects, timetables, calendars, and maps.

The descriptions of the language, self-help skills, cognitive ability and curiosity that relate to AS may represent a different quality of impairment from autism. Yet the core features of AS overlap with the core features of autism. In other words, people with Asperger syndrome have many areas of ability and may seem to function fairly well in most of the practical areas of daily life. In such cases, the term "high-functioning autism" is often used. In contrast, other individuals with autism may not function as independently early in life or develop self-help skills on the usual timeline. Both groups share the effects of social and communication impairments with restricted and unusual interests.

What Has Been Learned About Diagnosing Asperger Syndrome and High-Functioning Autism From the Experiences of Individuals?

People of any age who are currently receiving a diagnosis of AS or HFA often share some common patterns of experience. For example, they may be diagnosed at a later age than others on the autism spectrum. School-aged children with AS and HFA are typically part of the mainstream educational group, placed in general education classrooms. Both academically and socially, they may be able to be successful for a time with no diagnosis being sought despite the obvious social differences, or having a different explanation/diagnosis for their difficulties.

When schoolwork becomes more abstract, and less tied to memorization, learning problems may become more evident. As the social complexities at school increase, children with AS may not have the social awareness or social skills to fit in.

Underdeveloped communication skills, not "getting the message" from others and not expressing themselves in a way that peers expect or accept can result in teasing, bullying and being left out. Poor self-esteem, sadness and depression affect some children with AS or HFA who see there is a problem, but don't know how to fix it. Other children with AS or HFA may seem to be unaware of their problems, or unable to express how they are feeling (their internal state). New explosive or problem behaviors may be signs of the anxiety and frustration that these children may be experiencing.

Some unusual responses to others set people with AS or HFA apart from other children or adults of the same age. Their "aloneness" (or differences in social skills) may be viewed as shyness or satisfaction with their own company. Children with AS often relate well to adults. These adults quickly learn how to adapt to the special communication needs of the child or adults with AS and "fix" problems in social communication. Often the adults who are responding to the child with AS are unaware that they are making any communication adaptations. Their adaptations to the child's "differences" have been made gradually, over time, based on a desire to be helpful and communicate well.

Individuals with AS and HFA are often intelligent and capable in many areas. Their remarkable abilities often "mask" the severe language, social and sensory differences they experience. They may express a strong desire to have friends and be part of the group, but be unable (or seem unwilling) to do so. Their coping and adaptability compensate for some deficits, while other problems are very obvious. This adds to the confusing picture perceived by others.

Individuals with AS and HFA can be overlooked and misunderstood. They may be judged as aloof, manipulative, spoiled, shy, detached, obsessed, uncaring, unmotivated, oppositional and odd, instead of uniquely and multiply disabled. The unevenness in neurological development (being very good at some skills and very poor at others) is often misinterpreted. In many, many cases, the person with AS or HFA is first given a diagnosis of Attention Deficit Disorder, (ADD) and put on medication for that disorder.

In other cases, the difficulties and problems are blamed on the child or adult, who "could be successful if he wanted to" and "has a bad attitude." Sometimes the child or adult's aloof or unconventional interaction style is attributed to the personalities of the parents or poor parenting skills. One result of blaming the individual or the family instead of determining the true nature of the disability, is that in response, interventions are designed to control or punish unwanted behavior and attitudes. Punishment may be used in place of interventions that are more appropriately focused on unique neurological, learning and sensory processing problems.

Many individuals with AS or HFA have gone all the way through school without being recognized as having a disorder for which there is treatment. As adults, they are sometimes "loners" who notice and are upset by their reduced ability to create and sustain friendships in both work and personal life. They may spend most of their personal time engaged in a highly liked activity upon which they become intensely focused. Other people may view them as nice, but odd, sweet but egocentric, naïve, self-absorbed or as a person who is like an "absentminded-professor."

In adulthood, a person with AS or HFA who has never been diagnosed may be very gifted in some areas, and yet, experience social isolation. Many people with Asperger Syndrome "self-diagnose" as adults when they read or hear about the characteristics of AS, or sometimes when they are learning about their own child with an Autistic Spectrum Disorder. It is never too late to know that an individual has AS or HFA. Even later in life, an accurate diagnosis can lead to more understanding from family and co-workers, access to therapies and support, and a higher quality of life.

The lifelong outcome (prognosis) for individuals with AS and HFA can be very good. Once parents and professionals recognize the differences and begin to provide support and training, the individual can begin to make progress, develop and maintain relationships and become a more fully-participating and happy member of society. Many individuals have achieved these positive outcomes, with the help of loved ones and dedicated professionals.

Case Example from Barbara

One afternoon I was presenting a seminar to teaching staff at a Special Education school to help them work with a young man with autism who attended there. His mother, father and sister attended the seminar. During a break, the sister approached me. She was a beautiful young woman in her twenties. She walked up to me and interrupted a conversation I was having with someone else. She stood uncomfortably close to me. When I backed up, she stepped forward. She spoke in a voice that seemed to me to be too loud for the situation. She said, "No one ever said that autism is a spectrum and that you can have autism and be smart and pretty normal. Now that I heard you describe it, I know I have it! What should I do?"

I directed her to a university that specialized in the diagnosis of high-functioning people with autism or AS. Her self-diagnosis was confirmed. She began to attend social skills training and was able to find a job and social group that matched better with her skills and needs.

Two years later, she telephoned me. When I picked up the phone, she did not identify herself. She began talking. She said, "The best day in my life was the day I met you!" After a moment, I realized who it was and greeted her. I told her I was very flattered by her statement and appreciated that she took the time to tell me. When I asked her why she was glad to have met me, she said that once she got diagnosed, she was able to forgive herself for being what she had thought of as "inadequate." She was able to forgive her mother, whom she had blamed for her lack of social success. She had found language to use to describe herself and methods for learning how to be more socially successful. She now had a few friends and was better able to maintain herself in jobs.

Most of us know someone with Asperger Syndrome or HFA that we met when we were growing up. Did you know someone who had few (if any) friends and was excluded from your social group? Perhaps this person focused on one or two topics to the exclusion of others and was really gifted in these limited areas. He may have been mistakenly viewed as an odd loner who really didn't care about other people. Perhaps he was teased by the other children, but did not seem to be able to fight back from bullying. Perhaps the teachers liked him, but had less success communicating with him about things in which he was not interested. Sound familiar? There may be a much better reason for what is seen than the explanation of "unusual or shy personality." You may be working or living with a person with AS or HFA who was never diagnosed. Or, perhaps you are realizing that this description may apply to you.

Asperger Syndrome and High-functioning Autism: Same or Different?

It is a good question to ask whether "High Functioning" Autism and Asperger Syndrome are indeed different developmental disabilities. Officially, there is a distinction made in the DSM- IV, yet they are both under the "umbrella" of Pervasive Developmental Disorders. The two core social and communication deficits are considered the same and the restricted, repetitive behavior and interests in both disorders are similar.

This leads people to ask: "What *differences* are there between "high-functioning autism" and Asperger Syndrome?" We have discussed the differences in the features used in differential diagnosis of autism and Asperger Syndrome: no clinically significant delay in early language acquisition, that individuals with Asperger Syndrome usually have normal to above normal intelligence and learn self-help skills as expected. Others note a distinction between autism and Asperger Syndrome based on the age of onset. Symptoms of autism may appear by the second year of life. People with Asperger Syndrome are thought to have symptoms that appear later than age 2.

Uta Frith, of the MRC Cognitive Development Unit, London, points out that the actual language used by Asperger was that, "Parents did not recognize the child's problems until the child was age three or older." He did not say that the problems did not exist before that time. Yet many professionals use the age distinction to rule autism out or diagnose Asperger syndrome.

In fact, this and other aspects of the "same or different" question in the field of autism are actually quite controversial and still unresolved. There is disagreement among professionals who are among the most outstanding experts in the field. Even those who contributed to the DSM-IV are not necessarily satisfied with the current criteria and have their own points of view on whether AS should be considered a form of autism, or is a separate disorder.

In the book, *Asperger Syndrome*, edited by Ami Klin, Fred R. Volkmar, and Sara S. Sparrow of the Yale Child Study Center (Guilford Press, 2000), preeminent scholars and practitioners discuss their theories, research, and the fact that they continue to disagree on this "same or different" issue. The editors consider the current description of Asperger Syndrome found in the DSM-IV to be "still evolving," and ask whether AS is a valid and separate diagnostic concept.

Some professionals believe Asperger Syndrome and High Functioning Autism to be related, but separate. A different, but popular, view is that autism and AS are two different names used to describe a more mild presentation of the same disorder. Many conclude that HFA and AS are "essentially the same disorder, or are treated in similar ways."[6]

Lorna Wing, of the UK's National Autistic Society, comments on the situation, saying,

> *"It is perhaps ironic that, having been responsible for using the term 'Asperger Syndrome' in my 1981 paper, I am now arguing strongly against its existence as a separate entity. The reason for its adoption in my first paper on the subject was to avoid the label of 'autism psychopathy' used by Asperger when writing in German. In his language, psychopathy refers to personality disorder, but in English, it is often used as synonymous with antisocial psychopathy. I thought that 'Asperger Syndrome' was a neutral term that would suffice for the discussion but carried no particular implications for the nature of the pattern of the behavior...The trouble is that verbal labels have a strange tendency to take on an existence of their own, whatever the intentions of the coiner. If I were starting all over again, knowing what I know now, would I have used this label? Perhaps not."[7]*

Only a level of scientific knowledge that does not yet exist can give a definite answer to the "same or different" question. In the meantime, the disorders are grouped or "lumped" together. Spending an extraordinary amount of time, energy or money in distinguishing whether an individual has HFA or AS is not very useful. Many families have spent thousands of dollars and years of time going from one university developmental clinic to another to try to sort out if the child's most accurate label was PDD, AS, or HFA, when any one accurately described the child's characteristics and needs.

It is not a contradiction to state that an accurate diagnosis is necessary for services, but it is not always necessary to labor over it. Parents and staff need to continue to insist on an accurate, objective diagnostic label that describes the individual's characteristics, differences and needs and makes the individual eligible for services. Once that is obtained, energy, time and money is better expended in designing and delivering effective, individualized services that will make a difference in the quality of life for everyone from that moment on. One of the only reasons to push the point of "same or different" would be if the use of one term qualifies a person for services, while another term does not.

Attention Deficit Disorder and Autism Spectrum Disorders: Recognizing the Similarities

There are many individuals who have had a diagnosis of Attention Deficit Hyperactivity Disorder (ADHD), or Attention Deficit Disorder (ADD), for many years before the features of Autism Spectrum Disorders were recognized. How could this happen? How could diagnosticians "miss" characteristics that should have been recognized from an early age? Here are some thoughts on the subject.

Look at this list of features:

- Hyperactivity

- Short attention span

- Impulsivity

- Aggressiveness

- Self-injurious behaviors

• Temper tantrums

Most people recognize that the above characteristics are consistent with Attention Deficit Hyperactivity Disorder. In fact, this list is taken from the DSM-IV description of Autistic Disorder. In the section under "Associated Features and Disorders," the DSM states: "Individuals with Autistic Disorder may have a range of behavioral symptoms, including hyperactivity, short attention span, impulsivity, aggressiveness, self-injurious behaviors, and particularly in young children, temper tantrums." These symptoms are often seen in individuals with Autism Spectrum Disorders. In people with autism, these features may be considered not as a separate disorder, but arising from autism, as part of what autism is and how it affects an individual.

Autism Spectrum Disorders and Attention Deficit Disorders have several other characteristics in common

• Autism Spectrum Disorders include problems of focus, attention, sequencing, and organization that affect learning and performance; these issues of "executive function" are also seen in ADHD.

• "Hyperactive" behaviors in people with Autism Spectrum Disorders are often related to sensory issues and the diminished ability to tolerate and process sensory input from the environment. The response to feeling overstimulated by sensory input in the environment may look very similar to the "can't sit still" look of a person with ADHD. People with ASD often have difficulty staying in their seat, or completing their work due to sensory issues. They may seek sensory input by running, jumping and climbing, when it is not appropriate to do so.

• Inappropriate social interactions seen in autism spectrum disorders that stem from social and communication deficits may look like inappropriate behaviors seen in Attention Deficit Hyperactivity Disorder. Examples are pushing, interrupting and aggression. In individuals with Autism Spectrum Disorders, these behaviors can be attributed to deficits in socialization since, people with ASD do not always automatically learn through experience what is expected in social situations and do not automatically recognize or respond to social cues. For example, children with ASD may *not* learn to join in by watching the behavior of their peers and may make social mistakes in this type of situation. They can LEARN to join in if taught well!

- The "self-stimulatory" behavior seen in ASD can be similar to the physical "busyness" of hands and feet in motion in individuals with Attention Deficit Hyperactivity Disorder.

- In ASD, self-regulation of energy and attention is a recognized issue, and individuals with Autism Spectrum Disorders may be over stimulated or under stimulated by the cues of the environment. This may look similar to children with ADHD who are always on the go.

The DSM-IV recognizes the similarities in some features of ADHD and ASD. The last criterion in the DSM-IV for Attention Deficit Hyperactivity Disorder states that, "the symptoms do not occur exclusively during the course of a pervasive developmental disorder." *This means that before an ADHD diagnosis can be given, the diagnostician must either determine or rule out whether an Autism Spectrum Disorder or PDD accounts for the characteristics of the person or the problems they are experiencing.*

Refining the Distinctions

There are differences between the behavior and problems of people with ADHD and Autism Spectrum Disorders. Many differences may be described as *qualitative*. This means that while a feature may look the same at first glance, a closer look shows that there is a difference. Although they may be subtle, the differences can be significant and make sense in light of what is known about the communication, social and sensory issues in ASD. Here are some observations and possible differences noted through experience and discussion:

- While ADD and ADHD can cause problems in social interaction and communication, they are not the same type of problems that are part of

ASD. For example individuals with ADHD do not typically have problems in both verbal and non-verbal communication. Their ability to understand idioms and unusual patterns of speech are not generally affected, and both their tone of voice and rate of talking are likely to be the same as other people.

• Individuals with ADHD may not respond appropriately to the non-verbal cues of others, but they have the ability to easily and automatically learn what those non-verbal cues intend to communicate, even if they have problems paying attention to the cues. Their non-verbal communication (gestures and facial expression) is likely to be quite typical.

• Individuals with ASD do not spontaneously learn to respond to the subtleties of communication, such as, proximity and gaze, where individuals with ADHD do respond to these subtleties spontaneously and appropriately much of the time.

• Individuals with ASD may have tremendous focus for topics of interest to them. An area of difficulty for people with ASD is to focus on what others want them to notice or to shift focus from one area to another. Individuals with ADHD are thought to have difficulty paying attention and sticking with activities, even things they like.

• People with ASD may appear to be unable to stay on task, but sometimes, the problem is actually getting started. Once the person with ASD gets going, or is helped to get going, he may have no problem staying with the task until it is finished at least as well as someone else his age would be expected to do. People with ADHD may be able to get started on a task, but may be less able to see it through.

• Children or adults with ASD often have limited or no peer relationships, or limited successful social interactions, unless engineered by the adults around them. Children and adults with ADHD do have friends and two-way friendships that develop spontaneously at each stage of development.

- Individuals with ADD or ADHD sometimes have a favorite or highly liked topic. However they do not tend to be as restrictive and repetitive in their interests as individuals with ASD can be. People with ADHD may have new favorite topics on a regular basis.

- Individuals with ADD or ADHD have less difficulty in the use of imagination, predicting outcomes and identifying the possible internal states of others than do people with ASD. Distractibility in ADD/ADHD is often attributed to things or events in the environment. People with ASD report being distracted by their own internal images or thoughts.

ADD and ADHD seem to be the "diagnosis of the day." Professionals in the fields of neurology and psychiatry are recognizing and discussing the overuse of the ADD and ADHD diagnoses. The National Attention Deficit Disorder Association, an organization that educates and advocates for the needs of individuals with ADD/ADHD, notes concern that, "paradoxically, ADHD is both incorrectly diagnosed when it is not present and underdiagnosed when present."[8]

Many neurologists who treat ADHD report, and research supports, that when individuals are accurately diagnosed with an attention deficit disorder and the appropriate medication and interventions are given, improvement is often rapid, obvious and substantial. However, some people are being given this diagnosis and the medications used to treat it, but do not demonstrate improvement as expected. Children who take attention deficit medications and show minimal improvement in attention and learning over time, may not have an attention problem, or may have more than an attention problem, especially when a medication change or increase remains ineffective. In cases like these, it may be important to drop the "bias" of believing the symptoms are part of Attention Deficit Hyperactivity Disorder, and carefully examine whether another diagnosis could be more accurate. (This is often what happens when diagnosis in the autism spectrum is finally recognized.)

Questions to Ask

The following areas highlight the need to seek professional advice from someone well-informed in the area of ASD *and* ADHD to determine if a child or adult has an attention deficit or a collection of characteristics that are part of the autism spectrum, or both disorders. Think about the individual with an ADD or ADHD diagnosis and answer the following questions with "yes" or, "no:"

Socialization skills:

- Typical for that culture and family?

- Spontaneously improving?

- Developing appropriate social skills due to feedback and experience?

- Knows when he or another person has made a social mistake or is inappropriate?

- Friendships developing as expected with peers (even with peers with disabilities)?

- Sustains conversation and shifts topic when another person wants to?

- Seeks the company of others, especially same-aged peers?

- Withdraws from others when needed and appropriate to do so and/or before becoming upset?

- Knows how to join in a conversation or game without disrupting?

- Learns at an age-appropriate time which topics can be discussed only in private?

Communication skills:

- Uses non-verbal communication such as gestures, tone of voice, eye contact and facial expressions as you would expect?

- Joint references: shifts attention to a common object or event at the direction of another or by own initiation (such as an adult and a child looking at a toy together, as well as interacting with one another at the same time)?

- Responds to the non-verbal cues of children and adults as you would expect?

- Over time, spontaneously learns to interpret idioms and expressions without having them explained many times?

- automatically learns to ask questions to clarify or repair communication breakdowns (such as saying, "What?" or, "I don't understand you.")?

Interests and behavior:

- Has a wide variety of topics of interest?

- Develops new interests frequently?

- Becomes interested easily in the topics that others want to talk about?

- Changes interests and behavior to "please" others?

- Never did unusual repetitive actions with the hands, body or objects?

- Plays (or played) with toys in the usual functional manner you would expect?

- Seems to prefer to be with people most of the time?

- Plays imaginative games in childhood "pretending" to be someone else in another place or time?

- Easily deals with a variety of sounds, sights, textures, foods, schedules, etc.?

- Can "shift gears" and change topics or activities without much effort or upset?

- Displays age or developmentally appropriate flexibility when routines are disrupted or changed?

If you answered "No" to one or more questions in each of the three areas, then it is important to write down what you have observed and your concerns. Many people find that a diagnosis of ADD or ADHD explains some things. In other ways, it does not "seem to fit." ADHD, or any of its subtypes, may seem an unsatisfactory diagnosis if it leaves significant characteristics unexplained or unaccounted for. In this case, it is important to consult with a professional experienced in the field of ASD to find out if diagnosis in the autism spectrum will more accurately describe and explain the characteristics of the individual.

DSM-IV Diagnostic Criteria For Attention Deficit Hyperactivity Disorder

Here are the crieteria for ADHD. You may see how they relate to features of ASD but still leave other characteristics unaccounted for.

A. Either 1 or 2:

1. Six or more of the following symptoms of inattention have persisted for at least six months to a degree that is maladaptive and inconsistent with developmental level:

   a) Often fails to give close attention to details or makes careless mistakes in schoolwork, work or other activities.

   b) Often has difficulty sustaining attention to tasks or play activities

   c) Often does not seem to listen when spoken to directly.

   d) Often does not follow through on instructions and fails to finish schoolwork, chores or duties in the workplace (not due to oppositional behavior or failure to understand instructions).

   e) Often has difficulty organizing tasks and activities.

   f) Often avoids, dislikes or is reluctant to engage in tasks that require sustained mental effort (such as homework).

    g) Often loses things necessary for tasks or activities (toys, school assignments, pencils, books, or tools).

    h) Is often easily distracted by extraneous stimuli.

    i) Is often forgetful in daily activities.

2. Six or more of the following symptoms of hyperactivity-impulsivity have persisted for at least six months to a degree that is maladaptive and inconsistent with developmental level:

Hyperactivity

    a) Often fidgets with hands or feet or squirms in seat.

    b) Often leaves seat in classroom or in other situations in which remaining seated is expected.

    c) Often runs about or climbs excessively in situations in which it is inappropriate (in adolescents or adults, may be limited to subjective feelings of restlessness).

    d) Often has difficulty playing or engaging in leisure activities quietly.

    e) Is often "on the go" or often acts as if "driven by a motor".

    f) Often talks excessively.

Impulsivity

    a) Often blurts out answers before questions have been completed.

    b) Often has difficulty awaiting turn.

    c) Often interrupts or intrudes on others (such as butting into conversations or games).

B. Some hyperactive, impulsive or inattentive symptoms that caused impairment were present before age 7 years.

C. Some impairment from the symptoms is present in two or more settings (such as in school or work and at home).

D. There must be clear evidence of clinically significant impairment in social, academic or occupational functioning.

E. The symptoms do not occur exclusively during the course of a pervasive developmental disorder, schizophrenia or another psychotic disorder and are not better accounted for by another mental disorder (such as a mood, anxiety, dissociative, or personality disorder).[9]

ASD and Hyperlexia

Hyperlexia is a condition that is not found in the diagnostic manuals. It is a syndrome, or collection of characteristics. The American Hyperlexia Association describes the following characteristics that indicate hyperlexia:

- A precocious ability to read words, far above what would be expected at their chronological age, or an intense fascination with letters or numbers.

- Significant difficulty in understanding verbal language.

- Abnormal social skills, difficulty in socializing and interacting appropriately with people.

The word "hyperlexia" was first used in the 1960s to indicate word-decoding skills that were higher than word comprehension. Decoding involves being able to sound out and say, or recognize, the words that appear on paper. Children with hyperlexia often have amazing and gifted decoding skills and can read fluently from materials well beyond what would be expected for a person their age. Children as young as four or five who have hyperlexia may be able to read the newspaper or encyclopedia.

However, even though the young child appears to read very well and fluently, she does not necessarily understand the meaning of what is read. Since the 1970s, hyperlexia has been associated with learning disabilities. It seems ironic that a very young child who has a gift for decoding would also have a disability. The nature of the deficit areas may be masked by the fact that the child may "sound" like she understands. As the child develops, the gap in comprehension and other deficits in language, social skills and behavior begin to appear that impede learning.

Since the 1990s, hyperlexia has been associated with ASD. Exactly how they are associated is still under study. Many children who were hyperlexic when young have been later diagnosed with ASD. The description of children with autism in the DSM-IV specifically mentions hyperlexia as one example of the uneven development of cognitive skills, with ability or high ability in some areas and deficits in other areas. The types of problems in comprehension seen in hyperlexia are described in the features of autism. The DSM-IV, in the section under "Associated Features and Disorders for Autism Disorders," states:

"The profile of cognitive skills is usually uneven, regardless of the general level of intelligence (e.g., a 4 ½-year-old girl with Autistic Disorder may be able to read, i.e., hyperlexia). In many higher-functioning children with Autistic Disorder, the level of receptive language, (i.e., language comprehension) is below that of expressive language (e.g., vocabulary)."

Some children with ASD have hyperlexia, but it is still debated whether every child with hyperlexia has some form of autism. One theory is that the groups overlap, and clearly some of the characteristics are identical. Reading the following characteristics described by the Center for Speech and Language on the American Hyperlexia Association website, you will see the close relationship with features of autism.

"In addition, some children who are hyperlexic may exhibit the following characteristics:

- Learn expressive language in a peculiar way, echo or memorize the sentence structure without understanding the meaning (echolalia), reverse pronouns.

- Rarely initiates conversations.

- An intense need to keep routines, difficulty with transitions, ritualistic behavior.

- Auditory, olfactory, and/or tactile sensitivity.

- Self-stimulatory.

- Specific, unusual fears.

- Normal development until 18-24 months, then regression.

- Strong auditory and visual memory.

- Difficulty answering "Wh—" questions, such as "what," "where," "who" and "why".

- Think in concrete and literal terms, difficulty with abstract concepts.

- Listen selectively, appear to be deaf."

A child with hyperlexia will need supports and services to help him learn and be successful socially and academically. "Hyperlexia" is not a category of eligibility for special education services. Eligibility may be made in the category of Specific Learning Disability, Language/Speech Disorder , autism, or "Other Health Impaired."

In the determination of the areas of need and ability, it may be useful to include a differential diagnosis to determine if other conditions or disorders could be affecting the child with hyperlexia. This is an important opportunity to objectively examine whether a disorder such as ASD is present. The *"Questions to Ask"* in the section above on ADD and ADHD may be relevant. Parents of children and service personnel may find ideas in Chapter Three useful in identifying and describing the precise nature of the characteristics seen over time.

Case Example from Emily

This is my own case! Everyone who met my son, Tom, when he was a pre-schooler was absolutely amazed by him. When he was two years and three months old, sitting in a doctor's office, he pointed to the sign above the door and in a loud and happy voice exclaimed, to no one in particular, "EXIT! E-X-I-T!" I answered, "Yes, Tom, Exit." The man sitting next to me asked, "How old is that child?" I answered, "He just turned two, why?"

This was my first child, and I did not know that the other two-year-olds were not reading and spelling! Also at 2, Tom had memorized our car license plates, and when I bought gas I would ask him what the plate number was, because I could never remember. Tom's talents with letters, numbers and math continued at a great rate. At age 3, he and I used the sign language alphabet to play a spelling guessing game, and he solved puzzles on a popular TV alphabet game show before the contestants did. He could read just about anything, with expression, and read a book to the class on the first day of preschool. In kindergarten, he knew his times tables to nine.

While we recognized how bright Tom was, he seemed somehow, "socially immature." I had an excellent basis of comparison, for the twins who lived in the house behind mine shared Tom's birthday. We were often with this little boy and girl and differences in communication and social styles were apparent. Once, 3-year-old Ashley came to a birthday party, but Lindsey was home sick. When it was time to leave, Ashley asked me, "Can I have a goody bag for Lindsey? She's sick!" When she was 4 years old, Lindsey asked me, "Which dress do you think I should wear, this one or that one?" I remember being struck by both of those questions at the time. I was so impressed with the children's empathy, and I wasn't accustomed to being asked what I thought by a child. I have not forgotten those moments. They showed a qualitative difference to me, but I did not know what it meant.

One of the parents in our neighborhood preschool playgroup pointed out that she thought Tom was smart, but he did not seem to know how to play with the kids. We thought that maybe it was because he was too sophisticated to be interested in "kid stuff." Even though Tom could read and do math, the preschool teacher said he was not ready for regular kindergarten. On the advice of my sister, we chose a Montessori school that would allow Tom to excel in his areas of ability, give him a predictable routine and give him the opportunity to learn to play and be friends with the other children.

Barbara was always thinking about Tom and offering ideas about how to help him when problems arose. She even thought when Tom was age 5 that his differences fit the pattern of autism. I thought the idea was preposterous and was even angry that she suggested it. I told her that I was being the best mother I could be and she should *stop finding fault with my son and me. However, the pattern of academic strength and social problems continued and then worsened as elementary school progressed.*

Tom was born in 1983. When he was 11, Asperger's syndrome appeared in the DSM-IV. Barbara phoned. She said she had found a diagnosis that made sense and we needed to check it out. Lots of things about it did make sense to me, but some did not. I decided that we were doing OK without Asperger Syndrome. My kid did not have autism, not even a form of it. He wasn't like the character in RainMan and he didn't rock or flap his hands.

About a year later, however, I was anxious for a diagnosis. By age 12, things had spiraled into crisis for Tom and the whole family. We needed to know what the problem was. This time, when a professional at UCLA said, "autism," I was ready and actually relieved to hear it. It was a turning point, for the better, to finally accept that my child had autism.

Autism and Nonverbal Learning Disorder/Semantic Pragmatic Disorder

Some people say that Nonverbal Learning Disorder (NLD) and Semantic Pragmatic Disorder (SPD) are disorders on the autism spectrum viewed from the Speech and Language pathologist's point of view. Some people express concern that yet another discipline is looking at one piece of the ASD puzzle and adding more letters (and confusion) to the "alphabet soup."

Of course, speech and language experts and researchers would probably not agree with those views. Study continues to determine if NLD and SPD are separate diagnostic entities, or belong on the autism spectrum. Researchers are considering the correspondence between ASD, NLD and SPD and the neurological basis that may indicate whether these are distinct or related disorders. Refer to *references* at the end of the chapter to learn more about NLD and SPD.

If you or the child or adult in your case has a diagnosis of NLD or SPD and you feel that it is not a satisfactory explanation of all the characteristics and features that are evident, you may wish to refer to the section above "Questions to Ask" on ASD and ADHD. Answering the questions listed there may help in deciding if another professional opinion is needed. Remember that children and adults with NLD and SPD may benefit from many of the teaching techniques that help people with ASD.

Autism and Cognitive Disabilities

Some individuals with ASD have a cognitive disability, (sometimes called mental retardation) or cognitive impairment. This means that the individual has problems in learning, usually across most areas of learning and activity. Cognitive disabilities usually begin very early in life and have many causes. They occur on a spectrum, from mild to very severe or "profound."

The presence of a cognitive disability in an individual usually does not cause severe problems in the spontaneous development of social skills necessary as the foundation for relationships. For example, children with cognitive disabilities often look to those who are speaking, use gestures and facial expressions to communicate (sometimes later than their typical peers, but usually correctly) and seem to be able to "interpret" and understand the non-verbal communication used by others. Play skills in young children with cognitive disabilities are often quite social and reciprocal. Individuals with cognitive disabilities often have a variety of interests and tend to be less restrictive and repetitive.

Individuals who have a cognitive disability *and* an Autism Spectrum Disorder are at risk for being inadequately diagnosed. Staff and families may think that characteristics of autism that they see are "oddities" in the person with a cognitive disability. The features of an ASD could be mistakenly attributed to less intelligence, stubbornness, a desire to self-isolate, poor parenting or poor educational, residential or vocational programming.

It used to be thought that about half of all people with ASD also had cognitive disabilities. That percentage is being questioned now that it is possible to more accurately test individuals with ASD, and now that ASD is recognized as a spectrum disorder. We are not aware of any estimates of how many people with cognitive disability also have ASD, but our personal experiences and stories from staff and families indicate that there are many people with cognitive disorders who also have ASD being underdiagnosed.

Case Example for Barbara:

I was asked to a consultation regarding a man in his thirties named Jack, who had Down Syndrome with cognitive disability and profound deafness. He lived in a large group home in a metropolitan area. His parents were pleased with his residential placement and work program. However, they were upset that he continued to have "behavior problems" that did not seem to be resolved by any of the strategies used effectively by staff with other residents.

My observation confirmed the presence of what appeared to be characteristics of ASD. Down Syndrome, cognitive disabiltiy or deafness could not explain these observable behaviors. His parents were at first dismayed that staff would want to "give him one more diagnosis." In response to the parent's natural discomfort, we did not seek the confirmation of our suspicion from a diagnostician at that time. However, we got permission from Jack's parents to begin to change his programming as if he had ASD to see what would happen.

Staff learned to create routines that Jack could memorize. They began to use visual and spatial cues. They created an object schedule for Jack and began to incorporate more of his liked activities into his daily schedule. They stopped using behavioral programs where Jack "lost points" for doing something wrong. Staff began to focus speech and language goals on high-impact signs, and taught Jack to do some communicating with word and picture cards.

The improvements in Jack were phenomenal! His staff and parents were delighted. His parents continued to read about ASD and soon sought a formal diagnosis. Jack's life was greatly improved by recognizing the learning differences that are part of ASD and treating them with appropriate individualized programming.

How Important Is It to Diagnose ASD in an Adult with Cognitive Disability?

Very important! Most programs for adults with developmental disabilities in our country and abroad were designed for adults with cognitive disabilities, cerebral palsy and severe seizure disorders. Staff from these programs strive to meet the needs of the adults they support, even though staff to client ratios are often not adequate. Knowing that an individual has a cognitive disability *and* ASD can lead to staff and families making some simple, low-cost adaptations that improve the quality of life for the individual and everyone else around them. Staff working with adults can apply the information in this book to any adult who has the characteristics of an Autism Spectrum Disorder even if they can't get the diagnosis changed.

Case Example from Barbara

Staff from an adult service agency attended one of my seminars about ASD. They had come to learn how to provide services to a young man with autism who would be coming into their agency in the near future. During the discussion about characteristics and features, they began to realize that another person they served, Tim, might be a person with autism. We talked about the individual during the break and I agreed to meet him.

I observed features of ASD in Tim. We developed a plan to support him using some simple adaptations that work for people with ASD. They began to give him a printed schedule every morning so he would know who was coming to work with him, whether or not he was going to the workshop that day, if there would be visitors, if he was going out with the group in the evening, etc. They began to use more visual cues for him to help him keep working at the workshop and to help him distinguish his possessions from those of others. Staff began to speak to him in shorter, clearer, quieter sentences. They looked at his unusual interests in a new way and began to help him engage in more activities that he liked to do. They explained his differences to the other people with whom he lived and worked.

About one month later, a staff member called me. Tim's aggression had significantly decreased. They were working with the psychiatrist and reducing his medications that were prescribed for behavioral issues. His production at work had increased substantially. He seemed "happier" and more willing to be around other people than in the past. He had stopped taking other people's possessions. He had become a little more "popular" with his housemates. Since one of his highly liked activities was music, they had made him the DJ for the Friday night dances, events he previously resisted attending. They had changed his life for the better without additional money or staff resources. In viewing him as a person with autism and meeting his needs in a way known to help people with autism, they had accomplished what no simple diagnosis could ever do.

The lives of people with disabilities of any age and in any circumstance can be changed and improved when those who provide support have greater awareness and understanding. Knowledge shifts attitudes and a different attitude causes us to respond differently. Understanding that an individual learns as a person with an Autism Spectrum Disorder opens new avenues for teaching, communicating and improving skills. It leads the way to greater compassion and helps others more easily take the point of view of the person with the autism disorder. It is never too early or too late to learn about ASD and change how you interact with and support the individual.

CHAPTER 2 SUMMARY

- A parent, family member, teacher, school staff member, pediatrician or other medical professional, friend, neighbor or an individual with ASD may be the one to recognize the features of ASD, without knowing the correct diagnosis.

- The purpose of a diagnosis is to accurately describe and make sense of the symptoms and characteristics a person has. A professional opinion is needed to confirm ASD. The opinion formed will be based on the experience and perspective of the specialist.

- Differential diagnosis is the process of "ruling out" some disorders in order to obtain the correct diagnosis. This includes determining if any physical or mental illness or injury could be causing the symptoms being described or observed. Some people will have a developmental disorder such as ASD and another physical or mental disorder as well.

- Many people with ASD receive a separate diagnosis for each "piece" of the "autism puzzle" before the "whole picture" is seen and recognized by someone who knows. In other cases, families are confused when health professionals don't recognize and correctly identify what they are seeing. This may be due to limited training and experience, or the "overlap" of ASD with other disorders like ADHD, Hyperlexia, OCD, Nonverbal Learning Disorder and Semantic Pragmatic Disorder.

- It may be a good idea to be skeptical of a diagnosis that is not "satisfying." The correct diagnosis will accurately explain all significant features and will not "ignore" or fail to account for important characteristics or information.

- Lack of information can hinder an accurate diagnosis. It is important to collect and present all relevant information about development to create a "video" of the person's life instead of a "snapshot." This is especially important if the person has changed over time, has strengths that "mask" deficits or has received intervention through informal supports and accommodations from family or staff.

- It is never too early or too late to benefit from an accurate diagnosis.

- One individual may have an autism disorder and any other mental or physical disorder such as Down Syndrome, Cerebral Palsy, or hearing impairment.

- Professionals making a diagnosis may prefer particular terms such as PDD or Autism Spectrum Disorder. This may be personal preference training, local custom or done to be sensitive to parents who may be shocked by the word "autism."

- Parents, professionals, or individuals should persist in getting an accurate diagnosis that accounts for the characteristics present now and in the past. The correct diagnosis can help everyone view the person accurately work together, access services and strive for the best possible outcomes.

- To receive a diagnosis of "Autistic Disorder" using the criteria found in the DSM-IV, section 299.00, at least six criteria must be met in three categories: "social interaction," "communication," and "restricted, repetitive and stereotyped patterns of behavior, interests and activities."

- Pervasive Developmental Disorder, Not Otherwise Specified, can be diagnosed when there is "severe and pervasive impairment in the development of reciprocal social interaction or verbal and nonverbal communication," but the diagnostician feels the presentation of symptoms is not "typical" in some way.

- Criteria for Asperger's Disorder are found in section 299.80 of the DSM-IV and include guidance to distinguish Asperger's from autism. Asperger Syndrome is often diagnosed much later in life than Autistic Disorder.

- At the time of printing of this book, the *Wired* magazine website offers a self-administered screening, the Autism-Spectrum Quotient (AQ). Designed by Dr. Simon Baron-Cohen of the Autism Research Center of Cambridge, England, the AQ is available for free online at http://www.wired.com/wired/archive/9.12/aqtest.html. Results are tabulated by your computer to give an indication of the presence of ASD, but not a diagnosis.

SOURCES
For Chapters One and Two

American Hyperlexia Association, 195 W. Spangler Street Elmhurst, Illinois, 60126. Phone: 630-415-2212; FAX 630-530-5909. Website:http://www.hyperlexia.org.

American Psychiatric Association. *Diagnostic and Statistical Manual of Mental Disorders, Text Revision, 2000.* [DSM-IV-R], Washington, D.C., author, 2000.

Atwood, Tony, Ph. D. "Asperger's Syndrome as a New Diagnostic Category." Autism Asperger's Digest, November-December 2000, 23-25.

Atwood, Tony, Ph. D. *Asperger's Syndrome* Seminar at University of California, Los Angeles, June 6-8, 1998.

Bauer, Stephen, M.D. *Asperger Syndrome.* Found online at the O.A.S.I.S. Website: http://www.udel.edu/bkirby/asperger's/as_thru_years.html.

Center for Speech and Language Disorders, 195 W. Spangler Street, Suite B, Elmhurst, Illinois, 60126. Phone: 630-530-8551. Website: www.csld.com

Church, Catharine Critz, Ph.D, CPNP, and James Coplan, M.D. *The High-Functioning Autism Experience: Birth to Preteen Years.* Journal of Pediatric Healthcare, Volume 9, Number 1, 23-29.

Code of Federal Regulations,(C.F.R.) Title 34, Section 300 and following.

Donnelly, Julie A. M. Ed, and Edna Smith, Ph.D. *Overcoming the Barriers: Strategies for Educating Students with High-Functioning Autism/Asperger's Syndrome.* Victoria, British Columbia, May 1996.

Frostig Center, The, 971 North Altadena Drive, Pasadena, CA., 91107 www.frostig.org

The Frostig Center is a non-profit organization that specializes in working with children who have learning disabilities, and the study, diagnosis, and treatment of learning disabilities. 971 North Altadena Drive Pasadena, California 91107 www.frostig.org

Forrest, Bonny. *The Boundaries Between Aspergers and Nonverbal Learning Disability Syndromes.* Website: www.ldonline.com

Freeman, B.J., Ph.D. *Autism: A Biological Disorder.* Educational Workshop, UCLA Neuropsychiatric Institute and Hospital, August 1997.

Frith, Uta. *Autism and Asperger Syndrome.* Cambridge, UK: Cambridge University Press, 1991

Howlin, Patricia. *Children with Autism and Asperger Syndrome: A Guide for Practitioners and Carers.* West Sussex, England: John Wiley & Sons, Ltd., 1999.

Individuals with Disabilities Education Act (IDEA) Title 20 U.S.C. Sections 1400 and following.

Kanner, Leo. *Autistic Disturbances of Affective Contact.Nervous Child*, 2:217-280, 1943. Found online at the American Medical Association Website: http://www.ama.org.br/kannereng11anddisc.htm

Klin, Ami, Fred R. Volkman and Sara S. Sparrow, editors. (2000) *Asperger Syndrome.* New York: Guilford Press.

Lord, Catherine, Ph. D. *Pervasive Developmental Disorders.* (Chart) Sept. 1995.

Mesibov, Gary B. Lynn W. Adams and Laura W. Klinger. *Autism: Understanding the Disorder.* New York: Plenum Press, 1997.

Mesibov, Gary, Ph.D. *High-Functioning Autism or Asperger Syndrome: Why the Controversy?* Autism Asperger's Digest, November-December 2000, 16-18.

National Attention Deficit Disorder Association. *Guiding Principals for the Diagnosis and Treatment of Attention Deficit Hyperactivity Disorder.* 2000. Website: http://www.add.org/gp98.htm.

O.A.S.I.S.: Online Asperger Syndrome Information and Support. Website administered by Barb Kirby: http://www.udel.edu/bkirby/asperger/.

Ozonoff, Sally, Ph.D. *High Functioning Autism and Asperger Syndrome: What Research Tells Us.* Presentation at University of California, Los Angeles, October 13, 2001.

Rasking, M.H., Goldberg, R.J.; Higgens, E.L. & Herman, K.L. (2003). *Life success for children with learning disabilities: A parent guide.*: Pasadena, CA: Frostig Center. Available online http://www.frostig.org/LDsuccess

Schopler, Eric, and Gary B. Mesibov. *Diagnosis and Assessment in Autism.* New York: Plenum Press, 1988.

Siegel, Bryna, Ph.D. *The World of the Autistic Child.* Oxford University Press, 1996.

CHAPTER 3

BEGINNING THE PROCESS OF ASSESSMENT AND DIAGNOSIS

In this chapter you will learn:

- Options for getting assessments for children or adults.

- Emotions in starting the assessment process.

- How to prepare a personal summary to assist with the assessment process.

- Ideas for adults who want to refer themselves for diagnosis.

- What teachers can do and why.

Options in Getting a Diagnosis

Who Can Diagnose

A first step to confirm or rule out a diagnosis of an Autism Spectrum Disorder is to arrange for a comprehensive evaluation from a psychiatrist or neurologist experienced with ASD. In all states, medical doctors (pediatricians, psychiatrists, neurologists, etc.) can diagnose autism and related disorders. If they have had little training or experience about the population, medical and psychological personnel may be less likely to recognize ASD in children and adults. Parents, guardians and staff can contact university medical departments, developmental clinics, and local or national autism groups to get recommendations for diagnosticians experienced with ASD. Practitioners may specialize in diagnosing children under 3, school-aged children, or adults.

In some states, Licensed Clinical Psychologists (LCPs) and Licensed Clinical Social Workers (LCSWs) may give a diagnosis. You may wish to check with your state licensing board to determine which professionals in your state are qualified to make an official or "clinical" diagnosis.

In some states, school psychologists can legally identify a child aged 3 to 21, only for the purposes of educational eligibility. An educationally valid diagnosis means that supports, services and modifications in the educational program, including special preschool services, can be put in place. Additionally, it may be worthwhile to secure a diagnosis from another professional in order to qualify the individual for any other available services.

There is no medical test for autism, so the diagnosis is not clear-cut or easy to determine. Sometimes a visit to a professional, such as a physician, psychiatrist, psychologist or social worker results in a diagnosis, but sometimes it does not. Diagnosis is based on the information collected by the professional and her opinion on whether the person meets the diagnostic criteria for a disorder on the autism spectrum. Sometimes, a diagnostician may ask for the person to be brought back to them again at a later date. The professional may "rule out" some disorders (meaning they are no longer being considered as possibilities) or identify multiple disorders present at the same time.

The diagnostic process usually results in a report with conclusions and recommendations. One value of the report is that the official diagnosis can be used for eligibility to arrange supports and special education services from the school district and local agencies, depending on where you live. The recommendations in the written report usually help service providers and others assist the individual. The downside of a report from individual clinicians is that the report may be limited in scope. The report may not be specific enough or provide complete information about the skills and needs of the individual in all areas of functioning. There is a chance that the diagnosis given will not seem satisfactory. You may disagree with it.

Another option in diagnosis is to get a full team interdisciplinary assessment. This means that a psychiatrist or neurologist will be part of a team that includes a physician, speech and language pathologist, physical therapist, occupational therapist, psychologist, social worker, educational/learning specialist and others. The advantage of a team assessment is the coordinated effort that examines *all* aspects of functioning. Evaluations are usually done in the same location, such as at a school, university or in a clinic, although several visits may be needed to complete the process.

Families and staff should try to find a team with experience and knowledge in working with individuals in the Autism Spectrum. The diagnostic team approach is often offered at clinics that specialize in ASD. Diagnostic teams are offered at some universities and hospitals, particularly those that have a service called a developmental clinic. School districts usually use multidisciplinary evaluations to determine if a disability exists that interferes with a student's educational progress or participation.

Some governmental agencies offer team assessments for ASD. In some states, the Department of Mental Health or other government agencies will do a complete, multidisciplinary team assessment. For California residents, the Regional Center System provides full evaluation services at no cost for individuals thought to have ASD with an onset before the age of 18. In Illinois, the state Office of Developmental Disabilities can refer families to centers and clinics with experience in working with people with ASD. In Missouri, the Department of Mental Health has a special autism services section that parents and staff can contact for help. A local autism society or support group in your state or a nearby state may be able to provide references for team assessments done by professionals who have demonstrated expertise and sensitivity.

If the assessment is done privately, the family will be responsible for the fees of the professionals, and the costs can be substantial. Some insurance companies may pay for an assessment or evaluation to determine the presence of a developmental disability. Contact your insuarance agent before the assessment and ask for a copy of the terms of coverage, as well as a list of clinics or professionals that are service providers in your insurance plan.

Some insurance company employees are uncertain whether ASD is a medical or a psychological condition and may not know how to direct an inquiry. It may help to describe the condition as a developmental disorder, just as cerebral palsy and Down Syndrome are classified as developmental disorders. Employees of insurance companies who are not familiar with ASD are often more familiar with other developmental conditions and know where they fit into their programs. Most insurance carriers now consider Autism Spectrum Disorder as a medical, brain-based condition, and not as a psychological disorder or mental illness. When in doubt, ask to speak to a manager or supervisor and request that all decisions about what will and will not be paid for by insurance are sent to you in writing.

The Role of the School System

Another option to get an evaluation for children ages 3 to 21 is to go through your school system. While particular schools and school districts may have more or less experience in serving children with ASD, federal and state law requires that all school districts provide evaluation services as part of their mandate to provide a free, appropriate, public education to children with special needs. This is sometimes referred to as a "child-find" obligation, meaning that schools are required to, in a timely manner, identify and evaluate whether a child is experiencing significant difficulties learning because he has a disability or special needs.

School districts will provide a full evaluation of the student at no cost to the parents. Even if the child is a preschooler and not yet enrolled in or attending school, the local school district has the responsibility of conducting an assessment if it is believed that the child has special needs. The process gets under way when a parent or guardian submits a written request to the school principal or district head of special education services and requests a full evaluation to determine if a disability that impacts the child's education is present.

The response of the school district will be to form a comprehensive team to plan the necessary assessments. The team usually includes a general education classroom teacher, an administrator, and other personnel such as a school psychologist, speech and language pathologist, learning specialist, reading specialist, social worker, physical therapist and/or occupational therapist. The members of the team will select tests and assessments intended to identify if a disorder is present and to determine the nature of the problems that the child is experiencing. The expected outcome is that the team will be able to specify the child's educational needs and strengths then design supports and services to address them. School psychologists report the results of testing and assessments to the child's school team (always including parents.) The team can determine eligibility for special education services under "educational autism" at a Multidisciplinary Educational Eligibility Conference (MDEC).

The Role of the Parent

Parents are always a part of the assessment team, no matter who is doing the diagnosis and assessments. Parents need to look very carefully at the areas being tested and the types of tests being proposed in order to be sure the proposed testing is adequate to reveal the problem areas. Since most parents have very little experience or knowledge of the various areas to be tested and the tests used, they may need more help in understanding what it all means before signing the form consenting to the assessment process. Clinic or school administrators or staff should be able to answer any questions parents may have about the testing. (Chapter Five of this book offers specific information about testing and the assessment process.)

When evaluations are done by a school district, procedures, rights and responsibilities of the school and parents are covered by Federal laws contained in the

1997 Individuals with Disabilities Education Act, (IDEA) Public Law 101-476. This version of IDEA law is in effect in all 50 states until Congress re-authorizes a revised version in 2004. Schools are required by law to provide parents with special education rights information, but it is not always provided before the assessment process begins. This information should be provided early in the process, but if it is overlooked, parents should ask for it. Most states have a booklet for parents beginning any special educational process. It is usually titled something like "A Parent's Rights in the Special Education Process," or "Procedural Safeguards."

Another option for parents is to find and/or hire an educational advocate who is familiar with educational law and procedures and who knows about testing and assessment procedures. Other parents with experience are often willing to talk with "new" parents to help them negotiate the assessment process, and many states have service agencies that provide help to parents at no cost. Advocates help parents understand legal issues, their rights, and the process of serving the needs of a child with a disability. Area autism societies can provide a list of advocates and resources, while the state department of education or office of special education, will provide free materials that explain parental rights in the special education process. The only thing parents have to do is ask for the information. We recommend getting this material and reading it at the beginning of the assessment process.

Adults in the Care of Adult Service Providers or Agencies

If an individual is over 21 years old, or is no longer served by the public schools, parents and staff can talk to the director of the local agency that provides services to adults with developmental disabilities. Parents and staff can ask for information about professional diagnosticians in the area and contact them for information about adult assessments. Once the parent/staff has found a diagnostician with expertise, the parents can explain the need for an assessment and ask how to arrange it. If the adult is in the care of an agency, the agency staff can be asked to define, in writing, any barriers to getting an assessment, and agency management should help in removing those barriers.

Our best advice for staff and families is "be determined." Simply don't take "no" for an answer if you believe an assessment is necessary. If someone says it is not possible, speak to their supervisor. Find out who can make exceptions to rules and who makes final decisions, then talk to those people. Work all the way up to your state developmental disability agency if you need to. If you are still denied a comprehensive assessment, call your legislators or contact the governor's office in your state. All states require that "appropriate" services be provided to people with disabilities. You need to point out that "appropriate" services can not be provided without an accurate diagnosis based on a comprehensive assessment. This is true even if the person already has some other diagnosis.

Adult Readers

Some individuals reading this book may think that they have some or many of the characteristics of ASD. Some may consider, "I have made it this far and have been this successful in my life without knowing, so what difference would a diagnosis make at this point?" This is a very personal matter that may take some time to decide. Other adults may feel that a diagnosis would make sense and be a welcome explanation of many difficulties.

More and more adults are now seeking a diagnosis from qualified professionals. Adult readers may want to contact local or national autism societies and support groups, universities or diagnostic centers, and even their health insurance company for help in finding a practitioner experienced in recognizing ASD in adults. In the section that follows, we'll discuss preparing for the assessment process. Although much of the discussion is about schools and children, many of the ideas will apply equally well to assessments for adults.

Emotions and the Assessment Process

A Stressful Situation

There is no question that the assessment process is stressful. Often, at the time of evaluation, families or staff are in a state of crisis because of the seriousness of problems at home, school, work, or in the community. The person with ASD may feel anxious in general and be further stressed by being assessed, by having normal routines disrupted or by having to be in contact with unfamiliar people in unfamiliar places. This strain can make learning, social problems and behavior problems even worse, leaving the person with ASD feeling overwhelmed, and staff and family exhausted before the assessment has even begun!

The process of assessment can be very emotional for the family as well as the child or adult being assessed. Parents may experience a sense of loss, shock, or panic. Many have great difficulty accepting that ASD could be the problem, and they may be overwhelmed by having to face and name their child's deficit areas. It is natural for people to need time to understand it, or to feel reluctant or unwilling to look at the facts. Other parents tell of their worries about privacy, labeling issues and other fears. Add to this the fact that siblings and other family members may feel guilty, angry, embarrassed, overwhelmed or left out of the process entirely, and it is easy to understand why families feel anxious.

The amount of time that it takes to complete assessments is another strain on the family or caregivers. Many weeks and months may pass from the time that problems first arise until the need for assessment is agreed upon, assessments completed, meetings held and services begun. Families or staff may feel almost desperate for help, yet they must often wait for the process to be completed before getting the help they need. (If parents or staff think that harm may come to someone before the assessment is completed, they should ask for immediate, emergency services and help from the local developmental disabilities or mental health service providers.)

Parents may have feelings of anger and resentment toward school personnel or agency staff. Parents may blame them for not having intervened sooner to get help when so many signs were there. It is common for people to feel angry that time has been lost or wasted and that the child or adult has suffered as a result. In other cases, parents may feel anger or resentment when school or agency staff suggest that an assessment is needed and that some specific problems do exist.

From the point of view of the school or agency personnel, the assessment process has its share of difficulties. It may be hard to administer tests or get individuals to respond so that an accurate assessment can be made. Professionals may feel overwhelmed by the demands of working with the individual and question their own skills, competence or training. Special education and adult agency staff personnel often feel "snowed under" by legitimate, but ever-increasing, demands on their time and resources.

Additionally, school or agency staff may feel pressured by stated or implied expectations from the school district or adult provider agencies that seem to limit what staff can do or say if they suspect that a student or client is experiencing difficulties. Teachers and staff may experience frustration if parents appear uncooperative or unresponsive when the individual's problems are discussed. They may feel that their hands are tied when they are concerned enough to ask to do an assessment, but are told, "there is nothing wrong with my child."

Recognizing that the assessment process can be stressful and emotional for everyone involved can help both parents and staff to be rational, factual and understanding. As difficult as the assessment process is, it can be made better or worse by the degree of cooperation and mutual courtesy among those participating. If all parties remain calm and non-judgmental, it leaves the door open for communication without fear.

Trust is an important element in helping teams work well together, but it is not instant or automatic. Parents may worry about sharing private information and personal details about their family life with "strangers." Parents may be reluctant to "open up" in early meetings or during meetings with large numbers of staff. They may hesitate to confide in a professional until they know him or her better.

Staff can help parents feel more comfortable by explaining how privacy laws apply to confidential information. This can include mentioning how the information will and will not be used, who may and may not discuss it, where the written records are kept and how access to records is controlled and limited. Parents may respond well to sincere staff who recognize and empathize with parents' reluctance and fears and the fact that the whole process is new, confusing and frightening.

Professionals have the opportunity to be both sensitive and caring, and communicate openly with the family. Parents have the opportunity to give input, suggestions and support to the diagnostic team. This is the optimal scenario to which all team members should aspire within the confines of everyday reality! It certainly helps to try and work together as a team for the good of the individual. One expression regarding the process of working together as a team is to "check your baggage at the door!" Obviously, it's easier said than done, but still important to consider. It is especially helpful for all participants to put emotional responses to past events in the past and begin the assessment process with "a clean slate."

There are many ways for teams to learn to communicate more effectively. We suggest the use of accurate, non-judgmental language to describe behavior and features realted to ASD. The additional time it takes to communicate, as a team, will be saved many times over as problems are avoided or more quickly resolved.

How Parents Can Help Professionals With the Diagnostic Process

The diagnosis of autism is described as "retrospective." This means that detailed information about a person's past is needed to make the correct diagnosis, even if the person is an adult today. Recollections provided by parents about their child's development and behaviors at different ages and stages are crucial and may be the only source of this important information.

Parents may not feel confident about their own knowledge and ability in discussions with professionals who have formal training in education and disabilities. Parents may vary in their level of understanding of ASD, but there is no disputing that the parent is the expert when it comes to his own child. Parents can provide invaluable information about a child's past and current functioning, strengths and needs. Parental input should be welcome and invited in all phases of the collaborative process of identification, assessment and service delivery.

Case Example from Barbara

My friend Eileen recently phoned from another state. Last year, she had brought her son to me because she thought that there was "something wrong." Max, age 7, is as cute as a little boy could be and obviously bright and loving. He has a fantastic memory for facts and loves dinosaurs and transportation vehicles. However, Max was having difficulties that other bright and loving boys don't usually have. He showed repetitive behavior in watching the same videos over and over and making the same drawings many times without variation. He became very upset by changes in routine. He did not play with any child except his sister. On the playground at school, he engaged in a kind of tag and chase game, but other children never sought him out to do this. He had used echolalia (repeating what someone just said) much longer than most children who go through a short, but natural, stage of echoing. He was often confused by what other people said and his mother found herself giving more explanations to him than to his younger sister. He sometimes cried and said that something was wrong with him. It seemed very hard for him to focus and pay attention to schoolwork, yet his attention for things he really liked was sometimes hours long. He had difficulty getting organized and starting activities, finding his materials and keeping track of homework and other papers.

I clearly saw a pattern in Max, but I am not a diagnostician. I helped Eileen list the characteristics she saw in Max in an objective way. Then I told her to take the list to Max's teachers and ask for Max to be assessed and diagnosed by people licensed to either say he has a disability or he does not. I told her to ask them to try to see how Max is learning and to assess any areas where learning was particularly difficult for him. I told her she had a right to this service since Max was experiencing difficulties in school (no friends, difficulty working in small groups, often in trouble on the playground, difficulty participating in gym, often said things to teachers that were interpreted as "spoiled" or "rude"). Eileen and I were both afraid that Max was being labeled as "troubled" or a "trouble-maker," two labels that would be inaccurate and unfair.

Eileen called me to say that Max had a terrible year in third grade and to ask if she should consider home-schooling him for fourth grade. I asked what services he had received as a result of the assessment that she had requested. I was horrified to learn that Max had never been assessed, and, as a result, he had received no services at all! Eileen had gone to the school with her list. School staff told her that she was overprotective, not understanding how to "let Max go." They said that Max was "fine" in school and that the hours of homework he had to do every night resulted from his "stubbornness" and her "coddling" him. When Eileen mentioned the autism spectrum as a possible area to consider, a speech therapist and a learning resource teacher told her that Max did not have autism, and that they had seen plenty of children with autism before and that Max was not like any of them.

My heart broke for Max and Eileen. I encouraged Eileen to talk to the director of special education services immediately and to try to get an assessment completed before the end of the year. I encouraged her to seek a diagnosis outside of school.

What had happened here? Several things. First, school staff dismissed the concerns Eileen described last year because they did not see the same concerns, because she described them in an ordinary way, because they judged her in advance or because they did not understand her concerns. School staff did not pursue her request by making a home visit or asking Eileen to give them more information, possibly because they had already decided that it was all Eileen's fault! Two special educators "ruled out" a diagnosis of ASD, even though they are not licensed or certified diagnosticians. (By the way, they placed themselves in a position to lose their license or certification by doing diagnostic work when not certified to do so!) Eileen had little recourse to address the refusal to assess because it was not documented or put in writing.

The saddest piece is that now that Max has had such a bad year in school, he is really depressed. He describes himself as stupid. He says he is bad and that is why he has no friends. He told Eileen that his teachers do not like her! Eileen feels like *a failure and another year of Max's free, appropriate, public education is irretrievably gone.*

When parents seem "too helpful" or "too protective" of a child, it is often because they have seen that the child often fails without this help or protection. Parents who have a different style of parenting are often responding to the ways that the child is different. In more than 30 years in the field, I have met only one parent that was too protective for no reason. Our least dangerous assumption is that parents say and do what they believe their child needs and their beliefs are based on years of accumulated day-to-day experiences. Sometimes the child does better in the classroom because there are rules to follow and other children to watch to see what to do. The real proof of skills however, may be when everyone is not seated at a desk in a classroom.

School staff made many mistakes about Max and Eileen. Now Eileen is going to have to fight against the assumptions and conclusions that school staff have mistakenly drawn. I can only hope that these staff will open their hearts and minds and listen to her now.

I do not blame the school staff, however. In our special education training, we special educators are taught to make quick decisions and to know about children and adults and their needs. Staff also need to be trained to listen and respond to legitimate concerns; that training is not part of teacher education or special education at the college level in most places. School staff are frequently overwhelmed by the number of children presenting with problems that were rarely seen in the past. Perhaps we do not want to believe there are so many special needs children! Special education managers and supervisors must be sure that every concern of parents is actually addressed systematically, not "blown off" by overworked, but well-meaning staff. Max and Eileen's story highlights the fact that all schools need to have a consistent way to help parents describe issues and begin the assessment and screening process.

When in doubt, assess objectively. When in doubt, err on the side of believing the parent until you have hard proof that she is wrong. When in doubt, blame the brain,

> *not the child or the family, and seek to find ways that this brain is different and how it can be helped to function more efficiently. Learn to tell the difference between what is known and what people have decided to believe. I have made the mistake of not hearing parents in the past. These mistakes have led to the biggest regrets I have when I view my career in retrospect.*

Some parents and caregivers may not be skilled in using professional language to describe their children. However, no one knows a child better than his or her parents! **Professionals need to "listen deeply" to what parents have to say**, not to the way the parents say it. Professionals will do well if they can practice separating the content of the parents' statements from the emotion that propels it.

Recently, another issue in parent-professional collaboration has emerged. Some parents and other caregivers come to the table very well-educated and articulate regarding their son or daughter. They may have done months or years of research, sorting through pages of material, until they came upon a diagnostic profile that seems to "fit" their son or daughter. Professionals may have to hurry to "catch up" with parents, learning quickly about new topics and resisting the urge to dismiss what is unfamiliar to them.

Sometimes concerned professionals will have studied or done research in their dedication to finding a way to effectively serve all children and adults in their care. But in the beginning of the assessment process, it is important for both parents and professionals to describe features that are clearly observable in the child or adult, rather than begin by suggesting a diagnosis first and describing the features that fit that diagnosis.

Prepare a Written Personal Summary

In the process of diagnosis and assessment, parents or other caregivers are often asked dozens or even hundreds of questions about the child's development over the years. Similar questions may be repeated in preparation for several different assessments. We suggest that parents or other caregivers prepare a written summary of the child's development and health. It will be useful to you and helpful to the professionals who will be working to complete tests and assessments.

To prepare a detailed, year-by-year history of your child (or the child or adult in your care), use videos, photos, a baby book, journals, preschool reports, school records, etc., to bring back memories. Try to remember what the child was like at each stage. Think about things that were different about him, aspects that perhaps stood out when he was with other children of the same age. Include things that surprised, puzzled, worried, or frustrated you or others.

Describe the child, and write about what the child did, how the child communicated and the child's social life. Concentrate on one year at a time, from birth to the present. Use specific examples and anecdotes that show clearly what the person was like at a particular moment in time. Add writing samples, drawings, schoolwork, or even video recordings that show what you are describing.

Looking back at each year of life, include a note if there was any medical condition at each age, or other health issues. Note if medications were used for a significant period of time, whether prescription or over-the-counter, and what effects medication seemed to have. Include a comment if the child stopped doing something that he had done at an earlier age or seemed to "regress" and no longer used skills that she previously had used.

Talk to others and include impressions of friends and family who knew the child at various stages of development. Ask sisters, brothers and other relatives to tell about things that they remember about the child growing up. They may have some very specific memories, e.g., "I'll never forget the day I saw your child_____." The recollections of others may help you recall other significant events, behaviors or characteristics. For older children or adults, talk to previous service providers, parents, or family members if they are still living (even if they are no longer "involved" in the life of the person) and try to get copies of school records, hospital, work or medical records, etc.

Review school records, looking for notes from teachers who may have noticed differences or issues. Then organize the information in chronological order. One source of information for all children during their years at school is the cumulative file. This is a file of information kept at the school that contains many details about the child's experiences and problems from day to day and year to year. Graded writing samples are often kept in the cumulative file as well. The file may contain information that is not included in report cards. There may also be a separate "personal file," a "discipline file," or a "psychological file," that may contain important information or document significant events. Sometimes the issues described in these files have not been discussed with parents. The cumulative, personal, psychological or discipline files may include teacher comments that reveal a pattern of difficulty. These files are usually transferred along with a student if he changes schools and are sent from the elementary school to the junior high and the high school to form a continuous record.

The cumulative, personal, disciplinary, and psychological files may be valuable sources of information and should not be overlooked. Parents and other legally entitled caregivers can go to the school office to ask to see any and all files created that contain information about your child. You cannot know the value of the information they contain until you look. The school district is obliged to photocopy any pages that you would like to have copied, usually for free or for a nominal fee. If you find information in these files that you disagree with or feel is inaccurate, you may wish to add a letter with your comments to the contents of the file.

If your "child" is already an adult, the process of recording everything you can remember about their childhood is very valuable. One reason is that the history you prepare may be the only source of relevant information. It is important because of the changes that occur in individuals over time. An adult may have learned many ways to cope, cover-up, adapt and compensate for some aspects of the disability. The personal summary will likely reveal patterns in learning, behavior and communication that may not have been previously recognized.

Professionals and family members may have gotten into the habit of attributing the individual's characteristics to certain causes ("Oh, that's just because he has mental retardation." or, "He just prefers to be alone.") These opinions can interfere with presenting an objective and clear picture of the individual, past and present. Trying to look at characteristics in an adult or older child can be like looking at an "after" picture; the "before" that is no longer as evident needs to be clearly described. Although, it may take longer to prepare a personal summary for a teen or adult and it may be harder to recollect information, it is crucial.

The summary will not take the place of the questions that professionals will ask, but it can be a great way for parents to prepare for the diagnostic interviews and assessments. It will be helpful for finding needed information, or ideas you wrote while you had time to think. It will help to be consistent in giving answers to questions like, "At what age did your baby sit up?" or "Did he play with or alongside other children at age 4?" Details can be added or changed as they are recalled. You can later add answers to questions that you are asked that were not covered in your summary.

A word processor is a great help, but the summary can also be handwritten. If it seems like a daunting task, don't try to do it all at once. Break it into manageable pieces. It may be easier to organize parts of the summary in list form rather than use sentences. Don't wait to complete the summary before you begin to contact professionals and make appointments to begin the assessment process. There is usually a waiting period before the first appointment when parents or staff can gather their thoughts and information and put it down on paper.

Adults Piece the Puzzle Together

One of the best pieces of advice for an adult seeking a diagnosis is, "Ask your mother." If your mother or someone who was involved in your life on a regular basis is living and willing to talk with you about details from your childhood, she may be able to provide crucial information. Having a conversation or interview about yourself may be awkward, however, as parents may not want to say they thought that something was wrong. They may be feeling guilty, sad or responsible, or they may have difficulty remembering long ago. They may also confuse what one child did with what a brother or sister did.

To help get answers to the most relevant questions about differences in development or unusual characteristics, it is useful to ask specific questions. Instead of asking a general question such as, "What was I like as a child?," ask more specific questions like, "Did I get a lot of invitations to parties when I was in kindergarten?," "Did I play with the children or just play alone alongside the others?," or "What toys did I like to play with?" Any of the many sources of information suggested in the section above may help you gather information about yourself. Looking at the list in the section that follows about "what to include" in the summary will give ideas of the kind of information that is relevant in creating a developmental history many years after the fact.

Depending on the policy for record storage, your high school could have your complete cumulative file, starting with kindergarten. You may have to call in advance to have all of your files (including personal, disciplinary, and psychological files) retrieved from the archives, or put your request in writing. Find what was written in your yearbooks. What can you remember about outstanding events in your life? What fuzzy memories need clearing up? Try to organize these things on paper, year by year.

Case Example from Barbara

I began a few years ago to work with a man who had been diagnosed at age 28 with autism. His past diagnoses included Emotional Disturbance, Behavior Disorder, Learning Disabilities, Mental Retardation, Obsessive-Compulsive Disorder, Attention Deficit Hyperactivity Disorder, Tourette Syndrome and Oppositional Defiant Disorder. Why had autism been missed for all of these years, including 18 in special education services? One reason was because staff and family attributed what they observed in him to be the result of personality, will or another diagnosis.

For example, when he failed to develop appropriate social relationships, it was attributed to ADHD and his "lack of interest" in other children. His verbal and non-verbal communication difficulties were attributed to defiance and not paying attention. His restricted and repetitive behaviors were attributed to being spoiled and indulged by his parents and a lack of interest or respect for other people. Other behavioral issues were attributed to stubbornness, obsessiveness and poor parenting. (The first day I met his mother, she asked me if I was going to blame her again. She told me that when her son was five years old, a professional school employee told her that her lack of parenting skills was responsible for his difficulties. His mother was still thinking about that statement 23 years later!)

When I was able to help parents and former staff describe the individual objectively, in terms of what he did or did not do, the pattern of autism became clear. He had social difficulties, communication difficulties and restrictive and repetitive topics of interest. It became clearer that he had problems learning these skills and that what came automatically to other people did not come automatically to him. Once identified, he was then able to access autism related services for the first time in his life. He has made some progress and now has a job and some meaningful activities to do outside of his home. He seems to be a person with both autism and mental health issues, and it is not unreasonable to wonder if they are a result of never having received the proper type of treatment and services earlier in his life.

What to Include in the Developmental History

The list below includes some of the topics that are usually discussed in the diagnostic process. The list can be used to form comments to include in the summary you prepare for your child, an adult in your care, or yourself. Developmental "milestones" are always discussed in the diagnostic process. It is important to pinpoint the age the child was for the big "firsts" in her life: first smile, first words, first steps, etc. Apart from covering the milestones, a comment on the child's social interactions, language and behavior at each age will be very useful. Some items in the list may "stand out" helping you to describe what the child was like or how the child behaved at a certain point in time. If you just don't know, or can't remember something in particular, you may wish to write that you cannot remember or are not sure, or keep asking others until you find someone who remembers.

Developmental Milestones

When (or if) your child first:

- Smiled at you
- Recognized your voice
- Rolled over, including the way of rolling over
- Slept through the night
- Reached for a toy

- Ate solid foods (how did that go?)
- Fed himself
- Babbled, or made sounds
- Sat up
- Crawled
- Pulled to standing
- Walked
- Ran
- Hopped on one foot
- Jumped
- Balanced on one foot
- Used single words
- Put two or more words together
- Played baby games like peek-a-boo
- Was toilet trained for urine and/or bowels

Style of play:

At different ages, did the child, or how did the child:

- Play alone
- Play alongside others but not "with" them
- Join in group play
- React to your games
- Start play with you or others
- Pay attention to an activity
- Imitate others doing daily tasks
- Play make-believe, use imagination, or pretend
- Play dress-up
- Pretend an object was something else
- Take turns
- Share toys or objects
- Play games with others when older
- Participate in team or organized sports

- Develop motor skills, coordination and balance
- Follow rules
- Create own "play" using toys or objects in an unusual way

Describe at different ages the child's social style:

- Reaction to being held or cuddled
- Ability to be calmed when upset
- Style of seeking comfort
- Reaction to being separated from mother or father
- Sharing of pain and pleasure with others
- Understanding and reacting to the feelings of others
- Desire to direct parents' interest to some item or event
- Response when parent pointed out something of interest
- Ability to form and maintain friendships
- Interest in and connections to other children
- Reactions of the child to other children
- Reaction of other children to the child
- Reaction of the child to siblings
- Often giving more attention to objects than people in a family or other social setting
- Seeming to prefer being alone
- Atypical, unusual or surprising reactions to people/situations
- Interest and attachment to animals

Describe at different ages the use of communication and language

Did the child:

- Speak like others his age
- Use pronoun reversal (say "you" instead of "me")
- Have a flat tone, lack of expression or singsong voice
- Copy or repeat words or phrases from television or video
- "Echo" back what was heard, right away or later
- Let others know what he wanted or wanted to say

- Ask questions
- Repeat questions or statements over and over
- Use eye contact
- Turn or look towards someone who was speaking
- Understand common words and gestures
- Use gestures or sign language
- Respond to body language and facial expressions
- Respond to a sound sometimes and not at other times
- Appear deaf
- Respond to his or her name being called
- Seem fascinated with particular items or subjects
- Be hard to engage if it was not his favorite topic
- Follow directions as expected

Describe at different ages behaviors, interests, and sensitivities:

- Favorite things and things she really liked
- Strongly disliked objects/activities/people
- Dangerous or self-injurious behaviors
- Surprising skills at a young age (like read, balance, do puzzles, climb, stack items)
- Fears of particular objects, people or animals
- Lack of fear when it would have been expected to be present
- Problematic behaviors (including the circumstances)
- Response to expected and unexpected changes in routine
- Motor habits like rocking, flapping or pacing
- Repetitive habits, such as lining up objects, making lists
- Reaction to pain, temperature, pressure
- Strong reactions to taste, smell, touch, sound and light
- Response to large crowds
- Eating habits
- Sleeping patterns
- Ability to dress himself, brush hair, etc.
- Idiosyncrasies, things you noticed that caused you concern
- Things that you will "never forget" that made an impression

You may wish to make copies of the summary and provide it as part of the permanent, confidential record to be considered by the professionals and team members involved in the process of assessment and diagnosis. You can make additions and corrections to the history as information is remembered. You may want to continue adding to the history each year.

Case Example from Emily

I have helped many families sort and read their records looking for important information that would be relevant to a diagnostician. Matt's parents brought me a box of information about their teenage son. He had been in special education since the age of seven. He had assessments and a new diagnosis every year for six years, but was still doing very poorly at home and at school. Having read about ASD, the parents thought it could be the diagnosis that fit their child and explained his characteristics.

It was painful to see how this family had struggled and how much they had been through. They had put their confidence in many professionals who had different perspectives and came to different conclusions. But one report surprised me. It said that Matt had been talking in full sentences since 18 months of age. While the diagnostician writing the report could have suspected autism as a possibility, this diagnosis was inconsistent with such advanced language development. The diagnosis was not made.

I asked the mother, Carol, about this early language. She confessed that she actually did not know when Matt began to speak, that the doctor wanted answers on the spot, and that was the best she could remember. We discussed that this crucial piece of information needed to be clarified. Carol and her husband, Mark, took to heart the need to carefully document Matt's milestones and development. They went home and, over several weeks, watched hours of videotape. They went through medical and school records. They talked with relatives. It turned out that Matt was barely saying single words at 22 months. They used their computer to write an accurate chronological history of Matt. They took their document to a developmental specialist who took all the information into account and gave Matt what seems to be his most accurate and final diagnosis: ASD. Matt is now in a program tailored to his needs and the family is beginning to see real improvement. Carol and Mark now have a very complete understanding of their son and are relieved to have an answer that makes sense to them and gives them hope for progress.

Parents may not realize that a small error can have a big impact. This case illustrates the need for accuracy. Knowing what to expect and being prepared can make a huge difference in helping professionals gather information. Portions of several sample histories are provided here, adapted from actual summaries prepared by parents, to show ideas about organizing the information. All names have been changed. See 3.1, Matt's Story, 3.2, Laura's Timeline, and 3.3, About Alex. We hope that these personal summary ideas help parents, professionals, staff, and individuals provide an accurate description of the communication, socialization and behavioral history that diagnosticians need to know.

3.1 Matt's Story

Matt's family wanted to be certain about the timing and issues of Matt's development. The following is a sample of what his parents wrote after they "did their homework," watching videos, looking at records and talking with others.

Early Development and Milestones

Matt seemed to have normal growth patterns until approximately 6 months of age. At that time, he began to fall off the growth chart. A bone age test was performed and the results were normal. Matt has consistently been in the 10-20% range on the growth chart.

Matt walked at 14 months, although he exhibited difficulty in walking, falling frequently, swaying and holding onto objects to stabilize him. We cannot recall Matt reaching for or showing any fascination with mobiles or other objects in and around his crib. He would sit and stare for long periods of time, and when spoken to in an attempt to get his attention, he was unresponsive. He began frequently spinning in circles with his eyes rolled back at about 20 months. This behavior would continue until he could no longer remain standing and persisted until he was almost 4 years old.

3.1 Matt's Story continued

Communication and Language

Matt's ability to speak progressed relatively slowly. At 22 months his vocabulary consisted of 1-2 words which were primarily babble and perceptible only to mother and father. He frequently grunted and pointed instead of attempting to speak. When 2 ½ years old, he spoke only 2-3 words and developed persistent whining, pointing and grunting techniques when he wanted something. His speech developed at 2 years, 9 months to the point that he could speak 3-4 word sentences that were still very difficult to understand and had to be repeated several times to be understood, and usually were understood only by the parents. When he did begin speaking with regularity, he would consistently repeat exactly what we had said to him and speak in broken phrases.

It is very difficult for Matt to maintain eye contact when meeting and speaking to people. Matt underwent extensive, one-to-one speech therapy with an audiologist and intensive work in language development with a resource specialist at his elementary school, 2nd through 5th grades. Now Matt can speak fairly well, but he still mimics what is said to him frequently, pauses when speaking, inserting "uh" in most sentences. His speaking technique includes long pauses with facial distress until he can continue to express his thought.

Socialization and Behaviors

When around other children at approximately 2 ½ years of age, Matt would avoid them and if they would "invade" his space, he would become aggressive. In second grade, his peers would leave the table when Matt joined them for lunch. Last year in 8th grade, his gym clothes were stolen and thrown in the toilet of the gym. He was bullied and teased a great deal at the local middle school. One incident caused him to be kept out of school for a week for his own safety. His ability to engage in play with other children continues to be a concern. Except for three neighborhood children, Matt has never been invited to a birthday party, invited to get together for play or for sleepovers. To this day, he has no friends that he has any contact with outside of school, no best friend and no playmates, other than his younger brother who is 11 years old.

3.2 Laura's Timeline

To prepare this timeline, Laura's parents went back through their records to find all the times she had been assessed at school or seen by a doctor. They summarized all of the testing that had been done, all diagnoses, and significant facts and recommendations. They arranged the information as a timeline, from the earliest reports to the present. They realized that no one had ever looked at Laura's entire history as it progressed over time. The timeline effectively created a whole picture and a clear pattern. The sample below is just one part of the document. Readers will note that core deficits of autism were identified in Laura, but separated and given separate "labels."

Readers may also note that Laura had a diagnosis of PDD-NOS at the age of 10, but that fact was actually "lost" or overlooked. No one explained to Laura's parents that PDD-NOS was an Autism Spectrum Disorder, and they did not find this out until she was 13. She was also presumed at 10 to have borderline cognitive impairment, (such as mild mental retardation) but it turns out that Laura has gifted intelligence. All these things became clear when Laura's parents presented their information to a developmental pediatrician experienced in ASD who could take all the information into account in the diagnostic process.

April 28, 1998 age 10 years, 4 mo.
Evaluation by Dr. Blank
Identified as "At Risk"

Diagnoses:

1. Obsessive Compulsive Disorder (OCD)

2. Borderline intellectual function (presumed)

3. Mixed Receptive-Expressive Language Disorder

4. PDD-NOS

3.2 Laura's Timeline continued

Significant Findings and Recommendations:

Perseverative play and a lack of sustained reciprocal interaction.

Developmental history includes delayed language and gross motor skills.

Laura often does not seem to understand what people say to her or follow directions. She sometimes has great difficulty expressing her thoughts in words or in writing.

Laura was found to be at risk for significant social and academic disability.

Her comprehensive treatment plan should include placement in a flexible educational setting able to provide accommodations in curriculum, classroom structure, teaching method and therapies appropriate for Laura's diagnoses and specific academic and emotional needs.

3.3 About Alex

Alex is a young boy with autism, diagnosed late in elementary school. The description written by his mother includes many features of hyperlexia, meaning that Alex had a fascination and skill with letters and numbers beyond what anyone would expect for his age. Here is a sample of the information Alex's mom brought to the first interview with a specialist. The diagnostician thanked her and praised her for being so thorough and providing information he found essential.

Alex from age 3 to age 4

- Learned to use a computer game to play along with an alphabet TV game show. Developed a systematic line-by-line approach to solving puzzles. Could beat the contestants and other adults.

- Started preschool, still in diapers. Read a book to the class the first day.

- Began to memorize long texts with full inflection, such as the introduction to his favorite TV game show. Memorized entire books on tape from Sesame Street, including all character voices and sound effects. Memorized entire dialogue from movies on video.

- Often repeated words from commercials and videotapes in conversation.

- Favorite activities, TV and video. Read books of at least a second grade level.

- Not interested in "imagination" toys like cars and trucks. Did not invent games or pretend. Did not build forts, play house, school or firestation. Did not join in with other children in these activities at home, school or playgroup. Continued to play alongside others.

- Adored animals. He told me he was more interested to visit our friends' homes to see the animals than the people who lived there. Very emotional and loving towards cats and dogs.

- Did not appear curious, or ask, "why?" Seldom asked questions of any type. Was very annoyed when other children asked questions.

- Toilet trained after a rational discussion of the topic, around 3 ½. Still had accidents a few months more.

Alex from age 4 to age 5

- Second year at preschool. Very bored with dull curriculum. Put no effort into coloring letters of the alphabet. Teacher complained he would not color in the lines. She knew of his intellectual capacity, but told me that he was not ready for kindergarten.

- Liked addition and subtraction flashcards.

- Would not sit for "circle" time; needed to be cued to sit down and pay attention every day.

- Not emotionally connected to his little sister, now age 1. He did not harm her, but "got in her face" which still continues to the present.

- He was happy to hear friends were coming over, but when they arrived he did not play with them. The children we got together with for over two years did not seek him out.

3.3 About Alex continued

> - Seemed "self-contained," happy to be on his own; did not demand much attention.
>
> - Was happy to go to parties; participated in the entertainment. Did not speak to or interact with kids. Did ask adults for help or to get something he needed.

Professionals Can Help Parents Organize Information

Valuing parents' irreplaceable understanding and knowledge of their child, professionals realize that when parents share their knowledge and experiences in a clear and organized way, the assessment process is improved. If the parent does not wish to write a history, or is not able to do so, professionals can encourage parents to provide this information in a different way, such as answering into a tape recorder while someone asks questions or providing outlines or checklists for parents to use. Professionals can use the parent information to supplement and "round out" the information gained from formalized testing, evaluating and observing children or adults.

The Role of the Teacher

Parents may want to read the following section to understand a teacher's position and perspective and to recognize what an excellent ally a teacher may be in helping any child.

A Note to All Teachers: What You Can Do When You Notice Significant Differences in a Child in Your Class

As a teacher, you are an expert in child development. Every day, you witness the huge variations in development, ability, skills, socialization, communication and behavior among typical children in the same classroom. With experience, you have a clear view of the wide range of what is "normal" or "typical" at a particular age or stage.

Sometimes you recognize a child with variations that seem more significant. Some differences cause a reaction, making you stop and think about what you are seeing. Other differences in children cause disruptions and problems. Sometimes it is easy to determine what the differences are and what the cause may be. In other cases, a difference may be more subtle and harder to describe, quantify and explain.

As a teacher with concerns about a child, it is sometimes hard to know what to do. You may be unsure about what you are seeing and what the observable differences in a student might mean. Sometimes the school environment may not be conducive to "speaking up" about a child.

When you have concerns about a student, it may be helpful to get guidance about school or district policy and procedures in identifying students with a suspected special need. You could talk to a mentoring teacher, the school psychologist, the principal or district staff.

Record Objective Information

It is useful to gather information to share with other school staff and probably with the parents at some point. It is important to be objective and factual in looking at the differences that you are seeing. Here are some ideas to help you organize your observations and thoughts. Remember that these notes should be marked and treated as "confidential." Be sure to learn about and follow all rules and laws regarding student and parent confidentiality.

1.   Write (or speak into a tape recorder for later transcription) a description of the child, starting with physical characteristics and expanding to include more abstract qualities. How is he like other children? What makes him stand out as different? What does he seem to not understand or not know that may cause problems or set him apart? What seems really difficult for him? What about him is the most puzzling or unexpected?

2. Describe the behaviors (repetitive, inappropriate, stigmatizing, problematic, self-injurious or dangerous) that you see and any patterns you notice, such as the time of day when it occurs, the size of the group or location in which the problems are most obvious, the noise level in the room at the time, etc.

3. Describe anything else you are seeing that concerns you. Give specific examples and the details of what happened. This can include the circumstances, the outcome, and the reactions of others.

4. Describe and document what you are seeing in neutral terms. Avoid drawing conclusions. Do not assume you know what the child's behavior means or why it is happening. Avoid characterizing the child as disruptive, withdrawn, inattentive, self-isolating, etc., but instead report what you saw and heard. (Some people find it helpful to compare the process of objectively recording their observations to writing down what a video tape would have recorded at the scene.) A factual and impartial description will help everyone who reads your summary to be objective and consider all the possible explanations, rather than jumping to any conclusions.

5. Record your observations over a period of time. Record your observations using the following headings:

   • Communication

   • Socialization, friendship skills, responses to other children

   • Repetitive behavior, speech or interests

   • Inflexibility or problems with changes and transitions

   • Problem behavior (causes a problem for the student or others)

   • Sensitivity to elements of the environment like lights, sounds, or temperature

   • Unusual responses to people, objects and events

- Unusual behavior that makes you "wonder"

When you see a situation or observe a notable difference, write the incident down under one of the headings listed above. As you record more information, patterns may emerge, and you may be surprised by the frequency of some problems. Commit to "logging" observations about the child for a week or more, until you feel confident you have "documented" your areas of concern.

6.   You observe children daily and have a critically important role in providing "insider information" about a child in all school environments, in and out of the classroom. Teachers are not allowed to diagnose disabilities. Be sure you know and follow all of the correct procedures to request assistance from other staff or to refer a child for further assessment.

7.   Take all of your written information to the school psychologist (or other appropriate staff members). Support staff may want to observe the child and gather more information. They may observe a pattern of a specific disorder. School staff will advise the next steps to be taken, such as speaking with the parents, convening a case study team, or conducting a comprehensive assessment.

Seventeen Reasons for YOU to do *Something*, Rather than *Nothing*.

As a classroom teacher, you have vital information to share without making assumptions about underlying causes and without suggesting a specific diagnosis. You are often a child's best advocate. You may feel reluctant about mentioning the problems you observe in a particular student. While it may feel risky, here are some reasons why "speaking up" may be a good idea:

1.   **You are an expert in child development through training and experience.** You have had classrooms full of children to "compare,"

who provide a grand view of the wide range of expected development and behaviors. Parents, on the other hand, often have limited experience, especially if the child is their first child or an only child. They may not notice some things, or know that a child is significantly different from more typically developing peers.

2.   **Parents may be worrying.** Parents may be observing things that they think are "not quite right." They may be asking friends and family members if they think everything is OK. They may describe what worries them to the pediatrician. Their concerns may be explained away by others who say, "She'll be fine"or, "Boys are always less mature," or, "His father didn't talk until late...." Mothers may be accused of being overly concerned and nervous about their children. Sometimes one parent is able to see and acknowledge what may be a significant difference in a child when the other parent cannot see it or is not yet ready to acknowledge it.

Friends, family and medical staff may tell parents, "If there was something wrong, the teacher would be seeing things. Has his teacher said there is a problem? If not, then stop worrying." Your silence can be one more thing to discourage parents from defining the problem and finding out what their child really needs.

3.   **The differences may be qualitative.** A child may appear to be doing as well as his peers at first glance, but the quality of the interaction or behavior may be different, inappropriate or inadequate when more closely observed. Teachers may be able to give examples of significant qualitative differences that are masked when typical measures are applied. It is often a teacher who can "see" these subtleties.

For example, when measuring, "Works well with others," the rating may be "Yes," if there are no complaints from the other students, and the work is finished. However, your close observation during a group experience may reveal qualitative differences in the way the child interacts such as less flexibility, telling others what to do, repetitive speech or behavior, making statements out of context, appearing to not understand the perspective of the other children or having difficulty making and carrying out plans.

4. **You observe peer interaction on a constant basis.** Some children are able to interact better with adults who tend to mediate or support interaction. In many cases, the nature of children's difficulties is more apparent with the peer group. Is the student isolated? Does she know how to join in? Does he sound like the other children and talk about the same kind of things? In contrast, is the interaction very one-sided or "immature?" You may notice if the child is "left out" in class, at lunch and at recess.

5. **You may be aware of the reaction of other students to this child.** Is the child the last one picked to be part of the group? If he is picked early, is it because he is well-liked, or because he knows something that can give the group an edge? Do the other children seem to think him odd or laugh at him, particularly if they do not know that they are being observed by the teacher? Does the child spontaneously have same-aged peers to eat lunch with and play with on the playground? Do the peers seem tired of the child's "same old topics"?

    Children in the primary grades tend to be more accepting of others, especially in classrooms with teachers who model this behavior. As the students get older, they become more selective about friends, less tolerant of those outside their circle and less tolerant of those who seem "different." While younger students might invite the whole class to their birthday parties, older students, left to their own devices, do not. Some children are never or rarely invited to out-of-school activities. Parents will notice this and worry about the isolation their child is experiencing.

6. **Some "differences" may be more obvious in the school setting than at home.** "Home" is an adult-mediated, variable setting where individual differences are often gradually accommodated into the family routine. Over the years, parents may not even be aware of the number and types of accommodations they have made for their child.

   School is more structured and group-oriented. There may be more rules and expectations to be considered "typical." It is more obvious in school whether or not a student has the skills to "fit in." The classroom and campus settings place different demands on students and may reveal difficulties in organization, attention, behavior, communication and socialization not noticed at home or elsewhere.

7. **You may be the only person at this point in the child's life who can take the steps to help a child in need access services.** If not you, then who? Who else is in a position to observe and objectively report the difficulties this student is experiencing? Some diagnoses will make a child eligible for special education and other services. With a diagnosis, family life can improve and other family members may be able to access the services that *they* need. Interventions specifically tailored to the child can help close the gap between what the child has learned and what he or she needs to learn. As more time elapses, this gap becomes wider and harder to close.

   Particularly in the case of Autism Spectrum Disorders, a complete assessment and understanding of the child is necessary to design and deliver a systematic and comprehensive program. The alternative, just "adapting" to identified differences, is not enough to support the student and does not allow him to benefit from his education and becoming a contributing member of society.

   This is the first time in history that adults with Autism Spectrum Disorders are telling us in their writing and lectures about their educational experiences. Many of them experienced total social failure in school that led to an isolated and depressed adult life. Others mention the important "moment" when a caring professional acknowledged a difference and took the steps to help the child get the supports and services he needed. The teachers who helped are recalled as mentors, leaders and heroes who transformed the child and family's life for the better.

A formal diagnosis may make the child eligible for services from out-of-school providers, such as health insurance companies and local providers of disability-related services. A formal diagnosis may make the child eligible to participate in studies or treatment protocols that can be positive and supportive. A formal diagnosis may make the child and family eligible for mental health services that may be as important to the child and family's well being as the academic and adaptive supports. Stepping forward with your objective observations can be the first step in obtaining a diagnosis.

8. **Your information may be a "starting point."** There is a delicate balance between what you might want to say and what parents are ready to hear. Some parents may be very sensitive or even defensive when the teacher or school suggests that there may be a problem. Whether or not parents are ready to hear about a suspected special need, the teacher and school staff will need to present the information in a kind, clear and objective way.

Some parents will be relieved to have their suspicions validated. They will be grateful to have specific and concrete information provided by the school to help medical or health care providers have a more complete understanding of the nature of the child's difficulties in different environments. Some parents will be energized and ready to get started working on behalf of their son or daughter now that they have been given the information and direction that they needed.

Some parents may resist, or need more time to make sense of the information, seek advice, and come to a conclusion that they can accept. There is no good reason to delay providing information since it may take months or years for parents to become ready to act on the information.

Some parents may react with anger or accusation. You will need to remember that these parents love their child and the information may be particularly devastating to them if they had not observed differences in their child's development. Most often these emotions are in response to parents' shock, fear, confusion and disappointment. Emotional responses are a natural part of the process of learning and becoming ready to act. You may want to try to protect parents from these emotions, and avoid this difficult experience yourself. In fairness to the child, you cannot. You can, however, respond with caring, objectivity, support, kindness and empathy, recognizing that you might feel the same way if your child was observed to have special needs or disabilities.

9. **Children learn the best and the most early in life.** The plasticity of the young brain teaches us that it is important to begin interventions as soon as possible, for the best possible lifetime outcome. There is no good, brain-based reason to "wait and see." You may begin to observe the differences and problems caused by features of autism spectrum disorders as early as three years of age.

10. **The child and family may be headed for a crisis.** Follow your district procedures to check the cumulative file or the psychological file for this child. Have there been student study teams, conferences or meetings about problems at various times? Is there a pattern of problems, but no lasting solutions? If there is a history of difficulties, and you are currently seeing problems, consult with staff to address these issues before a real crisis or major incident happens.

11. **You can get help and support and so can the other children in the classroom.** Sharing information can lead to eligibility for services and a plan to support the child. This plan can include support for you. More students are being diagnosed with ASD than ever before, and more students with ASD are being included in general education classrooms. You will likely have a child with an autism spectrum disorder in your classroom now or in the next few years.

Most general education teachers do not have specific training about autism related disorders. While you have plenty of talent, education and flexibility, that is often not enough when it comes to meeting the complex needs of a child with ASD in your classroom. When a student has a diagnosis and educational plan, the plan can include information and training for you and time to consult with the specialists who are working with the child. A team approach with school and district staff can help you feel less "alone" and better supported to do your job.

When a child is identified to have a special learning need or specific disability, the other students in the classroom will be able to access more of your time. Specialized support may be provided in your classroom or via special "pull-out" services. You will have more time to devote to the needs of the other children in your room.

Special education and other support staff can help the typical students gain a greater understanding of their special classmate and learn how to access support for themselves if they need it. (Read about how to talk to the typical children later in our book.) Typical students will be able to use in adulthood what they learn in childhood about their special needs peers.

12. **School districts, or local education agencies, have a "Child Find Obligation" under IDEA law.** This means that "educational agencies have an affirmative duty and simultaneous obligation to identify, locate and evaluate those students who may be in need of special

education...."[10] While some parents who suspect their child has a disability may bring the child to the educational agency, the agency has a "dual responsibility" to bring a child with an actual or suspected disability to the attention of his parents.

The obligation under IDEA includes identifying the special needs of students from birth to age 21.[11] The child find obligation holds educational agencies accountable to identify any special need that may be interfering with a student's ability to access his or her free and appropriate public education. Teachers may comply with this obligation by bringing information to the attention of school staff when academic or social development seems outside the norm.

Some teachers may worry that there would be resistance to actively seeking to identify students with actual or suspected disabilities because it would be costly to the district. However, there can be a great cost to not complying with the obligation. First, there is the human cost, the time lost to a child who is not correctly identified and therefore does not have appropriate supports and services to benefit from his education. Being unidentified and underserved can cause the child and family to experience additional social, emotional or behavior problems

There can be a financial cost to districts or agencies found to have failed the child find obligation. In some cases taken to due process, hearing officers who hold the district accountable for failing to identify a student with a disability have awarded compensatory services to the child. The district or agency may also be ordered to reimburse parents for out-of-pocket expenditures for therapies and services that the district should have been providing. It is in the best interest for the children, the families and the educational agencies to comply with the law.

13. **Children in the autism spectrum will not automatically improve over time just by experience and imitation.** However, they will improve

when specialized, individualized services are delivered over time. Your attention to their needs may be the first step in getting a child with ASD the services he needs to improve.

14. **It is more cost effective to provide early, intensive education that results in a productive adult than to "pass the child along" through their educational life.** Adults with special needs are most likely to become contributing, independent tax payers when their needs are met as early as possible during their educational years.

15. **There is no entitlement to support services after a young adult leaves their free, appropriate, public education.** Students are entitled to an education, but not to services after age 21. If the student with whom you are concerned does not learn to become a contributing member of society during his educational experience, he may never have the opportunity and needed support to do so.

16. **The only way that school districts can advocate for sufficient special education and support personnel positions is by proving the need.** You may notice that special education and other support staff in your school have large caseloads and no "spare" time to meet the needs of one more child! You do your colleagues no favors when you do not refer a child for special services. In fact, you help your colleagues remain stuck in a situation in which there will always be more children than they can possibly, adequately serve. The only way that school administrators can justify the creation of new positions for special education and support staff in schools is by showing that the number of staff currently employed cannot meet the needs of all of the identified children.

When many special needs students began to be included in general education classrooms in the 1990s, administrators calculated that it would require less time, money and staff than the previous "self-contained" approaches did. They were wrong! It requires more specialized staff to support you and your special needs students in inclusive educational settings. Educational staffing patterns have not yet changed sufficiently to reflect current needs. When you identify children who may have need for specialized support in your classroom, you assist in the evolution of staffing patterns that can meet the needs of all children.

17. **It is never too late to find out how you and others can begin helping.** We have talked to many people who did not know that they had an autism spectrum disorder until high school. Although this was very late, it was still helpful to find out during high school so that intensive services could be delivered as quickly as possible to help the individual prepare for life after educational services ended.

What are the Risks to Teachers or Doing Something Rather than Nothing?

Doing something admittedly can have its risks. You may get a negative reaction for "stepping on toes." Some schools discourage teachers from speaking up for a variety of reasons. Both staff and parents may be angry at the suggestion that something is "wrong."

Doing nothing can be risky, too, because a child's needs may continue to be overlooked, ignored or misunderstood. It may be important to weigh the risk of what might happen if you talk about the problem versus the effects of the decision to stay silent.

If you fear you will be resisted in your efforts to help a child, you may wish to ask a qualified member of staff to help you start the process. You may wish to ask another teacher who has been through the same situation for advice. You can also encourage parents who express their concerns to you to follow up on their own worries by seeking a professional opinion.

CHAPTER 3 SUMMARY

- To begin the process of diagnosis of ASD, look for providers experienced with this population in the medical and/or educational field.

- There is no medical test for ASD; diagnosis is based upon professional opinion, observation, psychoeducational testing, and information provided by those who know the person well, over time, across environments.

- The joint efforts of an interdisciplinary team may be an effective option in getting a diagnosis whether at a clinic, government agency, or in a school setting.

- Federal law mandates and guides identification, assessment, eligibility and education of students with disabilities ages 3-21; "IDEA" law is being revised and re-authorized by Congress in 2003-4.

- Parents are always part of the assessment team. Parents may wish to find guidance in the assessment process from another experienced parent or support/advocacy group.

- It is never too late to seek a diagnosis. It may be useful to seek a diagnosis for an adult of any age.

- The assessment process can be upsetting or unsettling or even feel like a time of crisis for the person being assessed and the family, especially if the family is experiencing serious problems or feels desperate for help.

- Teachers and staff may also feel pressure and experience difficulties in the assessment process. A cooperative effort between parents and professionals is optimal.

- Parents can provide crucial information about a person's development, characteristics and difficulties over time. Preparing and providing a written summary of the child's development and health with focus on milestones, communication, socialization, behavior and sensory issues at every age can be a key to accurate assessment and diagnosis. Parents need to know what to expect. Prepared parents can make a huge difference in helping professionals gather information.

- Diagnosticians and special education managers and supervisors must be sure that every concern of parents is actually addressed systematically in assessments.

- In the beginning of the assessment process, it is important for both parents and professionals to describe features that are clearly observable in the child or adult, rather than begin by suggesting a diagnosis first and describing the features that fit that diagnosis.

- Adults in the diagnostic process will need to collect information about their childhood and development, as well as describe the quality of difficulties they are experiencing in work, relationships and daily living.

- Teachers have a very important role in identifying children who may have ASD. While it may seem uncomfortable to "speak up," there are many reasons why teachers have an indepth understanding of the child's functioning and subtleties and can be a child's best advocate.

- It may be helpful to organize information about diagnostic visits, test results and contact information, because there will be a lot of paperwork in a short time!

SOURCES

Freeman, B.J. Ph.D. *Diagnosis of Autism: Questions Parents Ask.* UCLA School of Medicine, 1993.

Recommendations of the Collaborative Task Force on Autism Spectrum Disorders: Best Practices for Designing and Delivering Effective Programs for Individuals with Autism Spectrum Disorders. Copyright 1997, California Department of Education, P.O. Box 271, Sacramento, CA 95814

COPAA, The Council of Parent Advocates and Attorneys *Child Find Requirements Under IDEA* http://www.copaa.net/

IDEA Law, Subpart B 300.125, Regulations from the Federal Register *Child find.* Once source to read this part of IDEA is http://www.ideapractices.org/law/regulations/searchregs/300subpartB/Bsec300.125.php

CHAPTER 4

"We judge ourselves by what we feel capable of doing. Others judge us by what we have done."
Henry Wadsworth Longfellow

THE ASSESSMENT PROCESS

In this chapter you will learn:

- Components of a thorough assessment.

- Challenges in assessing individuals with Autism Spectrum Disorders.

- Practical strategies to improve the assessment process.

- Preparing for the assessments.

- Ways parents and professionals can collaborate to improve assessments.

- What to ask about the qualification of those providing assessment services.

This chapter will discuss challenges in actually conducting assessments with people who may have ASD. We will discuss how parents can help with the assessment process and how to make the process more bearable to the person being assessed. We will suggest ways that parents and professionals can work together for the best outcome. Practical strategies are offered to improve the process for everyone concerned. Much of the discussion in this section describes the process of assessment as it relates to children and families. Many of the ideas about assessing children will guide parents of adults and adult services staff or help an adult who is referring herself for diagnosis.

The term assessment can be described as an information-gathering process. Evaluation is another word for assessment. The assessment process is crucial in determining how best to identify and address the needs of each unique individual. Thorough assessments measure and describe a person's level of ability and functioning on many levels. Good assessments also identify areas of strength and ability that can be used to build skills in areas of need.

The information learned from the assessments can be used to determine a diagnosis. Assessments can be done when a person already has a diagnosis. Results of assessments are the basis for designing a specific plan and choosing services, programs, interventions and therapies most appropriate to the individual's needs.

Another purpose of assessments for children ages 3 to 21 who are in school is to "shed considerable light upon the student's strengths and needs, the nature of his or her disability and how it effects educational performance and what types of goals and objectives should be established for the student."[12]

Reassessments take place after a time to measure the effectiveness of services and the student's progress. Depending on the results, services and plans will remain the same or be changed. 4.1, the *Assessment Cycle*, shows how assessment and reassessment are steps in a continuous process.

4.1 The Assessment Cycle

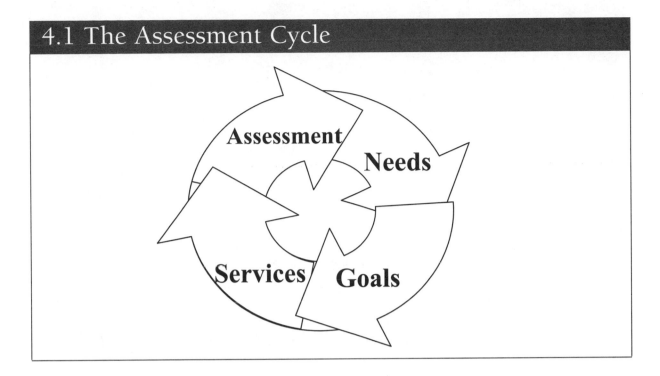

Components of a Comprehensive Assessment

Information about the development of the child, problems and concerns and areas of skill and need will be collected by a variety of professionals. A comprehensive assessment for a child or adult who has ASD, or when an ASD is suspected, usually involves several appointments taking place over the course of days or weeks, involving several professionals.

Collection of Information and Evaluations May Include:

- Background information about both parents and their families.

- Background information/social history/developmental history of the individual.

- Medical history of the individual and families.

- Review of previous testing.

- Review of school records.

- Rating scales and screening tools like questionnaires and surveys.

- Psychological evaluations including assessment of how the individual learns.

- Social-Emotional functioning assessment.

- Medical examination and testing.

- Educational, academic and skills testing.

- Comprehensive speech and language or social communication.

- Functional behavioral analysis of any seriously problematic behavior.

- Occupational therapy, including self-help, motor planning and organization.

- Sensory regulation and sensory processing.

- Physical therapist's assessment.

- Comprehensive hearing testing (not just a screening), including auditory processing.

- Vision testing (not just a screening), including visual processing.

- Play and leisure time activities assessment.

- Adaptive physical education assessment.

- Prevocational-vocational skills assessment (usually for people ages 12 and older).

- Community based skills assessment (may be done by parental/staff report).

- Assistive technology assessment.

Who Will Be Part of the Interdisciplinary/Multidisciplinary Team?

Several specialists may take part in the process of assessment and diagnosis. They may use tests, interviews, observation, and other methods to understand the abilities and needs of an individual. Ideally, the specialists act in a coordinated manner as a team. Parents or other significant caregivers are included in all aspects of assessment.

A person with expertise in a particular field will evaluate each particular area of functioning and ability. This is true whether a school, adult service agency or other provider does the assessments. Participants can include:

- A licensed social worker.

- A licensed speech and language pathologist.

- A licensed psychologist.

- A special educator.

- A classroom teacher in general education.

- A school nurse or other person concerned with medical/health issues.

- A physician, pediatrician, psychiatrist, or other medical doctor.

- A dentist.

- A licensed Occupational Therapist with certification or training in sensory integration assessment.

- A licensed physical therapist.

- A behaviorist, preferably with at least a Master's Degree.

Parents, staff or adults seeking a diagnosis face an overwhelming amount of new information during the assessment process. Parents often are not familiar with the many areas of specialty, and may not be clear of each specialist's role in the process. Even keeping all the names, faces, appointment times and locations straight can be overwhelming.

It may help parents to have a notebook to write down contact information and take notes on telephone or in-person conversations. Most professionals will offer a business card during an assessment appointment; ask for one if it is not offered. Make a note on the back to help you remember something about that person, such as "office with slides and swings," or "played ping-pong with Jessie." Another way to organize is to tape the person's business card to a 3x5" index card and write any notes about the person on the card. Keep the cards in a card file or on a ring.

For meetings with several professionals, bring some 4x6" index cards with you and a large black marker. Fold each card lengthwise (like a long tent) and write each professional's name and title on a card. Place this name card facing you on the table in front of each person. This will enable you to learn and remember the "players" more easily. Keep the cards after the meeting and bring them with you the next time you meet with these professionals.

Challenges in the Assessment Process for Professionals, Parents, and Individuals Who Have or May Have ASD

The assessment process for individuals who have or may have ASD may be challenging for many reasons. The possible effects of assessment on children and adults are described below. Any points that are relevant to you, your child, or an individual you will be assessing should be discussed. Other challenges that are not mentioned here can be added and addressed. Later in the chapter, we give suggestions for dealing with many of these challenges. Suggestions are offered to help parents and professionals improve the assessment process.

It is important to note that the sensitivities and difficulties for the person being assessed may be similar to the challenges that people with ASD face in everyday life. These challenges are relevant to more than the testing situation. Other social situations such as meeting new students, applying for a job, going to a new place for the first time, taking standardized tests or moving to a new home can evoke stressful responses in anyone, but particularly in people with ASD. Applying the suggestions contained in this chapter to other life situations may be of benefit to individuals with ASD and other people that you support.

Stress

The assessment process provokes anxiety in everyone. As it is likely that the child or adult has difficulty with new situations, he may feel very stressed during the assessment. The assessment usually causes a disruption to the routine, which may be even worse if the individual has not been told what to expect or cannot understand what has been told. Disruptive behaviors or other signs of stress often occur as a result.

Trust

The role of trust and familiarity is important to recognize. The individual may be uncomfortable or resist the assessor because she does not yet know or trust the person. Some people with characteristics of ASD have a very hard time getting used to "new" people. An individual of any age may feel vulnerable and not be confident that she is "safe" with the person doing the assessment. The need for trust for an individual with ASD may be much greater than for most people. In the assessment process, children and adults being tested may meet more new people than in every-day life. It may be difficult to "open up" to so many new people in a short period of time.

Defensiveness

Some children and adults with ASD tend to be sensitive to criticism. Many of them feel that there is nothing "wrong" with them. The testing process may be upsetting because they may perceive that they are being criticized, picked on, singled out, or are having their flaws pointed out.

The individual may become defensive and angry. These negative feelings may carry over into a feeling of dislike of the person conducting the assessment. The feelings may last much longer than the testing process. The person may be able to mask their negativity or anger. Sometimes, a person may not be able to control his negativity or anger. He may have great difficulty coping during the assessment process. Some individuals with ASD, who have been repeatedly tested in the past, may feel that they always "fail" these tests, repeatedly disappointing parents and loved ones. They may be reluctant to "fail" again.

Variability of Performance

It may be difficult to get an individual with ASD to demonstrate ability "on demand." This may be caused by "variability of performance" or "situation-based learning." A skill may be demonstrated spontaneously, or in an informal setting, and yet a person may not be able to demonstrate it during a formal assessment session simply because someone tells her to do it.

Problems with Generalization

People with ASD often have difficulty transferring what they know from one setting to another. In testing, this means that a child or adult may not be able to demonstrate a skill that he actually has during the assessment. However, a parent or other informant can report whether he is able to perform the same task at home, school or in another setting. Videotape or a description of the person using specific skills can be provided to the tester.

Attention

It may be difficult to get and hold the child's or adult's attention for an assessment. Or, the assessor may find that the individual gets "stuck" (some say fixated) on a particular detail or aspect of the process and has difficulty moving on. Attention problems are often reported by saying the participant "refused to cooperate," or "refused to participate."

Social Skills

Underdeveloped social skills may cause the individual to appear disinterested, rude or uncooperative during "testing." She may actually be engaged or listening even though she is not looking at the assessor, or showing attention in an expected way. It is important for the tester to know and recognize if the individual "listens" without looking toward the speaker.

Masking

Another, but less obvious, obstacle to getting a thorough and accurate assessment for some children and adults is the fact that many individuals who are "high-functioning" unwittingly mask their deficit areas. They have become successful using adaptations and coping strategies with the result that their true needs (deficits) may be hidden. For example, strong decoding skills (sight-reading) may mask a lack of comprehension. Strong memory for social rules of politeness may hide a lack of social correctness in real social situations, or a deficit in being able to respond to actual social cues.

Language

Individuals who do not use formal language to communicate (speech, print/picture systems or sign language), or who cannot speak, present particular challenges for assessment. Appropriate non-verbal assessment tools must be chosen. Informal, objective observations in multiple settings and interviews with staff and family may become a more important aspect of assessment for these individuals. Modifications may be necessary for non-verbal individuals or those with unusual language or speech problems such as a lack of understanding of idioms, sarcasm, inference and humor or for those whose speech does not accurately reflect what they mean (say one thing, but mean another).

All people communicate and almost everyone has some kind of language use. Professionals and parents should not accept language and communication assessments with results that state the individual "does not communicate" or "has no language."

"Borrowed" and Safe Responses

It is important to be aware during assessment that responses and behaviors that seem quite acceptable and appropriate may not be original. They may be responses or actions that were memorized from videos, television or life situations. The assessor may not know that the individual re-words the same "safe" response to answer different questions. Similarly, the individual may be repeating actions or dialogue from a movie or video that may be relevant to the testing scenario, and the person testing thinks that these are original thoughts. Or, an answer may consist of repeated dialogue that seems irrelevant and out of context.

Strength in Learning Things by Rote

Strong rote memory, or strength in memorizing facts, may hide the lack of higher level thinking skills such as analysis, abstraction, comprehension and generalization. Assessors must look to the quality of responses and may need to do a very in-depth analysis to discover the individual's true areas of need. A very detailed and systematic approach may be needed in addition to objective or standardized testing.

Sensory Sensitivities

Sensitivities to environmental stimuli may be heightened in a new, stressful situation, such as testing. The child or adult may have a hard time tolerating lights, sounds, being touched or handling new material involved in the assessment. Smells or other stimuli may be particularly upsetting. The time of day of the testing may influence results. If any of these situations occur, diagnosticians should note the need for any unusual accommodations that were necessary to help the individual participate.

Processing Problems

Deficits in auditory processing and auditory processing delays may put the child or adult at a disadvantage. The individual may not respond well or quickly to oral instructions or prompts. This may include difficulty following directions. Rapidly repeating or rephrasing things may make the situation worse. Strength in the visual modality may help the child or adult be more successful in assessments that use pictures and written material or visual cues, such as signs, gestures and other visual signals. Giving additional time for responses may be necessary.

Settings

Individuals with ASD often appear very competent, understanding and responding appropriately during an evaluation. A quiet, one-to-one session with an evaluator is usually the best possible situation for performance for a child or adult with ASD. Importantly, the one-to-one session may not provide an accurate picture of how the individual functions in real-life situations. Observing the child or adult in less structured, peer-mediated settings (lunchroom, playground, gym, indoor recess, small group work or in the classroom) may reveal areas of need that will not manifest in one-to-one, quiet, adult-mediated settings. Careful observation of peer interactions, or the lack of them, and observing and listening in play areas, physical education class and the lunchroom are important components of a thorough assessment.

Adding disruption, background noise or testing in a group setting may help to show more areas of need. We do not suggest that intrusions or interruptions be done so intensely that the individual being assessed cannot function or experiences emotional stress. Rather, the "disruptive" presence of music or sounds in the background or a planned knock on the door may give the professional a clearer idea of how the individual functions in settings that are not perfectly quiet and predictable. (If parents or staff have indicated that a particular sound or sight is aversive to the individual and causes such stress that the individual "shuts down" or becomes unable to function, we suggest that evaluators not add that stimulus to the testing session.)

Could Not Test (CNT)

Some individuals will be unable to participate in any aspect of standardized testing. For these individuals, we must not be satisfied with an outcome of "CNT," could not test. Professionals in the assessment process can collaborate with parents or other caregivers to devise plans to observe and discover information about the individual's learning style, memory, communication skills, fine and gross motor abilities, etc. The result of these information-gathering events can be added to the information gained by objective observation in multiple settings.

Improving the Assessment Process

Individualizing to Improve the Assessment Process

Once a parent (or legal guardian) signs the permission form for assessment to be done, in most cases, a "standard" procedure will be used. Logically, this includes doing assessments at customary times and places, or at times and places most convenient to the evaluators (people doing the testing). However, the standard ways, times and places may not be the best choices for the child or adult. Parents can help get a better and more accurate assessment by providing information about the individual and asking to have the evaluations more "customized" to the individual's needs. This is especially important if the individual seems to feel anxious about changes in routines, new situations, new people, etc.

Each professional who is working with a child, adult or family can improve the experience for everyone involved by describing what each assessment is intended to measure, how the assessments will be administered, and what to expect. Parents benefit when professionals are willing to clearly explain the procedures and terms in language that can be easily understood and remembered, before the assessment takes place. The information can be provided in person, in writing, or on audiotape.

Providing an explanation is of value to the professionals in planning for the actual assessment appointment and opening dialogue with parents about concerns, strategies and modifications. Parents, other caregivers and staff may have valuable suggestions about what works best with the individual child or adult. Most professionals are open to being flexible if it is likely to result in a more accurate assessment. Parents and others can explain preferable accommodations and why these would help the child or adult. Most professionals are very responsive when given important information about how to best assess a particular person, because it helps them to do their job well and that is what they want to do!

Parents and professionals can discuss whether or not the administering, the way that a test is presented or given, can be adapted or modified depending on the age, development, interests and needs of the individual. Modifications may include doing the assessment in a comfortable, known environment, breaking the assessment into shorter time sessions or using materials in which the individual has shown an interest.

An accommodation may be as simple as allowing the mother to be present in the room during testing or having her hold a young child on her lap. It does not change any content of the testing being done, but it helps the child be more "testable." Another accommodation could be to allow the child or adult being tested to respond in a non-verbal way, rather than only verbally. Any accommodations should be noted in the report written to explain the test results.

The circumstances in which some tests are given cannot be modified in any way without compromising the validity of the standardized score. The protocols are specified in the manuals that accompany the tests. In these cases, one option is to attempt the test without modifications to gain a standard score. Alternatively, sections of the test may be given to provide "informal" results for which no standardized score is given. If the team decides that what is learned about the child from the increased participation is more important than a standardized score, it may be acceptable or even desirable to use modifications that affect the standard score. Again, any changes made are noted in the test results.

4.2 Parent and Professional Collaboration for Optimal Assessments

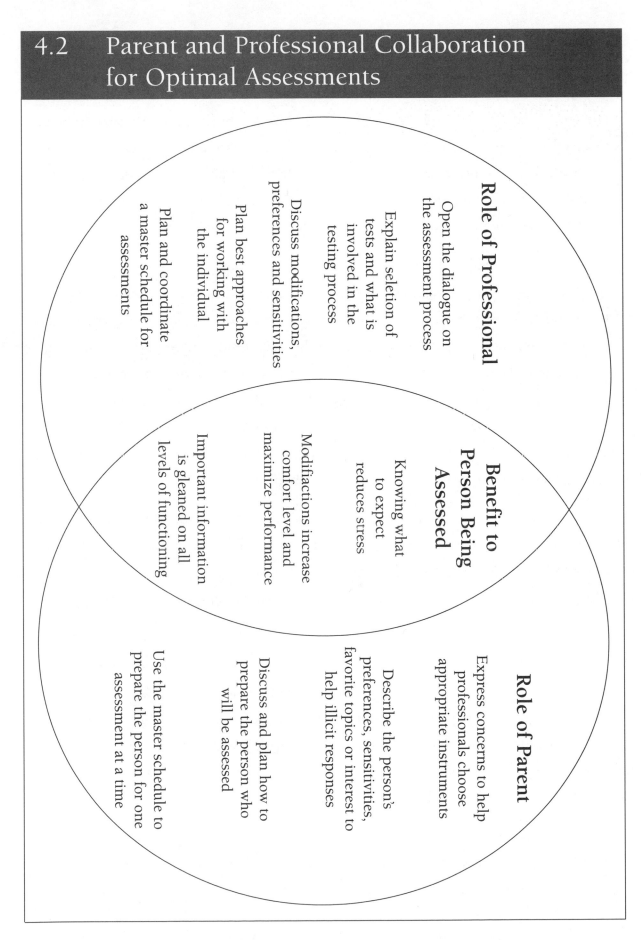

Role of Professional

Open the dialogue on the assessment process

Explain selection of tests and what is involved in the testing process

Discuss modifications, preferences and sensitivities

Plan best approaches for working with the individual

Plan and coordinate a master schedule for assessments

Benefit to Person Being Assessed

Knowing what to expect reduces stress

Modifiactions increase comfort level and maximize performance

Important information is gleaned on all levels of functioning

Role of Parent

Express concerns to help professionals choose appropriate instruments

Describe the person's preferences, sensitivities, favorite topics or interest to help illicit responses

Discuss and plan how to prepare the person who will be assessed

Use the master schedule to prepare the person for one assessment at a time

4.2, *Parent and Professional Collaboration for Optimal Assessments,* illustrates the value of parent-professional collaboration for the benefit of the person being assessed. In this Venn diagram, the contributions of parents and professionals can improve the efficiency and accuracy of the results of assessment. By helping the person being assessed know what to expect, stress may be reduced. Modifications that are agreed upon can help the individual feel more comfortable and able to perform at their true level of ability. Helping the individual to better tolerate the assessment experience aids in discovering information about all areas of the person's functioning.

If this is an "early" stage of collaborating and intervening for a particular child or adult, then possibly the parent-professional relationship has not yet been established. It is important to establish open communication and a good rapport before, during and after the assessment process, even if it seems difficult or intimidating. Parents may find, or professionals may suggest finding, an educational advocate or experienced parent-to-parent support person for advice and guidance. Classroom teachers, specialists and adult service providers may find support from a mentor teacher, the Special Education Department of the school district or the regional or state office that provides funding for services to people with developmental disabilities.

Creating accommodations and getting the assessment properly organized may make the assessment process take longer. It can involve more time or work, but is likely to be more productive. The suggestions that follow are based on assessments in which we have participated and on the experiences reported to us by parents, guardians and staff over the years.

Many of these suggestions are common sense and obvious. Others are novel and may not have been tried where you live. Some professionals may view a few of the special assessment adaptations unusual or cumbersome. Remember this: the incidence of autism and related disorders is increasing across the globe. Every adaptation that can be made on behalf of one individual with the characteristics of ASD will benefit not only that individual, but all who follow.

The education and adult services systems must begin the task of adapting to this population. The educational and adult services delivery systems have not been designed with the needs of people with ASD in mind, but many people with ASD are already in these systems. More are on the way. Each time any of us press the system to truly individualize on behalf of an individual being assessed, the path is paved for every individual, their staff and families to get the full benefit of accurate, comprehensive, individualized assessment. The value of this to the lives of people with ASD and those who love them is beyond measure!

Practical Strategies For Parents and Professionals to Improve the Assessment Process

In light of the challenges discussed above, professionals and parents will want to recognize and address the specific needs of the individual being assessed. To increase accuracy, efficiency, cooperation, and comfort, practical accommodations described below can be used that are appropriate to the situation. Many of these suggestions involve parents or staff, who know the person well, sharing information with professionals. Alternatively, professionals can look at the strategies and suggest that certain ones be used. Professionals can also ask parents or staff for specific information as described, if it is not offered.

1.   Do not discuss the individual's current issues or history in his or her presence or allow others to do so, even if the person seems to not understand or be paying attention.

2.   Schedule a separate appointment before an assessment to review the historical information and records with the diagnostician. This is often standard procedure, but if it is not suggested be sure to request it. It would be ideal if all the team members who will be assessing the individual could be present for this meeting at one time so that family members would only have to review the comprehensive child and family history once. An option would be to have this interview audiotaped or video taped so that others on the diagnostic team could access it as needed for review. Any such tape becomes part of the confidential record of the individual.

3. Provide a copy of the child or adult's detailed history that you prepared (see Chapter Three) to be included and taken into account as one of the records of the assessment process. Ask that each member of the diagnostic or assessment team be given a copy of it. Mark it "Confidential."

4. Find out who will be the "team leader" of the assessment team, and coordinate efforts through that person. It may be a school psychologist, social worker, lead special education professional, etc.

5. Ask for a written list of the assessments that will be given, and the names and titles of the people who will give them. Ask the team leader to pass on to all the other team members the useful information and accommodations that team members provide. Work with the team leader to schedule the assessments and keep everyone fully informed.

6. Ask each person who is doing an assessment to include recommendations based on the results they find. Ask them to add suggestions about supports and services to their written report. Ask for each area of deficit or need that is defined to be paired with a suggestion for a support or service to address it. While people doing evaluations in their field of expertise may have opinions as to appropriate or helpful therapies, etc., these opinions are often not included in the report unless requested. Also ask each assessor to write in any information about learning strengths or learning styles discovered during testing.

7. Plan the best times to do assessments. Depending on the individual being tested, some times are preferable, while others should be avoided. Let the team leader know if the individual is calmer, more cooperative, or worn out at a particular time of day. Let those doing the assessments know if the individual would be less or more stressed if "pulled" from a particular class or activity. Tell them about any class or activity that must not be disrupted.

8. Ask whether a parent or caregiver can or should be present at the assessments, as a silent observer, if this will be comforting or calming to the individual. As an alternative, ask parents to agree to be present nearby during the assessments in case team members have questions or the individual needs reassurance or help.

9. Individuals with very limited or unconventional communication skills should not be left alone with someone who cannot read their messages. For these individuals, a person who communicates and gets along well with the individual can be present or very close by to serve as "interpreter" as needed.

10. If needed, ask the people doing or scheduling the assessments to plan on several shorter sessions to complete the evaluations. The addition of extra "breaks" may allow an individual to participate more fully for a longer overall time.

11. Request and help to plan to use a variety of settings for testing and observation. Evaluations should include structured and unstructured settings. Ask to have your child or adult unobtrusively observed in settings you know to be difficult, such as sports practice, a group activity, playground, workshop, home or in specific community settings (church, the mall, etc.). Ask the person doing the assessment to videotape the person in some settings if that seems a better way to objectively observe. Consider providing your own videotape if it will give the other team members a better idea of how the child or adult functions in multiple settings.

12. Let the person doing the assessment know in advance that the child or adult may be anxious, stressed, sensitive to perceived criticism, angry, frustrated, etc., by the testing process. The person doing the evaluation may know effective ways to calm the individual or reduce stress through their experience or training. You may wish to warn the tester that the testing process may cause behavior problems or responses that may be considered rude or inappropriate.

13. If the child or adult sometimes uses threatening or dangerous behavior, let the person doing the testing know ahead of time. Tell them what types of actions or events can bring on these behaviors. Tell them if there are "warning" signs that the individual may become dangerous or strike out. Let them know any successful ways you have discovered about preventing dangerous behavior. (Sometimes it is simple: don't touch the individual in a certain way, allow them to hold a favorite object, etc.).

14. Tell the evaluators about any objects, foods, drinks or activities that motivate the child or adult to do a better job. Rewards are perfectly acceptable. Some professionals do not generally use tangible rewards (something the individual gets like food, a toy, a hug) for participation. However, if the individual is likely to pay attention and participate better when rewarded with potato chips, lemonade, playing with play dough or a favorite object, or having a back rub, be sure to tell the professional about this. Provide the snacks or materials, if needed.

Unusual but Important Considerations

These ideas may sound odd, but evaluators and families should discuss the need to make specific accommodations during testing based on what the individual can and cannot tolerate. Here are some real-life adaptations that evaluators have done or avoided doing in order to help the person most fully participate in the assessment process. You may choose to follow any of these that apply for the person you are working with:

• Don't wear any perfume, scented hair sprays or use room scents.

• Don't wear a particular color or type of clothing if the person has demonstrated a consistent dislike or avoidance of it.

• Don't use certain phrases or bring up certain topics that are known to upset the person.

- Avoid physical contact if such contact causes a negative response in the person.

- Don't ask particular questions if these are known to be upsetting to the person.

- Do not have certain objects in the room if the person has consistently shown an intense preoccupation or fear in response to them.

- Allow the individual to stand, sit in a rocking chair or swing during parts of the assessment.

- Let the individual identify and work towards specific rewards or prizes for participating in the assessment.

- Create a "game show" type of atmosphere in which the child or adult being tested earns points to "win the game" or "win the grand prize."

If any accommodations such as these are made to increase the individual's ability to participate, they should be clearly noted and recognized as part of the information resulting from the assessment process. They may later be used as the basis for program recommendations.

Home Visits Help the Assessment Process

One of the fastest ways for parents and professionals to break down barriers and establish communication as equal participants in the process is a home visit. Families can invite professionals to observe the individual in the family home. Arrange the home visit at a time that is mutually convenient.

Professionals often find that they can learn more useful and helpful information in a one-hour home visit than in the first several days or weeks of the assessment. Parents need to know that when they open their home to a professional that the professional is coming there to learn, not to judge, criticize or look at how the parents do housework!

An effective method for a professional making a home visit is to take a seat in the house, be quiet and then fade into the background. If the parents offer to make dinner or snacks for the visitor, politely decline. The goal is not to be a participant in home activities, but to be an observer and learner.

When professionals visit families in their homes, they are better able to design teaching strategies and plans that can be carried out at home, based on the types of activities and schedules that they see there. They become more sensitive to the demands placed on family members and the unending struggle and energy drain of having a beloved child with special needs.

Staff can learn how parents anticipate and/or prevent problematic behavior, how parents "read" unusual behavior for communicative value, and what skills need to be taught to the child or adult to increase the quality of life for the family. If notes are taken during the home visit, to increase trust, they should be shared with the parents before leaving the home.

For professionals working with adults, home visits are just as important. For example, staff working with an adult with ASD in a developmental training program should visit the individual home whether it is the family home, a group home or some other supported living arrangement. Residential staff should visit the adult at their work place or wherever the adult spends the day. Staff from all settings need to meet together regularly and make one entire team that provides services to one entire person! This is a critical component of a successful assessment that results in goals that improve life for the child or adult and everyone with whom he lives, works and plays.

Later in this book we provide more extensive information about making effective and respectful home visits. We provide forms for collecting important information. Be sure to read that section before you make your home visit. We hope you find it helpful!

How Parents Can Help the Child or the Adult Cope with the Stress of Evaluations

The assessment process may be annoying at best and overwhelming at worst to a child or adult being evaluated, particularly because of some characteristics of ASD. Some modifications or adaptations may make it easier to prepare the child or adult. Others will help to reduce anxiety and reward the individual for trying to participate. Reducing the stress of the person being assessed also helps reduce stress on the parents and family members, or other caregivers, during a difficult time.

Families and teams may want to try any of the practical strategies described below that seem appropriate. Some of these things can be done even if the individual "appears" to not be listening or to not understand. We never know what individuals are taking in. It is best to provide positive preparation whether the child or adult appears to respond or not.

Strategies

1. With your child or adult, (or within listening distance if she cannot fully participate) prepare a list of all the strengths that the child or adult has. Include nice features of their personality (helpful, shares, etc.). Include stories of things that the individual child did (does) that made you feel proud or happy. Share this with each diagnostician in the presence of the individual.

2. Do not discuss the individual's history or current issues, or your fears or concerns, with any diagnostician in front of the individual, or within earshot even if the child or adult does not appear to be listening or is judged to be not capable of understanding. This is an important rule—even if the child or adult is deaf!

3. Help the individual choose and plan rewards that will be given after each testing session. Do not make these rewards depend on the individual behaving a certain way in the session. Just tell the child or adult that the reward will be given when the session is over.

4.   Let the child or adult know that there is no "score" and that he cannot "fail."

5.   Let the child or adult know that no one will know about the testing. It is private information for the team. That is the law.

6.   Before each assessment, talk to the person who will be doing the assessment. Find out what tasks or steps will be involved. Explain, practice and role-play the routine to help your child or adult know what to expect. Help your child or adult know what to do if the real assessment is different from your practice.

7.   Talk about what won't happen in the assessment (no shots, no restraint, no punishment, no time out, no embarrassment, etc.). When the person with ASD is not sure what to expect, he may imagine something much worse is going to happen and feel afraid. Some individuals will have negative associations or fears about assessment based on where it is taking place or the clothes worn by the people there, or have some other worry associated with another upsetting event (like getting a shot at the doctor's office).

Humiliation and punishment are not humane practices and are not methods that should be used with people with ASD or with anyone else. However, they have been used and continue to be used in an attempt to control people with ASD. Over the past thirty years, restraint techniques, originally designed to protect people in situations of imminent danger, have sometimes been used inappropriately by staff and families in response to non-compliance or non-cooperative behavior with children and adults with Autism Spectrum Disorders. Most people would not dream of using these aversive techniques today, but it is important to recognize that if this has happened in the past, or still continues in some setting in the person's life, the person being assessed may be very apprehensive.

We suggest that these issues be discussed prior to assessment with staff or family members who know the history of the individual who is going to be assessed, particularly if the person being assessed has had a negative or traumatic incident in the past or is particularly fearful. Evaluators may need to reassure children and adults who are going to be assessed that aversive practices and other feared things will not be part of the assessment process.

8. Arrange for introductory meetings for your child or adult with the person who will be conducting the assessment in the place that the assessment will be done. No testing should be done at this time. The assessor can explain the steps of the assessment to the individual (and to you!), show some of the materials that will be used and get to know the communication style of the individual.

9. After coordinating with the team leader, make a master schedule of exactly when and where each assessment will be done and by whom. Prepare the individual one event at a time. Remind what the assessment involves and who will be doing it (see 6 and 7, above). Plan it as an event in the child's or adult's daily schedule. While the individual may be anxious knowing that an assessment is coming up, this is usually preferable to "springing it" on the individual without warning. Be sure to remind her of the reward she will get after the session.

10. Anticipating the assessment may be stressful for the individual and result in some problematic behavior. Staff and families can keep other elements of the individual's life consistent, routine and as stress free as possible during the days or weeks of the assessment process. Increase the child or adult's access to liked and calming activities during the assessment process.

11. Let the child or adult participate in a highly liked activity before and after each session regardless of their level of participation and cooperation. You are trying to create in the individual's mind a positive association between testing situations and nice things happening.

Qualifications of Professionals Doing Assessments

The qualifications of the personnel who will conduct the assessments have tremendous impact on the quality of the assessment process. Experienced professionals familiar with ASD should be assigned or selected to conduct the assessments. This is practical and realistic and such specialists can be found in almost every area of the country. Family members or staff of a person being assessed need to know about the qualifications and experience of the assessor. How do parents guardians, staff, or other concerned professionals know if diagnosticians and specialists are experienced and qualified?

Parents may be able to assume that the team members are qualified if:

- The assessment results in the accurate identification of the individual's areas of need.

- Other parents and professionals are having positive experiences with the assessment team.

- The team is working successfully with the child or adult.

- The team is sharing information across disciplines (such as the speech and language pathologist working with the occupational therapist during assessments).

- The team members use language that clearly, objectively describes their findings without blaming the individual or the family.

Parents may not feel comfortable asking about the professional qualifications of staff; this subject has been handled in various ways across the country. Now, however, the No Child Left Behind Act of 2001, (NCLB) gives parents the right to "request information regarding the professional qualifications of their child's teachers and/or instructional aides."[13] This federal law applies to general education as well as special education teachers. You may need to ask the school principal or district director of human resources how to request information and what information can be shared, such as the curriculum vitae or resume, etc.

If you are concerned about qualifications, you may want to ask for a special meeting with the professionals who have been assigned to be part of the team assessment. Tell them you would like to get to know them and something about their qualifications before the assessments start. Ask each person or the responsible district personnel to provide resumes before this meeting depending on how the NCLB law is followed where you live. Here are some things to look at and talk about when you review the resume and during the conversations:

- The type of degrees the person has, (B.A., B.S., M.A., M Ed., M.S., Ph.D., M.D.) how long ago the degree was obtained and from what school.

- If the person is licensed in their field, and if a license is available in that field.

- How many years of experience they have had working with children with special needs.

- Previous or current employment during which the person worked with children or adults with ASD or related disorders.

- Any courses they have taken on the subject.

- If she is a family member of people with disabilities.

Parents or Staff can:

- Ask team members to explain their working knowledge of ASD and talk about their experiences. (Remember, they cannot discuss other specific cases with you or violate the confidentiality of others by talking about them, but they can speak in general about their experiences.)

- Ask team members to describe any additional help they may need to be able to make the evaluation as successful as possible. Sometimes the assessment team members do need some support, but need the parent or guardian to ask for it.

• Ask if your name and number could be given to other families whose children have been assessed by these professionals. Ask if the other families could be asked to call and talk to you about their experiences if they want to.

• Meet with any professional privately and ask them in confidence if there is anything else you need to do to help the assessment team.

Note: Some people consider a professional to be qualified in the field if the professional belongs to many organizations in a particular field. However, most professional organizations allow anyone to join who pays the membership fee. This is not necessarily a way to determine professionalism or qualifications.

Some parents have had consistently negative experiences with team members, or are consistently being told that their child or adult is "untestable," or that the assessment team cannot "find any deficits." In these cases, the parent may do well to ask more questions before the assessment process proceeds. This "asking" is not done to intimidate or offend; it is done to be sure that the individual is getting the best possible assessment. A poorly done assessment often results in long time delays while new and possibly costly additional assessments are planned and carried out.

If a school district or local education agency does not have qualified personnel to do the assessments for children ages 3 to 21, parents have the right to obtain a private assessment at the expense of the district by going to a fair hearing or due process proceeding. Sometimes the school district will agree that a private assessment is the best option if school staff is not trained or experienced in the area of ASD. Be sure to negotiate and get agreement from the school district before arranging for a private assessment. Consult the special education rules in your state.

Sometimes professionals are asked to participate in the assessment process and do not feel qualified to do so. It is important for professionals to disclose their honest feelings to the team, ask for additional help or support and describe the areas of competence they possess. It is very gratifying when professionals make this sometimes painful admission. "No one knows everything!" In most districts, directors of special education and the personnel who work for them want to do the absolute best possible work. Team members must take personal stock of their own skills, identify areas in which they are not comfortable working and seek assistance.

Often as a result of such honest disclosure a person with expertise is brought in. The professional works with that person, acquires new skills and knowledge, and from then on can do an even better job. Most people in special services want to do the best possible job. Professionals should not expect themselves to have expertise in ASD, because even today there is very little training at the university level about ASD. However, professionals need only look at the increase in incidence of these disorders to know how much they must commit themselves to gaining knowledge and skills about ASD.

Many training opportunities are designed to give professionals the newest and best information while allowing them to accumulate professional credit hours needed to maintain their licenses or certifications. Educators and service providers can contact the local or state Autism organization (or a nearby state) to find out about training opportunities, best books and articles to read, specialized consultants in the area, etc. Excellent courses and other information on ASD are available on the Internet.

Parents and others asking for the assessment must ask for help when needed. Another rule of thumb is, "If you ask for no help, that is how much help you will get!"

CHAPTER 4 SUMMARY

- Results of assessments are the basis for designing an individualized plan and choosing services, programs, interventions and therapies most appropriate to an individual's needs.

- Components of a thorough assessment include a full medical and developmental history, family health history, review of existing school records, review of current and past academic assessments and testing, psychological testing, measure of social-emotional status, behavior analysis, communication, speech and language testing, evaluation of vocational skills, daily living and functional skills, occupational and motor skills, play and leisure skills, sensory functioning and processing, and an assistive technology assessment.

- A variety of specialists may do assessments in various domains of functioning based on their areas of expertise; an interdisciplinary team will consider all information learned about the individual, his capabilities and identified areas of need.

- The difficulties experienced in everyday life by people with ASD may present challenges in the assessment process. This can include heightened levels of stress, difficulty "trusting" unknown people, defensiveness, problems with change or new experiences, variability of performance, problems with generalization, inattention, poor social skills, lack of awareness of social expectations and poor eye contact.

- Communication and language problems may make it difficult for the person to understand and follow instructions or respond in a way that can be understood.

- "Masking" may occur when high-functioning individuals use adaptations and coping strategies, with the result that their true needs (deficits) may be hidden. Use of borrowed, memorized, or "safe" responses may have a similar effect.

- Sensory sensitivities may be heightened in the assessment process and present challenges.

- A one-to-one setting may not provide an accurate picture of how the individual functions in real-life situations. Adding disruption, background noise or testing in a group setting may help to show more areas of need. Observing the child or adult in less structured, peer-mediated settings may reveal areas of need that will not manifest in one-to-one, quiet, adult-mediated settings.

- Parents can help get a better and more accurate assessment by providing information to "customize" the assessment to the individual's needs. Collaborative planning between parents and professionals and discussion of accommodations improve the accuracy, efficiency, and levels of cooperation and comfort in assessments.

- An excellent way for parents and professionals to establish communication as equal participants in the assessment process is by making home visits.

- The assessment process may be annoying at best and overwhelming at worst to a child or adult being evaluated, because of some characteristics of ASD. Modifications or adaptations may make it easier to prepare the child or adult, help her know what to expect, reduce anxiety, and reward her for trying to participate.

- Parents can ask about the qualification of those providing assessment services to increase confidence.

- Less experienced professionals should ask for additional support and training.

CHAPTER 5

TYPES OF ASSESSMENTS AND WHAT THEY MEASURE

Parents wonder how the "experts" will be able to find out about their child's areas of needs and strengths and identify any disability. Staff want to be sure that all needed areas are assessed with appropriate methods. Whether a person will be assessed for diagnosis, for educational placement, to add services, or for the triennial review after three years of Special Education services, it is important to know what testing is done, why, what is involved and "what they are looking for."

In this chapter you will learn:

- Areas that are included in a comprehensive assessment.

- Types of assessment and testing tools.

- Methods used to conduct assessments.

- Skills relevant to each area that is assessed.

As you page through this chapter, you will notice many lists. It may look like something that is not too important for the child or adult who will be evaluated. On the contrary! This chapter was written in response to requests from parents, staff and professional evaluators who have asked:

- What do I need to look for in an evaluation to determine the presence of Autism Spectrum Disorder (ASD) or to determine educational planning or adult services?

- What tests will help us see the characteristics of ASD if they are present?

- How do we find the more subtle communication problems in high-functioning people with ASD?

- How do we identify the more subtle higher-level thinking skills problems in high-functioning people with ASD?

- What are the important skills to have in different areas of development and functioning?

Behavior as Skills

Behavior is defined as any observable action that can be described, measured or counted. ASD is behaviorally diagnosed. This means looking at how the person behaves. The purpose is not to judge "good" or "bad" behavior. For assessment and diagnostic purposes, behavior can be defined as **skills and abilities the person is able to demonstrate or skills and abilities the person does not have or use.**

Development is a continuous process. There is an expected and predictable path of human development. The purpose of testing and assessment is to identify the skills a person has along a continuum of growth. It helps to show what a person knows and can do and what he needs to learn next. Testing can also show whether a person has a pattern of development that is significantly unusual and falls under the category of developmental delay or disability.

Children develop in many areas of skills at the same time. Progress in one area can affect progress in another area. For example, children learn to talk and play at the same time, and skills in one area affect the other. We expect children to recognize the letters of the alphabet, before we expect them to read words. We expect them to express their needs, before they ask us how we are feeling. We need to be able to identify at what stage of development a person is at a given moment. Then we can help them move on to the next step.

Pinpointing Development

Several areas of development need to be assessed to get a complete picture of a person's progress and functioning. Many different evaluations and assessments may be needed, all at once, or over time to measure all areas of functioning in the child or adult with ASD. Assessments can be done in any of the following areas:

- Psychiatric or neurological.
- Medical/physical.
- Psychological/educational/learning.
- Communication/language.
- Social skills.
- Behavior.
- Occupational therapy and sensory integration.
- Adaptive functioning/daily living skills.
- Physical functioning including hearing and vision.
- Assistive Technology needs and use.

A section of this chapter will address each of these areas of assessment. In each section, the reader will find a description of the:

- Purpose of the assessment or evaluation.
- Methods, tests or techniques used.
- Skills that will be measured or evaluated.
- Results - the form in which information from evaluations is summarized or reported.

Purpose of Assessments or Evaluations: Why Do Them?

Assessments are designed to measure particular areas of skill and functioning. Evaluations are intended to measure the present level of performance, ability or skills in any given area. Each assessment is specific to a field, whether it is education, speech and language, occupational therapy, psychiatry or others. Professionals conducting assessments must be trained, qualified and/or licensed to conduct the assessments and evaluations they perform.

Specific tests are designed for a particular purpose. Scientific method is used to demonstrate that a test is effective in testing for particular traits, skills, etc. Research and trials confirm that particular tests are valid and appropriate for the purpose named and for use with specific age groups. You will often see that a test has an author's name and is dated or copyrighted. This information identifies the person or people that designed the test instrument and scientifically demonstrated its' effectiveness.

Methods: How Will we Measure?

A listing of assessment tools or methods used to gather information is included to help parents become more familiar and comfortable with the "jargon" of various specialty fields. It might look a long list of big words and too many abbreviations. But it may be better to see the titles and names of tests and techniques here for the first time rather than in the report about your child or adult! Over time, some of these terms may become part of your everyday vocabulary. Different methods of testing can include such things as an interactive play, filling in the blank on a written test, listening and giving answers or being observed in everyday activities.

Standardized Tests

We have included a list of standardized assessments, tests or evaluation tools to use to open the dialogue between parents and professionals. This list can be reviewed in advance to discuss which tests or tools will be selected. When a school district is going to test a child for the presence of a disability, or to get a complete picture of the child's abilities and needs in a variety of areas, the parents must first give their informed consent. Parents are often given a form that says, "Tests to be given may include, but are not limited to...." followed by a long list of things most parents have never heard of. It is very hard to consider the consent "informed," if no one explains which particular tests will be selected and why.

Parents can ask professionals to explain which assessments will be used and what is involved in a particular type of test. The explanation should be simple and clear. Parents need opportunities to have any questions about the assessment tools answered.

Standardized tests are "**normed.**" This means scientific method, research, and statistical analysis are used to tabulate how persons of a certain age perform on the test. Standardization allows the results for any individual to be compared to the results for other individuals of a specific age. Professionals rely on these instruments to help accurately measure the level of functioning and ability of a child or adult, and compare the results to others of the same age that have taken the same test.

Other assessments are "**criterion referenced.**" This means that the assessment is done to see whether a particular ability, skill or attribute is present or not. An example would be assessing to see whether a child can tie his shoes, or not. No comparison is made to what others of the same age know or can do.

Sometimes standardized tests can be used to help discover the skills and needs of an individual without concern for the score. As discussed in Chapter 4, a test score is not valid or accurate if the testing conditions are not or cannot be followed. But, there may be times when the information gained from the process of doing the test activities, or attempting the test, may be as valuable as a score. Standardized tests are normed for people of specific ages, meaning that there is no basis for comparison if a test is used for a person of a different age. However, some tests designed for children can be used to gather information about teenagers or adults with ASD, even if the "normed" score is not useful. These are decisions to be discussed by teams before testing.

Informal Methods

"Testing" alone will not give all the information needed about the child's or adult's development and functioning, areas of learning strengths and needs or shed light on services that may be appropriate. There is a great degree of subtlety in the deficit areas of some people with ASD. Some deficits may not be revealed with standardized tests or in formal settings. Other ways to test informally for the presence or absence of skills are often needed and can be incorporated into the assessment process.

Interviews are a method used to learn about the skills of the individual. Interviews may be conducted with the individual herself, family members, teachers and others who know her. Playground supervisors, bus drivers or attendants, lunchroom staff, sports instructors, activity leaders and workshop or residential staff can be interviewed. Checklists and surveys are sometimes given with an interview, and sometimes used alone.

Observation in various settings is another informal method to gather information. Observation is most helpful when the observer watches and listens and objectively records what actually happens without adding opinions or assumptions.

Share and Prepare

Dialogue between all parties about the formal and informal evaluations that will be used will help the parents or involved professionals prepare the individual for the assessment. It is more likely that the individual will perform best if she knows what to expect, what will happen and what will not happen. ("You will answer questions about spelling words; and it is multiple choice" or, "The lady is going to play some games with you in the play area.")

If the individual is not prepared in advance, the parent should ask the professional to allow extra time for the assessment. The time is needed to allow the individual to acclimate to the environment and materials. The individual and tester will need time to learn how to communicate best with one another. Time to process explanations may be needed before testing begins. Many professionals make these adaptations in the normal course of testing. People who possibly have disorders in the autism spectrum may need extra time.

Due to the nature of ASD, explanations and preparations may not result in an individual "knowing" what is going to happen or what to do, even if being assessed for a skill he has mastered. "Variability" of responses may mean that several observations and informal assessments should also be used to round out the picture. Refer to Chapter 4 for information on improving the assessment process.

Skills: What Do the Tests Measure and Reveal?

For each area being assessed, we have created lists of skills usually measured. The skill lists are based on the skills that have been found to be, or are thought to be, most relevant to the functioning and development of people with ASD. Skills listed have been selected either from the literature on typical development or from experience and familiarity with skills that are often a challenge for people with ASD.

These skill lists can be used as guides by both parents and professionals to focus on particular issues and areas of need. The lists may help teams be sure that all important skill areas are measured either formally or informally as appropriate to the individual's development and age. Parents and staff may use the lists of skills to indicate areas of concern they are aware of from observation and experience in addition to formal assessments. (Lists of skills are not provided for medical and psychological or intelligence testing, because they do not apply).

Our lists are not comprehensive: they do not include every skill that a person could demonstrate or every skill that could be assessed. They are not intended as a checklist to diagnose ASD. They are intended to answer the question, "What are we looking for?" when doing assessments. Parents or professionals may have reasons to test for items not on these lists. Additional information can be added or more testing done to address any other important areas of functioning. Professionals may have testing manuals that describe the specific skills measured using a particular test instrument.

In addition, any skills identified, through the lists and through assessment, that need to be learned can be broken down into the smaller steps that make up the activity. Each step can be taught until the activity is mastered. For example, if a person needs to learn to brush his teeth on his own, this may be broken down into taking the cap off the toothpaste, putting toothpaste on the brush, putting the cap back on the tube, brushing teeth in soft circles, rinsing the mouth, rinsing the brush and putting the brush away. Any other skill to be learned can include specifying the steps that are needed to accomplish it.

The skills listed are intended to include the school years approximately ages 3 to 21. This wide range is covered because levels of skill are often developed over time in an atypical way in children with ASD. In other words, the age of the child on the calendar and expected skills for that age do not always match. Children with ASD develop skills on their own timetable. A first-grader may be able to solve an algebraic equation, but may not pedal a tricycle. A seventh-grader may have reading comprehension many grade levels lower, but know the names of all the bones in the body. This type of development is called **asynchronous**, development that is "out of sync" with what is expected.

Adult services providers and caregivers of adults with special needs can use these lists to assess the skill areas of adults in their care. Most adults in the service delivery system will not have learned all of the skills listed. Staff and families can use the lists to assess and to help prioritize skills that need to be taught to the adult.

Results: What Have We Learned About the Person?

The section on results will describe the findings or information gained from testing or evaluation. The results can be reported or presented in a variety of forms or formats. The results are often in the form of scores, charts, graphs or percentages. The results may be written as a description and discussion. If the results are given in person as a verbal report, a written copy of the results should be provided at the same time.

Informal testing may be reported as a summary of observations, including who/did what/in what setting/under what conditions/with what result. Conclusions may be drawn or theories and assumptions stated as such.

Written and oral reporting of results must be given with adequate time for explanations by professionals and time for questions from parents and others. Parents or guardians do not have to "agree" with results, nor must they understand them all the first time they are heard. Discussion of test results may need more than one meeting with the various people involved. We recommend that test results and assessment findings be shared and discussed at an informal meeting of just a few team members before a decision-making meeting, such as, an IEP or IHP meeting. Parents and professionals need time to digest and think about assessment results before being asked to make a plan based on those results. If a meeting cannot be held to discuss the results before the IEP, professionals should be sure to provide copies to the parents or staff before the IEP meeting. Parents may request this is writing, if needed.

Standardized tests result in a score that can be reported in a variety of ways. It is important to know how the score is being reported and what the "number" means. Reading through the different types of scores below, it is easy to see that a person could get confused, or get a completely wrong idea from just "seeing a number" without knowing how it is used. Refer to 5.1, *Reporting of Test Scores* to get an idea of the many ways scores are interpreted.

Understanding the scores and results of testing can be very difficult. It is important not to proceed with planning educational goals and placements until the results of the testing are understood. Parents, a guardian or concerned staff can ask the person who did the testing to explain the results and what they mean. Another option is to schedule to meet with one professional from the agency or district responsible for the testing. The test results can be discussed in an individual session before the large team meeting. In this way, the information can be heard, processed and understood one step at a time.

Parents or staff may wish to discuss the results with an educational specialist experienced in interpreting the numbers and any graphs or charts used. Parents may also wish to consult with an experienced person if the results reported are not consistent with what they know about their child or conflict with information from other sources. Books and websites on education and advocacy are useful. Some are suggested at the end of this chapter. The suggested sites link to a variety of additional information sources.

Subtests and Averaging

In interpreting test results, parents and staff will want to be aware that many tests are divided into "subtests" that focus on particular areas. Some people with ASD will do well on some subtests, but have much more difficulty with other areas. Looking at the results of individual subtests can be helpful and revealing of strength and deficit areas.

Knowing that the subtest scores are important on their own, parents and staff will want to look at reports carefully to see how much variation there is within the subtests. Parents and staff must know whether the subtest scores were averaged, or combined, to get a final score. Averaging can be counterproductive when trying to clearly identify the deficit areas.

5.1 Reporting of Test Scores

Intelligence Quotient

(IQ)   IQ Score Intelligence tests result in a number being given for Intelligence Quotient, with 100 as the score for average intelligence.

Age equivalent

(AE)   A calendar age is given to reflect the level of ability, as in, "He is reading at the level of a child age 6 years, 3 months."

Grade equivalent

(GE)   A school grade year and month is given to reflect the level of ability, as in "she does math at the level of grade 4, 5th month."

Percentage

%   The percentage of correct answers; for example, "she answered 7 out of 10 questions correctly, scoring 70%."

Percentage ranking

(PR)   A measurement comparing the performance to that of others, as in, "He is at the 37th percentile." This means that 37 % of people tested had the same or a lower score and 63 % tested higher. The average score is 50 in a percentile ranking.

Raw score

(RS)   The number of correct responses out of the total number of questions; it is the test result at face value, before it is interpreted or converted for standardized comparison.

Standard score

(SS)   Found by applying a mathematical formula to a raw score; "100" is average, and performance is measured above or below 100.

"Z" score

Measure of performance above or below a standard of zero.

"T" score

Measure of performance above or below a standard of 50.

Stanine score

Test results given as a value of one through nine; 1, 2 and 3 are below average, 4, 5, and 6 are average, and 7, 8, and 9 are above average scores.

Here is an Example From a Reading Test:

An 11-year-old boy scored at age 15 for reading on the subtest for decoding, that is being able to sound out words, recognize words, etc. On the subtest for comprehension, the boy scored at the age level of a 7-year-old. Looking at the subtest scores alone, one can see an 8-year gap between the ability to read and the ability to understand what is read. But the person reporting the scores added together 15 and 7, and divided by 2, to get an "average score" of 11 years. The conclusion was that there was no concern in the area of reading, because an 11-year-old boy was performing "on average" as an 11-year-old boy. Averaging can smooth out the very peaks and valleys that we are trying to identify and address!

How Assessments May Overlap

There may be a degree of overlap between various types of assessments. For example, hearing tests often involve the use of language — an area of overlap with a speech and language assessment. Social skills assessments evaluate social use of language. Language evaluations may also reveal the ability to use higher-level thinking skills and solve problems.

This type of overlap is normal and acceptable and may provide additional information about the functioning and skills of the individual. For example, a student may score very high on a test of vocabulary and yet not be able to use those words to make a simple request in a social situation. Looking at skills from a variety of perspectives and in various real situations may help the team understand more about what skills the person has and can use.

Duplication That Should Be Avoided

In some circumstances, two different professionals may wish to use the exact same assessment tool or test. However, duplicating tests within a certain time period can invalidate the standard score results. This is because a "learning effect" takes place each time a person takes a test. If the person takes the same test a short time later, they will usually have a better score because they will have "learned" the test. Parents and professionals should be clear in advance about what assessments will be used. It is helpful to keep a list of the assessments to be done by each assessor, so duplication can be spotted and discussed. The written report provided after the assessment will also specifically name the assessment tools used and the results.

Areas of Skills, Abilities and Needs In Diagnosis and Assessment for Autism Spectrum Disorders

Psychiatric or Neurological Diagnostic Evaluations

Purpose

A psychiatrist, neurologist, developmental pediatrician or other qualified medical professional will evaluate the individual's features or symptoms to try to distinguish an emotional, behavioral or mental health disorder from a neurological, developmental disorder like autism. The evaluations are usually done in an office or a clinic. More than one visit may be involved. Sometimes more testing will be recommended. An official diagnosis (sometimes more than one diagnosis) is often the result.

Physicians may wait and postpone their diagnoses until further development (of a child) is observed. They may also want to "rule-out" another diagnosis. (Rule out "depressive disorder" for example, means that the evaluator will look for all signs and symptoms to definitively say that the individual does not have a depressive disorder. When a disorder cannot be ruled out, it is then diagnosed.) "Waiting" and "ruling out" may be done to increase accuracy and find the correct diagnosis.

Method

The medical professional will do an extensive interview which may last several hours. Parents or those responsible for the person usually provide the needed information. The interview may include:

- An account of the pregnancy of the mother and birth of the child.

- A full developmental history of the individual, from birth to the present.

- Health history and medical issues.

- Parent and family histories.

- Description of family and social relationships.

- Descriptions of current functioning at home, work, school and community.

- Description of current problems, issues and concerns.

- An interview with the child, adolescent or adult.

- Interviews with family members or caregivers.

Parents or others may bring written records or personal notes with them. Copies of important information can be provided to the diagnostician for the permanent file including a written history of the child or adult (as discussed in Chapter 3). Additional information that is provided may not be read during the interview. Most professionals will read it later as part of researching and preparing their reports. In other cases, the professional will want to discuss the material and ask questions to be sure she understands the information. If you are unsure about how much information to provide, err on the side of providing too much, not too little.

Tools

When ASD is suspected, the professional may use standardized screening and diagnostic tools. These tools assist professionals in identifying people with autism spectrum disorders. Screening tools are used to verify that there is reason to suspect that a child may have ASD and follow up with an in-depth look at the person's development and functioning. Diagnostic tools often use rating scales, checklists or interviews with parents or staff to assess the development and functioning of the child or adult. Some tests involve structured, planned, interaction with the child or adult. Diagnostic tools may have scores or other indicators to help arrive at the correct diagnosis.

The psychiatrist or neurologist may select one of the diagnostic tools listed below. Before the first appointment, you can discuss which will be selected and what is involved. Different assessment tools are chosen depending on the age and verbal/communication ability of the individual being tested.

Screening Tools:

- Checklist for Autism in Toddlers (CHAT).

- The Ages and Stages Questionnaire.

- The Brigance® Screens.

- Infant-Toddler Developmental Assessment (IDA).

- The Child Development Inventories.

- The Parents Evaluations of Developmental Status.

- Autism Screening Questionnaire.

- The Screening Tool for Autism in Two-Year-Olds.

Diagnostic Tools

- Asperger's Syndrome Diagnostic Scale (ASDS)

- Autism Behavior Checklist (ABC)

- Autism Diagnostic Interview- Revised (ADI-R)

- Autism Screening Instrument for Educational Planning-Second Edition (ASIEP-2)

- Batelle Development Inventory

- Childhood Autism Rating Scale (CARS)

- The Diagnostic Observation Scale-Generic

- Gilliam Autism Rating Scale (GARS)

- Prelinguistic Autism Diagnostic Observation Schedule (PL-ADOS or Play-Dos)

- Pervasive Developmental Disorder Screening Test- Stage 3 (PDDST-3)

- The Parent Interview for Autism

Note: There are two "do it yourself" or self-administered screening tools for ASD to mention. They can be used to screen yourself, or can be answered about another person, such as your child or student. The first is the Autism-Spectrum Quotient designed by Dr. Simon Baron-Cohen of the Autism Research Center of Cambridge, England. It is available online at: http://www.wired.com/wired/archive/9.12/aqtest.html. This screening has been validated, meaning that it has been methodically proven to identify the characteristics of Asperger's Syndrome in those who have it and not in those who don't.

The second screening tool is the Australian Scales developed by Dr. Tony Attwood. It can be found online at http://www.tonyattwood.com/paper6.htm. It can be a useful reference point and may be accurate, but has not been validated by scientific method to identify people with Asperger's Syndrome.

In either case, it is advisable to seek a professional opinion if the results of a self-administered screening tool indicate the possibility of Asperger's Syndrome in you, your child, your student or an adult in your care.

Results

The findings of the psychiatric or neurological evaluation are written in a report sometimes called a "**formulation.**" It includes a summary of the individual's history, description of problems, a specific diagnosis and recommendations for treatment. The formulation is often presented at an appointment after the assessment, so that parents or staff can discuss the findings and ask questions. The discussion about this and all findings should be done when the child is **not** present. An adult who presents himself for diagnosis may want to bring a friend or family member when the results are presented and discussed.

Medical Testing

Purpose

There is no medical "test" for autism. There is no way, at present, to identify the disorder based on blood tests, genetic tests or imaging of the brain. Even so, a thorough medical exam should be done to determine if there is a physical cause or any other explanation of the symptoms that are being observed. Schools and adult service providers do not generally provide these valuable evaluations. Health insurance providers can help to determine what is covered in particular policies.

Methods

Interview to discuss:

- Health history of child.
- Developmental history of child.
- History of mother's pregnancy and delivery.
- Health history of each parent.
- Health histories of family members of each parent.

Tools

Full physical examination should include laboratory analysis of blood, feces and urine.

The examination includes measurement of the head and limbs and observation of:

- Any unusual physical features.
- Gait (how the person walks).
- Muscle tone.
- Style of play.
- Reactions and reflexes.
- Mental status.
- Use of verbal and nonverbal language.
- Vision screening.
- Hearing screening.

Other tests are sometimes done when a physician, geneticist or neurologist feels there is a need to do so based on the history given, screening and observations, and professional judgement. However, none of the listed techniques are intended or able to find a "marker" or sign that proves a person has ASD. They can be significant to detect any other co-existing abnormalities or disorders. Some examples are:

- Genetic screening and/or testing to rule out Fragile X syndrome or other genetic conditions.

- Chromosomal analysis, screening for genetic disorders.

- Metabolic tests: blood and urine screening for amino acids, organic acids, lactate and pyruvate, thyroid function, liver and kidney function, uric acid.

- Rubella/CMV assay.

- Magnetic Resonance Imaging (MRI), creating a detailed image of the brain.

- ElectroEncephaloGram (EEG) a measurement of brain waves, used especially if seizures are reported or suspected. May reveal tumors or other abnormalities of the brain.

- PET/SPECT, colored images of the brain as it "thinks," related to heat/blood flow.

- Computer Assisted Axial Tomography (CAT SCAN), used to detect structural abnormalities of the brain.

Nutritional and allergy-related medical testing can include:

- Urinary peptides.

- Food/environmental/medication allergies.

- Nutritional analysis.

- Gluten/casein sensitivity.

- Screening for the presence of heavy metals (lead, mercury).

Results

Findings from medical testing are usually presented in the form of a written report explained verbally to the parent or guardian. The report may include a diagnosis, data, analysis of findings and recommendations.

Educational and Psychological Testing

This type of assessment, also called psycho-educational evaluation, is done to understand how a person thinks, learns and functions on a daily basis. Several methods and tools are usually selected to test a full range of abilities in this area.

The purpose of educational and psychological testing is to measure and assess:

- Academic ability (current level of skills and knowledge in school content areas).

- Learning strengths and skills, style of learning (sometimes called modalities, intelligences or learning preferences).

- Adaptive, self-care and daily living skills.

- Attention span and style of attending.

- Cognitive skills related to:

    — Learning: amount, types, speed and style.

    — Thinking.

    — Understanding.

    — Processing.

    — Recalling, remembering.

    — Reasoning.

    — Inferring.

    — Generalizing.

    — Problem Solving.

- Personality traits related to:

- — Preoccupations.

- — Mood.

- — Defensiveness.

- — Aggressiveness.

- — Depression, etc.

- Executive Function skills related to:

  - — Planning.

  - — Organizing.

  - — Inhibition of impulses.

  - — Attention.

Methods

Standardized Tests

Several standardized tests are normally selected to measure the full range of intelligence, thinking and learning. Most will be given in an environment prescribed in the testing manual for each test. It is usually a quiet, undisturbed, one-to-one environment. In testing an individual suspected of having ASD, the introduction of noise or distraction may lead to a more true measurement of the person's functioning in daily life. The option of adding sound or disruption should be discussed by those requesting the assessment and the person conducting it.

Play-Based Assessment

Play-based assessment is another method that can be used in psycho-educational testing. It is especially useful for young children or non-verbal children, but can be used with any child or adult. Interactions between the professional and the child or adult being tested are planned and carried out. Often, a second person observes the child's reactions and responses and takes notes or videotapes the session.

Sometimes the assessment is structured, and the tester goes through a series of planned activities using specific toys and materials. Other play-based assessments are more spontaneous, or unstructured, following the interests and the lead of the child or adult. Play-based assessments are used to understand a child's or adult's emotional and cognitive development and her style and skills in communication, socialization and play.

Observation

Direct observation is another method used in psycho-educational testing. Sometimes a natural setting is used, and the professional doing the observation takes notes or takes data on what is observed. Other observation can take place in a clinic or office. Rooms with a one-way mirror are sometimes used, so the observations go unnoticed by the children or adults being observed.

Interviews and checklists

Interviews and checklists are can also be used to round out the collection of information. Input is usually sought from parents, teachers, siblings or staff. Checklists may be done on the spot or are sometimes taken home and returned to the practitioner to be taken into account with all the other information collected.

Educational/Psycho-Educational and Intelligence Assessment Tools

Educational and psycho-educational tests are specially designed to be appropriate for individuals of particular ages and stages of development. These tools are used to test for things that a person of a certain age is typically expected to be able to do or to know. Educational professionals are often familiar with the tests that are age-appropriate for younger children, older children and adults. Brochures and manuals used with standardized tests, state the age group for whom the test is normed.

In the case of many individuals with Autism Spectrum Disorders, the level of ability is not as closely related to age as it may be for other people. The individual with ASD may have limited communication and/or social skills. These are important factors to take into account when selecting the most appropriate assessment tools.

Informal assessment of learning strengths, needs and style may be done for individuals who cannot participate in standardized IQ testing. Particular testing methods can be selected for people who are non-verbal.

Tests are chosen to measure at least the following areas of ability:

- Intelligence (Intelligence Quotient, or IQ).

- PIQ: Performance Intelligence, or planning and reasoning skills.

- Non-verbal IQ: measure of intelligence not based on ability to use language.

- Tests of verbal intelligence: use of language (expressive and receptive), speech, sign language or picture/print systems.

- Auditory memory (remembering what is heard), immediately or later.

- Reading (if the person is able to read).

- Mathematics, from number recognition, to sequencing, operations, measurement and more complex forms of math.

- Assessment for comprehension.

- Assessment for level of symbolic representation (does the individual know that the word "tree" in print refers to a tree outside, or recognizes that a picture of a tree or a black and white line drawing does the same).

- Sequencing events using pictures or print.

- Application of material to own life experiences.

- Looking at pictures, then telling a story.

Tests for Learning and Thinking

Some frequently used tools to assess learning and thinking are:

- *Bayley Scales of Infant Development, revised as Bayley II.
- Beery-Developmental Test of Visual-Motor Integration (VMI).

- Differential Ability Scales (DAS).
- Kaufman ABC Test (K-ABC).
- Kinetic Family Drawing.
- Woodcock-Johnson Revised Tests of Achievement (WJ-R).
- Wide Range Assessment of Memory and Learning (WRAML).
- Gray Oral Reading Test-3 (GORT-3).
- Peabody Picture Vocabulary Test-Third Edition A (PPVT-III).
- Preschool Learning Scales (PLS).
- Stanford-Binet Intelligence Scale (4th edition).
- Thematic Apperception Test (TAT).
- Test of Written Spelling (TWS-3).
- Vineland Adaptive Behavior Scales (VABS).
- Wide Range Achievement Test-Revision 3 (WRAT-3).
- *Weschler Preschool and Primary Scales of Intelligence, Revised (WPPSI-R).
- Weschler Intelligence Scale for Children-III (WISC-III).
- Psychoeducational Profile-Revised (PEP-R).

* These test instruments may be appropriate for children who do not speak at all or have limited ability to speak or use language in some form (are non-verbal or have limited verbal skills).

Skills

Educational and thinking skills may be evaluated in a comprehensive educational assessment using a variety of the tools mentioned above as developmentally/age appropriate to measure the ability to:

- Follow oral directions.
- Follow directions with visual cues.
- Follow written directions.
- Understand directions.
- Shift attention.
- Form concepts.
- Solve problems.
- Draw conclusions.

- Synthesize information, bring learned material together.
- Understand cause and effect.
- Remember.
- Match.
- Sequence.
- Order.
- Compare.
- Contrast.
- Categorize.
- Memorize.
- Use long-term memory.
- Use visual memory.

Examiners may note or consider:

- Amount of time needed for response.

- If responses are based on comprehension (not memorized, "safe" answers).

- Originality of responses (not "borrowed" from television or movies).

- Whether and how the child or adult "compensates" for an area of need with an area of strength.

Educational Testing

Educational or academic testing may include assessing what a student has learned compared to what he is expected to learn and what others of the same age have learned. Academic testing is age-appropriate, and students are not responsible for material that have not been taught; however, the testing may reveal if the person knows more than what is expected.

Reading Skills Assessments (as age-appropriate) Measure the Ability to:

- Match pictures to objects.
- Use pictures to communicate.

- Use pictures to follow a sequence of steps or a schedule.
- Attend to words when presented with pictures.
- Recognize and respond to print and/or pictures in the environment.
- Recognize letters of the alphabet.
- Understand that print has meaning.
- Use print to gain information.
- Follow a printed list to complete a task.
- Know sounds associated with letters.
- Recognize rhyming.
- Recognize words.
- Point to a picture when a word is said.
- Identify objects in pictures.
- Figure out unknown words using phonics.
- Understand word meaning.
- Understand multiple meanings of a single word.
- Figure out the meaning of a word from context.
- Understand a story.
- Identify main ideas.
- Identify supporting details.
- Remember details from a story.
- Recognize a plot.
- Recognize the beginning, middle and end of a story.
- Identify the climax and resolution of a story.
- Retell the plot in their own words (summarize).
- Predict outcomes.
- Draw conclusions.
- Invent a different ending for a story.
- Recognize the moral, lesson or point of a passage.
- Understand motivation of characters.
- Describe characters beyond physical traits.
- Understand events beyond their own experience.
- Infer.
- Understand concrete facts.

- Understand abstract concepts.
- Imagine future events.
- Distinguish fantasy from reality.

Wrting Skills (as age-appropriate) can be measured using handwriting or assistive devices such as keyboards. Assessment measures the ability to:

- Use print to express an idea.
- Respond to print when presented with it.
- Use printed words (or word cards) to express ideas.
- Combine words (or pictures) to express ideas in print.
- Organize thoughts into sentences.
- Use words appropriately.
- Use a variety of words.
- Vary sentence structure.
- Organize cohesive paragraphs.
- Follow rules of grammar.
- Identify parts of speech.
- Follow rules of mechanics, like punctuation, capitalization.
- Use supporting detail.
- Be original.
- Be creative.
- Use imagination.
- Put ideas into writing.
- Use penmanship skills.
- Follow the sequence of writing:

    — Pre-writing.
    — First Draft.
    — Revising.
    — Editing.
    — Final Product.

Mathematics assessments (as age-appropriate) measure the ability to:

- Understand one-to-one correspondence.
- Use numbers in functional daily tasks.
- Use concepts of less and more in daily life.
- Count forward and backward.
- Write numbers.
- Order numbers.
- Use computation skills, such as,

    — Addition.
    — Subtraction.
    — Multiplication.
    — Division.

- Measure.
- Order objects by size or weight.
- Understand money.
- Understand time.
- Discriminate shapes.
- Understand spatial relations (next to, under).
- Recognize patterns.
- Make a coded message.
- Read code.
- Estimate an answer.
- Estimate an amount.
- Figure out what does not belong in a set.
- Use fractions.
- Understand decimals.
- Calculate percentage.
- Understand and interpret graphs.
- Make and use tables.
- Do geometry.
- Solve algebra problems.
- Solve word problems.

- Use mathematical language.
- Explain how to solve a problem.

Determination of learning style looks at the ability to:

- Learn by imitating.

- Learn by following verbal direction.

- Learn by using peer support.

- Learn in a variety of environments.

- Learn with a variety of environmental elements in place, such as noise, a variety of lighting, music in the background, the close proximity of other people, etc.

- Apply recently learned material to real life situations.

- Apply recently learned material to academic activities.

- Use immediate, short and long term memory.

- Use visual, kinesthetic or auditory modalities, etc., as a primary processing modality.

- Use coping strategies for learning new things quickly or under time constraints.

- Use movement, music, poetry, logic, sequence or other elements to improve learning.

Results

Some results of educational testing will be presented mathematically as percentages and/or scores. Graphs and charts are also used. The report should include narrative sections that describe why and how the testing was accomplished, observations of the child or adult during testing, a discussion of impressions and recommendations for specific types of services. Scores should be interpreted to identify areas of strength and areas of need. Scores help to establish where an individual is on the continuum of skill development and highlight what needs to be taught and learned.

Results may include a number score for "IQ" with the number 100 representing average intelligence. The score of the individual can be compared as average, above average or below average. Sometimes the results of the intelligence testing are described as a "mental age." The mental age from testing can be compared to a person's actual calendar age. This gives a comparison of whether the person is functioning at, above or below the level expected for a person of that age.

Some test results will be reported in the form of observational notes or understanding gained from watching how the individual learned in the testing situation. Some results will be reported as "anecdotes" or stories told to the tester about what and how the individual has learned in the past. This kind of reporting is just as important as formal scores and should be considered and discussed by the team. Parents and family members may have important information to share about the learning style and processes of the individual. If there is debate, situations can be designed to "test" a learning theory about any individual.

For example, staff or family may have learned that the individual learns best when a printed list is provided. This information may help the team design and implement some printed lists that the individual can learn to use independently, decreasing the need for on-going interpersonal support at every moment. If lists have been shown to be an effective way to help the individual learn, then lists could be used to help teach social skills or to gain greater control over impulses.

A Note About Intelligence:

After seeing "the number" from an intelligence test, parents and staff often report that the individual with ASD is actually "smarter" than what the standardized IQ test indicates. THEY ARE RIGHT! Intelligence testing is a measurement of what someone knows compared to other people their age. If the child or adult has developmental and social issues, they are likely to have acquired less information than their same-aged peers. Their mental focus may have been more directed at understanding and functioning in a confusing and/or upsetting world or focused on specific areas of interest.

To best take an intelligence test, the person being tested needs good communication skills to understand what the tester is saying. The person being tested must interpret and act upon instructions and give information and answers in a way that can be understood. A second set of skills that helps a person to take an intelligence test is social skills, some of which are meeting, adjusting to, getting to know and responding to an unknown or little-known person. Finally, to concentrate on intelligence testing activities, the person being tested needs to be able to know what important aspects of the room, test and tester on which to focus attention on. He needs to be able to be "led" by instructions and directions, switching from one task or activity to another, at the direction of another.

As is probably obvious, the skills needed to do well on standardized tests are skills that people with ASD often do not have. Children or adults with ASD acquire degrees of social and communication competence. Their communication and social skills may not be sufficient for the task of showing their full mental ability in a testing situation. Because of these obstacles to testing, it is not surprising that people with ASD may have unexpected or inconsistent results in intelligence testing.

Professionals who conduct the IQ testing may themselves declare the results of an IQ test invalid when the test results are clearly inconsistent with a level of intelligence demonstrated in other ways. For example, one child demonstrated ability in mathematics at university level when he was in junior high school. His IQ test gave a result of normal or average intelligence. Most thirteen-year-olds of normal to average intelligence cannot do math at university level, so the tester declared the IQ test score to be invalid. However, it did have value for showing different areas of strength and need outside of mathematical abilities.

What does this mean? We should all continue to recognize, celebrate and use every intelligence trait that every individual has. It is great to consider everyone to be "smart" in some ways, even if not in all. (Who of us is?) Remember that the standardized IQ score is not a measurement of the person's overall capacity, or potential to learn or of their willingness to do so. This fact reinforces the need to do assessments in multiple environments, and under a variety of social conditions, to have a better understanding of a person's true abilities.

Speech, Language and Communication Assessments

What is the difference between speech, language, and communication? There are many definitions, but here is a basic description of each:

- Speech is the ability to make sounds with your mouth in a way that causes other people to understand the message you are trying to send. Speech includes articulation (how sounds are pronounced), rate (how fast or slow you talk), tone of voice, volume and rhythm.

- Language is the ability to use symbols (spoken or written words, sign language, pictures, etc.) to send messages and to understand the messages that other people send to you (using spoken or written words, signs, pictures, symbols, etc.).

- Communication is the process of selecting and forming a message and sending it to someone (the receiver). Communication includes skills like watching for understanding or a response from the communicative partner, reacting to their reaction, correcting any problems in understanding each other and knowing when and how to change conversational topics.

Purpose

Speech, language and communication assessments are designed to look at all the skills needed to communicate effectively with same aged peers and/or adults. This is probably one of the most important areas of assessment due to the many effects of ASD on speech, language and communication.

It is important to know that, ironically, some of the effects of ASD can be so well compensated for by higher-functioning people that they appear to be communicating typically at first glance, or in a one-to-one or highly structured setting. This type of "masking," while not intentional, can be misleading. Standardized testing may be of limited value in identifying the communication deficits in a person with ASD. Since comprehensive assessment is essential, it may be necessary to use a variety of assessments in more situations than usual in order to find all the subtle, but important ways that the features of ASD affect the person.

Speech/language/communication assessments measure the ability to:

- Speak and use the sounds of speech in combination.

- Use language symbols (pictures, word cards, etc.) for the purpose of communication.

- Understand the meaning of language symbols presented to him.

- Formulate phrases and sentences.

- Organize thoughts into language or speech.

- Read and write.

- Use low or high technology devices to communicate (low tech might be pictures, high tech might be an electronic voice device).

- Understand what is written.

- Understand and respond to spoken language.

- Use and understand gestures, facial expression and body language (non-verbal communication).

- Communicate socially, in pairs, small groups and large groups.

- Appropriately use the space in the communication situation (not too close or far away, facing the person you are talking to, etc.).

Methods of Assessment

Should include assessment of:

- Articulation: how speech is made.

- Phonology: how speech sounds.

- Semantics: understanding words and the meaning of language.

- Syntax: sentence construction, grammar and word order.

- Pragmatics: communication and conversation skills.

In speech, language and communication assessment, the quality of the response or skill may be measured, as well as ability to:

- Comprehend words, signs or symbols.

- Use words signs or symbols singly, in phrases or in sentences.

- Take part in a conversation and keep it going.

- Make himself understood in more than one way.

- Perceive and respond to non-verbal cues, such as, gestures, facial expression and proximity.

- Re-tell a story in her own words.

- Assemble words into a sentence.

- Sequence and interpret the story behind pictures or drawings.

- Identify facial expressions and their possible underlying emotional content in photos, videotapes or people.

- Listen to a story to predict outcomes, interpret feelings or intentions of the characters.

- Recognize words and their meaning (vocabulary).

- Understand word relationships, like antonyms and synonyms.

- Understand the meaning of words, phrases and sentences that do not literally make sense, (idioms), such as, saying that something is "cool," but not referring to its temperature, or saying that it is "raining cats and dogs," but knowing that there are no cats or dogs coming down.

- Follow rules of conversation with adults, peers and in a group setting.

- Remember what someone else said while planning an answer.

In addition, the person doing the assessment with a person with limited speech will want to:

- Identify the communicative functions (reasons to communicate such as requesting, protesting, negating, informing, asking, etc.) for which the individual has an effective way to communicate.

- Identify the communicative functions for which the individual has no apparent way to communicate or communicates in an appropriate way.

** Be sure to look in the Appendix at the Communicative Functions Grid. The Grid is the work of Anne Donnellan, Ph.D., from the University of Wisconsin, Madison. Suggestions for the use of the Grid are given in the appendix.

Tools

Here are some assessment tools that may be used based on age and the level of speech and language a person has:

- Assessing Semantic Skills Through Everyday Themes (ASSET).

- Clinical Evaluation of Language Fundamentals-Preschool (CELF-P).

- Clinical Evaluation of Language Fundamentals (CELF-3).

- Kaufman Speech Praxis Test (KSPT).

- The Nonspeech Test for Receptive/Expressive Language.

- Sequenced Inventory of Communication Development (Revised) (SICD-R).

- The Test of Language Development, Primary (TOLD-P:2).

- Test of Language Development-Intermediate: (TOLD I:2).

- Test of Pragmatic Language (TOPL).

- Test of Problem Solving (TOPS).

Apart from standardized tests, play-based assessment may be used. Observation of the individual in small and large groups, with familiar and unfamiliar people, and in structured and unstructured settings, will each yield important information about how the individual speaks and/or sends and receives messages to communicate.

Taking a language sample is another way to assess language and communication. The speech and language pathologist may listen and take notes on the conversations and interactions for a short period of time in a variety of natural settings. This helps to round out the picture of how well language can be used when needed in real life situations as compared with a private, quiet test environment. The team may decide if anyone beside the speech and languge pathologist should take language samples, such as, parents, teachers or instructional assistants. Language samples are useful in identifying the problem language areas in situations that are often difficult for the person being tested. The language sample may also show the language patterns the person uses and whether they are working well or not.

An interview with the person being assessed is useful as is the "double-interview" technique. In double-interview, the person doing the assessment first does an interview, and then invites the person being assessed to "conduct" an interview of her own. Interviews with parents and teachers will shed light on problem areas and circumstances when difficulty with communication arises. Checklists can also be used to identify areas of need and levels of skill.

Part of any communication assessment should include an individualized analysis of the possible communicative message underlying any problematic, stigmatizing or dangerous behavior that the individual displays.

Skills

Articulation and Phonology

This includes the ability to:

- Make sounds.

- Make others understand you by making certain sounds.

- Speak.

- Speak so that anyone can understand what is said.

- Create sounds or words.

- Imitate sounds or words.

- Show interest in sounds.

In addition, the quality of the following may be assessed:

- Prosody (or rhythm) of speech.

- Melody (if the voice sounds flat, natural or sing-song).

- Volume: appropriate loudness of speaking, whispering and laughing.

- Stress: monotone or "robotic."

- Pitch: very high or low.

- Expression.

- Pronoun use.

- Use of word order in a sentence.

- Use of echolalia (immediate or delayed repeating of words or phrases said by another).

- Occurrence of agnosia (word deafness).

- Impairment of word reception (understanding words).

Semantics: Making Sense of Communication

This includes understanding and interpreting the communication cues and behaviors of others and using words and non-verbal cues to be understood. Measurement of receptive and expressive language includes the ability to:

- Use, recognize and respond to facial expressions.

- Use, recognize and respond to body language.

- Understand and appropriately use posture in communication situations.

- Understand and use gaze to communicate.

- Understand and use space between people during communication.

- Understand and use gestures.

- Tell appropriate gestures from inappropriate gestures.

- Recognize the feelings of others.

- Show or explain feelings in a way that others can understand.

- Identify the intentions of others.

- Make own intentions known to others, verbally, using print or pictures, or using sign language or objects to communicate.

- Identify the motivations of others.

- Identify and tell others about own motivation.

- Recognize deception.

- Infer what another person means.

- Understand humor.

- Use humor appropriately.

- Understand and use figures of speech, expressions and idioms.

- Use and understand metaphors.

- Use and understand sarcasm.

- Use and recognize social conventions and habits for use in different social circles, such as the Interact with peers or adults.

- Use and recognize irony.

Pragmatics: What to Say, How to Say It, and Getting Along with Others

This includes interacting with others, including developing and maintaining relationships, being successful with peers and playing. Assessment examines the use of language to:

- Get the attention of another.

- Respond when another initiates.

- Relate to others.

- Approach or initiate contact with others.

- Share ideas and interests.

- Make appropriate comments.

- Make appropriate choices.

- Engage and form friendships with others.

- Respond to feedback from others.

- Make a request.

Conversation Skills

This includes the ability to:

- Respond in any way to his name being said.

- Turn towards someone who said his name.

- Use an object to raise a topic.

- Answer when spoken to.

- Engage the listener before speaking.

- Use eye contact.

- Look toward the person speaking (gaze).

- Turn the body toward (orient to) the speaker.

- Stand at a correct distance to others.

- Begin a conversation.

- Keep a conversation going.

- Take turns in a conversation.

- Avoid interrupting.

- Listen to others.

- Choose appropriate topics.

- Move from one topic to another based on cues from communicative partner.

- Notice cues in conversation, such as, whether the listener is bored.

- Move off a favorite subject of conversation.

- End the conversation.

- Ask for clarification.

- Check with the speaker to be sure that he understands what has been said.

- Use "repair strategies" when the conversation breaks down or when there is misunderstanding.

- Reflect: understand and/or restate the other person's point of view.

- Ask appropriate questions.

- Answer questions.

- Limit using pedantic or memorized speech.

- Avoid echolalia.

- Use appropriate voice inflection.

- Use appropriate volume.

- Express ideas coherently.

- Keep conversation relevant.

- Talk on the telephone.

Interacting with Others

This includes the ability to respond to the communication of others and express ideas. Assessment will measure the use of language and the ability to:

- Know what to say and do to start an interaction with another.

- Know what to say and do to join in a conversation.

- Know what to say and do to join in a game.

- Know how to join in a group activity.

- Know how to continue working within a group.

- Ask for help.

- Inform someone else of the intention to do something.

- Let others know where he is going.

- Follow instructions.

- Give instructions.

- Ask for a favor.

- Ask permission.

- Use words or other symbols to describe something that happened.

- Use words or other symbols to describe feelings.

- Recognize internal states.

- Express emotion appropriately.

- Communicate wants.

- Control impulsiveness.

- Use correct posture to convey underlying meaning.

Reacting to Others

This involves knowing what to say and do particularly dealing with intense feelings and quick responses. Assessment can measure the use language to:

- Be aware of others' reactions to her.

- React to the people and events around her.

- Move away from something or someone disliked.

- Move towards someone who can help or protect.

- Recognize a dangerous situation or environment.

- React in a self-protecting way to the presence of something or someone dangerous.

- Know when to let authorities know that a dangerous person or event is present.

- Give compliments.

- Express appreciation.

- Express affection.

- Acknowledge authority.

- Give negative feedback appropriately.

- "Edit" thoughts and decide not to say something that would be hurtful.

- Deal with the justified complaints of others.

- Know how to apologize.

- Deal with criticism.

- Deal with anger.

- Deal with the anger of others.

- Deal with annoying behavior of others.

- Deal with teasing.

- Deal with embarrassment.

- Deal with failure/imperfection.

- Deal with frustration.

- Deal with being left out.

- Deal with boredom.

- Resist giving in to peer pressure.

- Stand up for himself.

- Defend others.

- Avoid trouble.

- Negotiate.

- Take the perspective of another.

- Predict what another might do next.

Results of the Speech and Language Assessment

These will be presented, in the form of a report that may include some standardized scores, some analysis and explanation. Sometimes a score is given called **Receptive Language Age** (the developmental level of understanding of what is said, shown in pictures or print or signed in sign language in some cases) and **Expressive Language Age** (the developmental level of being able to convey ideas using language to others). These scores compare the child's level of ability to typically developing children. The speech/language assessment can describe the individual's overall level of success in communicating in everyday life. It must identify situations in which the individual is **not** successful.

Sometimes speech/language specialists or other assessment professionals assume that children or adults with characteristics of ASD are "choosing" not to communicate effectively. The report of the assessment might sound like the child or adult could do better if they wanted to, or if they tried harder, or if the parent provided more consequences.

Professionals may react this way because they observe the variability of performance of people with characteristics of ASD. They "know" the individual has the skill, because they have seen it with their own eyes at another time or in another place! It is essential for speech/language staff and others to find the true causes of variability and not assume that it is the result of the conscious will of the individual with characteristics of ASD.

Adults with ASD tell us that there are many reasons why they cannot demonstrate communication skills at certain times. Lighting, sounds, changes in routine, confusion, fear, proximity of others, stress, level of demands, etc., all can effect the person's ability to use the communication skills they have demonstrated elsewhere or in the past. This does not imply that the individuals with characteristics of ASD do not have "will" which they can use. They do! As professionals, it is more helpful to look beyond "will" to root causes.

Social Skills

Most people would have a hard time naming ten social skills. Social skills may be taken for granted by most people, since they are acquired naturally through relating to others. Social skills include the capacity to:

- Interact with others.

- Develop and maintain relationships and friendships.

- Be successful with people your own age.

- Be successful with people older or younger than you are.

- Learn and apply social conventions appropriate to the local culture.

- Understand "social hierarchy" and where you fit in.

- Use language and non-verbal social cues with individuals and groups.

- Change, be flexible or "self-correct" in response to feedback from others.

- Use self-control and appropriate behaviors.

- Develop play, leisure activity and relaxation skills.

- Participate in structured and unstructured activities.

- Learn to "read" who wants your attention and who does not, and respond appropriately.

Purpose

Social skills assessments are designed to look at the skills needed to interact effectively with same-aged peers and/or adults. This is probably one of the most important areas of assessment due to the deficit in socialization that is a part of ASD by definition. Social skills assessments can overlap with speech, language and communication assessment. Without some kind of language or communication, there can be no social interaction! It may be useful to refer to the sections on Speech, Language and Communication that are also relevant to social skills assessment.

Method

One-to-one evaluations between the professional tester and the child or adult being assessed are useful to see if the child or adult understands social conventions, manners and the language of social interaction. Evaluations planned with and without background noise, the close proximity of known or unknown other people and interruption will help to show how the person functions more realistically.

Objective observation and analysis of social skills in natural settings in one-to-one and group interactions with peers, one-to-one and group interactions with familiar adults, and one-to-one and group interactions with others (strangers, authority figures, etc.) will give a different picture than a clinical evaluation. Skills demonstrated (or not demonstrated) in a group setting controlled by members of the group are particularly important to assess.

Social skills cannot be evaluated in isolation. Assessment needs to determine whether skills that are understood or can be demonstrated in the clinic or in a one-to-one setting can be used in natural social situations, without additional support or accommodations and particularly with peer. Evaluation and observation must take place in small and large group settings and in multiple environments. Those doing the assessment will want to monitor participation in group activites, observe and take notes and even take some language samples. Places to assess include small and large social functions, such as, group work in the classroom, assemblies or sporting events, gym, outdoor play, lunch or meal time, large group work areas, the family home and in community settings, such as, a restaurant and the local shopping mall.

Observations in multiple environments will complete the picture of social ability. Highly structured environments (such as a classroom, auditorium, a formal meeting, or church) will give an idea of how the individual communicates and functions. Observations in unstructured environments such as a playground, the gym, the break room at work or the food court at the mall may yield significant and different information.

Tools

The testing instruments used to diagnose ASD will usually contain social assessment since the social deficit is a core symptom of autism spectrum disorders. You may wish to ask the diagnostician to share specific results of any testing related to social skills, social skills scales or observation that can help to pinpoint what the child or adult knows and what he or she needs to learn.

The following tools used by Speech and Language pathologists may also describe and measure understanding and use of social skills:

- Test of Language Competence, (TLC).

- Test of Pragmatic Language, (TPL).

- Test of Problem Solving-R elementary. (TPS-R).

- Test of Problem Solving-Adolescent (TOPS)

Here are some assessments specifically related to evaluation of social skills:

- Walker-McConnell Social Skills Rating System (SSRS)

- Walker-McConnell Scale of Social Competence and School Adjustment

- School Social Behavior Rating Scales, 2nd Edition (SSBS-2)

- Home and Community Social Behavior Scales (HCSBS)

- School Social Skills Rating (S-3)

An additional resource for assessing the social and play skills of children ages 3-12 is material found in the book Peer Play and the Autism Spectrum by Dr. Pamela Wolfberg. Specifically tailored to the needs of young children with ASD, Wolfberg's research-based program includes methods and tools to identify and understand important developmental features of play and childhood socialization.

Results

The evaluator may provide a printed report with standardized scores, and a description of observed interactions. Descriptions of the reactions of others to the individual being assessed should be included. The evaluator should be able to list specific social skills deficits and strengths without judgment pertaining to the cause of these observable actions.

Skills

Issues discussed above in the section on social use of language, particularly semantics and pragmatics, and particularly with peers is part of the social skills assessment.

Having Relationships with Others

Assessment will determine the level at which the individual is able to:

- Acknowledge the presence of others in an observable way.

- Respond in an observable way when others initiate.

- Initiate with others in a non-threatening way.

- Initiate with others in a way that others enjoy or accept.

- Follow the lead of others.

- Keep "pace" with the other person in an interaction.

- Monitor if the other person is keeping pace with him.

- React differently to known and unknown persons.

- Show things to others (such as a toy or other object) to share pleasure.

- Have safe and effective ways to get and hold the attention of others.

- Say and do nice things for others.

- Share and take turns with games, toys, food or other items.

- Allow others to interfere or interrupt activities without overreacting.

- Seek the company of particular children or adults.

- Be physically affectionate appropriately with others.

- Have manners, and use words like "please," "thank you" and "you're welcome."

- Use proper table etiquette.

- Not talk with the mouth full.

- Be culturally appropriate, such as, knowing to say "excuse me" if he burps at table.

- Be friendly and welcoming to others.

- Have empathy.

- Know what makes a good friend and how to be one.

- Understand the expectations and point of view of others.

- Understand different social settings and contexts.

- Seek out and enjoy the company of others.

- Understand and be aware of peer pressure.

Self-Organization

Being organized is a social skill for the home, classroom and work environment. Assessment will determine the level of ability to:

- Keep objects orderly.

- Find something in the place she is at.

- Follow directions to go out of the room to find something.

- Know where items are kept.

- Scan the inside of a closet or cabinet to find something.

- Know which items are needed for which activities.

- Have needed items ready for an activity.

- Create routines or rituals to self-organize.

- Respond to and follow the routines created by others.

- Respond to picture or print schedules to self-organize.

- Use picture or print lists to self-organize.

- Put things away where they belong.

- Begin, do and end a task in an organized way.

- Understand time.

- Prioritize.

- Set goals.

- Make and/or use schedules, lists and calendars.

- Keep appointments.

- Understand what a deadline is and keep it.

- Delay gratification, that is wait for a reward, or work towards a goal.

- Confirm or verify details of time and place of an event.

- Keep promises.

- Remember special occasions.

- Follow through and finish projects.

- Follow routines without being too rigid.

- Determine the use of free time.

Personal Skills

This includes the ability to:

- Function independently in a variety of settings.

- Function interdependently with specific supports in place.

- Meet his needs for daily necessities, such as, toileting, getting a drink, making a snack, etc.

- Maintain self-control when experiencing a variety of emotional states.

- Move self to a safe place when experiencing emotional overload.

- Keep personally safe (avoid accidents, not be a victim).

- Cross the street safely.

- Handle tools and implements safely.

- Keep possessions clean and put them away when not in use.

- Judge safety issues at home, at school or work and in the community.

- Keep personal privacy as appropriate to age and situation.

- Maintain personal hygiene (independence in this area can be a priority focus).

- Respect the privacy of others.

- Ask before touching others or their possessions.

- Recognize own strengths and weaknesses.

- Weigh the "pros" and "cons" to help make decisions.

- Concentrate.

- Let others know where he is going.

- Accept a "yes" and a "no" answer differently.

- Respond to a command, such as, "stop" or "move."

- Accept criticism.

- Recognize signs of internal stress.

- Consider options in handling stress.

- Calm himself.

- Learn coping skills.

- Use coping skills when under stress.

- "Talk through" problems and consider options for resolution.

Functional Behavioral Analysis

A variety of problems related to behavior can arise due to the characteristics of ASD. A functional behavior analysis is an assessment that looks at the functioning of the individual in many settings along with the circumstances when problems do and do not occur.

Purpose

A functional behavioral analysis is intended to discover and explain the underlying causes for problematic behavior. This information forms the basis of a plan to modify or change behavior. Some problematic behaviors can be described as:

- Aggression or hurting others.

- Self-injurious behavior.

- Property destruction.

- Running away.

- Wandering away.

- Inappropriate undressing.

- Hyperactivity.

- Emotional outbursts ("tantrums").

- Difficulty adapting to social changes.

- Difficulty adapting to changes in the physical environment.

- Being resistive (uncooperative).

- Fecal smearing.

- Touching others inappropriately.

- Setting fires.

- Non-compliance.

- Eating inedibles (things that are not food).

Methods

Depending on background of the behaviorist and the training she has received, various methods may be preferred. Behaviorists will often use several of the following:

- Informal observation of everyday tasks or play in both natural and contrived situations.

- Structured or standardized observation.

- Interviews with parents, staff and others.

- Data collection and analysis.

Any functional analysis of problematic behavior should begin with a comprehensive physical examination. A person with ASD may not be able to indicate if he is ill or in pain. In many cases, the underlying cause of serious, problematic behaviors has actually been an unrecognized or untreated medical condition.

Whatever methods are used, the essential components of a functional analysis of problematic behavior include:

- A complete description of the target behavior: the behavior to be changed.

- Data collection and analysis.

- The development of a reactive strategy: a planned response that everyone can use when the target behavior occurs to prevent harm to anyone and to end the episode quickly.

- A complete history of the target behavior.

- A complete history of all consequences that have been delivered in response to this target behavior.

- A time line that compares major life events to changes in the target behavior.

- An analysis of the possible effects and side effects of any medication being used.

- An analysis of conditions under which the target behavior is likely to occur and conditions under which it does not occur.

- Assignment of meaning to the target behavior: a "guess" at what message the person is trying to send with the target behavior, also called an analysis of the "communicative function" of the target behavior.

- An intervention strategy that tests that "guess."

- Continued data collection and analysis to gauge the effects of the intervention strategy.

Tools

Some standardized tools such as data collection sheets, graphs and charts can be purchased. They are described in materials specific to the field of behavior analysis.

Skills

The word comprehensive is used with "full functional behavior analysis" because understanding behavior involves looking at all areas of a person's functioning. Many behavior problems are caused by a lack of skill or understanding of what should be done. Evaluation in a variety environments of can include defining the level of ability to:

- Communicate: express and receive messages.

- Understand time and sequence.

- Process and recall verbal information.

- Ask for help.

- Protest and refuse without using dangerous behavior.

- Know his own possessions from those of others.

- Regulate emotional output based on presenting situation or stimulation.

- Handle changes in routine.

- Cope with feeling overwhelmed in certain circumstances.

- Be self-aware, physically.

- Recognize own feelings and internal states.

- Tell others about own internal states.

- Be aware of the feelings of others.

- Know how to respond to the emotions shown by others.

- Know what she needs to feel safe and calm.

- Keep self-control.

- Control aggressive behaviors.

- Control temper.

- Cope with daily situations.

- Deal with a variety of stresses in daily life.

- Use coping strategies.

- Adapt to novel situations.

- Have skills to "repair" situations, especially when stressed.

- Process information when stressed.

- Identify options and choices.

- Choose appropriate options.

- Follow rules in a way that is not too strict or too lax.

- Be tolerant of others or flexible.

- Deal with winning and losing.

- Use time well.

- Wait.

- Cooperate.

- Move away appropriately from a disliked stimuli.

- Any other skills related to controlling self and others.

A functional behavioral analysis must include an analysis of how the people in the environment respond to the communicative signals used by the individual. The premise is that we must accept some non-standard forms of communication as long as they are not harmful or stigmatizing. We must show the person that their communicative signals are working and have an impact on the environment. If the individual sees or thinks that he has no impact on the environment when using non-harmful strategies, he may be required to escalate to more dramatic and harmful ways of communicating to affect the environment.

For example, if the child or adult indicates he needs a break by standing next to the door of the break room (a clear and non-dangerous signal), does he get a break, or is his signal consistently ignored or refused? If the individual is consistently asking for a break when it is not the time for a break, do staff "tell" the individual that it is not time, or create a visual schedule so that the individual will "know" when it is break time? If communication is ignored, problem behavior may result.

Results

Results of the functional behavior assessment will include a report about the objective observations, interviews, data collection and summaries and analysis of the data. Conclusions may be drawn based on objective facts, and possible theories may be stated if there is uncertainty. The report should not ascribe blame or contain subjective (unproven) assumptions about the willingness of the individual or any (unproven) assumptions about the internal state of the individual. For example, the report should not conclude that an individual is not "trying" or "does not care about others" or "is spoiled and attention-seeking."

A report may identify a variety of possible problems that underlie problematic behavior such as:

- The need to learn a specific skill.

- A high level of anxiety.

- Inability to know how to relax or to use relaxation techniques when needed.

- Dependence on routine and need to have more information about routines changing or being interrupted.

- Lack of ability to predict and anticipate the actions of others.

- Lack of understanding of time and concepts such as "not yet," "in a little while" or "next week."

- Lack of ability to predict events outside of the usual routine.

- Memory problems.

- Need for a change to be made in the physical environment or schedule.

- Need for additional information to help the person understand what is going on around her, perhaps provided visually as well as spoken.

- The need for additional, appropriate sensory input.

- The need for sameness, being upset by changes in routine.

- Coping by using repetitive motor responses (like flapping hands or arms).

- Finding certain circumstances overwhelming.

- Sensory sensitivities or issues.

- Depression (that could explain apparent "lack of motivation").

- "Executive function" problems, such as, problems in planning or carrying out plans.

- Inability to communicate effectively in either or both sending and receiving information.

- Inability to communicate effectively under certain circumstances.

- Insufficient response from the people in the environment to the communication of the individual.

- Need for staff and family training.

- Insufficient control and influence the individual has in the environment.

- A symptom of a physical, neurological or medical disorder.

- Other underlying causes for the problematic behavior.

The report will also contain elements of a plan and describe:

- The new behavior the individual will be taught and rewarded for using instead of the target (problematic) behavior.

- Teaching methods and steps to use to teach the alternative behavior.

- A description of how parents and staff are to respond should the problematic behavior occur (reactive strategy).

- A description of and practice in any techniques that will be used that involve physical contact with the individual.

- Plans to have the individual seen by any needed professionals such as neurologist or nurse.

- A summary of the data collected and the analysis of that data.

- New data collection information if needed.

- Plans to train all staff/family involved.

- Plans for frequent team meetings until the behavior is eliminated.

Occupational Therapy and Sensory Integration Assessment

Occupational tasks can be described as the "jobs" of daily living. This may include activities and skills involved in play, home, school, work or community activities. Sensory integration refers to how an individual tolerates and responds to sensory input from the daily environment. Specialists in this field are often trained in both areas.

Purpose

The purpose of assessment is to determine the individual's ability to physically function in daily living at home, school, work or the community. Occupational and sensory integration assessments identify areas of need that can be improved through therapeutic activities for individuals or small groups. Assessment includes an evaluation of:

- Adaptive and self-care skills.

- Independence and self-reliance.

- Self-organization skills.

- Control and tone of body and muscles.

- Coordination of body parts and movements.

- Motor planning.

- Fine motor skills.

- Gross motor skills.

- Response to the physical environment.

- Self-regulation.

- How the senses perceive and respond to stimuli.

- How the brain organizes and processes sensory input.

Method

The occupational therapy/sensory integration assessment may include:

- Observations.

- Interviews with caregiver/teacher/job coach, etc.

- Standardized testing.

- Rating scales.

- Physical tasks and exercises.

- Clinical observations.

- Completion of personal history surveys by caregiver and/or teacher; possible follow-up interview with caregiver.

Tools

- CDER Evaluation Element.

- Sensory Profile Questionnaire, completed by caregiver for children ages 5 to 10.

- Sensory Integration Praxis Test (SIPT Third Edition) for children ages 4 to 8 years, 11 months.

- Test of Visual-Motor Skills-Revised (TVMS-R) for children age 3 to 13 years, 11 months.

- Test of Visual-Perceptual Skills-Revised (TVPS-R) ages 4 to 12 years, 11 months.

- Peabody Developmental Motor Scales-2 for children from birth to age 6.

- Bruininks-Oseretsky Test of Motor Proficiency for children ages 4 1/2 to 14 1/2.

- Developmental Test of Visual Perception (DTVP-2) for children ages 4 to 10.

- School Function Assessment (SFA) for children grades kindergarten through grade 6.

Skills

Activities of daily living:

- Self-care skills; The ability to:

    — Use the toilet.

    — Brush hair.

    — Keep personal hygiene, including self-care during menses.

    — Dress herself.

    — Feed herself and eat.

- Self-organization; Ability to:

    — Take care of belongings.

    — Know and say own name, address and phone number.

    — Organize and use materials for school or work.

    — Use planners, schedules, checklists, calendars, timers, watches, clocks, etc.

    — Work independently in a classroom or work setting.

— Participate in small group activities.

— Respond to teacher, parent or employer requests.

— Follow directions.

— Use personal learning strengths to support learning needs.

• Vocational/pre-vocational/community (as age appropriate); Ability to:

— Do household tasks and chores.

— Prepare or cook food.

— Make the bed.

— Wash dishes.

— Handle money.

— Make change.

— Anticipate costs.

— Budget.

— Handle a checkbook and bank account.

— Use a credit card.

— Spend money responsibly.

— Make purchases.

— Order food in a restaurant.

— Use public transportation.

— Open containers.

— Open packages.

• Fine motor: The ability to

— Use hands.

— Use arms.

— Use tools.

— Use scissors.

— Use proper grasp holding a pencil, pen, chalk, paintbrush, art supplies, etc.

— Color, cut and paste.

— Use materials correctly.

— Manipulate objects.

— Copy figures, such as, a circle, square and triangle.

— Draw a simple figure.

— Trace.

— Print.

— Write in cursive form (script).

— Use a keyboard /use computer.

— Do buttons, snaps, hooks and other fasteners.

— Tie shoes.

— Assemble and disassemble items.

• Gross motor: Ability to:

— "Cross the midline," moving arms or legs past the center front of the body.

— Climb.

— Crawl.

— Creep.

— Walk.

— Pedal.

— Hop.

— Skip.

— Run.

— Gallop.

— Roll, throw and catch a ball.

— Use playground equipment.

— Carry items while walking.

— Hold items while stooping or bending down.

— Use upper body strength.

— Lift.

— Carry something with substantial weight using only one hand/arm/side and still being able to walk, talk, etc.

• Having strength and endurance to do daily activities:

— Energy level.

— Muscle tone.

— Balance.

— Strength (upper extremity, hand).

• Self-regulation:

— Awareness of arousal and alertness levels.

— Coping strategies and techniques for dealing with overload and stress.

— Use of calming and relaxation techniques.

Sensory Issues: Determining Sensitivities and Reactions to Sensory Input

- Hearing: auditory sensitivities, auditory defensiveness, and auditory distractions.

    — Distracted or fascinated by sounds.

    — Vocalizes or makes sounds too often, almost continuously or from time to time in an unusual way.

    — Finds some sounds painful or bothersome.

    — Problems identifying the source of a sound when the source is not in view.

    — Avoids or protects against some sounds.

    — Difficulties screening out background noise.

    — Difficulties attending to one voice when other people are speaking within ear-shot.

- Vision:

    — Sensitive to light.

    — Seeks unusual visual input.

    — Watches bright objects.

    — Has a hard time distinguishing a figure or object from its background.

    — Difficulty with depth perception.

    — Difficulties in low lighting or bright light.

    — Sensitivity to some types of lighting, such as, fluorescent tubing.

- Smell:

    — Upset by some smells.

— Very sensitive to smells.

— Avoids or protects against some smells.

— Seeks out certain smells.

— Seeks out smells that others find distasteful or awful.

• Touch:

— Resists being touched unless initiated by him.

— Dislikes touching certain things.

— Some textures and clothing are bothersome.

— Avoids or protects against some textures or situations involving touch.

— Is oversensitive to pain or pressure.

— Is under-sensitive to pain or pressure.

— Seeks sensory input by holding or carrying certain objects.

• Taste:

— Some foods seem very hot or cold.

— Dislikes certain foods because of texture.

— Eats non-foods (sometimes called pica).

— Avoids or protects against some foods.

— Touches mouth, lips, teeth or gums frequently.

— Touches or plays with saliva.

• Responses to movement:

— Does not liking having his feet off the ground.

— Engages in excessive movement such as spinning, jumping and climbing.

— Gets carsick.

— Prefers sedentary activities

— Seeks crashing, bumping or rough movements.

— Seeks pressure, likes tight wrapping or bundling.

— Seeks a particular sensory input most often such as swinging or spinning.

Results

A written report is prepared detailing the methods, tools and circumstances of testing. Standardized scores may be used as well as observational notes and impressions. Recommendations should include suggestions for types and frequencies of exercises, treatments or therapies to address each deficit identified in the assessment process. A meeting is held to explain the results and to help all team members understand the sensory or occupational source of any issues previously viewed as "behavior problems." Team members will most often need support in the report and in person to prioritize interventions, and to learn, to think and describe observable behavior in terms of the underlying sensory or motor causes.

The assessments may reveal:

• Unusual movements or tics.

• Fine or gross motor issues.

• Planning and task issues, such as, motor planning deficits.

• Difficulties organizing materials.

• Strength and endurance issues.

• Difficulties in performing everyday tasks.

• Difficulties with self-care and self-help skills.

• Weakness in some muscle groups.

- Sensory processing issues.

- A heightened need or desire for some forms of sensory input.

- Sensory defensiveness or avoidance of some stimuli.

Adaptive Physical Education

The neurological differences inherent in ASD can affect physical functioning and coordination. This may negatively affect the individual's ability or skill level in many typical activities. Occupational and physical therapists will examine many areas of physical functioning and movement. An adaptive physical education, or APE, evaluation may be done for school age children. (Reminder: the word "motor" refers to physical movement of the body.)

All students who participate in Physical Education class receive a grade for performance. They receive a grade for effort that includes citizenship or sportsmanship. The social aspect of participation in physical education activities is an important component for students with the features of ASD. In the past, adaptive PE was mainly concerned with accommodating the needs of individuals with physical disabilities. Identifying social issues, like sportsmanship and communication, may not be automatically connected with an APE assessment, but should be considered for students with ASD.

This may mean that the APE assessor will work with the occupational therapist, or speech and language pathologist or other staff. Together they can look at the social and communication issues involved in successful participation in Physical Education. If a school district is not accustomed to looking at both the physical and social aspects of participating in PE, parents can request that this be done. Or, the speech and language evaluation can include observation in Physical Education and suggestions for improving social skills in this setting.

Purpose

- To determine a child's ability to participate in physical education activities.

- To determine if modifications are necessary to enable the child to participate in P.E.

- To identify areas of need that can be improved through physical activities implemented individually or in small groups.

- To determine how the child participates in group games, including sportsmanship, taking cues and signals from others, understanding and functioning in teams, taking turns, waiting and cheering for others.

Method

Physical activities are structured to measure areas of skill such as Perceptual Motor Functions, Motor Development and Fitness. Surveys and checklists may also be used to report or record physical activity. Observation of performance with peers in natural settings, and surveys with parents and teachers can be included to identify the social aspects of participation.

Tools

- APEAS: Adaptive Physical Education Assessment Scales.

Skills

- Physical skills:

  — Balance.

  — Imitation of body postures.

  — Hopping and jumping.

  — Catching, throwing and kicking.

  — "Cross the midline," moving arms or legs past the center front of the body.

  — Arm strength.

  — Coordination.

— Endurance.

— Strength.

— Reflexes.

— Eye-hand coordination.

• Social skills:

— Turn taking.

— Sharing.

— Waiting.

— Following rules.

— Coping when others do not follow rules.

— Being a good sport.

— Learning to join in.

— Coping with being left out.

Results

A chart format may be used listing the physical activities attempted, the score and the percentile rank of the student. This compares the student's performance and level of skill with that of same-aged peers. A report should explain the findings, point out areas of strength and areas of need. Suggestions may be offered about therapeutic activities to develop the motor skills, physical skills and social skills needed to participate in physical education activities. Adaptations and modifications needed to help the child participate in P.E. are detailed. Results from surveys and observations can describe the social aspects of participation in P.E. Any areas of difficulty will be noted and goals selected to address them.

Audiology

It is important to be sure that individuals hear well and that nothing is interfering with hearing all the time or part of the time. It is important to be sure that individuals do not have ear conditions that cause them constant or intermittent pain. Individuals with ASD seem to have more middle-ear infections and ear problems than the general population. Many took antibiotics and/or had "tubes" put in their ears as young children to help to alleviate the problems. Into childhood, adolescence or adulthood, people with ASD can continue to have middle-ear issues that interfere with their ability to hear consistently from day to day. It is important for people with a history of middle ear problems to be assessed by a licensed audiologist to determine if middle ear trouble is present or if the chronic middle-ear problems have resulted in permanent damage or hearing loss.

Hearing screenings performed at schools or agencies are not the same as comprehensive audiological testing. Hearing screenings are not as precise or controlled as a full evaluation. Screenings are intended to indicate if a hearing problem could be present, but are not specific about the nature of the problem. A screening may not detect mild (but significant) hearing problems, problems in only one ear or inconsistent hearing ability. Every person who fails a hearing screening should be referred for complete audiological testing.

Purpose

Audiology is the science that measures the ability to hear and discriminate sounds and words. Testing is done to rule out or identify any hearing problems that affect the person with ASD. This includes measuring the ability to:

- Distinguish similar sounds, such as, big and pig.

- Hear and discriminate in the presence of background noise.

- Repeat the correct sequence of heard or spoken sounds (elephant or "ephelant").

- Understand words and phrases that are heard.

• Hear equally well with both ears.

• Localize sounds: know from what direction a sound is coming.

Method

Audiometric tests are done in a soundproof booth by a licensed audiologist. The audiologist can see the individual being tested through a window at her control panel. For more precise testing, the individual wears a headset (earphones) and listens to tones and responds when he hears each tone. Audiologists test both ears together and test each ear separately. Individuals may be asked to point to the ear in which they heard the tones. While wearing the headset, the audiologist may say words and phrases and ask the individual to repeat what was heard.

The audiologist will "condition" the individual for testing. This means the audiologist will teach the individual how to respond. If the individual is unable to give consistent responses, or cannot yet tolerate a headset, the audiologist will put sounds of various levels and types into the sound-proof booth, and watch the reaction of the individual to try to determine if the sounds were heard or if the words spoken were understood. This is called **"sound field testing"** and can determine the general hearing level of the individual and sensitivity to sound. It cannot determine how each ear functions separately.

Tests for the function of the middle ear are part of comprehensive audiological testing. A test can be given to show the flexibility of the eardrum and whether or not it is likely that the middle ear space is clear or occluded (for example, blocked by fluid). The test is done by putting a small instrument in the ear canal and sending a puff of air (it doesn't hurt) against the eardrum and recording the action of the eardrum on a graph called a **tympanogram**.

"Bone conduction" testing can be done if the person can tolerate wearing a small headset and responds upon request. This is another way to determine if something is wrong in the middle ear.

Tools

• Audiometric Tests: measuring hearing, middle ear function.

- Transient Evoked Otoacoustic Emissions (TEOAE).

- Test of Auditory Perceptual Skills (TAPS).

- The Listening Test.

- Children's Auditory Performance Scale (CHAPS).

Skills

- Reacts to sound.

- Can identify the direction from which sound is coming.

- Turns head or eyes to sound.

- Responds to voices.

- Recognizes words that sound different (cat and door).

- Recognizes words that sound the same (cat and hat).

- Understands the meaning of what is heard.

Results

Results are usually provided in the form of a graph called an audiogram that displays how the person responded during testing. Sometimes a printed report will be attached. The report can describe both what the individual heard and what he understood. Audiologists discuss their findings in detail with parents or professionals.

On the audiogram, hearing levels will be described in decibels or units of measurement that tell how loud something is. The person's "**threshold of hearing**" will be described by saying at what level of loudness (how many decibels) the person responded. A first decibel level is used to show how loud it has to be for the person to be aware of a speech sound. A second number indicates how loud it has to be for the person to understand words that are being said. Marks on the audiogram indicate how the individual responded at each frequency (pitch of the sound) from very low-pitched sounds to high-pitched sounds.

If the individual was able to use the headset and respond to pure tones, different marks on the audiogram will indicate the hearing level for each ear. Usually people hear somewhat differently in each ear. The audiologist will mention if there is any need for concern.

If a test of the eardrum flexibility and middle ear space was done, the audiologist will have a tympanogram, a graph that shows the results. If the line on the tympanogram is fairly flat, there may be fluid or infection in the middle ear or a problem with the flexibility of the eardrum. If the line on the tympanogram is very curved (looks like the traditional "Bell" curve), then the audiologist may assume that there is not a problem with fluid or infection in the middle ear.

For individuals tested who have limited ability to respond, the audiologist may have to give general impressions about hearing levels and understanding, such as:

- Did it seem the person used one ear better than another?

- At what level of loudness (decibel level) did the person consistently react?

- Did certain types of sound seem to cause a more noticeable response?

- Were there any sound frequencies that you noticed a negative response to? (Did low pitched or high-pitched sounds seem to bother the person?)

- Did the individual seem to hear male or female voices better?

- How can we "train" or prepare the individual so she will take a better hearing test next time?

Could Not Test

Sometimes the results will be the letters "CNT" on the audiogram. This means "could not test." If it is possible that hearing loss may be a concern for an individual who has limited ways to respond, contact your state licensing board for referrences to audiologists or a professional association of audiologists. Some audiologists specialize in assessing difficult-to-test individuals. These specialists may have methods that staff and family can use to teach the person skills that will help them be more "testable" in the future. One friend of ours helped his son be more testable by practicing wearing a headset to watch his favorite video. For individuals with difficulty responding, staff and families may provide the audiologist with notes and observations about when the individual appears to hear or not hear in daily life situations.

Auditory Processing

Even when hearing is normal and all the parts of the hearing system are functional, some people have a limited ability to process sound. This means that while sound is heard, the person may have difficulty recognizing sounds or telling sounds apart. Other problems involve paying attention to sounds and understanding what is heard. These are **auditory processing problems** and involve how the brain interprets sound. In-depth assessment of auditory processing is usually only done when hearing is found to be normal, but a person does not respond appropriately to sound or seem to understand what is said.

Purpose

An audiologist will conduct Auditory Processing Assessments to determine whether a person has an auditory processing problem. Assessments will look at:

- Auditory discrimination, recognizing sounds and words as same or different.

- Auditory memory, remembering and recalling information that was heard.

- Auditory sequencing, remembering and reproducing sounds in the order they were heard.

- Auditory blending, putting sounds together to form words.

- Listening to and understanding speech in the presence of other sounds.

In cases when testing of the cochlea or auditory nerve is necessary, testing using specialized equipment can be done as described below.

Method

An auditory processing evaluation is typically done using a headset. It can also be done in a sound field, where sound comes through speakers. Testing involves measuring response to a human voice. The testing can be done using the voice of the audiologist or of a parent or recorded voice. Tests can be modified to include prompts that the person usually responds to.

Otoacoustic Emission Testing can be done to measure the sensory functioning of the cochlea of the ear. The person being tested wears a tiny microphone in the ear, that looks like an earplug and holds still for 20 or 30 seconds.

In some cases precise and sophisticated testing is required. Testing called **auditory evoked potential** (AEP), or **auditory brain response** (ABR), is done by a medical professional or audiologist specializing in this area. Electrophysiologic (EEG) equipment is used to directly measure auditory nerve function from the cochlea to the upper brain stem. It is a painless procedure, in which the person wears electrodes and earphones and rests. Sedation is often required because the person being tested must lie perfectly still for about 90 minutes or go to sleep. These tests are designed to determine if the brain is reacting to the sounds and speech the ears are "hearing."

Tools

- Auditory Continuous Performing Test (ACPT).

- Lindamood Auditory Conceptualization Test (LAC).

- SCAN-A: Test for Auditory Processing Disorders in Adolescents and Adults.

- SCAN-C: Test for Auditory Processing Disorders in Children, Revised.

(Note: the four tests above are also used in speech and language or language processing assessments.)

- Brain Stem Evoked Response (BSER).

- Auditory Brainstem Response (ABR).

Results

A report is prepared detailing the procedures used and the results found. Charts and graphs of response levels are interpreted. The report will indicate if signs of a processing disorder are found.

A Note About Hearing and ASD

It can be very difficult to test an individual with ASD. The individual may need some "training" prior to testing to help him learn the steps involved in taking the tests. Many teachers of children who are deaf know how to "condition" or prepare an individual for hearing testing and could be contacted for assistance. Discrete trial lesson plans or other systematic and routine instruction may help the person being tested understand what to do in the testing situation.

We know of individuals with autism who responded as if they were deaf on tests of the brain and later were found to have normal hearing! We know of some people with autism who have used hearing aids for years, only to find out that their hearing had been normal all along and now was deteriorating due to so much amplification.

People with ASD may be more inclined to have ear infections and fluid sometimes building up in the middle ear space. This is not only uncomfortable or painful, but can cause a severe difference in hearing abilities from one day to the next.

Children with hearing loss can have autism. Children with autism can have hearing loss. Due to the difficulties in administering formalized tests, objective observation in multiple environments and objective description of hearing abilities by staff and families is extremely important. It is important to separate what was observed objectively (Amy did not look up when Victor screamed) from any subjective, unproven judgments (because Amy does not care about her peers). Subjective and unproven information will distract the team and may impair the team's ability to get an accurate hearing assessment.

Vision

Vision is tested as part of a full assessment to be sure that the eyes are healthy and the person is seeing properly. The vision assessment can determine if eye problems are affecting the person with ASD.

Purpose

Eye examinations are done to determine:

- Visual acuity, or the ability of the eyes to see and sharpness of sight.

- If both eyes are working.

- If both eyes work in unison.

- If there is any eye disease.

- If the individual needs corrective lenses (glasses) or other aids or devices.

Methods

A board-certified ophthalmologist tests the individual in a darkened room. Sometimes drops are put in the eye. Individuals are asked to describe what they see and respond to questions. The eyes are examined to look for any indications of disease or problems.

There are methods that family or staff can use to help individuals who cannot respond easily or tolerate the eye testing procedures. Some of the strategies described in *Chapter Four, The Assessment Process,* may be useful. In most states, some eye doctors specialize in working with people with disabilities, and have developed special methods to test and assess. Contact a university child developmental clinic in your state for a referral.

Results

The physician will discuss any findings with the individual, staff or family. Recommendations will be made for treatment if needed. Corrective lenses will be prescribed if needed. Information about eye safety and health may be shared.

Visual Processing

Even when sight is normal and eyes are functional, some people have a limited ability to process what they see. This means that while sight is accurate, the person may have difficulty recognizing letters, numbers and words or telling them apart. Other problems involve paying attention to visual stimulus and understanding what is seen. These are **visual processing** or **visual perception problems** and involve how the brain interprets what the eyes see. In-depth assessment of visual processing is usually only done when sight is found to be normal, but a person does not respond appropriately to what is seen or understand what is seen. A related issue is how sight is used to guide movement of the whole body and the hands.

Purpose

A visual processing assessment measures:

- Visual Discrimination, the ability to:

    — Recognize objects or symbols and tell one from another.

    — Distinguish an object from the background.

    — Differentiate between foreground and background.

    — Differentiate between similar-looking numbers, letters, shapes, objects or symbols, like p, d, b and q.

- Visual Closure, the ability to:

    — Recognize objects or symbols when only a part of it is visible.

    — Recognize objects or symbols when a part is missing.

- Visual Memory, the ability to:

    — Recognize familiar objects.

    — Form visual representations of what is seen (visual memory).

    — Make a connection between a visual memory and an object being viewed.

    — Retrieve visual memories.

    — Integrate and synthesize visual stimuli into a recognizable whole.

- See whole/part relationships, the ability to:

    — Recognize a part as a piece of a whole object.

— Recognize that a whole object is made up of separate pieces.

• Visual coordination with movement:

— Visual-motor integration: use of sight to guide movements.

— Large-motor: body movement, coordination and dexterity.

— Fine-motor: hand use, eye-hand coordination.

Method

A professional experienced in visual processing disorders can conduct an evaluation.

Skills

• Explores the environment by looking around.

• Follows moving objects.

• Looks for an object that disappears from sight.

• Responds differently to different objects.

Results

The medical or certified professional will write a report describing what procedures were used and the results of the process. The report will indicate if there is a visual processing problem and may recommend therapies or exercises to address it.

Assistive Technology Assessment

What is Assistive Technology?

Assistive Technology (AT) refers to a broad range of devices, services, strategies and practices that are designed to increase the functional competencies of persons who have disabilities. An assessment answers the question, "Which technologies and strategies can be used to improve function during a specific activity?" Assistive technology can be "low tech" or "high tech" and range in price from a few dollars to thousands of dollars. There are many assistive aids and devices that can benefit people with ASD and allow them to access the curriculum at school and the workplace.

Purpose

To find an appropriate assistive technology solution, parents, teachers and therapists must look at a child or adult and his needs in a new and different way. Most children and adults with disabilities receive services that focus on remediation and/or rehabilitation. In other words, we want to "fix" the individual — make the disability less of a factor in their lives. That way of thinking is called the medical model approach to service delivery.

But, AT does not work to fix the individual. It fixes the environment, the space around the child or adult, the place where he works, learns and does things. "Environment" in this case means any place that the individual happens to be: in his bed, at the lunch counter, in the story circle, on the school bus, on the playground, at work etc. The goal of assistive technology is to let the individual participate and become part of whatever activities happen around him.

Assistive technology for people with ASD might enable the person to communicate and participate more in the activities in his environment. They may help the person be more organized or understand and follow a schedule or plan. They may enable the person to complete her work.   Other examples include voice output devices, slantboards for writing, pencil grips and note-taking devices.

Method

Best practices include consideration of many factors such as assessing where the person will use a device, the user's expectations in those environments, the necessary supports for device use and individual preference in device use. The evaluator should also compare the unique features of a variety of devices to decide which device(s) might meet the individual's needs.

The best procedure any evaluator can use to find out if a device will work is to actually have the user perform the desired activity using the device in their natural environment. The evaluator should carefully document the degree to which the device provides the desired outcomes; it makes for an almost irrefutable justification for the device recommendation. While evaluators can yield some information from a structured evaluation setting, typically the fact that the user has so little time with a device, and in an unnatural environment, makes the data less than optimal.

Using a loaned or rented device over a longer time, like a few weeks, in a natural environment, provides powerful data to support the need for and effectiveness of a particular device. An evaluator who presents "real-life" observations in a recommendation is far more persuasive than one who presents only a theoretical rationale.

Be cautious if evaluators use volumes of standardized testing data in areas such as cognition, visual acuity, auditory acuity, range of motion, fine and gross motor, receptive and expressive language, etc., as the basis for their device recommendation. There is no denying that standardized testing in traditional areas is helpful. However, in technology assessments, it should not form the sole basis for a recommendation.

If a school district is going to pay for a device, "best" is not the standard by which they must measure. IDEA, the federal law that governs special education, only requires schools to provide what is "appropriate." Likewise, in an ADA case, the legal standard is to achieve "effective communication." In vocational rehabilitation, the legal standard is "necessary for employment." For Medicaid to cover the device it must be "medically necessary." Make sure that your evaluator understands the legal standard upon which his device recommendation must be based.

Who Does AT Evaluations or Assessments?

Someone who is recognized by public and private funding agencies as a provider of AT services can provide a formal AT assessment. Currently, there is no licensure available for AT assessment. Evaluation providers are often licensed in related fields such as Physical Therapy, Occupational Therapy, and Speech/Language Pathology. Rehabilitation engineers, while not certified and licensed, have engineering or technology backgrounds. Other persons who provide evaluation information often include AT specialists or practitioners who have identified themselves as having experience and knowledge in AT.

Occupational therapists, physical therapists and speech and language therapists are professionals who have training and expertise in clinically recognized areas. All practicing therapists must pass standardized tests and be certified or licensed in their field. However, there is no special requirement for assistive technology applications, and a therapist may or may not have experience and expertise in assessment and recommendation for AT. You will need to ask if your therapist is qualified in the area of AT.

Rehabilitation engineers are providers who have engineering and/or technology backgrounds and are very familiar with assistive technology devices. You will need to ask about their experience and expertise to determine if they are able to meet your needs for assessment or recommendation. "Rehab" engineers most often provide services in non-medical related areas such as home modification, work-site accommodations and computer adaptations.

Assistive Technology practitioners or specialists are individuals who have identified themselves as having knowledge and experience in assistive technology. Generally speaking, such persons have a clinical background in working with persons with disabilities and have specialized in AT applications. Most provide complete assessments and training with devices. AT Specialists usually charge for their services.

Those doing assessments will need a working knowledge of assistive technology foundations, devices, and applications and be able to complete a formal AT assessment. If the AT will be funded by a school district or agency, a formal assessment is often required to be performed by individuals with particular credentials. You will want to ask about the individual's experience and expertise to determine if the provider is appropriate for your needs and has qualifications that comply with any requirements set by the funding source.

> *(This information is adapted from the Illinois State Board of Education Assistive Technology Resource Manual Website: www.isbe.state.il.us/assistive/general_at_evals and the Illinois Assistive Technology Project Website: www.iltech.org. Used with permission.)*

Tools

Here is a list of tools, resources and contacts for AT assessment:

- SETT is an acronym which stands for the following: S=Student, E=Environment, T=Tasks, T=Tools. The SETT framework can be accessed via the internet at: www2.edc.org/NCIP/workshops/sett3/index.html. This is an online workshop created and facilitated by Joy Zabala. The goal of the framework is to guide teachers, specialists, clinicians and parents to work together collaboratively to select assistive technology for an individual student who has disabilities.

- Assessing Students' Needs for Assistive Technology: A Resource Manual for School District Teams by the Wisconsin Assistive Technology Initiative (WATI). Online at: www.wati.org/. This is the first manual developed by WATI to help school district service providers such as teachers, speech/language pathologists and occupational therapists. The Assessing Students' Needs for Assistive Technology (ASNAT) is a collection of information about assistive technology. It is arranged around the tasks that children need to be able to do such as writing, communicating, reading, studying, etc.

- "Navigating the Process: Educational TECH Points for Parents." This 1997 article is by Gayl Bowser and Penny Reed from *Closing The Gap*. It provides a framework to help parents work with their school district to assess the need for AT and obtain it. On the internet at: www.ldonline.org/ld_indepth/technology/bowser.PM.pdf. (This document is in PDF format and you need Adobe Acrobat Reader software to download or print it.)

- "Assistive Technology Assessment: More Than the Device," by Andrew R. Beigel. This article written in 2000, outlines a helpful process for AT assessment that attempts to keep the student at the center of the process. Available at LD Online: www.ldonline.org/ld_indepth/technology/at_assessment.html

- "Technology Evaluation Guide For Students with Learning Disabilities." This online guide offers several tools to assist with the evaluation process: a form listing areas to be considered and an accompanying list of critical questions for consideration, plus a quick guide to "No Tech/Low Tech/High Tech materials, equipment and technology tools." (This article is in PDF format only and you need Adobe Acrobat Reader software to download and print.) Link: www.ldonline/ld_indepth/technology/evaluation.pdf.

- "A Functional Approach to Assistive Technology." University of Kentucky Assistive Technology Project online at: http://serc.gws.uky.edu/www/ukat/function.html#implications.

- Lifespace Access Profiles: "Assistive Technology Assessment and Planning for Individuals with Severe or Multiple Disabilities," and "Access Profile Upper Extension for Individuals with Physical Disabilities." Profiles are client-centered, team-based tools to address the physical, cognitive, emotional and support issues of individuals using AT. The profiles come with a manual for detailed instruction on completing each section of the profile. To purchase profiles or for more information contact: lifespace40729@aol.com or Lifespace Access, PO Box 52724 Irvine, CA 92619. 949-733-2746 voice or 949-552-1348 fax.

- "Assistive Technology Screener, Form B." A sample from Texas Technology Resource Center, a project of Technology and Inclusion, Administrative Offices & Technology Center, 1715 FM 1626 W, Suite 106, Manchaca, TX 78652; Mailing address, Box 150878, Austin, TX 78715. http://www.taicenter.com/screener.html

Resources

- "Smart Tech Tricks - Ideas to Frame Your Thinking." Online at http://www.ihdi.uky.edu/projects/tech_tools/tricks.htm.

- "The Pros From Dover . . . Using "Experts" to Justify an Assistive Technology Need." From the Illinois Assistive Technology Project Home Page: www.iltech.org.

- "Quality Indicators of Effective Assistive Technology Services." Online at: http://sac.uky.edu/~jszaba0/tamkeynote.html.

- "Standards for Assistive Technology Services." Online at: http://sac.uky.edu/~jszaba0/sampstandard.intervention.html.

- "Evaluations of Effectiveness: Standards for Assistive Technology Services." Online at http://sac.uky.edu/~jszaba0/sampstandard.evaluation.html.

- "Selecting and Obtaining Assistive Technology." Iowa Program for Assistive Technology. Online at: http://www.uiowa.edu/infotech/SelectAT.htm.

CHAPTER 5 SUMMARY

- For assessment and diagnostic purposes, behavior can be defined as skills and abilities the person is able to demonstrate or skills the person does not have or use.

- The purpose of testing and assessment is to identify the skills a person has along a continuum of growth. It helps to show what a person knows and can do and what he needs to learn next. Several areas of development need to be assessed to get a complete picture of a person's progress and functioning.

- Assessments may be done in these areas: psychiatric and/or neurological; behavioral; medical/physical; physical functioning, hearing and vision; social skills; assistive technology, psychological/educational/learning; communication/language/speech; occupational/motor/sensory integration; and adaptive functioning/daily living skills.

- Professionals can use a variety of methods, tests or techniques to measure specific skills and abilities; results of the assessment will be summarized as "findings."

- Professionals conducting assessments must be trained, qualified, and/or licensed to conduct the assessments and evaluations they perform.

- Standardized tests are "normed." This means scientific methods are used to suggest how persons of a certain age should perform on the test. Standardization allows the results for any individual to be compared to the results for others of a specific age.

- At times, the information gained from the process of doing or attempting test activities may be as valuable as a score.

- Some assessments are "criterion referenced." This means that the assessment is done to see whether a particular ability, skill or attribute is present or not.

• Ways to test informally for the presence or absence of skills are often needed and can be incorporated into the assessment process. This can include interviews, observation in various settings, and surveys for "reporting" from parents, teachers or staff.

• People with ASD may have development that is uneven or "out of sync" with what is expected for a person of a certain age. For this reason, a variety of testing methods may be needed to measure the full range of ability and need.

• Standardized tests result in a score that can be reported in a variety of ways. It is important to know how the score is being reported, and what the "number" means.

• The results of individual subtests can reveal specific strengths and deficit areas.

• Beware of averages or the "average range." Averaging can be counter-productive when trying to clearly identify any deficit areas by smoothing out the very peaks and valleys that we are trying to identify and address!

• Lists of skills provided in this chapter can be used to understand what assessment in a particular area is intended to measure. The skill lists may also inspire other ideas about what to include in gathering information in a particular area.

• Lists of assessment tools and tests in this chapter are provided to open dialogue between the person doing the testing and the family and individual being tested. This helps families know what to expect, give informed consent to testing and lends direction to the family in preparing the individual for the testing procedure.

• Discussion about the findings and results of testing should be done when the child is **not** present. Parents, guardians and staff can include an adult with ASD as appropriate. An adult who presents himself for diagnosis may want to bring a friend or family member to the meeting when test results are presented and discussed.

Chapter Resources

American Academy of Neurology. (2000). *Practice Parameter: Screening and Diagnosis of Autism Spectrum Disorders*. A Multi-Society Consensus Statement. Website. (Very technical language.)

American Academy of Child and Adolescent Psychiatry., (1997). *Comprehensive Psychiatric Evaluation, Facts for Families*. At www.aacap.org/publications/factsfam/eval.htm

Assistive and Adaptive Computing Technology in Education: Assessment Instruments. Online at http://at-advocacy.phillynews.com/data/assessinfo.html, http://www.flash.net/~brainwks/assess.html, and http://www.scilearn.com.

California Departments of Education and Developmental Services., (1996). *Recommendations of the Collaborative Task Force on Autism Spectrum Disorders: Best Practices for Designing and Delivering Effective Programs for Individuals with Autism Spectrum Disorders*.

Center for Autism and Related Disabilities (CARD). *Diagnosing and Evaluating Autism: Part 1*. Fact sheet Number 3, 1999.

Center for Autism and Related Disorders (CARD). *Diagnosing and Evaluating Autism: Part 2*. Fact Sheet Number 4, 1999.

Folse, Rene Thomas. PAUSE4KIDS Special Education Advocacy Seminar Series, 2001. *Lifespan Development*, and *Understanding the Math of Psychological and Educational Assessments*. www.childpsychologist.com.

Fouse, Beth. *Creating a Win-Win IEP* Arlington, TX: Future Horizons, 1996.

Functional Assessments for Students with Behavior Disorders www.ldonline.org/ld_indepth/special_education/quinn_behavior.html

IDEAL: Identify, Define, Explore, Anticipate and Act, an approach to problem solving as outlined in the book *The Ideal Problem Solver: A Guide for Improving Learning, Thinking and Creativity*, by John D. Bransford and Barry S. Stein.

Second Edition, W.H. Freeman and Company, New York, 1993. Online information at www.ihdi.uky.edu.

Illinois Assistive Technology Project, Springfield, Illinois. Phone/TTY 800-852-5110 ; FAX 217-522-7985. Website: www.iltech.org.

Illinois State Board of Education, *Assistive Technology Resource Manual* Website www.isbe.state.il.us/assistive/general_at_evals.

Isaacson, Stephen L. *Simple Ways to Assess the Writing Skills of Students with Learning Disabilities* in The Volta Review, 1996, Volume. 98, No. 1, pp. 183-199; Adapted at the Learning Disabilities Online Website, http://www.ldonline.org/ld_indepth/writing/isaacson_assessment.html.

Macleod, A.K. *Assistive and Adaptive Computing Technology in Education: Assessments Various Speech and Language Assessment Instruments.* http://at-advocacy.phillynews.com/data/assessinfo.html. Written by a parent, to explain testing.

McLoughlin, James A. and Rena B. Lewis, *Assessing Special Students 4th Edition*

MEDLINEplus Medical Encyclopedia. (2001). *BAER-Brainstem Auditory Evoked Response.* Online at: http://www.nlm.nih.gov/medlineplus/ency/article/03926.htm.

National Center for Learning Disabilities. *Visual and Auditory Processing Disorders,* (2002). Online at: http://www.ldonline.org/ld_indepth/process_deficit/visual_auditory.html.

Parker, Stephen J. and Barry Zuckerman. *Therapeutic Aspects of the Assessment Process.* In, *Handbook of Early Childhood Intervention*, S. Meisels and J. Shonkoff Eds. (pp 350-359). New York: Cambridge University Press, 1990.

Osterling, Ann. Speech and Language Pathologist, Champaign, Illinois.

Pierangelo, Roger and George A. Guiliani, *Special Educator's Guide to 109 Diagnostic Tests.*

Rapin I. *Autism.* New England Journal of Medicine 1997-337:97-104 Reprinted in Andolsek, Kathryn M., *Characteristics and Symptoms in Patients With Autism, Tips from other Journals.* <u>American Family Physician</u>, February 15, 1998, v.57, n4, p.809 (2).

Score! Educational Centers and Newsweek Magazine. *How to Help Your Child Succeed in School,* (1998.) *Score! Grade-by-Grade Parent Guide* pp. 73-168. The Score! Guidelines are based on information provided by The National Association of Young Children, *Developmentally Appropriate Practices in Early Childhood Programs* (from birth to age 8) NAEYC 1509 16th St. NW Washington, DC 20036-1426. Phone 800.424.2460, Fax, 202.232.8777.

Taylor, Ronald L., *Assessment of Exceptional Students 4th Edition*

Tri-City Herald Online *Central Auditory Processing Disorders in Children.* www.tri-cityherald.com/HEARNET/disorders.html, 1998.

Waterman, Betsy, *Assessing Children for the Presence of a Disability.* National Information Center for Children and Youth with Disabilities (NICHCY) website, http://www.kidsource.com/NICHCY/assessing.1.html.

Wiznitzer, Max, M.D. *Assessing the Assessment: An Approach to the Evaluation of the Individual With Autism/Pervasive Developmental Disorder.* (Handout in outline form, not dated).

Wright, Peter W.D., and Pamela Darr Wright.(2000). *Understanding Tests and Measurements for the Parent and Advocate.* Online at http://www.wrightslaw.com/advoc/articles/tests_measurements.html.

CHAPTER 6

DIFFERENCES OF OPINION IN DIAGNOSIS

This section is about questions that result from the diagnostic process. Read this section to answer any of the following questions:

What can I do if:

- An Autism Spectrum Disorder is not diagnosed and I think it should be?

- I think that the testing/evaluation results are not accurate?

- The individual has been given a diagnosis in the autism spectrum and I do not agree with it?

- I am given a diagnosis in the autism spectrum and I do not think it is correct?

- I am told that the person does *not* have ASD and now I doubt it too?

- I find that the person actually does have a different disorder than autism?

- I do not agree with any diagnosis given?

- An adult in the care of adult services may have an incorrect diagnosis; who changes it and how?

Why Would There be Disagreement About Diagnosis?

Autism Spectrum Disorders are "behaviorally diagnosed." Diagnosis is made by observation of what the person does and how they act (their behavior), as well as by looking at the early years of development. Sometimes a diagnosis of ASD is missed because there is a barrier to diagnosis. As described in Chapter Two, certain circumstances will hinder accuracy. Consider if any of the following situations are relevant:

• Some diagnosticians (people who specialize in finding a diagnosis) have not had recent training in autism and related disorders. Therefore, they may not recognize these disorders. Instead, they may give a diagnosis of a similar or overlapping disorder based on a point of view influenced by their own training, experience and area of expertise.

• The characteristics of ASD may manifest in a variety of ways and have some features in common with other disorders. Staff and families need to consider whether the diagnosis given "explains everything," and seems to account for all the characteristics of concern. Be aware if some important features are not accounted for by a particular diagnosis.

• A very young child, who is still developing speech and reasoning skills, is very difficult to assess.

• If the individual already has another diagnosis, (such as, mental retardation, behavioral disorder, Down Syndrome, Attention Deficit Hyperactivity Disorder, visual impairment, hearing impairment, etc.) features of an ASD can be attributed (mistakenly) to the other diagnosis.

• Professionals or families may have misconceptions about what ASD is and how it "looks" in different people and at different ages. Professionals may or may not recognize characteristics that the family has adjusted to and no longer think are unusual. Family members may have supported the individual so well that she appears to be "typical" in some settings, in particular when communicating with supportive adults in a quiet and structured setting.

- Sometimes the inaccuracy in diagnosis arises when a qualified professional does not have enough information. Sometimes, only limited aspects of a disorder may be observed while an individual is in a clinic or office for an assessment. This means that a diagnostician will only see a part of the problem, or will not have enough information to draw an appropriate conclusion. Observational opportunities in different settings may have been too limited.

- Sometimes diagnosticians use rating scales to arrive at a diagnosis. Parents and staff who do not want to "make their child look bad" may answer the questions with less clarity than is needed. Sometimes the questions are confusing or ambiguous, and parents are not sure how to respond.

- Parents or staff may have difficulty remembering, or may not realize which events in the child's development are significant and relevant to the diagnosis. They may inadvertently supply inaccurate information.

- Staff or parents may not know how to objectively describe the individual's characteristics to the diagnostician, resulting in an inaccurate or incomplete picture being presented.

- An assumption may have been made that there is "nothing wrong", except willfulness and defiance on the part of the child, and poor discipline and parenting skills on the part of the parents.

What Can I Do if ASD is Not Diagnosed and I Think it Should Be?

Here are some things to do if staff or parents think that a disorder is present, but has been "missed:"

- Look at the barriers to recognizing autism listed above and described in Chapter Two. Have any of these barriers affected the diagnostic process for the individual? If so, these areas need to be addressed or revisited.

• Insist that only objective information be considered in the diagnostic process. Look again at the records and reports to see if the individual has been described in an objective way. Make sure if an opinion is given that it is labeled as an opinion. Look to see if subjective opinions have caused bias, misinformation or false conclusions. For example, one child was described in his assessment as "not wanting to interact with the other children." Later, when asked, the child explained that he wanted very much to interact with the other children, but did not know how to do it. The opinion that he did not want to interact should never have been stated as a fact. All facts can be observed by more than one person and can be verified.

• Ask each member of the diagnostic team, separately, what he thinks about the accuracy of the diagnosis that was given. If any team members agree with your impressions, ask them to go with you to talk with the other diagnosticians to share these views.

• Ask diagnosticians to describe in detail all aspects of ASD that were observed in the individual. Ask for specific examples. Ask the diagnostician to tell you why that is a feature of ASD and not just an individual personality trait. Ask the diagnostician to describe what features or characteristics of an Autism Spectrum Disorder that the individual did *not* have. Ask what they were looking for that they did not find. Ask diagnosticians to put detailed answers to these questions in the written report they provide. If their report has already been written, ask them to write a letter explaining the answers to these questions. Most diagnosticians do not mind explaining their diagnosis in detail.

• Think about the explanation from the diagnostician. Consider if any of the following steps would clarify things. If so, ask that they be done. Would it help if:

    1. The diagnostician was invited to observe the individual at a time when the individual demonstrated a particular characteristic? Some behavioral responses are easier to see in social situations in community environments and harder to observe in a quiet,

structured office. Behavior such as running away in the mall, straightening everything in the house when it is moved, not responding in an age appropriate way to the initiation of a peer, having problems with change, or a variety of characteristics are best viewed in natural situations.

2. The diagnostician was invited to meet more family members? This may be helpful if it is your assumption that the features the diagnostician observed are "just like the rest of us in the family."

3. Were photographs, audiotape, or videotapes shared with the diagnostician? This may be an excellent way to show events, characteristics or behaviors of concern. Or, ask the diagnostician to interview more people who know the individual well, such as, siblings, former teachers, relatives, etc. Ask if others who know the individual well can answer the questions to any rating scales that were used to see if another person could better describe what is observed.

What Can I Do If I Think That the Testing or Evaluation Results Are Not Accurate?

Many parents and staff report that they do not agree with the results of testing or evaluations. For example, it may be reported that a child cannot count to ten on an assessment, when a parent has seen him count to 21 at home. Or, a student may test "in the average range" for verbal language, but not know how to have a conversation with peers. Standardized testing for people with Autism Spectrum disorders may falsely identify problems that are not there or fail to reveal problems that are there!

As has been explained in detail in other parts of this book, this difficulty may arise from the challenges of testing people with ASD. They may not perform to their true ability, their responses may be inconsistent or their strengths may mask areas of weakness. But when the results are not completely accurate or telling, false conclusions may be drawn about the person's areas of ability and areas of need. Such conclusions may hamper recognition or diagnosis of ASD, or an accurate picture of abilities and needs.

If parents or staff receive test results that just don't seem to make sense, let it be known. Tell those who did the testing that the information from the evaluations does not match what you know about the person. Give information and examples of why the test results do not seem to be an accurate reflection of what the person does or does not know.

In response, professionals can choose other assessment tools to look at particular areas in depth. This may help to measure the skills and characteristics of the person more accurately. It may even make a difference in recognizing the deficit areas that are characteristic of ASD and affect the diagnosis.

In other cases, parents or family may question the person's experience, competence or qualification to do an assessment or make a diagnosis. There are several options regarding the appeal process depending on who is providing the assessments. If a school district is doing the assessments, the right to seek a private assessment at public expense may also be relevant. These issues are described in Volume Two of this book in the chapter on the IEP process.

Parents also have the option of getting another opinion from a professional at their own expense, or paid for by insurance. The findings of the professional would be submitted to the team and the team is required to take the information into account.

What if the Individual Has Been Given a Diagnosis of ASD and I Do Not Agree with It? What If I Am Given a Diagnosis of ASD and I Do Not Think It Is Correct?

Parents or staff may disagree with the diagnosis of ASD and feel like it is a mistake. Individuals who receive a diagnosis as adults may find it hard to accept or believe. Many teachers and staff report that they sometimes do not "believe" or agree that a student has ASD.

Looking at the Facts

The first thing to do is ask, "Why don't I agree?" Try to pinpoint what it is about the diagnosis that does not seem to fit the individual. Try to be objective and think about what you have observed. You may know something about the person that does not seem consistent with ASD. In the case of adults, you may have specific concerns that make you think that the diagnosis is not correct. Then, share these thoughts with someone who knows a lot about ASD to see if you may indeed be right.

On the other hand, be prepared to look at the possibility that misconceptions, or a lack of information, are causing the "it can't be" reaction. Sometimes parents, adults and staff just need to know more, or have some things explained in more detail before they can agree that the diagnosis is correct. Parents may know their child better than anyone else. Teachers and staff may have excellent opportunities to see how a person learns and functions on a daily basis. Adults feel that they know themselves better than any "outsider." But parents, staff and the average person are not usually experts on ASD. It is important that doubts be expressed so information can be shared. The diagnosis needs to make sense compared with what parents, staff and individuals see and know.

In one case, a mother felt that ASD was the wrong diagnosis because of "reciprocity of emotion." It was the one thing that nagged at her and did not seem to make sense. She felt that her daughter had good reciprocity of emotion with her — that there was "give and take" and understanding of feelings. She reasoned that since her daughter did have reciprocity of emotion, she could not have an Autism Spectrum Disorder.

She arranged to speak with an experienced advocate. The advocate helped the mother to notice that the reciprocity of emotion was very limited; the mother-daughter relationship was the only place this feature could be seen. This contrasts with typical development in which people are able to identify, understand and respond to the feelings of just about anyone, not just one person. The mother realized that reciprocity of emotion was indeed a legitimate concern.

During their conversation, the advocate realized that the mother had a mistaken idea about diagnosis. The mother thought that her daughter had to meet all of the possible criteria and have every characteristic in order to have a diagnosis of ASD. When the mother was told that only a certain number need to be met, and that no person has all the characteristics, she felt far more accepting of the validity of the diagnosis.

Two Case Examples from Barbara

I met a man who had become involved in the field of autism because his son had been given the diagnosis. Recognizing some of the same features in himself, the man went to a university clinic that specializes in autism and was diagnosed with ASD. Even though he recognized the features in himself, he could not "accept" or believe the diagnosis. He had built a very successful career and had a happy marriage and good home life. He was devoted to his children. Although he did not have a wide circle of friends, some family members and extended family members filled his need for friendship. How could he have autism? Everyone knows, he thought, that a person with autism cannot grow up, be successful in business and have an excellent home life! Over time, he came to realize that "what everyone knows" is largely wrong.

He looked back more objectively and thought about the loneliness of his young days in school. He thought about the names he had been called and his lack of a spontaneous social life, especially compared to his siblings. He began to think about all that his mother had done to assist him in a different way than how she helped his brother and sister. He realized that he had "decided" early in life that he was different, because he was very smart, not because of a social disability.

Although he did not want to think of himself as having a "label," he decided to use some of the techniques he was learning to teach his son. He was surprised and delighted by things that seemed small, but made a big difference to others, such as telling others what topic he wanted to discuss before starting to discuss it, informing others of his plans in advance and giving more compliments. In overcoming his fear of a "label" or "disability," he was able to become happier and better accepted by his peers at work and socially. His family continued to love him as they always had, but now had a greater understanding of what he needed and who he was.

In another situation, a mother learned about ASD because of her children. When other family members pointed out that she had similar characteristics, she became very angry. She did not want to believe that there was a name for the difference that she had always experienced. Her mother had told her many times that she was just smarter and more sensitive than others. Surely that explained everything. Over time, this woman was unable to consider that she had a special need that could be addressed in a positive way. She became more angry and depressed and isolated herself more from friends and loved ones. Eventually she needed to receive mental health services related to anxiety and anger management. Those of us who knew her did not blame her and tried to remain supportive.

Emotional Barriers

A range of emotions from fear, to denial, guilt, anger and blame may keep parents and adults from "believing." Sometimes parents and individuals are just not "ready" to believe that the diagnosis is correct. Other parents, people diagnosed as adults and health professionals will tell you that this is perfectly normal. Taking time to work through these feelings helps to be objective in looking at the information that has been presented.

Sometimes a lack of confidence, or conflicts with the people doing the evaluations, may cause parents and staff or adults being diagnosed to be skeptical of the results. Many times, parents feel uncomfortable because they have never met the evaluators. They have to trust their child's welfare to people they barely know. Adults may also have issues of trust and feel unsure about the diagnosis. These things may make it difficult to accept the results.

Often, teachers, other staff or family members think that the diagnosis is an "excuse" for poor self-discipline and poor parenting. Staff members who think that blame for problems lies with the family may resist "believing." In other cases, staff may be concerned that too many people are being frivolously diagnosed with ASD and it is the "disease of the week." A backlash is to be expected, especially with the rise in incidence and diagnosis of ASD that is being reported in all parts of the U.S. and the world. As much a part of human nature as they are, neither of these attitudes is a legitimate reason to refuse to look at the facts.

Language Barriers

In some situations, the difficulty with understanding the diagnosis and agreeing with it may be related to language. First, the technical and professional jargon used in the diagnostic process can be a barrier to understanding. There is a lot to learn in a short amount of time while at the same time working with a variety of new people. The center of all this is a dearly loved person and a serious and emotional issue. Sometimes this combination is overwhelming and confusing. Misunderstandings may occur, but they may not be obvious until later.

People often joke, saying, "Can you say that again, but in English this time?" When it comes to a serious matter like assessment of a developmental disability, there is no joke involved. Professionals need to remember that parents are hearing what they say for the very first time, and use the clearest language possible. Parents or staff need to feel comfortable asking to have terms explained in the moment or later.

Many people who do not speak English as their primary language may have great difficulty with the entire diagnostic process. They may not be able to follow discussions or understand jargon, terminology and new vocabulary. Parents, individuals or staff who are deaf and use sign language as their primary way of communicating may also feel "lost" if they cannot follow conversations and have access to all the information they need in a way they can understand it.

Both English language learners and people who are deaf and use sign language are entitled to the services of a professional interpreter for discussion and planning related to assessment, treatment, education and services. The Americans with Disabilities Act also requires that all publicly funded services must be "accessible" to people with disabilities. This includes access to information about diagnosis and services, for the individual or the family members responsible for decisions. It may be up to staff or school personnel to offer to arrange to provide an interpreter, as the parents or family may not be aware of their right to have one.

Language and communication needs come in addition to all the other "traumatic" things families experience in getting a diagnosis. If there appears to be disagreement or misunderstanding, or to prevent it, it may be helpful to have meetings with the interpreter present just to explain and discuss assessments and findings, with extra time planned for clear explanations and answers to questions, before it is time to make any decisions.

What Can I Do If I Am Told That the Person Does Not Have ASD, and Now I Doubt It Too?

You could make an appointment to talk in private with the diagnostician. Tell him what topics or aspects of the diagnosis are problems for you. Ask for more explanations or more examples. It is easier to take in and consider information in a one-to-one discussion than when findings are "presented" to a whole team or group.

If an individual has **any** features in the autism spectrum, address them; do not ignore them. For example, if a child is having problems in social interactions, but does not have issues in verbal and non-verbal communication or restricted repetitive interests, she will not meet the criteria for ASD. She will still have significant problems that could be helped with interventions such as social skills training.

Sometimes when no formal diagnosis is given, staff and families become more subjective and tend to blame the child or adult, considering their difficulties as a personality trait or choice. This is very dangerous and team members need to help one another avoid this attitude. When in doubt, assume that any individual would do better if she could do better. Rather than slip into blaming the child (or family, or teachers, or therapist, or other students, etc.) begin to focus on what needs are presented by the deficits the individual displays. Think about services that could help to meet those needs. Gain eligibility in any legitimate way possible. (For example in schools, eligibility might be under "speech and language needs" or "other health impaired.") Then get to work teaching the individual new skills.

What Do I Do If I Find That the Person Actually Does Have a Different Disorder?

Get busy and learn about *that* disorder. Try to find a support group for people and families who are interested in that disorder. Ask the diagnostician if she has any information for you about the disorder and contacts you can make to learn more. Try to meet other people who have been given that diagnosis to find out what has been helpful. The Internet is a terrific resource. If you cannot access the Internet yourself, people at your local public library can help you find the information you need. No matter what "diagnostic label" is given, the individual is the same person that he was before the diagnosis was given. Now you may be able to find some new ideas and techniques that will better help and support him. Do not be afraid; just start learning all you can.

What Do I Do If I Do Not Agree With Any Diagnosis Given?

Parents or staff could consider selecting the diagnosis that seems to fit the best and gain eligibility to services. Start working with school or adult agency staff to make an individualized plan to teach the individual new skills. Perhaps you will need to postpone finding the exact diagnosis for the moment. Put your energy into identifying the deficit areas that the person has, listing his needs and getting services designed and implemented to address those needs as soon as possible under any legitimate eligibility that you can.

Perhaps you can take a brief "diagnostic rest" and focus on getting appropriate services delivered as long as the child or adult is not at risk. During this time, you could continue to learn, talking to people who know about different conditions, reading and surfing the web. It would be helpful at this time to learn to be really objective about the individual, and keep objective notes about what the person does or does not do to help future diagnosticians.

When an Adult in the Care of Adult Services Has an Incorrect Diagnosis, Who Changes It and How Is It Changed? Is It Important to Change It if They Are Already Receiving Services Anyway?

If an adult is already eligible for services, changing the diagnosis may not be necessary for eligibility. However, it is very important for staff to know if they are working with an adult who thinks and learns as people with ASD often do. Knowing that the individual has ASD provides a framework for viewing the individual in a new and more appropriate way. New interventions can be tried that have been proven successful for people with an autism spectrum disorder. Communication issues can be understood better and communication programs designed to be more effective for the person with ASD.

As in children's services, one size does **not** fit all. If team members know that the person has ASD, then team members can make changes and modifications in all aspects of programming that will help the individual have a better quality of life and greater success. Many of the changes that are suggested that benefit adults with ASD who are already in the developmental disability (DD) service delivery system are low cost or no cost changes.

Many helpful accommodations for adults with autism in the DD system require a shift in thinking and attitude and some environmental adjustments. Most staff are able and willing to learn how to think and behave differently when they are given an opportunity to understand autism and related disorders.

A Case Example from Barbara:

Paul, a 38-year-old man with developmental disabilities (seizure disorder and mental retardation), was diagnosed with autism at a clinic. The clinic asked me to provide an in-service for staff to help them understand how autism affected this individual and what staff could do to help him. Staff loved Paul and had worked with him for more than 20 years. It was a pleasure to see how staff interacted with him, patiently participating in his repetitive humor and using kind and gentle management techniques.

Paul did better in the presence of some staff in particular. This was attributed to his "liking" those staff. Paul was able to access some community environments, but everyone at his service agency "knew" that he should have been doing better. When they brought him to the clinic, it was for support for some behavioral issues. They never thought that they would find out that Paul had ASD!

I provided a day of training for the staff focusing on understanding how Paul might best learn and what teaching and communication ideas might work the best. We really did not have much time to talk about his behavioral issues that day.

About three months later, I received a note from the staff. They wanted to thank me for my help and to let me know how well Paul was doing. He no longer took behavioral medications and was no longer having the behavior problems that he had in the past. Paul had changed dramatically in reaction to the changes that the staff made.

Staff had started being more visual and concrete in the way they communicated with Paul. When he asked repetitive questions, they wrote down the answers and created a card file for him of "need to know" things. They put a calendar in the kitchen of the group home and wrote down items that they knew would be of interest to Paul. Staff had decided to increase his access to liked activities and places. They established supportive routines that helped Paul function with less personal support.

To everyone's delight, Paul was talking more and echoing less. He was producing more work at the workshop. He had fewer problems with his housemates. Staff said, "he just seems happier!"

Paul changed because staff found out that he had autism and were able and willing to change their ideas and interventions. One staff member said that her only regret was that they did not recognize the features of ASD sooner so that the needed changes could have been implemented. She commented that the changes were not hard or expensive and the most important change was that everyone had a better understanding of how Paul learned.

Readers might think that this case reads like a "fairy tale," but it is a true story that illustrates the power of:

- Learning as much as possible about autism disorders and how people with ASD might think and learn.

- Using this knowledge to view the individual in a new and more positive way.

- Being encouraged by others and supported by management to try new interventions that could not harm the person and might actually help.

- Having staff who are willing to change what they do and how they do it.

- Having staff who want people with ASD to have a better quality of life and feel the joy of celebrating the improvement.

Paul's story shows us the powerful effects of staff interactions on the quality of life of people with autism. We hope that an example like this will encourage staff (in schools and community settings) and families to see the many opportunities they have to improve lives and make a real difference. There is a saying, "If you always do what you always did, you'll always get what you always got." We say, "If you want to get different results, do something differently." It is your choice.

CHAPTER 6 SUMMARY

- If you disagree with a diagnosis, or when ASD is not diagnosed when you think it should be, consider whether the following may have occurred:

  — Professionals involved have not have had recent training in the autism spectrum.

  — Features of ASD have been (mistakenly) attributed to another diagnosis.

  — Those involved have misconceptions about what ASD is and how it "looks" in different people and at different ages.

  — The diagnosticians do not have enough information or have inaccurate views.

  — Rating scales were confusing or ambiguous to those who completed them.

  — A false assumption caused a biased view that there is "nothing wrong," except the child's willfulness, defiance and lack of trying and/or poor discipline and parenting from parents.

- If any of the above "errors" have occurred, take steps to clarify and revisit the issues.

- If you feel that testing or evaluation results are not accurate, tell those who did the testing that the information from the evaluations does not match what you know about the person. Give information and examples of why the test results do not seem to be an accurate reflection of what the person does or does not know. Make a plan to clarify and resolve the issue.

- In cases of disagreement about assessments done by educational agencies, IDEA law specifies how to appeal. In some cases of due process, the educational agency may be required to pay for a private assessment. Parents may have the option of getting a diagnosis or a second opinion from a professional at their own expense or paid for by insurance.

- Parents or staff may disagree with the diagnosis of ASD and feel like it is a mistake. Try to pinpoint what it is about the diagnosis that does not seem to fit the individual.

- Be prepared to look at the possibility that misconceptions, or a lack of information, are causing the "it can't be" reaction. Determine whether a range of normal emotions from fear, to denial, guilt, anger and blame may keep parents and adults from "believing."

- Whether or not a diagnosis is given, if an individual has **any** features in the autism spectrum, address them; do not ignore them. Think about services that could help to meet those needs. Seek eligibility in any possible legitimate way.

- If you find that the person actually does have a different disorder, get busy and learn about that disorder.

- If an adult is already eligible for services, changing the diagnosis may not be necessary for eligibility. However, it is important for staff to know if they are working with an adult who thinks and learns as people with ASD often do.

CHAPTER 7

"Acceptance is, in fact, the first step to successful action. If you don't fully accept a situation precisely the way it is, you will have difficulty changing it."
Peter McWilliams, Life 101

REACTING TO THE DIAGNOSIS

This chapter will discuss:

- The reaction of parents and staff to getting a diagnosis for the child or adult.

- The process of understanding and believing a diagnosis (how we define "accepting") and getting down to business.

- The reactions of siblings and other family members on receiving a diagnosis.

- The reactions of adults who are just identified as having ASD.

- Family issues that affect families with a son or daughter with ASD.

- Reactions of professionals and staff to a diagnosis.

Reacting to the Diagnosis

This section discusses the variety of reactions and emotions experienced by parents and family members who have a cherished child of any age diagnosed with ASD. We describe some of the varied reactions and feelings of adults identified in adulthood and the effects on extended family members.

Professionals and staff may gain valuable insight and perspective by reading about the family's process of understanding and believing a diagnosis. The last part of the discussion describes the reaction of professionals, such as teachers and adult service providers. Parents may wish to read this to gain insight into how the diagnosis affects people outside the family.

Parents Receive the News

Receiving a diagnosis of autism for your child can be a shock, something that you never expected or could be prepared for. In fact, it may leave you numb, confused, or disbelieving. Autism is an "invisible" disability. At birth, parents are overjoyed to have a perfect and lovely new baby. There is usually no indication that anything might be wrong. As the child grows and develops, he looks like all the other children. It is what he says (or doesn't say) and does (or doesn't do) that signals an alarming difference.

Each parent notices their child's differences and begins to worry to varying degrees. Some are mildly concerned, and some are distressed. Many parents do nothing because they think or are told that the child will "grow out of it." Some parents are referred for assessment and diagnosis with no idea of what the problem could be. Other people suspect that an Autism Spectrum Disorder could be the problem. Even if parents have some hint or idea of what the cause of their child's difficulties may be, there is little way to be prepared to hear the actual diagnosis and find that it is now "real."

Realizing that your child has ASD can be painful and distressing. The reaction of shock and disbelief is understandable. Parents never dreamed that they would have a child with autism. They are not prepared for difficulties they had never imagined facing. They do not know enough about autism. They fear the unknown and what life will be like in the future. Even when the diagnosis is no longer "brand new," parents continue to have mixed feelings and reactions for some time.

Psychologists recognize stages of reacting to a diagnosis similar to any emotional trauma. Many parents experience a range of emotions during the process of understanding and accepting that their child has ASD. Sometimes this is called the **grieving process**, and some people refer to it as the **coping process**.

Many parents express the need to go through a grieving period after getting a diagnosis. Some people explain that getting a diagnosis is like experiencing the "death" of the child that will never be, as if their child is lost to them or taken away. Others feel the sense of loss for what might have been. This may mean realizing that they will have a different life for the child and themselves than the one they had expected and planned.

The stages of grieving are identified as denial, disbelief, helplessness, guilt, blame, anger, and finally, acceptance. While "acceptance" is the goal, it may not mean that one emotional stage is replaced by the next. The varied feelings may be felt in any "order" or all at once. Parents may need only a short time to move from emotional overload to acceptance. Or, it can be a much longer process.

The intensity of emotions may be different for each parent as well. Each person will work through their thoughts and feelings at their own rate. It is important not to deny your feelings, or feel guilty for having "negative" feelings.

The individual nature of reacting to the diagnosis may mean that each parent can be at a different emotional stage at any given time. This can complicate communication and understanding between a couple and between parents and other team members. When conflicts arise, it may help to be aware of the fact that each partner is experiencing different emotions. For example, if the mother is feeling guilty and the father is feeling angry at a given point in time, things can be very difficult. It can be helpful if each partner can "allow" whatever emotion the other is experiencing and permit free, safe expression. Over time, it seems that expressed emotions may not hold the individual in as tight a grasp as suppressed emotions.

The "information gap" may have an affect on how each parent will react to the diagnosis. Sometimes both parents feel completely in the dark about what ASD is. Often, one partner may have more awareness or knowledge, while the other partner knows very little. Having different amounts of information and understanding can affect how each person responds to the diagnosis and to one another.

It is important to realize that the reality of having to help your child or adult who has ASD comes on top of whatever the other realities of your life are. The news of the diagnosis is one more thing to cope with. It is a big thing with a very big impact. It is not just one piece of news that upsets your already perfect world. The diagnosis is "added to" other issues, such as whether you are a single parent, have relationship problems or problems in your marriage, stress from your job, money problems, personal problems, physical or mental health issues or issues with other children or family members. Your personal circumstances affect the process of understanding, reacting to and accepting the diagnosis.

Your personality and personal style also have bearing on the coping process. Are you a fighter? A "fixer?" Are you easily overwhelmed? Are you going to read everything you can get your hands on? Do you seek comfort and understanding from others, or withdraw into yourself? How much time and space do you think you need to begin to recover from the shock? Can you offer the same to your partner? Do you express or repress your emotions? Do your emotions keep you from being objective? How patient are you?

It may help to recognize, identify and express your feelings and where you are in the coping process, whether it is to your spouse, a friend, another parent who has a child with ASD, or a therapist, psychologist or psychiatrist. Do not be afraid to seek guidance from a professional to help with the process of receiving the diagnosis, understanding the effect on the family and preparing yourself for what to do next.

Many families have shared some of the thoughts that they had after diagnosis, the questions they asked themselves and the many emotions they felt. Here are some of the thoughts that they expressed. Many readers will identify with these ideas and experiences:

- Denial

  It can't be true.

  This must be a mistake.

  How could this happen?

  Not me, not my kid.

  Maybe after I wake up tomorrow, it will be gone.

  Doctor, you are wrong.

  Not autism!

  I don't believe it.

  I feel like I am in a dream.

  These people do not really know my child.

- Feelings of guilt, blame, and shame

  Why me?

  Why my child?

  What did I do to deserve this?

  I must have done something wrong.

  Whose fault is this?

  Is it my fault?

  This is all my fault.

  This is _____'s fault.

  I should have known sooner.

  Why didn't I do something sooner?

Why didn't someone help us/tell us sooner?

Is God punishing me?

I bet this is an inherited disorder from his/her/my side of the family.

What will other people think of this?

What will the neighbors say?

People will think that I did something wrong.

- Anger and resentment

  This isn't fair!

  This is an innocent child!

  I did not ask for this burden.

  My life would be so simple if I did not have to deal with this.

  I am stuck with this problem.

  People missed this all along and now look at where we are!

  How could our pediatrician not have seen this?

  Don't you tell me something is wrong with my child.

  I told you something bad would happen if you_____.

- Fear, anxiety and worry

  I am not sure if I can cope.

  I feel all alone with this responsibility.

  What will the future be like?

  What is autism?

  What will happen to my child?

What will his life be like?

What will my life be like?

How will this affect our family?

What do we need to do to deal with this?

How will I find out how to help my child and myself?

What will happen when I am gone?

How can she have a good life now?

- Feelings of being overwhelmed and helpless

    This is all just way too much.

    I can't cope with this.

    This is a disaster.

    Things are out of control.

    I do not know what to do.

    I will be responsible for my child with autism for the rest of my life.

    I cannot face "autism."

Depression and Sadness

Because receiving a diagnosis is linked with the process of grieving, sadness is often experienced by parents. A sense of loss may cause sad feelings or depression. Feeling worried or unable to cope can cause feelings of depression. Some parents feel sad because they feel something bad has happened in their child's life and their own. Parents feel a loss of control over the situation that can lead to sadness or depression.

Even when you accept that your child has autism, you may wish for things that will probably never happen. In spite of the fact that you are adapting and coping as well as you can, every day may bring a reminder that your child has ASD. Hopefully, the sad moments will be balanced by progress and possibilities for the life of your child.

Depression as a phase of the grieving process is normal and even expected. But severe or long lasting bouts of depression can be devastating. When depression is a problem, it can be difficult for a person to recognize or acknowledge it in oneself or in a partner. Depression is a condition that usually requires professional help. No one should feel ashamed to ask for help. There is no blame attached. Reestablishing well-being is a priority to help the parent and the family to function and thrive. Remember, it is unlikely that you will be able to meet the needs of your child or adult child with autism, if you are not well yourself and have your own needs met.

A Message for Parents:

While it is reasonable to keep in mind that nothing you did has caused your child to have an Autism Spectrum Disorder, sometimes feelings of guilt remain, especially at the time of diagnosis. A mother may worry that habits and behavior during pregnancy may have caused the child to be born with autism. However, no correlation between maternal behavior during pregnancy and autism has been established.

If the cause of autism is genetic, the parents are not to blame any more for autism than for eye color. No one has knowingly passed autism on. The genetic research is still inconclusive. There is some evidence that particular family members may have "shadow syndromes," showing some characteristics of autism, but not having the disorder. However, having "odd," family members is not responsible for causing ASD in others.

If the cause turns out to be environmental and if you acted with no knowledge of any potential hazard, you cannot hold yourself responsible for having been exposed. If vaccines turn out to be a cause, and you did not know that that was possible, you cannot blame yourself for following recommendations of the medical profession.

Getting a diagnosis of ASD can be very emotional and upsetting. It is important to give yourself time to learn about the disability and learn to cope. We encourage you to find a support group of people who understand what you are going through. Avoiding self-recrimination for the amount of time it took to get help is important; you are doing the best you can with what you know.

Acceptance

Parents wonder if they will ever accept that their child has a disability — has an autism spectrum disorder. There is often a surreal feeling to the idea, and it feels like it could not possibly be true. Sometimes it feels so difficult, parents think that they may not be able to move on. Strong, overwhelming feelings can be paralyzing.

Acceptance is expected to be the outcome of the grieving process. After experiencing the feelings of denial, anger, blame, shame, fear and sadness, beginning to understand and accept can be an emotional turning point. Coming to terms with the diagnosis can be very powerful. Parents already have the motivation to move on, and that is love for the child. Feelings of acceptance help parents to find the strength, the courage and the energy to help their child.

Acceptance is a process. Steve Meckstroth, the father of a boy with autism, gives a perceptive view of parental emotions and "acceptance." Mr. Meckstroth made a little device for a presentation that deeply impressed everyone. He used the format of a spinner for a board game. Instead of numbers on the sections of the spinner, he put emotions. His spinner could land on elated, depressed, accepting, rage, hopelessness, joy, pain, guilt, fear, contentment and many others. Mr. Meckstroth told his audience that being the parent of a child with ASD means that each day is like another spin of the arrow. Emotions can change constantly.

Sometimes professionals give parents feedback (either intentionally or not) that these emotional states indicate a "lack of acceptance." They suggest that parents "move on" and get busy with all of the steps necessary to get helpful services. When parents sense that they are doing something "wrong" by having all kinds of varying emotions, it simply adds to their burden.

It is normal and very typical for families to have wide variations in emotional responses from day-to-day or even hour-to-hour. This does not mean that the family is not "accepting" the fact that the child has a disability. If acceptance is defined as "liking" the situation and never feeling negatively again, most people will not be accepting. Parents can accept the diagnosis and continue to experience a variety of emotions. Acceptance can be understanding and believing that the diagnosis is correct and beginning to take active steps in a positive direction. That does not mean that pain, sadness or blame will just disappear.

Two Steps Forward, One Step Back

Often, after all the upset and tumult of getting a diagnosis and getting services, families settle into a good routine and life proceeds more calmly. The emotional roller coaster levels off and things go more smoothly. However, even parents who understand and accept their child's diagnosis can be emotionally jolted when changes occur. Transitions, such as moving from pre-school to elementary school, moving from one school district or service provider to another, losing a support person, and moving from school life to adult living can be very stressful. Changes in services or service providers are unsettling. Parents often say that these things can trigger strong emotions similar to those felt at the initial diagnosis. Usually, the crisis or uncertainty passes and the family re-establishes balance more quickly than the first time.

One couple who plays in a symphony orchestra have a daughter who is both deaf and blind. The mother says that sometimes when she hears a beautiful piece of music and knows that her daughter never will, she cries. She says at that moment she "hates it" that her daughter is deaf and blind. At the same time, the family has been working continuously to help their daughter access high quality services. They love her and are planning for her future knowing full well that she will most likely always be deaf and blind. Do they accept it? Not at some moments. They do recognize the realities of her disability and are taking active steps to help her.

Parents can understand the situation and move ahead without really liking the fact that they must. This is based on a definition of acceptance as "recognition and action." If a family is seeking services for their son or daughter, it is likely that they are accepting the situation to the degree necessary to get moving to the best degree that they can at the moment.

The positive side of a diagnosis:

A Sense of Relief

Parents report that several positive things can come from getting a diagnosis. When the diagnosis seems to really "fit" the characteristics and behaviors that they have seen, it can be a great relief to finally identify and understand what is happening to the child. This is particularly true when a person has had several diagnoses that did not explain or account for all the features parents were seeing. A diagnosis that makes sense can be a positive thing. Even when a diagnosis comes as late as adolescence, getting the information helps both the parent and teen to understand and identify his needs. Individuals diagnosed as adults may share a sense of relief described by parents. Here are some of the positive thoughts parents have shared:

- A source of hope and direction

    Somebody knows what to do about this!

    We have been living with something for years. Now it has a name.

    You think you are alone until you find out you're not.

    I am not alone.

    We are not alone.

    Other people understand what I am going through.

    There are other children like my child.

    My child can have a good life.

- Validating parents' feelings and insight into the problem

    Finally, someone believes me!

An expert I trusted was listening to me.

"Someone who knows" understood what I was trying to explain.

I was right about my child.

My persistence paid off.

Now we can move on to get some support and make some progress.

I am relieved to know I did not cause the disorder and I am not to blame

I am not crazy. This was not all in my head.

People can stop blaming my child for what he cannot do.

People can stop blaming me (or us).

Some Things Are not Really Different

One intuitive mother said that getting the diagnosis did not really change her child, herself, or her life. Living with her child was the same the day before the diagnosis and the day after the diagnosis. The diagnosis did give a name and an explanation to their experiences and an idea of what to do next.

Eligibility

Parents may also be relieved to know that an official diagnosis of autism or ASD may make the person eligible for special education and other services. In this case, the diagnosis serves a purpose and holds promise of accessing what can be done to help the person learn and improve.

What Parents and Staff Can Do

If getting a diagnosis is numbing, even paralyzing, doing nothing is not an option. Knowing what to do and where to start can be overwhelming. Here are some ideas to help parents focus and move forward with the plan for their loved one with autism.

Hope For a Good Future

Have high hopes for the individual with ASD. Tell the person that you have dreams for them and that you will help them to reach their dreams. Be sure to speak positively in this way to the person with ASD even if he does not appear to be able to understand everything that you say. Share your hopes and dreams with friends, professional staff and extended family.

If someone predicts that the individual with ASD will "never" be able to have desired outcomes for their life, ask the predictor to give you next Saturday's lottery numbers. If the person can predict what will happen years in advance, surely they can give you a couple of numbers this week!

This is a light-hearted way to respond to dire predictions that are painful and limiting for the family, child and staff. It can help everyone realize how ridiculous it is to pretend that anyone can predict the future. "Where there is life, there is hope" is our motto. Hope can lead to action and action can lead to the accomplishment of goals that will help the individual with ASD. Parents are not misguided, unrealistic or foolish to have high hopes. No one should treat them as if they were, or take hope away from any parent.

A Case Example from Barbara

When I was teaching deaf children in the early years of my career, I met Tim, a very special boy who had lost his hearing due to meningitis. One day he was a "normal" two-year-old and the next, he was profoundly deaf with a damaged balance system.

I loved working with Tim's family. They did not allow anyone to decrease their high expectations for Tim. Some of Tim's family members were pilots. One day his father told me, "I would like for Tim to be able to fly a plane someday." I thought, "Wow, this Dad is really unrealistic! Tim can hardly walk across a room without stumbling and he cannot hear. There are no deaf pilots anyway." However, a wise college professor had taught me to honor the hopes that parents have for their children. So I decided to do whatever I could to help nourish that hope. I suggested that Tim learn more about math and physics and that his father teach him everything he could. When he was in his twenties, Tim became the first deaf pilot in his state!

Tim's father came to me again one day and said, "You know, I think these computers are going to be something important in people's lives some day. I want Tim to learn about them." (Remember this was about 1975. No one had home computers and very few businesses had them. At that time, a computer could take up all the space in a large room!) Once again my first reaction was to dismiss what Tim's dad said. I applied my "hope" standard instead and told him that I would do anything I could to help Tim learn about computers. The family bought and set up a huge computer. Today, Tim earns his living as a fantastic computer graphics professional designing award winning websites, while raising his lovely children with his beautiful wife.

Perhaps Tim might not have become a pilot. During the process of learning, he may have learned enough to be able to discuss flying and planes with the pilots in his family. While learning about computers, Tim would have acquired very useful information that his father's foresight had predicted to be important, even if he did not use computers to earn his living. The hopes that were preserved, honored and promoted gave Tim's father new energy and a forward-looking perspective. I like to think that some of the sadness over the loss of Tim's hearing was "balanced" with the hope for a wonderful future. The belief that there was hope for Tim may have been self-fulfilling and like a domino-effect, may be what set the tone and direction for what was to come.

ASD can bring with it some limitations for people's futures. But many people with ASD have happy and productive lives. Your loved one with ASD can be successful.

Continue to Learn Everything You can about ASD

Attend lectures, seminars or training sessions. Ask others for titles of useful books and resources. Renew your library card, or learn to use the Internet if you do not know how. Thanks to all the information that is available and accessible in so many forms, your expertise can grow in a short period.

Some people say that beginning to learn about ASD is like drinking from a fire hose, overwhelming. It may feel that way at first. You may need some time to take it all in, but knowledge is the key to making progress.

Do not turn away helpful information just because it is not specifically about ASD. Ideas about learning in general may be helpful for people with ASD. Helpful information may be found when searching for information with subjects, titles, key words or guide words such as disabilities, pervasive developmental disorders, advocacy, special education, learning modalities, etc.

Sometimes ideas that are helpful to most people may also help an individual with ASD. The person with ASD is first and always a person. An example of a "generic" idea is a planning calendar that many people use. Although it was not specially designed to be used by individuals with ASD, it can be very useful to them as it is to anyone else.

Throw Blame Out

It is perfectly natural to want to know why the person has autism or who "did this" to them. The causes of autism and ASD are unknown. There is no one to blame for autism and related disorders. It can be a relief to get rid of the need to blame someone, including yourself.

Research shows no evidence or reason to blame parents for their child's ASD. Parental behavior does not cause autism. Even if causes are discovered in the future, parents cannot be blamed for doing something that they did not know could be harmful. Parents must not judge themselves harshly for doing things that are widely done by others without apparent harm. Reading Chapter Ten on "Cause and Cure" can help parents understand the science about ASD and help them to stop feeling guilty, blamed or blaming.

Blame and self-blame are not only a waste of precious mental energy, it can be harmful and destructive. Parents who blame themselves are less capable of doing what their child needs. They may be less able to learn and accomplish what they want to do. Neither should parents be judged or blamed by others. Professionals who blame families or family members are less likely to be objective enough to provide help to the family.

Emily says that since Tom was born, she has thought long and hard about what "she did" to cause Tom to have autism. This is perfectly natural to do. Over time, she spent less time thinking about that (although she still wonders) and more time thinking about what could be done to help Tom. At a certain point, it makes no sense to continue to look for someone or something to blame.

As research in genetics progresses, we may find that some of us carry a genetic marker for autism. We may have passed that on to one or more of our children. However, we cannot blame ourselves for that either, just as a parent cannot be "blamed" for the child's hair color or height. A father of a child with ASD recognized in himself many of the characteristics of his son with autism. He said, "Oh my God, I did this to him!" He was very sad and had to work with a counselor to free himself from this unjustified blame. The truth is that most parents wish they could pass on only their best traits to their children. But no one can control genetic material or physiological development to determine whom a child becomes.

If, as a parent, you continue to blame yourself or someone else for your child's disability, you may wish to seek counseling for yourself. As a parent of a child with special needs, you only have so much energy. It is important to channel your efforts into the most productive areas you can. You need to protect and preserve your own mental health to be able to take care of yourself and your family. A good counselor may help you find positive direction.

Find Others Who Can Help You Make a Plan

Parents are usually not experts on disabilities, special education, or adult services, unless they happen to be working in those fields. (Barbara can attest to the fact that when it is a person in your own family, even being a professional in the field is not always enough!) It is very natural that parents and staff will need guidance and help to find out what they need to do. While autism may be brand new to you, many people with knowledge and experience can provide support and guidance.

Know that you are not alone. Every school district has a Special Education department. Personnel can guide you through the process of designing a program to meet the needs of the student. Every county has adult services agencies that provide supports and services to adults with disabilities. Personnel can help you find out what services the person is eligible for and how to get them. They may be able to help with filling out any required paperwork and link you to community resources.

Communities may have a variety of organizations and resources available. Support groups are a wonderful resource that brings local parents, staff and families together to share information and lend emotional support. Many local and national organizations are dedicated to helping families. One way to get started is to find out whom to call, and make that first phone call. If you live in a small community with limited resources, or in a big city, the internet is also a wonderful place to connect with others and find the information and support you need.   There are resource lists at the end of this chapter and at the end of the book.

Use Compassionate and Accurate Terminology, and Ask Others To Do So

Person-first language is a new concept to many people who are not familiar with disability issues. However, it is a central issue for people with disabilities. In fact, a section in the federal disability law encourages the use of person-first language. People with disabilities are people, first and foremost. Their disability is only one aspect of who they are. It is important to use language that is respectful and accurate.

People are not "autistics." They are people with autism. We do not call people "retards" or "spastics" anymore and are horrified at the thought. Yet that was common terminology in the past. Somehow, referring to people as "autistics" lingers on. Could it be because many people with autism cannot speak up for themselves to ask to be referred to with more respect and compassion? Parents and staff can model the use of respectful language and consider asking others to do the same.

In this book we have intentionally avoided describing people as "autistic." We use phrases such as "person with autism," "child with autism," or "adult with autism." We consider this a small, but important, way to focus on people and emphasize the fact that ASD is one significant part of who a person is, but not their entire being.

Many people describe the behaviors of people with autism with judgmental language. Simply changing the term used to describe the event can lead to more compassionate thinking and more appropriate interventions. For example, when a person with ASD has an extreme, emotional episode, some people call it a "tantrum." The word "tantrum" implies a naughty, self-centered child who just wants to "get his own way." In response to a "tantrum," staff or family members may be encouraged to ignore the episode or even punish it. When people who do not have ASD or other disabilities have an emotional crisis, it is rarely called a tantrum if the person is more than 2 or 3 years old. Taking away the judgment and negativity of the words we use is the first step to help discover the cause of the distress, comfort the person and make accommodations to teach and help them.

Get Organized

Keep a diary or notebook about your activities on behalf of your family member with ASD. There is just too much information to keep it all in your head! If you have one notebook or binder in which to write names, dates, phone numbers and other information, you will be better organized. Retrieving information later will be much easier.

It is a good idea to take notes when speaking to educational or service providers, whether in person or on the telephone. Write down the name, title and phone number of the person you talked to. If you are not sure of something, ask them to repeat it for you. Include the time and date, what you requested or discussed and the response given to you. You may need to refer to these notes later to support your efforts to get, change or improve service delivery.

You will also need to organize all the records and paperwork that is generated in the process of diagnosis and after. Many people use a large 3-ring binder and keep records by subject. Other people like to use an accordion folder and file by subject. If you have just gone through the process of diagnosis, you will have many papers to file already. Some headings may be:

Assessments	Child's History	Diagnosis	Local Programs
Medical	Notes	Parent Rights	Psychologist
Resources	School District	Speech/Language	Support people
Test Results			

Some parents and staff prefer to use a chronological system, filing papers in the order that they were received and notes in the order in which events occurred. Getting organized from the start keeps you from having to sort through a daunting pile of paperwork and keeps you from losing time looking for things. Find a method that works for you, and get started being organized! It is never too early or late.

Be a Cautious Consumer

Claims of "cures" for Autism Spectrum Disorders come around every few years. Sometimes, people claim cures after working with only a very small group of people. Parents and others interested in ASD are now a "targeted market," and there are some people taking advantage of parents' natural desire to take the burden of ASD away from their children. To make money, some people are willing to use untested, experimental products and procedures with your child or adult with ASD.

There are good methods and techniques that can help people with ASD learn, improve and have good lives. None of them will make the person "normal." There is no research to show that the use of a particular drug, technique, teaching method or behavioral program "cures" everyone with autism. It is wise to be skeptical about "miracles" and "cures."

"First, do no harm" should apply to any considered technique, product or service for the child or adult with ASD. Parents, guardians and responsible staff need to consider ALL possible outcomes before they agree to any service or product. If there is any risk, parents need to consider carefully. Parents will see the outcome of their decisions for years after the decision is made. They will have to live with the outcome long after others have forgotten about it.

It is important for parents and staff to keep balance and not become zealots or extremists about any intervention or promised "cure." Open dialogue and discussion with people with opposing views may help in getting a well-rounded perspective when considering options and interventions. Decisions should be made carefully. Families and teams should do what works for them and change their minds and methods as needed.

Avoid Fanatic People.

People who believe that there is only "one way" of thinking about ASD may have stopped learning, growing and changing. They may feel the need to try to "convert" others to the point of view they prefer. It can be exhausting and time consuming. Seek others who are open, willing to share and willing to learn. Research in the field of ASD is very important. As a parent, you will need to know the criteria to separate "valid" research from "faulty" research and arguments.

Put Time and Energy Into Developing Positive Relationships With The Professionals and Staff Who Will Be Working With You, Your Child or Adult, and Your Family

People who choose careers in education, special education and related services are obviously not in these fields for the money and the glory! Teachers, special educators, and staff are most often people who want to help others. Each of them sets out in their career with the goal of doing something good and making a difference. They deserve to be valued and respected. They bring experience and perspective to their work, and can be very helpful to you and your family.

Emotion is often an obstacle that interferes in establishing relationships with personnel. While it is natural for parents to be emotional about the child or adult they love, sometimes strong emotions get in the way. When trying to develop a service or education plan with others, it is important to focus on the fact that everyone's priority is the person who needs help. Anything to help strengthen relationships is in the best interest of that person. Divisiveness and negativity undermine the process. The solution for everyone involved is separating feelings from objective facts. While parents, teachers, administrators and service providers will not always agree, keeping your cool and focusing on facts can help everyone be more productive.

Sometimes parents report that they are frustrated when teachers and staff do not know enough about ASD. While parents are learning what they need to know and have ideas in mind about services and supports, sometimes personnel do not appear to understand. Keep in mind that many people teaching or working in schools today may have had very little education about autism and ASD. Even today's college graduates in education may have as little as sixty minutes of discussion about autism during a two-year teacher's program. The "information gap" that exists within families also exists in the schools and the community.

While frustration over this situation is understandable, it is counter-productive to be angry about it. Instead, parents can share information and encourage teachers and staff to attend training and seminars with them. Parents and staff together can highlight the need for more information and encourage their school districts or service agencies to provide learning opportunities.

There is a saying that you can attract more flies with honey than with vinegar. Sometimes staff and service personnel have a negative attitude about emotionally extreme parents who are "angry" and "aggressive." Staff may knowingly or unwittingly resist such a parent. Parents do not have to take "no" for an answer and can be pleasant while getting what the child needs! Staff often have a great deal of respect for parents who are informed and persistent, but calm. Remember that everyone has a right to be spoken to with courtesy.

Ask for Help

Sometimes living or working with people with ASD can be overwhelming or throw life out of balance. Parents and staff need to recognize when help is needed, and ask for it. It is not likely that someone will just offer to help solve your problems if they do not know what is going on. Parents and staff must often seek out and ask for help.

A first step is to identify the need, or a specific problem that you are having. If you can, identify what kind of service might help you. Then find out whom to ask, and ask for help.

If the person you ask cannot help you, ask them to refer you to someone who can. If you are told that there is no help for your problem, ask to speak to a supervisor, director or another person who is in charge of the whole service delivery system. Talk to other families and ask them how they got the help they needed and how you can do the same.

Here are examples of times when help is needed:

- Any member of the family or staff is often angry, depressed, agitated or aggressive.

- Communication between family members or staff is ineffective or reduced.

- Mental or physical health problems seem to be occurring, because someone in the household is under too much stress.

- Siblings of the person with ASD are angry, often away from home, have failing grades or changes in personality or attitude.

- There is not enough money or resources to meet the needs of all family members or all consumers of the agency.

- The presence of, or behavior of, the person with autism interferes with the needs of others in the family or household or restricts the family's opportunities.

- One person is usually solely responsible for the person with autism.

- Some aspect of the family situation is critical and dominating daily life.

Getting a Diagnosis as an Adult

Some people do not get a diagnosis of an Autism Spectrum Disorder until adulthood. In fact, many adults are now recognizing the signs of ASD that have always been present in themselves and seeking a professional opinion. Many parents recognize characteristics of ASD in themselves when their children go through the process of assessment and diagnosis. Other adults are learning about ASD and considering whether the information applies to them, describes them, or explains a lot about them, now and in the past. In other cases, adults become aware of the possibility when loved ones, friends or staff bring it up, or they watch a television show or read an article about autism or Aspergers syndrome. All of these scenarios are more common due to increasing publicity about the spectrum of ASD and the range of effects. This awareness about ASD may help academic, mental health and developmental programs identify people with ASD more efficiently and earlier.

How an Adult May React to Getting a Diagnosis

There is a wide range of reactions for adults who learn that they have ASD. The feelings of grieving and coming to accept it may be similar to what parents experience with a personal intensity. Some of the most immediate issues are often denial, blame, stress, anxiety, anger and regret. Three of the most positive long-term outcomes are often pride, gratitude and determination. Here are some thoughts on these topics that some adults with autism have shared.

Denial

No one wants to think that something is "wrong" with him. It is hard for anyone to accept the news that he has ASD. When a doctor, a family member, or staff bring it up, it can be a big shock. Some people have their feelings hurt by the suggestion. It is very hard to believe it is true. Then it takes time to understand and admit that it is true.

In other cases, adults think that something could be "wrong." They may wonder why some things have always been so hard for them. They may think of problems that have continued for years and wonder, "what is going on?" It may take some time before a person is ready to talk about it, figure out what is going on and get help.

Blame

Some people have gone through life blaming others for problems they have experienced. They may blame their parents for doing what appeared to be a poor job of raising them. They may blame their teachers for not knowing and recognizing a lifelong need. They may blame themselves and feel inadequate, stupid or anti-social. These feelings of blame can be viewed as a natural part of reacting to important information about oneself. In most cases, feelings of blame diminish when the individual begins to understand the diagnosis and gets to work learning and teaching others.

Stress and Anxiety

Some adults feel very stressed when they find out that they have ASD. They worry if they will be OK. They might worry that they are not OK. Adults are concerned about how ASD affects their personal life, career success and their future. When people first find out, they may worry whether things can turn out well.

Some adults worry that others will judge them or think less of them. They worry about how they are "different." Some adults feel that the diagnosis singles them out and are concerned that they will treated differently if other people find out about it.

Some adults feel overwhelmed by being in charge of the information about the diagnosis. It can feel like a big responsibility to make decisions about getting help. They want to know that other people can help them find out what to do.

Anger and Regret

Many adults feel very angry when they find out they have ASD. Sometimes, they blame other people, either for the fact that they have it, or for the fact that it took so long to find out about it. The person with ASD may have struggled all their lives, but no one else knew what was wrong or did anything about it. This can cause feelings of regret, because so much time was lost or wasted before the person's needs were recognized.

Pride

Some people feel proud of themselves after a diagnosis. They take pride in the fact that they have been doing so well in spite of not knowing. Having a disability can be like an obstacle, and overcoming it can make a person realize how much he has going for him.

Getting a diagnosis can help a person feel more aware of what is hard for her and what is easy. Then she can ask for help when she needs it; this is called **self-advocacy**. Learning about the features of ASD can help individuals make positive changes that can result in better relationships, lifestyle and productivity.

Gratitude

Some people who get a diagnosis feel thankful to others who have helped them over the years. Many parents did as much as they could for their child without ever knowing or asking, "Why?" Some friends, neighbors and teachers helped by instinct. People who reach adulthood before they are diagnosed probably had a good support network of caring people to help them get so far. That is something to appreciate.

Determination

Some people feel a sense of determination. They decide that they want to make a success of their lives in spite of their difficulties. They feel certain that they can overcome obstacles. They want to use their talents to make up for their difficulties. They understand that a disability is only one part of who a person is — not the whole person.

Some adults find that they have the opportunity and ability to help others. Many families with young children with ASD wonder what life is like for adults with ASD. Parents wonder what the future may bring. Adults with ASD can tell about their experiences and feelings. They can describe what they experienced growing up and what would have helped them. This helps everyone understand better.

Some adults with ASD have written books to share their stories and experiences. Temple Grandin, John-Paul Bovee, Donna Williams and Jerry Newport are some well-known authors and speakers. Other adults with autism have written magazine articles, been on television, given lectures or have their own websites. Many adults with ASD are glad to know that they are not alone or the only one with ASD. Other adults find support groups very helpful. In a support group, you can meet other adults who live in your area who also have ASD. Using the internet is another way to connect with others and get support and information from people all around the world.

Need for Support

Understanding and support are essential to help an individual who is diagnosed in adulthood. Psychological counseling can be invaluable. Educational materials are important for these individuals, their spouses, families, teachers and employers.

Together, the individual and the people in his life can find support services specific to the needs of adults.

Getting a Diagnosis as a Teen

Typical teenagers struggle with issues like being caught between the world of the child and the adult, struggling with independence and individual identity, fitting in and belonging. Life for teenagers is often full of uncertainty and emotion. Teens tell us that it is a heavy blow to get a diagnosis at this time of life. Some reactions of teenagers may be child-like; some are similar to what adults experience, and other reactions may be unique to those living through the teenage experience.

Teens, family, or staff report that teens diagnosed in their teen aged years with ASD often:

- Become more aware of their own strengths and areas of need.

- Feel frustrated in the attempts to be socially successful.

- Find out they are "different" when blending-in is prized.

- Feel stressed or anxious by the teen social scene.

- Worry that others will judge or will reject them if they know about the diagnosis.

- Suffer when treated cruelly by others.

- Feel pressure to do well academically, but feel limited in their ability to keep up.

- Worry about the future.

- Feel isolated.

- May blame or feel distrustful of adults.

- Want a girlfriend or boyfriend, but do not understand relationships.

- Are confused by emerging sexuality, sexual identity and sexual urges.

- Feel sad and depressed about their situation.

- Cannot conceive of a happy future for themselves.

The reactions of each teen will differ based on their age, their ability to understand what ASD is and how they are personally affected. Their self-esteem, self-concept, and level of awareness are also factors to consider. The way a teenager is told, the information that is shared and the words that are used are very important. For that reason, the idea of "telling" the teen and anticipating the possible reactions is discussed in detail in Chapter Nine.

The Reactions of Children to Being Told About Their Diagnosis

When children are told about their disability, there are many possible reactions. The reactions of each child will differ, based on their age, their ability to understand and their self-esteem and self-concept. The way a child is told, the information that is shared and the words that are used are very important. For that reason, the idea of "telling" the child and anticipating the possible reactions is discussed in detail in Chapter Nine.

Other Family Members and Siblings

Like parents, family members may need time to accept the fact that the child or adult has ASD. At first, brothers and sisters, grandparents, aunts, uncles and other relatives may experience denial or unwillingness to look at the facts. Denial may be based on the fact that relatives may have misconceptions and may need to know more about ASD. One little girl, the sister of a boy with autism, said, "Mom, you expect me to understand the way you do. But I'm just a kid."

Sometimes conflict arises when some family members do not "believe" that the diagnosis is correct or do not believe that the family member really has a disability. They may continue to blame the parents for the child's problems. Siblings and other family members may feel guilt or shame, be overwhelmed or feel left out of the process entirely. The family dynamic can be thrown out of balance for quite some time until all family members begin to learn about and understand the situation.

This situation has an impact on grandparents as well as other relatives. Some grandparents are sensitive to the fact that both the child they love, and the grandchild they love, may be struggling to face and live with ASD This may intensify their own reaction. There are now support groups for grandparents with grandchildren with ASD which is a great step forward.

Step-parents may find themselves caught in a balancing act learning to understand and meet the needs of the child with a disability. In cases of shared custody, various people may care for the child in more than one place. Step-parents may walk a fine line between what needs to be done and the many people who need to be involved in decision-making. Parents and step-parents of various marriages and partnerships are suddenly a team, having to get information, make decisions and provide consistent care to the child.

Step-parents who are responsible for the day-to-day care of the child often feel that the biological parents question their role and authority. Step-parents may love the child with ASD like their own and feel frustrated when their authority or "connection" is challenged, openly or in a subtle way. Other step-parents may feel pressured by the responsibility of having to care for a child with disabilities who is not really "theirs."

The Reaction of Teachers When a Student is Diagnosed

It may be a shock for a general education teacher to find out that a student with ASD will be joining the class or is already there. Preconceived notions, and a lack of experience or training, can affect teachers as it does family members, leaving them feeling unprepared and worried. If a student with ASD is to be included in the class, as more and more will be doing in the years to come, it is normal for a teacher to wonder if he can cope. Autism and ASD can be "labels" that make people afraid!

To make the experience successful for everyone involved, teachers will have to advocate for themselves! Teachers are entitled to help and support. Learning what you need to know includes finding out how to help the child with ASD communicate, socialize and behave appropriately.

Teachers will collaborate with the many specialists who provide services to the student. These same specialists can provide support to teachers by sharing information and strategies. Classroom teachers can learn a tremendous amount by contacting and meeting with the teachers and staff who have worked with the student in previous years. Teachers can ask to attend training at the expense of the district. Parents of the child can be an excellent source of information and support, as they want the experience to be as successful and beneficial as possible, not just for their child, but for everyone involved.

Sometimes teachers and staff "resist" the diagnosis as if it is an "excuse" for poor self-discipline and/or poor parenting. In other cases, staff may be concerned that too many people are being frivolously diagnosed with ASD, and it is the "disease of the week." A backlash is to be expected, especially with the rise in incidence and diagnosis of ASD that is being reported in all parts of the United States and the world. As much a part of human nature as they are, neither of these attitudes is a legitimate reason to refuse to look at the facts. Teachers and staff may need more information and a more complete understanding of ASD to be comfortable with the diagnosis, get over initial reactions of denial, guilt or blame and move into understanding and positive action.

If a teacher does not "believe" that a student with a diagnosis of ASD is correctly diagnosed, she can ask to meet with or talk on the phone with the diagnostician. (She may need the parent's permission to do this if the diagnostician is not a school employee.) There are so many myths in our culture about what ASD is or isn't! It can be very helpful to openly state your ideas to a person with specialized knowledge in this area and listen carefully to the response. Teachers and diagnosticians can work together and help one another understand and provide appropriate support. We ask teachers to **ask** until you understand and are ready to take positive action. We ask teachers not to wonder and wait! Teachers are entitled to all the information they need to do what they dedicate their lives to do: effectively teach **all** of the students in their classes.

CHAPTER 7 SUMMARY

- Parents and family members experience a variety of reactions and emotions when a loved one is diagnosed with ASD. The first reactions are often shock and disbelief.

- The range of emotions in reacting to a diagnosis can be similar to responses to any of life's emotional traumas. This is called the **grieving process** or the **coping process**.

- The stages of grieving are identified as denial, disbelief, helplessness, guilt, blame, anger, and finally, acceptance. The feelings may be felt in any "order," all at once, time and again.

- An individual's style and personality, the amount of information the person has, their rate of working through difficult situations, along with the other issues and realities of life, will affect how someone reacts to and copes with the diagnosis.

- Even when the diagnosis is no longer "brand new," parents and other family members continue to have mixed feelings and reactions for some time or stages of emotion that peak and subside. It is important to give yourself time to cope. You are doing the best you can.

- Do not be afraid to seek guidance from a professional to help with the process.

- After experiencing the feelings of denial, anger, blame, shame, fear and sadness, beginning to understand and accept can be an emotional turning point.

- Coming to terms with the diagnosis can be very powerful. Positive outcomes can include a sense of relief to finally understand the child and identify his needs, a sense of hope and direction and validation of a parent's insight and persistence. An official diagnosis may make the person eligible for special education and other services.

- Parents can focus and move forward with the plan for their loved ones with autism by dreaming and planning, learning, throwing out blame, finding others who can become a guide, using "person-first" language and accurate terms, getting organized, being a cautious consumer and avoiding fanatic people.

- Parents and professionals who will be working together benefit from putting time and energy into developing positive relationships, acknowledging what they don't know and asking for help when needed.

- There is a wide range of reactions for adults who learn that they have ASD, including intense feelings of grieving, coping and coming to accept it. Some of the most immediate issues may be denial, blame, stress and anxiety and anger and regret. Three positive long-term outcomes are often pride, gratitude and determination.

- Teens may find it a heavy emotional blow to get a diagnosis in that phase of life. Understanding, support and psychological counseling can be invaluable.

- Like parents, other family members such as grandparents, step-parents and siblings need time to accept the fact that the child or adult has ASD. The family dynamic can be thrown out of balance while family members learn, understand and work through emotions.

- The reactions of children finding out about ASD will differ, based on their age, their ability to understand and their self-esteem and self-concept. The way a child is told, the information that is shared and the words that are used are very important.

- Professionals and staff may gain valuable insight and perspective by reading about the family's process of understanding and believing a diagnosis.

- It may be a shock for a general education teacher to find out that a student with ASD will be joining the class or is already there. Preconceived ideas, myths about ASD and a lack of experience with children with ASD may cause teachers to feel unprepared and worried. Teachers will have to advocate for themselves to get the information and support they need to succeed with all of the students in their classes.

CHAPTER 8

"To the world you might be one person, but to one person you might be the world."

Unknown

SUPPORTING THE FAMILY OF A PERSON WITH ASD

In this chapter you will learn:

- How to recognize the emotional needs of parents, siblings and other family members.

- Services and supports to help families cope.

- The need for supports in all environments and across the lifespan.

- Practical steps to prepare for the future.

- How educators and support professionals can help families.

- Training and education for staff and parents.

- Why parents and staff need to become politically savvy.

Emotional Issues and Needs

Having a child with autism affects the entire family, whether it is a traditional or a non-traditional family. All families have various issues and difficulties. Families with a person with autism can have added levels of stress, anxiety and problems. The relationships between partners, parents-to-children and sibling-to-sibling can be seriously out of balance due to the difficulties in living with, and meeting the needs of, the person with autism. The process of getting a diagnosis, understanding the diagnosis and getting appropriate supports and services can be especially traumatic. Families face practical, behavioral and emotional problems that can leave them feeling in crisis much of the time.

Many families try to handle the needs of the person with ASD all on their own. In some cultures, parents are encouraged to hide the child with disabilities, or to pretend like nothing is wrong. In some cultures, parents are blamed for the problems of the child. Sometimes a single caregiver (often the mother) is expected to handle or is left with the sole responsibility for the complete care, training, supervision and support of the child with disabilities. In such cases, it is likely that the child with disabilities, the mother and the entire family will struggle or suffer.

It is in the best interest of everyone involved to do what it takes to keep families together and help families cope while assisting the family member with ASD. Families of persons with ASD need support in order to be able to function in a healthy and successful way. This section describes the types of problems many families face and the supports that are essential to help them. Not every family would need every service, but it is important to know what some of the possibilities are and to seek out what the family needs.

Parents or Partners

Some of the intense and unexpected feelings that parents may have when they have a child with ASD or any disability can get in way of daily functioning. This can hinder the parents' ability to cope. The personal suffering and strain on relationships that can result is immeasurable. Parents may need access to psychological counseling to work out these feelings. They may need help to recognize their own capabilities, find hope and feel empowered to act.

Marriage counseling is often needed. The rate of failed marriages is higher when a family member has a disability such as ASD. When a person with a disability is part of the family, issues in the marriage that may not have been a problem before may come up. This is not because of the person with a disability. It is because living with the disability creates demands and a need to make choices that neither parent expected.

Both parents have to make many decisions that they may not feel qualified to make. In sorting through information and services, parents are suddenly required to communicate effectively about topics that are unfamiliar and emotionally charged. If small problems in the marriage were masked in day-to-day life, these problems will surface when parents have to cope, learn, decide and interact quickly on behalf of their child.

Problems can arise between partners when one parent "believes" that the individual has this disability and the other partner does not. If one parent does not understand or believe that ASD is the cause of the child's difficulties, he may think that his partner is looking for excuses. One partner may blame the other for the problems. They may think that problems are really due to lack of discipline; the result of something the other partner did or inherited from the other side of the family. Neither partner may know that he or she harbors such blame deep inside.

Couples need to be on common ground and stand united in their support for one another. They need to get together in their understanding of ASD, their approach to the family member with autism and the rest of the family. Most families will not be able to manage all of this without support and counseling. When these services are not offered or used to the family's advantage, the marriage and the family can disintegrate each day bit-by-bit.

A Case Example from Emily

(I have permission from the people involved to share this story and I have changed the names and other identifying facts.)

A couple, Dan and Lori, were going through the process of diagnosis for both of their sons, ages 7 and 13. They had been struggling with the symptoms and behaviors for years, and as for most people in this situation, it had been a strain on the marriage and the family. Lori began to reach out for information, direction and support and was making progress. She relayed information to Dan on a regular basis, telling him about the newest thing she had learned, a person she had met or a service or therapy that might help one or both of their sons. Lori was very excited to find a local support group, because she needed it and was ready to go! She asked Dan to come with her, and although he was somewhat reluctant, he began to attend the group regularly with Lori.

At one meeting, each member was invited to talk about whatever was on his mind, and the others would actively listen. When it was Dan's turn, he said that foremost on his mind was how hard Lori was working to help their boys and their family and how much it meant to him. He was worried that she had so much responsibility. He wanted her to know he appreciated all her efforts and knew that she was keeping their family glued together.

Those of us listening were reminded of how meaningful and important it is to express our appreciation to our partners. Lori was very happy when Dan said he appreciated her and says this knowledge helps her keep going. She realized when he expressed his concern that he wanted to help, and that she could suggest ways he could share more of the work.

In spite of the challenges they were dealing with and the exhausted state they often found themselves in, Dan and Lori did many things well. They were learning together, they were both willing to do their part and they made a real effort to keep communication open. Together they reached out and asked for support from people who cared and knew how to help. These may be difficult challenges for a couple, but may make a real difference to help the marriage or partnership strengthen and keep the family together.

Siblings

Brothers and sisters of the person with ASD face their own emotional issues. Beyond typical sibling disagreements, brothers and sisters of a person with ASD may have other problems. These can include feeling angry or jealous that the person with ASD is the center of attention and the focus of parents' energies. Other children in the family may feel resentful that the person with the disability has his needs considered first. Siblings may feel that discipline in the home is not fair, and that the parents favor the child with ASD.

Brothers and sisters may resist making accommodations for the person with autism. They may not understand or believe that the behaviors and problems at home are related to the disability. They may think that the child with autism has control over his behavior and could change if he wanted to. They may observe the variability in day-to-day performance that is characteristic of people with ASD and believe that their brother or sister is "using" the disability.

Siblings may be disappointed, sad, embarrassed or humiliated when their sibling is not like other kids' brothers or sisters. They may wish the sibling was like everyone else. They may worry that others think that they are also disabled. Kids sometimes have misconceptions, such as they might get ASD too. They may not have enough information to understand the disability. They may not have words to explain their brother or sister to others in a way they all can understand. They may suffer ridicule because of their sibling and be told by their parents not to complain, but to be glad that they are "all right."

Siblings may feel guilty that they are all right and the sister or brother is not. They may experience a sense of loss because they don't have a "big brother" or "little sister" relationship like others they see. They may be disappointed or hurt when their sibling with autism does not have a close relationship with them.

Brothers and sisters of children with Autism Spectrum Disorders may be teased or bullied because their sibling is "different." At the same time, brothers and sisters may have a strong desire to protect and defend their sibling. They may feel defeated or ashamed if they are not able to do so.

Siblings may be truly distressed or victimized by the actions of the person with ASD and feel there is no remedy and no one to whom they can turn. Brothers and sisters need to feel safe and be protected from harm. While siblings need to have tolerance, there should be a limit to what they are required to tolerate. **No child should have to endure hitting or other physical violence from their sibling with ASD or have their property destroyed.** Physically harmful behavior is not the only behavior that affects siblings. One child who felt traumatized told his parents, "I can't be patient and accepting when she is so annoying!"

The effects on siblings must be considered in dealing with the behaviors of the family member with ASD. Brothers and sisters are often told to "accept" and "help" their brother or sister. This expectation may cause a non-disabled sibling to become the "good child." The "good child" tries to reestablish balance in the family by never being any trouble at all. The good child may repress her own needs and feelings in order to save the parents from any more pain or burden. This harmony comes at a very high cost to that child.

Some children will act out to get attention — becoming the "bad child." Parents need to be aware if one or more of the children is reacting in those ways and seek help in understanding and supporting that child.

In the long run, siblings may be the best source of lifelong support for the child with autism. Over time, siblings have a level of understanding, compassion and experience that cannot be duplicated. Brothers and sisters make many wonderful contributions to the well being of their family member with ASD, the whole family and the community.

Many siblings want to share in the responsibility for their brother or sister with ASD. Siblings tell us, however, that *it is important for parents not to "expect" it or require it of them*. Siblings need to grow up being comforted and taken care of like any child. They need to have their own needs met without being burdened with responsibility too early in life. Siblings should not be expected to act as a "second mother" or another "parent" of their brother or sister.

Be sure that siblings know that they will not have to be responsible for their brother or sister with ASD when parents die or become disabled. An eleven-year-old girl who had a brother with autism said that she could not get married when she grew up. When questioned about it she said, "What boy is going to want me and my brother?" Whether or not the parents had told her that she was responsible for her brother, the child believed that it was true. It is important to find out what siblings are thinking and "free" them to be children, with plans for their own independent futures.

Parents can help the children in the family to understand and cope with living with a family member with ASD. It is important for children to know that they can talk freely with their parents, even about "negative" feelings. Siblings need to know that their problems are real and that they are listened to. It helps if brothers and sisters know that they can ask questions either to parents or other trusted adults. Sharing thoughts and information helps families recognize and include the needs of all the family members. More information should be shared over time as the siblings get older and are better able to understand. Usually it is best to share information and feelings when the child or adult sibling with ASD is not present, even if she does not appear to understand what is being shared.

Siblings of people with ASD can benefit greatly from individual or family counseling. Family counseling is a forum to identify the specific problems that have upset the family balance and come up with practical and effective ways to help resolve them. Individual counseling helps each sibling recognize and understand the emotional issues that effect them and deal with them. Counseling is available in most communities through schools or community mental health centers. Services are usually available at no cost, low cost or on a sliding fee scale.

A Personal Example from Emily

Meeting the special needs of one (or more) children, while keeping the rest of the family intact and healthy, is a daily struggle requiring continuous effort. At two particularly difficult times, our family life was seriously out-of-balance and we asked for help. Both times we were eligible and received family therapy.

In one session, each of us was asked to draw a picture of our role in the family and explain what it meant. I drew a picture of myself as the person who spins plates on long, thin rods at the circus. I felt my job was to constantly make sure each person in the family was "OK." I put so much time into meeting the needs of each child and my husband (keeping the plates spinning so none would "crash") that I was left feeling exhausted! I had never really described my perspective until I was asked to. The therapist was able to help each family member recognize the situation and decide what to do about it. I felt encouraged to speak up for myself, ask for help and tell everyone when I was at my limit! It was gratifying to see how each member of my family came to my aide and began to step in and provide support — each in an individual way.

I tell this story to many other plate-spinning parents that I meet and we have an empathic laugh. Behind the smile is the knowing look about the fact that parents are subject to huge demands and responsibility. Sometimes we are better able to handle it than other times. Sometimes we need help to carry on.

The second time we had therapy, the sessions focused on sibling relationships. The conflicts were more complex and upsetting than "typical" issues brothers and sisters experience. Each week, over several months, we had in-home sessions that lasted for hours. Our therapist, who was a behaviorist, in effect "held a mirror up to us" that helped us understand the issues of what we were doing and why. Each one of us had a "breakthrough" of some kind and "thought some new thoughts." This was followed by learning new ways of doing things that restored balance and promoted harmony.

Thank goodness for both of these therapies and therapists. I had to do research to learn that such things as family therapy existed and then find out how to apply. We had to be evaluated to see if our need was "great enough." Next, we had to wait several months for a therapist to be available. Of course, the progress in therapy was gradual and took months, not days. But I shudder to think where we would be without it and am grateful to the professionals who helped us to accept, understand and value one another and do what we can to keep our family strong.

Other Family Members

Aunts, uncles, cousins and grandparents (extended family) may have concerns and needs that should be considered. Sometimes extended families do not recognize that help is needed. Their opinions may be outdated. In their years of experience they may have seen people with disabilities "improve" from methods that are no longer considered appropriate or state-of-the-art. They may be skeptical, critical, judgmental or angry and need help to come to terms with the diagnosis and be supportive of the family.

Sometimes grandparents see that there is an issue for a child in the family, but are in the awkward position of not being able to convince their son or daughter of the need for action. They may not know how to help their son or daughter. Involved extended family members may know other children and adults with ASD and want to talk to the parents about this, but are afraid to do so.

Government will never be able to afford to pay for every service needed by every individual with autism. Extended family can provide lifelong support to people with autism. Extended family members are often willing to help and remain in the life of the person with the disability but do not know how to help. These important people are likely to benefit from being involved and professional support and information.

Services and Support to Help Families Cope

Support Groups

Parents, siblings and extended family can benefit greatly from support groups. Many families feel isolated when they have a family member with autism. Support groups provide a tremendous service. Families can share both their problems and their solutions with other families with similar circumstances who can understand in a way that no others can. People who attend support groups usually feel a great sense of relief to find that they are not alone and that others care and know "what it is like." Many fathers or mothers have never forgotten the first support group meeting they attended and the positive impact it had on them.

A support group offers the opportunity to network. Participants get to know other families with children or adults with ASD. This presents opportunities to socialize and make new friends who understand your issues. Families can plan fun outings and activities that can include the individuals with ASD.

Support groups often focus on sharing practical information, usually with people who live in the same area.　Group members discuss the services they receive and service providers who have been responsive. Families are often anxious to find doctors, dentists and other medical providers who work well with people with ASD. Parents share experiences about school districts, educational and adult services. Participants describe what the child or family needs, and support group members may be able to suggest useful ideas and local resources.

Extended family members and concerned friends can and should attend the support group that the parents attend, or another one if that is more appropriate. Often, extended family can provide tremendous help to families, but do not know how. In a support group, members can share effective ways to provide help and benefit everyone.

Many support groups are organized and run by parents. Sometimes schools and/or agencies provide a time and place, invitations and a coordinator. That may be all that is needed for families to find great comfort and support. Some organizations that advocate for individuals with ASD and their families offer support groups or can recommend one in your area.

Every day, more and more families will get a diagnosis of autism for some family member. Community support can make the situation more bearable. Information can be shared to help people become more aware of what they can do to help themselves and their children of any age.

A Note from Emily

I am very active in my support group and have met parents of children with ASD of all ages and on all parts of the "spectrum." I have attended support group meetings for years and feel it is worthwhile every time. The "group" consists of whomever of our 100 or so members can make it to a meeting at a regularly scheduled time and place. Group composition varies from month to month. We try to accommodate peoples' work schedules and childcare needs by having more than one meeting per month, including one where children are welcome. We encourage couples to attend our evening meetings together. All groups are different, but our group emphasizes letting everyone say what is on his or her mind, being good listeners and "rallying round" with support.

Sometimes we talk about why our support group means so much to us. There is a tremendous sense of relief to be with other people who share common elements of our experience. When someone who needs us, finds us, we are happy for them. They are so relieved to meet people who understand them without the need for extensive explanations. Some people say that their friends at our support group understand and accept them and their children with autism better than their own family members do. Keeping our conversations confidential contributes to the feeling of comfort and trust.

Feeling like you are in the right place with "safe" people usually leads to the next step: unburdening yourself. We don't plan it, but it happens that most people have a good cry the first time they come to our group, and we have the tissues handy. It can be a heartbreaking cry full of emotion, and sometimes that is all the person can do at their first meeting. Most of the time, the person wants, needs and somehow manages to tell their story to empathetic listeners. While we comfort the new person, each of us remembers what it felt like when we were the new person, talking for the first time about our child's diagnosis and just starting out in our journey with ASD.

Another benefit of being in a support group is getting a "roadmap." People who are just learning about their child's diagnosis need guidance and direction to find out what it means, what to do and where to get help. Our group values sharing information and resources to help one another. This is important for newly diagnosed families as well as for families facing new challenges and stages of life as our children grow up or go through a "rocky patch."

Each person brings their experience and expertise to the group, and we are our own "network." Some of us took classes from a lawyer and understand educational law.

Others know a lot about services and local providers—the good and the not so good. Some know about early intervention and preschool services, while someone else may know a lot about transition services or adult living. A few people follow current events, legislation, and other issues and keep us informed. Our collective knowledge is considerable, and we share it in a newsletter and website.

We can't solve everyone's problems, but we can have productive conversations to suggest strategies, ideas and resources. For those with suggestions, it feels good to be helpful and know that sharing your experience or advice might make someone else's life easier or better! Those being supported are often overwhelmed in a good way with the possibilities and perspectives of people who have "been there" and "done that" and care enough to help. People seem to "take turns" offering support at one meeting and needing it at another. We take time to share success stories that are inspiring and often keep us all going.

Fellowship is another benefit of our support group. Many support group members have established friendships and get together socially at other times and places. Many families do babysitting exchanges and playgroups for the children with ASD and for siblings. We have whole-group events and parties where things that might upset "outsiders" don't concern us. Younger and older children get to know each other better. Siblings meet other "typical kids" who share the experience of having a brother or sister with special needs. In addition, all these things create opportunities to help our children get to know and feel more comfortable with families who might be called upon to step in an emergency.

Getting to know the children of support group members has been a real pleasure. We have clapped and cheered at meetings when good news is reported about children we have come to know and care about. Other members have told me that they enjoy meeting my son, Tom, who is older than many of their children. They like to talk with him and hear his perspective. Sometimes they ask if he can explain what their own child might be thinking and feeling in certain situations. Members enjoy meeting and applauding the involvement of other family members, the concerned grandparents, aunts, uncles and siblings who show they care by taking an active part.

I encourage parents to find a support group to help you through "the process." Why do it alone when you can find some very wonderful people to share the journey? Groups are often associated with autism organizations or other disability and advocacy groups. Local school districts, universities and hospitals may sponsor groups. Groups may be formal, with a moderator such as a mental health professional or social worker, or informal and led by parents. You may need to ask around to find one or check in the newspapers under "support groups." If an existing group does not meet your needs, you can always form your own group by starting with a membership of two like-minded people. Our support group has the form and function it does, because our members shaped and created it to meet our own needs.

Ways to Help a Support Group Grow

Sometimes support group meetings have a low turnout over time or only the same families attend every time. Here are some ideas to increase attendance at support group meetings:

- Ask the school district to send an announcement of the meeting home with every special education student. The district may not give the names and addresses of families to you, but they may be allowed to send home an announcement to the families of children in their special education programs.

- Ask your local newspaper to publish the date, time, place and topic for a meeting a day or two before the meeting is scheduled. Put an ad on your local access cable TV station. Many local radio announcers will advertise your meeting for no charge as part of their "community calendar." Some religious groups will announce your meeting or put it in their weekly services handout.

- Early in the formation of the group, choose a place and time that seems to work well for the members of the group. Then stick to the same place, day of the month and time. When meetings become predictable, family members may be able to attend at the last minute without having to try to find the flyer with a different place or time on it.

- Survey families to identify obstacles to attending. Try to overcome as many of those obstacles as you can. Sometimes parents need someone to pick them up if they do not have transportation. Sometimes parents cannot leave their son or daughter with autism at home and need childcare to be provided. Other obstacles could include not being able to afford to pay a babysitter. Ask parents and find out what could be done to help more parents attend.

- Try providing childcare. Many high schools and colleges have child development classes. Those students may volunteer to help. Students may be able to get credit for a class that they are taking or use the care of children with ASD during the meeting as a topic for a class assignment. Parents may want to "pass the hat" at the end of the meeting to provide a little payment for their child care workers. Sometimes siblings of children with ASD can be involved in child care during the meetings and be rewarded with special time with their parents or other rewards.

- Choose a location that is easy to find and well known in your town or city. Be sure it is a safe location with adequate and well-lit parking areas. We know of many religious groups who have allowed family support groups to meet in the areas used for "Sunday School" or other services for children. Some churches have classrooms with toys and VCRs that can be accessed by the children and their caregivers when the parents are meeting.

- Invite participants to bring snacks, "Pot Luck" style as an inexpensive way to provide refreshments

- Be sure to let fathers know that they are welcome and that other men will be there. Sometimes support groups seem like a "woman's" group meeting. Fathers benefit from support group meetings and enjoy meeting other men who share some of their experiences and concerns.

- Set a tone for support group meetings. Do not allow them to become only an opportunity to complain about the school district or other providers. Parents need to express themselves and share their burdens, but everyone should know that the support group speaks with respect about everyone, tries to take the perspective of others and proactively works to solve problems rather than assign blame.

- Once you are organized, you can invite speakers such as members of the school district administration, school board or adult provider agencies' administration to talk to them about the perspective and needs of the families in your community. These informal discussions and may attract new members can help administrators feel more informed in policy and decision-making.

Inviting Professional Staff to the Support Group

Often, support groups have meetings when speakers come to share information and strategies. Members of the group may want to invite staff who work with their family member to attend. Here are some of the possible benefits of having parents, family members and staff attend support group training or information sessions together, outside of the school or work environment:

- Parents and professionals can get to know one another as complex human beings who are generally doing the best they can.

- Parents and professionals can learn together, develop commonly understood goals and use terms and language with which everyone has become familiar, helping to improve communication back in the "team" meetings.

- Professionals can find out how much parents know and vice versa.

- Professionals can listen and learn about the real obstacles and issues that families have in a setting that does not require that the professionals make immediate decisions or immediately address the issues presented.

- Parents and professionals can discuss decisions that need to be made.

- Parents and professionals can brainstorm together ways to positively change the system and maximize the use of limited resources.

- Professionals can share information about resources with which parents may not be familiar.

- Professionals can share valuable lessons and information learned from other parents (with permission when necessary).

- Parents can share their concerns and issues more freely in a general group meeting than they might feel willing to do at a meeting just of their own child's team.

- Parents sometimes are professionals in the field; they may already be attending regular support group meetings and can share their unique perspective and expertise.

Sibling Support Groups

Sibling support groups can be an excellent source of support for brothers and sisters. Siblings of people with disabilities can share their experiences with others who understand, learning that their various emotional responses are "normal" and shared by others. Siblings discover that they are not alone in their efforts to understand and help the person with ASD. They find out that other children have the same concerns they do. Siblings can share ideas of how to cope and learn to recognize and take pride in their helpful contributions and loving efforts.

Sibling support groups should be monitored by a trained mental health professional. Children or adult siblings can be invited to share their concerns or just listen. Emphasis should be placed on honest expression of emotion and positive action planning. Age-appropriate activities and outings can be arranged to build trust with the professional leader and interpersonal relationships among the various participants. Sibling groups can be held with only the siblings or sometimes with parents in attendance. Some sibling groups include the siblings with ASD on occasion so that the typical children can meet other children with ASD.

Rest and Respite

Having a child or adult with ASD at home can be exhausting. Depending on the level of functioning of the individual and the behavioral issues, parenting can take every ounce of energy a person has. Parents need a break and to rest. They need to know that a trained caregiver can come into the home on a regular basis. The parents can be relieved of some responsibility for just a while. The time can be used to do important business, to spend with the other children in the family, for spiritual support, to sleep or rest or have recreation or physical exercise.

No one wants to do a job that never has a day off! Parenting a child with autism, who cannot be left with "just anyone," means that parents may never get a break. Not having trained caregivers to rely on, many parents feel trapped in their own homes. When a parent wakes up in the morning it is likely that they think about their child with special needs and the care and support the parent must provide that day and everyday. Knowing that a respite worker, who knows what to do, is coming to help during that day or week can be a great relief to any parent.

Two Types of Respite Care:

- In-home respite means that a respite worker comes into your home. The respite worker can do daily tasks, teach or just "be" with the person with ASD. Parents or other family members are free to take care of tasks at home or out of the home.

- Out-of-home respite means that the individual with ASD goes to a licensed and certified environment for a period of time. The out-of-home site may be a family home, a group home or even camp. Family members can rest, do activities outside of home or take care of business.

Respite is not the same as babysitting or childcare, because the respite worker is *only* responsible for the child or adult with ASD, but not any other siblings or family members. Respite care can be arranged privately, with a person you know and choose, train and pay. Some service agencies provide staff for respite. Some agencies will train and pay respite staff that you find, even if they are your relatives. Some service and government agencies may pay for respite services depending on where you live.

Hiring a babysitter is something else parents can do to make time for themselves. A support group may be an avenue for finding someone to occasionally take care of your child. After spending time with a family that has a family member with ASD, you may be able to begin to exchange childcare. Older siblings of children with ASD may be able to provide babysitting services once they get to know your child and family. The same type of exchange can work for older children and adults who may need someone to watch them or a place to spend the night on occasion.

Due to publicity and reports about abuse and neglect, most parents are aware of the need to be cautious and selective about people they trust to care for their children or adult children with special needs. This is a very important consideration when finding a caregiver for a family member with autism. People with ASD, even as adults, may be particularly vulnerable to abuse or neglect, especially when in the care of a person who is inexperienced or overwhelmed by problem behaviors or other challenges. The situation may be worse if the person with ASD does not understand when something "wrong" is happening, or is unable or has not been taught to tell others about it.

We urge parents and other concerned persons to take precautions when selecting a caregiver, such as checking references or checking for a criminal record. Parents may wish to be vigilant by "stopping by" at a care center unexpectedly or coming home early to see what is going on. In their own homes, some people may wish to use monitoring devices, recorders or cameras to ensure that their loved one is well cared for and secure. Sad to say, these precautions may be advisable even when the person with ASD is cared for by a family member or friend.

Families may need to speak up and let it be known that they need respite. Educators and community service providers can become more aware of the need for respite during home visits, or by careful interviewing, and can match families with the community resources to assist them.

Any parent may need support, help or respite even if they:

- Have high functioning children (or adult children) with ASD.

- Have some financial resources.

- Do not complain.

- Do not ask for help.

- Seem to be able to "handle" everything all right.

A Note to Families

If you need help, speak up! If you do not ask for help, no one may offer any help to you. No parent needs to be responsible alone for the life of a person with ASD. Parents who try to do too much without help often end up feeling exhausted, depressed or ill.

Supports Across All Environments

The purpose of education for all students is to prepare children to be competent, happy, useful citizens and members of the workforce. Education is both academic and social. In the case of students with ASD, what is learned at school must be taught at home and in the community. This is because people with ASD usually do not generalize what is learned in one setting to a different setting. Problems at home and in the community are obstacles to education. When parents and educators design effective educational programs for school, the home and community settings must not be overlooked.

Sometimes teams suggest that something that is a problem at home or in the community is not the responsibility of the school or agency. A problem that an individual experiences anywhere is a problem that the whole team needs to address. Providers of educational and adult services need to take responsibility for the quality of the individual's life overall—not just a certain number of hours per day.

As an example, a child with autism may have a very restricted diet that could compromise his health. This is an educational issue, even if the child eats sufficient food to make it through his school day. Intervention at home by professional staff may be required to establish eating behaviors that support the child at home and school and elsewhere in the community.

An adult living in a group home may have only one or two places she can go successfully in the community. This becomes a concern for the entire team, even those who support the person in her workshop. The whole team can plan and implement programs to make more environments accessible to this individual by teaching new skills and coping strategies.

If a student can perform a skill, task or behavior at school, but not at home, then the process of learning is not complete. Intervention by trained staff in the home may be needed to improve functioning and assure that skills are maintained in all environments. If an adult can perform a skill, task or behavior in one environment, but cannot demonstrate it in another environment, then learning and programming are not complete or sufficient.

Some of this needed support can be provided by making videotapes of the individual performing successfully at school or work and sending these videotapes home for family members to watch. Inviting parents or staff from other settings to school or work to observe the teaching strategies being used can be helpful. Role-play and modeling, when the individual with ASD is not present, is a method that staff and families can use to share successful techniques across environments.

Another way to assist families is to address social issues in context for people with ASD. Support staff could accompany people with autism to social events, such as sports activities, scouting and church until the individual is demonstrating acceptable behavior and social connection in the community. Simply telling the person what to do, in a clinic, agency or school setting, does not result in the person with ASD being able to carry over the correct behavior into the natural setting. Simply telling the parents what to do will not automatically result in the parents knowing how to apply the information in another context no matter how capable and motivated parents may be.

If a person with ASD is physically capable of playing baseball, for example, he may not be accepted or included on the team. This may be due to the fact that the player with ASD does not know the social rules and steps of how to be a team player and how to interact with his peers. The person needs to learn social skills to use at the baseball practices and games, and learn and practice needed skills in clinic and educational settings and then supported in using those skills in natural settings.. The need to teach in the natural setting is based on the individual's performance in that setting, not on how well the individual performs in the clinic or therapy room.

Support For People With Autism Through the Lifespan

Once formal education is finished, and the person with ASD reaches adulthood, she should be prepared to be a productive member of the community. She should have functional skills for daily living, vocational skills to do productive work using skills and abilities and a safe, comfortable place to live. She should have recreational and leisure opportunities and take part in community activities. Some people with ASD may want to go to college. They may be capable of doing so, if they are supported, socially and academically and in any other way that meets their needs.

ASD is not outgrown and does not disappear. Functioning, skills and behavior can and will improve throughout the lifespan when appropriate supports and services are provided. Depending on the severity of the effects of ASD, individuals may continue to need various levels of support as adults. This fact must be taken into account, and appropriate services and supports planned, for the lifetime of the individual if needed. This is especially important because parents will age, become ill or die. When this happens, the important support they have always given the individual is gone.

It is well recognized that adult developmental disability services are in a crisis state in many parts of our country. Funding for adult services is not a priority in most states. There is no entitlement to adult services and no funding levels that must be maintained by law. Concerned members of each community need to work together to find additional funding and to make the best use possible of public funding and private money. Remember that legislators need to earn your vote. People concerned with adult human services need to be sure that their legislators are listening and responsive.

Practical Steps to Prepare for the Future, Starting Now

1. **Be sure that, from as early in life as possible, your child can be left in the care of trusted adults (trusted by you and the child) whom you have trained to provide childcare.** It will not benefit your child to think that he can only be alright if he is with a parent or only one or two other people. Have potential careworkers come over and spend time at the house with you and your son or daughter with ASD at times when you will be staying home. That way, the trusted person can watch you interact with your child, learn issues about communication, meals, TV, video games, siblings, etc., and be taught how you would like them to intervene. When leaving the person with ASD alone with a new care provider for the first time, be sure to carry a cellphone or pager or call in regularly. Go out only for a very short time the first few times. Later, you can gradually increase the amount of time you spend comfortably away from home.

2. **Make plans for emergency care for your child before an emergency occurs.** What if you were hospitalized tomorrow? What is the plan for your child with ASD? Where would she go? Would she go to someone else's house or stay in her own home? Who would stay with the child with ASD? These types of plans need to be organized before anything happens.

3. **Plan how to avoid dangerous situations.** If your son or daughter has extremely dangerous behavior, such as aggression or severe self-injury, ask professionals to help you make a plan so that you will know what to do and when to do it. Identify dangerous behavior, plan ways to de-escalate and avoid crisis situations and make a plan for crisis intervention in an emergency.

   One kind of emergency plan is called a Reactive Strategy. This is a plan for staff and/or family that tells them what to do whenever a seriously problematic behavior occurs. To create a Reactive Strategy, staff and family members need to decide what the most appropriate and most safe response to the problematic behavior is. Everyone comes to an agreement regarding exactly what will be said and done when the problematic behavior occurs. The Reactive Strategy, is designed to provide protection, prevent injury and "fix" the situation as quickly as possible. All people, who would be likely to use the Reactive Strategy, need to have a written copy of it and be allowed to practice completing the steps (without the child or adult with ASD present).

Prevention of seriously problematic, dangerous behavior should be a top priority for everyone. Safety issues should override other goals such as compliance and conformity. Parents and staff who support individuals with ASD may need intensive, expert training in de-escalation techniques and the safe use of emergency interventions. People with ASD need to be taught calming and self-regulating skills as a high priority in any individualized educational or training plan. It may be a good idea to get to know the people at the emergency crisis line of your community mental health center and be able to call them, as needed, rather than to talk to "a stranger" on the phone during a crisis.

There are some times that it is better to call the police than to allow something really terrible to occur that cannot be undone. When there is immediate danger, a crisis or a true emergency, calling 911 may be the only option. In less dire situations, where people and property are not at risk, calling the police to intervene may be considered as a last resort after all other interventions for avoiding problems, de-escalating or calming have been tried.

Many times parents are "at the end of their ropes" and think that calling the police will help. Parents expect the police or sheriff to have expertise in dealing with the types of crises experienced by people with ASD. They think the police would "teach their child a lesson" and help him "see the consequences of his actions" or know special techniques for crisis intervention.

Law enforcement officials will respond to the best of their ability and use the skill they have to be as effective as possible. Sometimes the outcome will be fine. However, in most communities, law enforcement officials have not had specific training about ASD. As a result, they may use techniques that upset or escalate the person with ASD. Officers may misinterpret slower processing styles or other behavioral characteristics as defiance or disobedience to police commands. It is an unfortunate fact that calling the police sometimes results in an undesirable outcome, such as bodily harm or a police record that cannot be erased. "Guidelines for Dealing with Conflict," a section in the book "Navigating the Social World" by Jeanette McAfee, may also be helpful to teach important skills and behaviors to avoid problems and de-escalate conflicts.

4.   **Make a plan for guardianship of your child in case something unexpected happens to you and/or your partner.** Be sure to follow the requirements that make your wishes legally binding. Even if you child with ASD is a toddler, it is best to decide now who will care for him if something happens to you. Discuss this with the person or people who you would like to have guardianship. Be sure they agree to accept the responsibility. Write out your wishes for the child's life and anything you would want the guardian to consider.

Many organizations, including the Autism Society of America, can provide you with some guidelines for planning for the care of your son or daughter with ASD after (not if) you die. Remember that if your wishes are not known, a court may decide what happens to your child. The delay, conflict and suffering by the child can be avoided by making a plan.

5.   **Do careful estate planning to make sure eligibility for services is not affected by leaving property or money to the child with disabilities.** A local, statewide or national advocacy group can give you references of people and groups who are near where you live to help you with

this. The idea here is that ownership of certain amounts of money or property can interfere with an adult with ASD accessing publicly funded services. Do not wait until you are sick or very old to do this. After you make your plan, be sure that trusted family members or friends understand the plan, know where the paperwork is and what your requests are.

How Educators and Support Professionals Can Help Families

Families have a lot to think about. Many of these same issues concern educators and support professionals. There are many ways that staff can help families. Families appreciate staff that understand the emotional and complex issues in family life. Sensitivity, support and assistance from staff can dramatically improve the quality of life for people with ASD and their families.

Professionals and staff may have opportunities to use the information in this chapter to bring up difficult subjects when it appears that families are struggling. If families seem resistant, it is probable that they may be afraid or unsure. Let them know that you are there to talk to them about these issues "whenever they feel ready."

Many conversations between parents and staff "plant a seed" in the parents' mind. For example, a teacher may mention a behavior that concerns him. The parent may not immediately act on that information. The parent may need time to think about it or have her own evidence and understanding of the situation to make it seem "real" to her. Sometimes the parent will come back long after the initial conversation and appreciate your willingness to help her when she is ready.

Ways that Professionals Can Assist Families

1. **Remove the burden of judgment from yourself and the families that you support.** Assume that families are doing the best they can with the resources and demands that exist. It is likely that any one of us would be overwhelmed by the situations in which many families find

themselves. If you see that a family is not doing well, don't blame—ask and tell. Ask what is going on and if there is anything you can do to help. Tell the family about resources, make referrals or put then in contact with others for help and information.

2. **Strive to understand the entire family system**. If you can, help parents identify resources for other issues in the family, even if not directly related to the needs of the individual with ASD. Individuals with ASD will have a better life if the needs of all family members are met.

3. **Familiarize yourself with all the services in your community, not just those provided by the group that employs you**. This may include mental health supports, such as counseling and therapy, to help the family communicate, problem solve, deal with emotional issues and plan. You may also need to provide information about social work services designed to help families find the help they need in their communities, find financial aide and assist with family issues and needs. Professionals may be able to help parents get information about guardianship, estate planning and other important topics. If you do not have access to get this information, try to provide the contact information for at least one local organization or person that can make connections and provide the information parents need.

4. **Help families identify sources of stress**. Listening carefully you may identify the effects that stress is producing in family members and possible options for dealing with stress.

5. **Help families prioritize goals and activities**. No family can do everything well all of the time. Help families give themselves permission to put siblings' needs as a top priority sometimes. Help families recognize that time relaxing with family members is as important for every family member as goal-directed activities.

6. **Preserve the role of parents as parents of all the children in the family**. Do not ask parents to implement unrealistic programs that do not take into account the time demands placed on the parents by other children and other responsibilities.

7. **Give parents "permission" to do what works, even if it is somewhat unconventional**. For example, some families do not always attend parties or functions together. Sometimes, one parent will take the individual with ASD to one activity, while someone else takes the other children to a different place. Some people would object to this saying that the whole family "should" do everything together. Others would tell you that by sometimes doing things separately, each member of the family gets their needs met more fully. Accommodating the individual with ASD at other times becomes easier.

8. **Allow and promote a "hopeful" attitude in family members regarding their child with ASD**. Do not label families as "unrealistic" or "in denial" if they are hopeful for an active and successful life for the child or adult with ASD. Assist them in taking all possible steps towards goals they have chosen for the individual. If the goal turns out to be unrealistic, families will recognize this themselves over time.

9. **Parents and professionals need to have lifetime goals for each individual**. A lifetime goals planning session could be an annual event for teams working with individuals with ASD. Of course, the individual should be included in the planning process to the greatest extent possible. In the lifetime planning meetings, everyone discusses the interests, abilities, preferences and wishes of the person with ASD and envisions the best possible life outcome for this child and the family. A lifetime plan gives staff and parents a basis upon which to discuss and make decisions about curricular content, types of activities, intervention strategies, communication goals and skills training. Over time, lifetime plans will naturally change. "The Personal Future's Planning Model" from Minnesota is one way to plan for the lifetime of

the individual. We give references for lifetime planning in Volume Two of this book.

10. **Professionals need to model positive interaction when they are with the individual with ASD.** Family members need to see professionals modeling responsiveness, flexibility and sensitivity to non-verbal communication. Efforts to understand the individual's behavior as communication helps the family to do the same thing. Demonstrating understanding of the unique sensory processing challenges and needs that each individual with ASD has helps families to be sensitive and aware. Professional interaction should model respect and unconditional acceptance.

11. **Professionals need to model relationship building as the primary goal of interacting with individuals with ASD.** Relationships and communication are core deficits in ASD. Relationships need to be carefully nurtured and protected. Basic relationship building qualities are trust, listening, understanding, helpfulness, caring and acceptance. Success in life may have more to do with having quality relationships than with simple compliance and academic knowledge. This is something for teams to think about.

12. **Professionals need to share realistic and accurate information about the laws affecting the institutionalization of people with disabilities.** Currently, in many states, criteria for institutionalization are, "danger to self, and/or danger to others." To ensure a lifelong place in the community for every individual with ASD, dangerous behavior must be understood and effectively treated until it is no longer part of what the person does. Professionals can help staff and parents recognize the dangerous and potentially dangerous behaviors that can put the person with ASD and others at risk. Professionals can teach parents and staff effective ways of anticipating and preventing dangerous behavior, de-escalating problems and dealing with a crisis.

13. **If you are a professional staff person, you have tremendous power to improve lives.** Be instrospective and learn about your own motivations and needs. Become the best listener and communicator that you can. Cultivate objectivity and non-judgmental language and thoughts. It is a wonderful moment when a family member turns to you and expresses their gratitude for what you have done and understood or for your kindness and courtesy.

14. **Remember the wise words of teacher Haim Ginott**: "I have come to the frightening conclusion that I am the decisive element in the classroom ... as a teacher, I possess a tremendous power to make a child's life miserable or joyous ... In all situations, it is my response that decides whether a crisis will be escalated or de-escalated and a child be humanized or dehumanized."

No one can do everything that is needed to help all families. In the past it was not always clear what services needed to be available and how to best present these services to families. Now we do know what to do and how to do it. Families of children and adults with autism and other disorders are telling us what is needed.

A Case Example From Barbara

We were having great success at school teaching Ahmed R. to use the toilet. Mrs. R., his mother, honestly reported to the team that she was having no success at home and was keeping him in diapers. She said she could not "get" him to even sit on the toilet. The team did not judge her and simply accepted her story as her facts, although we were not having the same issues at school. A three-step approach was decided on:

First, Mrs. R. would come to school and sit quietly in our room and watch what we did at toileting time. We knew that Ahmed would be initially upset by her presence, but hoped that over time he would get used to it. (He was and he did!)

Second, we videotaped the toileting routine and sent the tape home (labeled with Ahmed's name, the school address and the word "confidential"). We asked Mrs. R. to watch it when he was asleep and ask us any questions.

Third, after the first two steps had been done, staff volunteered to make a home visit. While in the home, staff watched Mrs. R. work with Ahmed and provided coaching to Mrs. R., while she was toileting Ahmed.

The results of our three-step approach were wonderful: Ahmed became fully toilet trained at school and at home before the end of his preschool year. Mrs. R. expressed greater confidence in her ability to teach Ahmed new skills. Mrs. R. expressed her gratitude to staff in many ways, not the least of which were the wonderful snacks that she brought to us!

The current service delivery system for children and adults does not always provide the services that are most needed. One reason is the assumption that some other entity will do it. Providers of services in a community need to work together to be sure that the services that parents tell us are important and helpful are provided. To plan, design and implement needed services, agencies and schools can create groups of professionals and family members to work together. No school or agency should have service planning and development groups that do not include parents, siblings and extended family members.

Training and Education for Parents and Staff

Parents can be the best, lifelong asset of a person with autism or other disabilities, by commitment to his or her welfare. "Knowledge is power" is true in the case of families with a person with an ASD. Parents need information about the characteristics of autism, educational and treatment options and strategies to improve daily life. Parents want to know what services are most appropriate for their child, how to get them and what their role will be to ensure progress. Parents need help planning for the future, getting services and finding support persons.

Staff and Parents Learning Together

We often hear complaints from staff that parents do not know what they need to know. We hear from parents that staff do not know what they need to know. We hear both staff and parents complain that they do not understand one another and do not use the same terminology or have the same knowledge base. Why is this a surprise? Across the country we have seen the practice of separating parents and staff for training. It is time to do things differently!

On the subject of ASD, staff often need to know the same information that parents do. The practice of training parents, teachers, aides, respite workers, adult agency staff and others together makes sense. Training that is held for staff and educators should be made open to parents. Since both parents and professionals are working in the best interest of the individual, they benefit equally from opportunities to learn more and work together.

Parents are the true team leaders. Parents need to be encouraged and taught how to exercise their leadership role within teams. Joint training for professionals and families helps everyone develop compatible skills and vocabulary for effective teamwork. Parents and professionals can practice the courtesy and skills of active listening, providing feedback and checking intent and understanding during the communication process.

Sometimes staff object that they will not be able to "express themselves fully" in the presence of parents. That can be a symptom of a deeper problem in communication. If staff cannot ask questions or make comments in the presence of parents, they may need to find a better, more acceptable way of framing their ideas and issues. This does not mean avoiding the truth. The presence of parents can cause all of us to say what we mean, be clear in what we mean, and say what is defensible. If staff and parents have problems in communication, training together can focus on topics such as taking emotionally charged words out of communication, focusing on building on current strengths, active listening, dealing with conflict, recognizing underlying emotions, etc.

Here are some options for schools and agencies for providing opportunities for training that includes parents, family and staff:

1.   Ask parents and staff in the community what topics are most important to them for training. Use the information to plan training events and select speakers.

2. Assess and meet families' needs related to training such as transportation, childcare or the need for training to be held weekends or evenings.

3. Videotape each training session (with permission) and create a training video resource library available to staff, families, students and others.

4. Audiotape each training opportunity (with permission) and create an audiocassette resource library.

5. Create lending libraries on various subjects of interest to parents and staff.

6. Arrange for parents and staff to participate in training via video teleconferences.

7. Find public or private sources of funds such as regional centers, "wrap-around" services, foundations or grants to pay for trainers.

8. Offer to waive fees for some parents to attend conferences on ASD and other topics.

9. Hold local training sessions with trained professionals from the local schools or agencies.

10. Ask people to volunteer to come to open training meetings and share what they have learned.

11. Offer meeting rooms or conference rooms for training purposes.

12. Arrange for special courses at nearby regional colleges or adult education centers.

13. Invite local experts and professors from area colleges to speak to parents and staff.

14. Teach parents and staff how to use the Internet, or ask your local public library to provide Internet training and to allow them to access equipment if needed.

15. Provide specific one-to-one training. This is relevant in cases, such as, when a behaviorist is required to intervene in cases of self-injurious or dangerous behavior. The parent must be individually trained in what to do and how to do it to reinforce and respond in a consistent manner.

16. Set up "parents teaching parents" sessions where parents take turns sharing techniques and strategies with one another.

A Case Example from Barbara

I work with a fantastic director of special education services, Mrs. White. Mrs. White is a creative and dedicated person who drives herself and her staff to provide the best possible services. She is extremely creative in finding and using resources, including the resources that parents bring to the district. Training in her district is almost always open to staff and families. Requests from parents for specific programs or strategies for their children with ASD are not judged as not possible, but rather as a possibility to be pursued.

When Johanna first began to work as a director of special education, with her openness and willingness to learn and change (and cause staff to do the same!), there was some resistance. How could we express ourselves, staff said, if parents were present? How could parents express themselves if staff were there? How could she expect overloaded and overwhelmed staff to learn more and do more than they already were doing? There were heated discussions, always within the bounds of common courtesy, as everyone "regrouped" and learned to think more openly about roles and responsibilities.

Over time, the resistance faded as parents were recognized as knowledgeable and as capable contributors and as staff were given opportunities to learn and grow and share their extensive knowledge. As Mrs. White learned more from her parents and staff, she planned for even more innovative and exceptional programs to be implemented, still staying within the budgetary limitations imposed on her by the administration. She demonstrates that parents are not "them," but rather just another kind of "us." It is a delight for parents and staff to live and work in her district. One mother told me, "Mrs. White saved my mental health. It was not so much the changes that were implemented but more the way she truly acknowledged me as a person who could know something of value and as a mother with high hopes, not symptoms of denial. She helped the staff understand my perspective and that was a tremendous relief to my whole family."

The Need to Build Political Awareness

One last important idea for parents, professionals and other significant people who support the individual with ASD: Contact your elected representatives. Let them know how services are delivered or *not* delivered where you live. Tell them what is working and what is not. Let them know about barriers to service delivery. Give them your ideas and impressions about what would work better. If you want to, volunteer to give testimony at hearings about children or adults with disabilities.

Elected officials can often use their influence on behalf of their constituents. In fact, many of them want to be of real service to the families in their area. Go to them with problems, issues and proposed solutions both for your own family and for the system in general. You can take your son or daughter with ASD to meet your elected representatives if possible. Officials need to be able to think of and remember real people when they make laws and rules, not just numbers or descriptions.

Keep up with the laws that affect special education and services for children and adults with disabilities. Contact lawmakers to let them know how important these issues are and that voters hold them accountable to make the best possible choices. As policy and budget affects everyone involved, affecting political policy by reaching the politicians is an important way to make a difference in the life of the person you care about and millions of others.

Many advocacy groups and national organizations have political action committees to give a voice to people with disabilities, their families, educators and support staff. It is in the best interest of everyone involved to support these efforts in any way possible if and when you are able to do so.

CHAPTER 8 SUMMARY

- Families of persons with ASD need support to function in a healthy and successful way. It is in the best interest of everyone involved to keep families together and help them cope.

- Parents may need psychological counseling to work out their feelings and get help to recognize their own capabilities, find hope and feel empowered to act.

- Marriage counseling is often needed. Statistics show a higher rate of failed marriages when a family member has a disability, such as ASD.

- Brothers and sisters of the person with ASD face their own emotional issues. They may need counseling, as well as information, to understand and relate to their sibling.

- Family counseling is a forum to identify the specific problems that have upset the family balance and come up with practical and effective ways to help resolve them.

- Parents, siblings and extended family can benefit greatly from support groups. Families can share both their problems and their solutions with others with similar circumstances who may understand in a way that no one else can.

- There are many potential benefits of having parents, family members and staff attend support group information sessions together outside of school or work.

- No one wants to do a job that never has a day off! Families may need respite care, to take a break from responsibility while a trained person takes over for a period of time.

- If you need help, speak up! If you do not ask for help, no one may offer any. No parent should try to be solely responsible for the life of a person with

ASD. Parents who try to do too much without help can end up exhausted, depressed or ill.

• It may be necessary to teach students with ASD how to do what is learned at school "across environments," at home and in the community. Include this in the educational plan.

• Once formal education is finished, and the person with ASD reaches adulthood, she should be prepared to be a productive member of the community. Depending on the severity of the effects of ASD, individuals may continue to need various levels of support as adults. Appropriate services and supports should be planned for the lifetime of the individual.

• Take practical steps to prepare for the future, starting now.
(We suggest 4 ideas).

• Educators and professionals can help families. Sensitivity, support and assistance from staff can dramatically improve the quality of life for people with ASD and their families. (We suggest 13 ways to help).

• Parents need training and information about the characteristics of autism, educational and treatment options and strategies to improve daily life. Parents need to learn what services are most appropriate for their child, how to get them and what their role will be to ensure progress. Parents need help planning for the future and finding support.

• Staff often need to know the same information about ASD that parents do. The practice of training parents, teachers, aides, respite workers, adult agency staff and others together makes sense.
(We suggest 16 ways to do this!)

• Parents, professionals and other significant people who support the individual with ASD need to keep up with the laws that affect special education and services for children and adults with disabilities.

• Contact your elected representatives to let them know what issues are important to you.

SOURCES

Berli, Shane. *A Handbook for Families of Children (With Disabilities) From a Counseling Perspective*. (Master's Project). Published by the California State Council on Developmental Disabilities, 2000 "O" Street, Suite 100 Sacramento, CA 95814 phone 916-322-8481TDD 916-324-8420 FAX 916-443-4957

Powers, Michael D. Psy. D., Editor *Children With Autism A Parents Guide*. Bethesda: Woodbine House, 1989. *Chapter Five Children with Autism and Their Families*.

RESOURCES

Andron, Linda, Editor. (2001) *Our Journey Through High Functioning Autism and Asperger Syndrome: A Roadmap*. Philadelphia: Jessica Kingsley Publishers.

Harris, Sandra L. *Siblings of Children with Autism: A Guide for Families*. Topics in Autism Woodbine House, Second Edition 2003.

Lavin, Judith Loseff. *Special Kids Need Special Parents*. Berkley Publishing Group 2001.

McAfee, Jeanette. (2002) *Navigating the Social World: A Curriculum for Individuals with Asperger's Syndrome, High Functioning Autism and Related Disorders*. Arlington TX: Future Horizons.

Meyer, Donald J., Editor. (1997) *Views from Our Shoes: Growing Up With a Brother or Sister With Special Needs*. Woodbine House. Reading level ages 9-12. Stories from the experiences of 45 children. A book for siblings, about disabilities in general.

Meyer, Donald and Patricia F. Vadasy. (1994) *SibShops: Workshops for Siblings of Children With Special Needs*. Baltimore: Paul H. Brookes Publishing Co. Also a website, to find 200+ Sibshop locations nationwide: www.chmc.org/sibsupp/sibshoppage.htm.

Myles, Brenda Smith and Simpson, Richard L. (1998) *Asperger Syndrome: A Guide for Educators and Parents*. Austin TX: PRO-ED. (See Chapter 6: "Understanding Asperger Syndrome and Its Impact on the Family" for family perspectives.)

Naseef, Robert A. (1996). *Special Children, Challenged Parents: The Struggles and Rewards of Raising a Child with a Disability*. Secaucus, NJ: Birch Lane Press, Carol Publishing Group.

Nollette, C.D., Lynch, T. et al. (1986) *Having a Brother Like David*. South Minneapolis MN: Minneapolis Children's Medical Center. For siblings, about autism.

Siegel, B.; Silverstein, S.C. (1994) *What About Me? Growing up with a Developmentally Disabled Sibling*. New York: Plenium.

CHAPTER 9

SHARING INFORMATION ABOUT PEOPLE WITH ASD

In this chapter you will learn:

- The many factors to take into account when sharing information about your family member, student or the adult in your care with ASD.

- Distinctions between personal information, privacy, confidentiality and secrecy, and laws regarding confidentiality.

- Ideas to help in deciding who needs to know, what to say and ways to say it.

- Ideas to help explain about ASD to a child who has it.

- Ideas to help the individual with autism share information with others.

This chapter is about sharing information about ASD. This is a sensitive issue for many people. Deciding whether you will tell others, who to tell, what to say and how to say it are very difficult decisions. They are matters of personal choice having a lot to do with each person's own situation and experiences.

Many parents describe how conflicted and nervous they feel about this topic. One nagging worry is about how others will react when they "find out." Other parents do not see or understand the need to tell others. A parent's own understanding and acceptance of the diagnosis will affect whether she wants to talk about it to others. It takes time to decide what to do. Parents and staff can take the time needed to think about the issue. We encourage teams to address this issue and not avoid it.

Once parents decide that they want to tell others, they are not sure who to tell or what to say. They are not sure who needs to know. This includes when and how to tell the child himself or when and how to explain the diagnosis to adults with ASD.

There are many points of view to consider. Each individual situation is unique, and you will want to seek support and advice of others who know you and your child very well. This can help in deciding what information to share, with whom and how. A variety of ideas and suggestions are presented in this chapter. Discussion and examples give ideas of what you can do and help you make a plan.

Deciding how to share information is complicated by the awkwardness of approaching people. What makes it so difficult and uncomfortable to discuss autism or ASD? Part of the answer to the question has to do with how autism was thought about only recently. People who are adults today were often raised with the idea that autism and disabilities were something to hide, to be ashamed of, to be kept secret or someone's fault.

As we grew up, most people with disabilities were educated separately, or lived away from home. We did not get to know them or know about them. Many parents are shocked to realize that their own child is the first person that they have ever known who has ASD!

Many preconceived notions and generalizations surround autism and reinforce limited or mistaken ideas. In the fifties and sixties, it was believed that autism was caused by a "refrigerator mother"— a cold, uncaring woman — who caused her child to have autism, because she failed to bond with him. This type of misinformation lingers on and has not been discredited in every community. Autism and ASD are something that most people really know very little about even if they think they do. Sometimes what is believed or "known" is absolutely incorrect.

If we choose to say little or nothing about the child or adult with ASD in our care, the old notions and limitations continue. Keeping the "secrecy" around autism prevents other people from becoming informed, sensitive and aware. Sharing information is a chance to change ignorance to understanding. It helps to dispel bias, prejudice, pre-conceived notions and inaccurate information.

ASD is an "invisible" disability. Many people with ASD look like everyone else and there are few, if any, physical signs of difference. At the same time, some things can be observed that will make the difference apparent. Some behaviors, communication and reactions look "different" than the norm. These things will not make sense to others unless they are explained as being caused by, and part of, ASD.

When people do not know the real reason for something that they observe, they often draw their own conclusions which are wrong. Seeing or sensing a difference without understanding it sets people apart. Without the knowledge of why a child or adult behaves a certain way, children and adults in the environment may not understand or try to be helpful.

Understanding differences helps people to be accepting. Then they can move beyond the obstacle of "difference" to discover what they have in common. They find out that they can be friends, work together and have fun with people who have ASD. Their insight helps them to be sensitive and empathetic.

To many people, getting the information will have a big impact. Having information, they can know how and why to be supportive. They will think differently, feel differently, and act differently because of understanding and acceptance. It does not matter if these "listeners" are a minority or a majority of the group; their understanding will make a difference.

There is the risk, even the probability, that when information is offered, not everyone will "hear" the message. Some people will not be empathetic or supportive with or without information. It has nothing to do with you or your family member or what you say or do. Some people, even parents, "don't want to know." They may not welcome or accept information or want to hear about it.

Sometimes providing information causes a negative reaction in some people. Some people will decide to avoid you and your family because they are not ready to deal with the information, or choose not to. You do not need to spend too much time feeling bad about that. Do not take responsibility for the reactions of others. Allow these people more time to think and learn and grow. In the meantime, move on to find more receptive and understanding people.

Friends and family members who normally would be supportive may be uncomfortable as the family progresses with the process of diagnosis. Often, friends and extended family members spend more time away from the family not wanting to "say the wrong thing" or "do something that will hurt your feelings." Families need to be empowered to call friends and relatives, invite them back into the family's life, tell them that they are wanted and needed and that everyone can learn about ASD together.

Confidentiality vs. Secrecy

When defining confidentiality in the context of special education, adult services or a diagnosis, it can be defined as "protection of privacy." Confidentiality means that no one else can share information about a person's diagnosis or other personal information without permission. When children are minors, that is under the age of 18, parents have the right to:

- Share information about their child with others.

- Not share information about their child.

- Allow others to share information about their child.

- Refuse to allow others to share information.

- Specify what information can be shared.

- Decide what information will not be shared.

- Be involved in deciding how information will be shared.

- Prevent others from identifying the person as having a disability.

- Keep all medical, educational and legal records private.

"Children" over the age of 18 are adults, and like all other adults, are entitled to privacy. Adults are responsible for any choices about confidentiality. An exception to this is when a person over age 18 is part of a conservatorship. This is a formal legal agreement that keeps parents or guardians involved in the decision-making process concerning adults with disabilities.

It is up to parents, guardians or the adult with ASD to decide if, when and how to share the diagnostic information with other people including the individual himself, siblings or others. Many circumstances in everyday life will "demand" that decisions be made. For example, when people see someone use gestures instead of speaking, they may ask, "Why?" Or, if a person does not answer when classmates or roommates speak to her, they will want to know, "Why not?" When a little sister says, "Why won't Bobby play with me?" how will you answer? If your child behaves in an unusual way at school and the children ask the teacher "Why did he do that?" what should the teacher say? Who else should be able to answer, and what do you want them to say?

The reaction of some people to such situations is to say nothing, or keep "secret" why the person is different or having a problem. One reason for this is that autism and ASD seem difficult to explain. Other people think it is no one's business, "why" and they don't owe an explanation to anybody.

The fact is that people are going to think about and talk about your child or adult based on their interactions or in response to what they see. Since many situations bring forth the need for understanding and explanation, it is a good idea to learn where your comfort level is, decide what you want others to know and how you want to say it. This includes allowing and instructing teachers, paraprofessionals and others in the school or adult-care setting to know how you want such situations handled and what words are to be used when situations arise and you are not present to personally explain. Staff and parents will need to make a plan that can change over time as the person changes and grows.

Compare the situation of a person with ASD and people with other issues. No one would give a person insulin shots and restrict her diet, but not tell her she has diabetes. If the person with diabetes goes to a party and cannot have sweets, would it make sense to let the other people know? If someone doesn't tell others at the party that she can't have cake, or why she can't have cake, they will probably keep offering sweets. Keeping the information a secret can cause a lot of confusion and even harm.

No one would consider "including" a child or adult who had vision impairment and not mentioning it to the others in the environment. Such an omission would surely lead to problems in interaction, interpersonal misunderstandings and perhaps even dangerous situations arising.

Most people have no difficulty talking about disorders like diabetes. The facts are fairly easy to understand and explain. The disorder is thought of as physical. There is no confusion, blame or guilt attached. There is often some level of discomfort in talking about ASD in a way that seems different from talking about other disorders and disabilities. Yet ASD is a physical condition. ASD is related to the functioning of the brain, central nervous and other body systems. ASD can be treated as matter-of-factly as any physiological difference. Understanding and being factual about ASD can help take away the stigma and undertones about autism.

Most school districts and adult service providers will *not* invite parents to share information about their child or adult. Some districts or providers require parents to sign a waiver of confidentiality to share any information. This shows that the school or agency is upholding the rules of confidentiality.

Since confidentiality is a right, staff may feel that agreeing to "tell" is asking the parent to give up their right. That is not the case. Confidentiality does not mean keeping all information a secret. Confidentiality means that no one outside the individual's team has a right to know information about the individual, unless, and until, permission is given to share this information. Information is usually shared, with permission, when others in the environment "need to know." Agreeing to carefully choose and plan how, when, where and with whom to share information respects the rights and wishes of parents, upholds the law and allows information to be shared as needed.

Issues About Diagnostic Labels

Sometimes language is an obstacle to sharing information. This includes whether or not the actual diagnostic term (Asperger's Syndrome, autism, pervasive developmental disorder, ASD etc.) should be used to describe or explain a person's differences. Parents and professionals may have issues about whether or not it benefits a person to have a "label" used to describe them. There are arguments for and against the use of diagnostic descriptions and labels. Here are a few of the various opinions about diagnostic labels.

"I Do Not Like the Word 'Autism'!"

It can be difficult for parents and family members to become comfortable with the word "autism," even when they agree with it as the diagnosis. Many parents prefer to avoid the words "autism" or "Autism Spectrum Disorder," because they know about the connotations most people associate with those terms. Using the word, "autism," may set the scene for a lengthy explanation of a complex subject.

It may be a relief to parents and staff to know they can use any words they agree upon. "Autism," "Asperger's Syndrome," and "Autism Spectrum Disorder" do not have to be used. There is often no need to use the "official diagnostic term" except for "official" reasons, such as eligibility for services.

For the purpose of helping others understand, families and staff can **explain what the diagnosis means** using whatever terms and language are most appropriate. In discussions with friends and family, use the diagnostic label, words or descriptions with which you are most comfortable. Some families prefer to use PDD or "complex, multiple learning disabilities." A shorter version may be, "She learns differently," or "He has special learning needs."

In our family, at first, Emily was not comfortable using the word "autism" as an explanation of Tom's learning and behavior. She found that she had to immediately explain away people's misconceptions about autism. She found it easier to say that Tom had Asperger's Syndrome because most people had never heard of it. She was able to explain what Asperger's was, rather than what autism wasn't. Later however, Emily became more comfortable using the word autism. She was sure to always use his official diagnosis for educational eligibility, because it helped Tom get the services he needed.

Currently, the phrase "autism spectrum disorder" or "ASD" is becoming more commonly used and accepted in many parts of the world. The average person is becoming more familiar with it as articles about ASD appear in newspapers, television, movies and magazines more often than in the past.

Many parents have learned a technique for answering the tough questions children ask, like "the birds-and-the-bees" questions: only tell them as much as they need to know when they need to know it. This approach may be helpful in many situations when you wish to share limited information about your family member who has ASD, especially in casual encounters or with people you do not know well. Parents don't always have the need, the desire or the energy to tell everyone "the whole story!"

Instead, you can explain the person's behavior and needs using words that you are comfortable with. Use statements such as "my son has difficulty understanding what people say to him," or "my daughter wants to play, but is still learning how to join in." These are practical and factual ways to explain differences and needs. These simple statements, relevant to the situation at hand, help other people have an idea of how to interact with or react to your child. People often respond to statements such as these by asking, "What should I do to help?" presenting the opportunity for a positive teaching interaction.

Case Examples

David was a fifth-grade boy in the process of getting a diagnosis of Asperger's Syndrome. His peers were very aware of his differences and pointed them out in mean and humiliating ways. He was picked on, harassed and left out. No one had thought of telling the other kids about David. David felt terrible and came home from school upset almost every day.

David did not have the communication or social skills to defend himself. He had no way of explaining himself, to himself, or to the other children. Later, David's mother said that this was one of the biggest regrets she had. One thing could have changed her son's life for the better—if the other children had understood David rather than rejecting and being mean to him. This understanding may have led to greater acceptance and the possibility of developing relationships with the other children, that is, having friends.

Kristy was a kindergarten child in the process of being diagnosed with autism. Parent helpers in the classroom asked the teacher, "What's wrong with that child?" and "If she doesn't have to finish her work, why does my child have to finish his?" The teacher did not respond to those questions in order to maintain confidentiality. The classroom helpers drew their own conclusions and discussed them among themselves. This child was labeled by others as uncooperative, poorly behaved, poorly parented, disruptive and "out of control." The parent helpers did not want to let their children play with Kristy, because of how they had judged her. They formed their own opinions about Kristy's parents.

Kristy's parents became aware of these misperceptions. They wrote a letter to the families in the class explaining Kristy's differences in very easy to understand language. They asked for the support and friendship of the classmates and their families. Kristy's parents sought the help of the school district's Inclusion Specialist, who spoke to the classmates, teaching them to understand, accept and play with Kristy. The reaction was positive and encouraging. One mother telephoned to talk at length because her child was also in the process of being diagnosed with ASD.

A five year old girl was asked what she thought about her kindergarten classmate, Tony who had ASD. (No one had talked to the children about Tony.) The little girl drew her own conclusion and answered, "Well, I guess he just has a bad mother!" Another student answered the same question, saying, "Well, Tony sure doesn't like kids much!"

Some sixth graders had been in the same school classes with a boy named Mike (who has Asperger's Syndrome) since first grade. They were asked to tell the reasons why they thought Mike was different. Reluctantly, one girl finally confessed that they had all talked about it a few times. They decided that probably Mike had been hit on the head with a rock when he was a little boy. Interestingly, they said they were sure he could not help "being that way" and that they were pretty sure it was not his fault.

When Barbara went to a group home to do a consultation for an adult with autism who lived there, a resident met her at the door. She asked, "Are you here about Gregory?" Barbara said yes, she was. The resident continued, "Could you get him out of here? He is wrecking our lives!" Staff did not acknowledge that Gregory was different from his housemates with other kinds of special learning needs. They did not adapt for him or explain his behavior to his housemates. He was an unknown person in his own home.

Knowledge is power, and without the knowledge of why a child or adult behaves a certain way, children and adults in the environment may not have the power to be accepting, understanding or helpful.

"If my child, or the adult in my care has a label used to describe them, then other people will know that he is different."

The features of ASD are behavioral. The features show up in what the child or adult does. People around a person with ASD can already see and hear the differences, just as you can, even as early as four or five years old. Describing how the disorder affects an individual can make clear to others why he does what he does.

Consider this: you meet a man. You extend your hand in greeting, but he does not take it. He stares off into space and does not make eye contact with you. When you point to the table you want to use, he does not respond. You think, "Wow, this guy has bad manners! I think he doesn't even care about what I have to say or what I want."

If you had known that the individual was blind before the introduction, you would know how to interpret things that he did that were unexpected or unusual. You would not have been confused or caught off guard. ASD causes people to behave differently. Others can see the differences. They need to know why.

"If I label my child, people will be biased against him/her."

Parents are sometimes concerned that a diagnosis is a label that will hurt their child in some way. It is a fact that others may attach preconceived notions to a person's diagnosis. It may be a good idea to find out what others are thinking and dispel misinformation. The alternative is letting others continue to believe things that are not true.

A mother of a child with autism said that no one in her child's school knew that he had ASD, because she hadn't told them. Therefore, she explained, no one could be biased against him and limit what he or she expected him to do. When the child was observed objectively with his classmates, it was clear that the other children did not initiate play with him or seek his company. When he did something unusual, the other children made faces at one another behind his back. Sometimes, when he was loud, the other children appeared to be afraid of him and moved quickly away from him, unlike their responses to other loud children.

It may be unrealistic to think that because no one knows *why* the child is different, that no one knows *that* the child is different! Teachers and children in the environment notice all kinds of differences and will draw their own conclusions as to why the child does what she does. If you want them to draw the right conclusions, you will want to empower them with information and explanation. **No label changes who your child is**. It describes how she functions and helps others to view the child more accurately.

"Once you give a child a label, you can never get rid of it."

Many teachers and school staff share this concern. They worry that when a child improves enough, a label can do more harm than good. Children and adults with ASD should continuously improve and make progress. But ASD is a lifelong disorder, and it will not just "go away." It is rare that an autism or ASD label is "removed," and when it is, that sometimes turns out to be only temporary or to have been incorrectly given in the first place.

"If I use a label, my child or adult's access to services will be designed the same way it is for everyone with that "label." I want an individualized service package, not a generic one."

It is very wise to guard against the use of a label to make decisions about programming, interventions and especially placement. State-of-the-art providers know both best practice and educational law supports that placement decisions be based on an individualized analysis of the person's deficits, strengths and needs and what services are most likely to be able to meet those needs.

In the Cory H. lawsuit in Illinois, the courts ruled that no child could be placed or served only on the basis of a disability or eligibility label. That means that a child with autism cannot be placed in an "autism" program based solely on a label. Throughout this book, staff and parents are encouraged to look at individuals, not as a group. However, if a child or adult has a diagnosis or label of ASD, it can be helpful in selecting and using specific teaching strategies, communication supports, and educational programs based on an assessment of that particular individual.

"If the teachers and staff know, they will tell people who I don't even know."

School staff is required by law to maintain privacy and use the information about the diagnosis only as a way to help your child. Adult services staff must follow the same laws of confidentiality. Parents will want to maintain control over how the information is shared and with whom. Parents may share the information with anyone as they see fit and are not restricted by confidentiality laws for their children under 18.

A situation may arise at school when teachers or staff would like to explain something about the student. Perhaps the children will be taking a field trip or are doing "buddy" activities with another class. Perhaps a noisy, crowded assembly is scheduled that will be hard for the person with ASD to tolerate. Does a chaperone need to know that your child might be very afraid of certain animals or smells at the zoo? Will your child try to "escape" during the assembly in front of the whole school? There are times when it is wise to have people in the school or care setting know about the person and understand their needs. Giving permission to share information with people who need to know is not a license for gossip. Parents can specify who is to know, how they are to be told and what words to use.

"How could a label be of any benefit?"

Some professionals in the field of autism have found that a diagnostic label can actually be in the best interest of the student. For example, as described in the work of Church and Coplan, many children with autism progressed to the point of being "delabelled," having the autism designation "removed." Other students were "relabeled," focusing on specific deficits such as "speech impairment," etc.

The researchers found that the students were caught in a "zone of misunderstanding," because teachers and staff attributed the student's problems and difficulties to personality and willful behaviors, rather than having a clear understanding of how the student's ASD affected his behavior and performance. Using the correct label to clearly understand a student's needs and sharing this information among staff is useful, efficient, and can prevent misunderstanding and wasted time.

An Analogy from Barbara

If I were going to play a sport, I would need to know the name of the sport that I was going to play. If the name was baseball, that would mean that I would dress in a particular way, gather particular "baseball" materials and equipment, show up at the baseball diamond and play according to the rules of baseball. If I did not know the name of the sport, it would be very hard to prepare for the game. How would I know what equipment to bring or purchase? How would I know where to go to play the game? If I did not know the name of the sport, how would I know which set of rules to apply? Applying the rules of basketball, when the game was really baseball, would be disastrous!

I am not comparing our loved ones with ASD to a game. I am saying that in a complex world, teachers, children and agency staff may really need to know which type of disorder the individual has, so that they will be best "equipped" with appropriate communication and teaching "equipment," and so they know what "ball park" they are in.

Who Needs to Know About the Diagnosis

Parents and staff can educate and inform those involved with the individual. The goal is to help others understand the features of ASD and learn how to best communicate and interact with the individual. Don't let your child or the adult in your care live in a world where only one or two people understand him. Consider whether you wish to only describe the patterns of ability and need, or if you also want to tell that the pattern has a name and what it is called.

It would be overwhelming to "tell" everyone at once (although it would be efficient!). It is more realistic to think about who needs to know, based on the daily activities and routines the person follows. Here are some of the people who may need to know about the individual and his needs:

- The person himself.

- Parents, stepparents, foster parents and all those in a parenting role.

- Siblings.

- Grandparents.

- Other relatives.

- Teachers in other classrooms.

- School personnel, like the nurse and substitute teachers.

- Agency staff.

- All those who will be providing support services.

- Instructional Assistants.

- Classmates.

- Schoolmates.

- Roommates or housemates.

- Co-workers.

- Neighbors.

- Friends.

- Local police, firefighters and rescue workers.

- Security staff from the shopping center and some stores.

- Bus drivers.

- Activity leaders, like scout leaders.

- Teammates and people in individual's extracurricular activities.

- People from church or community activities.

- Sports coaches.

- Doctors and dentists.

- Hair salon employees.

A "circle of friends" model may to help decide who needs to know and how to tell them (See 9.1). The "circle of friends" looks like a bulls eye with the person himself in the very center. In the nearest circle to the center are parents and close family. This circle can also include others that interact with the person with ASD everyday, such as teachers, the bus driver, etc. The next circle is extended family and friends, and other people who frequently interact with the person such as neighbors, classmates, teammates and workmates. In the outer circle are people who are acquaintances, who do not know the person very well or who interact only occasionally.

9.1 Circle of Friends for Talking About ASD

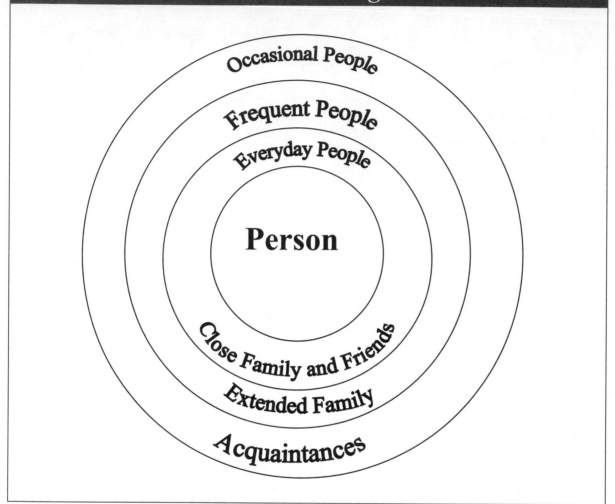

There are different reasons that each group of people would need to know about the features of ASD and how the person is affected. Some people will have everyday or in-depth relationships and will need a significant amount of information. Some encounters will be occasional, and some interactions will only be in an emergency. As the relationships differ, how much information is shared and the way it is shared, can be different.

It is realistic to recognize that you cannot educate every person who sees your child in public. By modeling the understanding, tolerance and acceptance that you hope others will learn, parents can send a message, even to strangers. What parents do and say in their interactions in public can positively impact and influence the perspective of others.

How Do We Tell Them?

It may be useful to decide what to say by answering the questions: "What will help the person to understand?" or, "What does the person need to know?" Does the bus attendant need to know that the child is sensitive to heat and light? Does the scout leader need to recognize signs that the child is becoming overwhelmed? Does a job coach need to understand the unique way the person communicates? Does a substitute teacher need to know that the student will need extra time to think and answer a question or take a walk in the hallway to remain self-regulated?

It is helpful to make sense of what people see, in context, by discussing how ASD affects the person. Most children and adults are kind and want to be helpful. Giving suggestions to others about the best ways to respond and support the child or adult with ASD can be very effective.

Parents and staff have used a variety of methods and materials to share information. Parents and staff can provide the information themselves, or ask another parent, a member of a support group, or a staff person with experience to lead the way. Here are some ideas:

- An informal, one-to-one discussion.

- A discussion and providing printed materials for the person to read later.

- A small group meeting.

- A family meeting.

- A meeting to show a video about autism, ASD or related disorders and discuss it.

- A private meeting with a coach or activity leader who then presents information to his group.

- A meeting with another family, a civic group, or church group or other group.

- A meeting/information session conducted by a professional.

- A presentation from the person with ASD or from another person with ASD.

- A letter from the parent or from the family.

- A letter written from the child's point of view.

- Sharing printed material such as articles about other people with ASD.

- Sharing a summary you have prepared about the person.

- Booklets.

- Reading a book to children or the class and discussing it.

- Books for adults.

- Videos.

- Websites.

We also provide two sample formats for "Talking to Typical Kids about Autism Spectrum Disorders," at the end of this chapter that you may wish to use or adapt. We provide sample letters and handouts, 9.2, 9.3, 9.4, and 9.5

A Case Example from Emily

I knew that my friend Rene was struggling because her son Mike, a sixth grader with ASD, was having a hard time with the children at school and in the neighborhood. My son Tom was asked for his opinion and said that sharing the information with families who need to know could make a big difference.

Rene took Tom's advice to heart and decided to talk to the parents of Mike's classmates, explain the situation and ask for their support. She arranged with the teacher to speak to the other parents at "Back to School Night." Rene and her husband adapted the letter shown in this book (9.2, Letter to Classmates and their families). One important sentence added to the letter was that Mike knew about his diagnosis, but did not really want to talk about it. That gave the other parents guidance about how to encourage their children to understand Mike and be a friend to him, but not press the issue of his diagnosis.

Rene excitedly phoned to tell me how emotional it was, but how well it went, and how relieved she feels to have shared the information. Now Mike comes home from school talking about the other children who invited him to play - a new and happy event for this child and family.

Rene and I have talked about the fact that sharing information is not going to make everything in Mike's life perfect. But Rene's family agrees it has made a big difference. Deciding to share is a brave thing to do especially because of vulnerability and trust issues. She was relieved that good things had come from it, and there have been no negative results or reactions.

Parents will have to decide for themselves what is right in their circumstances, when they are ready, who they should talk to and what they will say. Sometimes talking to other parents or staff who have been successful can be motivating, and parents can learn from the successes and obstacles others have faced in talking about ASD.

9.2 Letter to Classmates and Their Families

Dear Parents of Room 11,   September 2004

It is truly exciting for us that our daughter, Carrie, will be in Mr. Smith's class. We are looking forward to all the pleasures of second grade for her — that she will learn, make friends, have fun and be happy. That seems to sum up what all parents want for their children, and for us, this is like a dream come true. We have always wanted our little girl to be "just one of the kids."

This is the first time that Carrie will be in a "regular" classroom. Because she is a special learner, Carrie has been in a special education classroom. Seeing her, you might never guess this is true. You might not even be able to pick her out in a crowd. She likes to play as all children do. But while she looks typical, Carrie was born with a developmental disability that makes her different in some ways.

Our family and the staff at North School have planned how to help Carrie be successful in Mr. Smith's class. Carrie is well-behaved and will have an "aide," or instructional assistant, to help her when needed so we don't expect Carrie to be disruptive or need too much of the teacher's attention.

We think it is important to mention this, not to set Carrie apart, but to make sense of some of the "differences" that can be observed. We know that when children have the information they need, they become understanding, accepting and supportive. We are very hopeful that your son or daughter will be a friend to Carrie. It benefits all of the children to grow up together learning to respect and appreciate everyone's "differences."

We would like to ask for your support in helping your child to understand and get to know Carrie. On the back of this page are some of the things that your child may notice about Carrie and ask you about. We offer information to answer the questions, to help everyone be comfortable with the facts. You are also welcome to talk with us in person or by phone, or drop us a note if you have any concerns or questions. We are happy to answer and we'd love the opportunity to get to know you better.

Sincerely,

Carrie's Mom and Dad

Answers to Questions Your Child May Ask

1. **What is "wrong" with Carrie?** After Carrie was born, the doctors found out that her brain works differently. It may take longer for her to learn some things. Some things that are easy for you are hard for her. But, she is also very good at some things.

2. **What are some of the things that are hard for Carrie to learn?**

   — How to join in and play with kids; how to take turns.

   — How to ask for help.

   — How the schedule works at school and how to know when it is time to do things.

3. **Why does Carrie talk differently?** Carrie is still learning to talk, because her brain works differently than yours. Even if she cannot say words clearly, Carrie understands when people talk to her. She may "communicate" with you without using words. It is fine for you to talk to Carrie, even if she does not always answer.

4. **What should I do if I don't understand what Carrie says?**

   — Ask her, "Can you say that again?" Or ask another child or adult to listen with you.

5. **What should I do if Carrie doesn't understand what I am saying?**

   — Give her more time to think about it.

   — Show her what you mean.

   — Use different words that make it clearer.

   — Count to seven in your head and then repeat what you said.

   — Ask another child or an adult to help you.

6. **Why does Carrie get upset by loud noises or crowds?** Carrie is extra-sensitive. We all know what it feels like when something is really bothering us, like the fire alarm. Many things that don't bother you can bother Carrie and make her upset. Some people call this a "sensory problem" or a "processing problem."

7. **Carrie does not look at me when I talk to her. She does not look in my eyes. Is she mad at me?** No, Carrie is not mad. Carrie can be listening, even if she is not looking at you. And, Carrie wants to have friends, but is still learning how. You can help her learn by being a good friend to her, even if you aren't sure she notices.

8. **Does Carrie have mental retardation?** No, Carrie is very smart. She can learn many things. But it will take her a little longer. She will grow up to have a job and be successful like you.

9. **Is Carrie the only one who has these kinds of special needs?** No, about 1 in 500 people have this pattern of growing. They also need help to learn, communicate, make friends and follow rules. There is even a name for this, it is called having autism. But having autism is only one part of who Carrie is. She is a very nice girl, who likes what all the kids like and wants to make friends and belong. When we understand that she is still learning, we can be friendly and helpful.

9.3 What I Would Like You to Know

What I Would Like You to Know About My Son Who Has Asperger's Syndrome…

Confidential notes to help you get to know Jim:

ACADEMICALLY

- He is a good, cooperative student who wants to do well and follows the rules.

- He has strengths in some subjects, especially concrete and factual areas.

- Written comprehension and language are difficult for him.

- He may have difficulty understanding and following instructions.

- He may become confused or overwhelmed or have a strong reaction to change.

- He finds it hard to organize his materials and stay on task.

- These difficulties are due to the effects of his developmental disability, and not due to unwillingness or lack of cooperation and effort on his part.

SOCIALLY

- Although he seems likeable, especially to adults, he has a hard time making friends. He is aware of his lack of friends and frustrated by it.

- Other children often bully him because they perceive he is different and he does not know how to defend himself. He will need extra protection from adults.

- He may choose inappropriate ways to gain the attention or respect of the other children, because he does not know how else to do this successfully.

- He has more success communicating and socializing with adults than children.

EMOTIONALLY

- He knows about and understands that he has Asperger's Syndrome.

- This helps him to understand his difficulties and behavior.

- He is relieved that adults are aware of his difficulties and are being supportive.

- He may be sensitive, fragile or embarrassed when he makes a mistake.

STRATEGIES FOR HELPING … Here are some ideas to try

- Give clear, short, specific instructions. Give him time to "process" and respond.

- After waiting, re-stating works better than repeating.

- If a difficulty arises, you can "lead him out of it," with specific directions, such as, "Now you need to do this…"

- Don't ask him what he should be doing. If he knew, he would be doing it. Tell him gently what to do, rather than ask him.

- Allow extra time to complete tasks when feasible.

- Use his learning style and interests to advantage in academic or social areas.

- Match him with partners and teams who are supportive and empathetic.

- When possible, let him "shine" in his areas of knowledge for self-esteem and peer recognition.

- Avoid "putting him on the spot" for quick answers or inferences, as this may be frustrating or embarrassing.

Please communicate with me about his progress and needs. I appreciate your support and interest tremendously.

Jim's Mom.

9.4 A Letter From Angie

A letter from Angie (and her dad)

To the students and families of Mrs. Good's Class

Hi, my name is Angie. I am nine years old and I am going to be in Mrs. Good's class this year. I love to do spelling, but I don't like math so much! I really like to play jump rope at recess.

When you meet me, you may notice that I cannot talk. I am still learning. It is something that is very hard for me. I use pictures to let people know what I want and to answer people when they talk to me. I understand a lot and I am paying attention. It is just that I have a hard time forming words.

Last year all my friends learned how to talk to me using my picture book. They think it is fun. You can look at my book of pictures and you will see that we can communicate without words. I am so happy when the kids in the class are my friends and are nice to me. I try to be a good friend too.

Well, I am looking forward to a great year and having a good time in Mrs. Good's class! See you there!

Your friend,

Angie

> *P.S. My dad says if you or your parents have any questions, he is happy to talk to you, just phone or email us!*

A sample letter from an adult with autism to his new group home "roommates" who have developmental disabilities. This letter could be read to the residents and discussed before "Trevor" moves into the house.

9.5 A Letter From Trevor

Hi everyone!

My name is Trevor and I am going to live with you starting on September 1st. I am looking forward to becoming friends.

We all have special needs but I wanted to tell you about my special needs. I have autism. Autism makes it hard for me to do some things. My staff is continuing to teach me what to do. My mom and Dad have been helping me learn since I was a baby.

I have a hard time when I do not know what is going to happen next. Sometimes I ask the same questions over and over again! I do not mean to bug anyone; it is just that I can't remember the answer. If someone writes the answer down for me, I can remember better and can stop asking so many questions.

I have a lot of curiosity. I want to know what people have in their desk drawers or in their clothes dresser. Sometimes I forget to ask before I look at other people's things. I just want to look. I promise I won't take anything. If you do not want me to look at your things, say, "Trevor stop. Leave my things alone." Get the staff to help you if you need it.

I love music. All kinds of music. I hope that we will enjoy listening to music together. I love to dance and like dancing by myself or with other people.

Sometimes I need a break. I go to my room and rock in my rocking chair. I am not mad at anyone when I do this. I just need a rest from everything. Then I will come out of my room and I will be okay.

If I get mad, I might scream. Do not be afraid. I won't hurt anyone. Sometimes I just start screaming and I can't make myself stop for a couple of minutes. I know this upsets people and I am trying to learn to use my words to stay calm and tell people what I need so they can help me.

I have a couple of favorite topics that I like to talk about. I like to talk about trains and electricity. You might get bored with me when I talk about these things too much. Just tell me, "Stop talking about trains until later" and then tell me what time I can talk about trains again. I am learning to like to talk about new things, but it is really hard for me.

I do not like kisses and hugs, but you can pat me on my shoulders or we can shake hands if you want. I am sure I will like all of you, but my brain just does not like a lot of touching.

I promise to be a good roommate. I am really tidy and like to do the dishes, put away the groceries, arrange the videos in order and make all the beds in the whole house! I know we can be friends and be happy living together.

Your new friend,

Trevor

Timing the Approach

If you feel fairly sure about a method that is appropriate for sharing information with a particular person or group, when do you do it? Here are some considerations:

1. Plan a time when the individual will not be present. It could be very awkward or upsetting for the person to sit and hear his needs described. Others may not feel free to ask questions if the person is present. Unless there is a very good reason that the person should be there, it is usually best not to have him attend.

2. The best time to have a family meeting is maybe after parents have had some time to understand the diagnosis and begin working on behalf of the child or adult. It will help if staff and family members have been living or working for some time with the individual and will be well aware of the characteristics and features they have been seeing.

3. Plan a time to meet when there will be no pressure or conflict of commitments. For example, don't plan to share during a parent-teacher conference or during an IEP or annual planning meeting. Although that is private time with the teacher, others are waiting for their turns. Make a separate appointment.

4. Decide if the information should be shared before the group gets to meet the individual, or after. If any type of dangerous behavior is involved, adults or group leaders will need to know in advance. In other cases, it may be a good idea to have people meet and get to know the child or adult first, and then come back and explain the differences that they noticed. Waiting a few weeks into the session may help make clear what problem areas will be, and what needs to be done about them.

A Case Example from Emily

In one case, a mother decided to share information about ASD with the dance teacher before the child enrolled. The dance teacher became very nervous and worried that she could not handle having the child in class. Later, when she met the girl, she thought the girl fit in very well and was a pleasure to work with. As the teacher got to know the girl, she was able to use some of the strategies suggested by the mother to help the other dancers befriend the girl. The teacher was able to draw on her own training and education to help the girl with some motor issues. Although telling initially seemed like it was going to produce negative results, in the end, the informed teacher was able to use the information wisely.

In another case, a young lady was enrolling in drama class. She attended a few classes. Later, her father went to the group when the girl was not present. He asked the other drama students if they had noticed anything different about her. As it turns out, they had noticed several features of ASD. The parent was able to expand on their observations to explain ASD to the kids and ask them for their support and friendship.

Due to the desire and legal obligation to educate students with disabilities with their non-disabled peers to the greatest extent possible, students may have had the opportunity to get to know other students who have disabilities. While this may help them to be more prepared than in the past, the peer group will still need information and support to make the most of the time spent together. Sharing information early in the school year, or at the beginning of a placement may prevent students and those who interact with the student with ASD from drawing the wrong conclusions about his behaviors or communication style. This also gives the most caring students a chance to respond postively from the start.

Don't wait too long to tell people who are involved in activities with the child or adult. The longer you wait, the more likely it is that some confusing things will happen that are misunderstood. Having information helps people make sense of what they are seeing. It is also better sooner, rather than later, to suggest practical techniques to help the individual be successful.

It is never too late to tell! It is better to provide some information, even years after people have been living or working together, than to continue to have the person be misperceived.

A Case Example from Barbara

While on vacation in Florida, I was asked to talk to a group of junior and senior high school students about students with social and cognitive differences and other differences that we can't see. The principal had asked me to come, because he was becoming more certain that several high school students had true social issues. He had referred these students for case studies. In the meantime, he wanted the students to know something about social differences so that they could be more supportive.

I talked to the students for about 30 minutes. At one point, I told them about a student that I knew who, by eighth grade, had never gotten invited to a party or gotten a phone call from another student. I asked them what that might be like if it happened to them. A silent pall fell over the group as they considered the impact of being left out. Finally, one boy said, "Wow! That is about the worst thing that could happen to a guy!"

After the talk, three very interesting things happened. The first was that a boy approached me, introduced himself as Stan and told me that perhaps he had "some kind of autism." He explained that he really wanted friends, but seemed to make the other kids not like him no matter how hard he tried. He said he had no true friends, felt very lonely and had tried everything he could. He was tired of this situation and wanted to change. Fortunately the school counselors and principal had been present for my discussion and so I encouraged Stan to talk to them. Stan and his parents could ask to see if he had "some kind of autism" so that he could get some help and instruction about how to make and sustain friendships. He agreed and asked me to accompany him to talk to the counselor and the principal. I agreed to do both, starting with talking with the principal in private that afternoon, and talking to the counselor the next day.

Next, a teen-aged girl, that I guessed to be about 16, approached me. She was a lovely child with the kind of gentle beauty that I associate with Grace Kelly. She said, "You know that child that no one called in his whole life? I am so sorry that happened to him!" She put her arms around me, hugged me and patted my back gently. Then she said, "I promise you that no child will be left out ever again if I am around!" I believed her and tried not to cry at such a sincere outpouring of empathy and caring.

Finally, I went to the principal's office, as I had promised to do, to mention Stan to the principal. When I arrived, I said, "I am here to talk to you about a student named..." Before I could continue, the principal said, "Josh, right? I get it now, he really needs an assessment. You described him to a tee." I was startled and told him no, that I was talking about Stan. The principal sat in silence for a moment and said, "You know, we have always thought about Stan and Josh as being bright, kind of egocentric and a little spoiled. What a limited view! I better refer them both to be assessed." We did not have a parental release of information so the discussion stopped there.

Whether or not Stan and Josh both met the criteria for the diagnosis of ASD, I am convinced that their lives took a turn for the better that day. Faculty and students were likely to be less judgmental and more understanding than in the past. Whatever assessments were completed would likely yield information, about special learning needs that could then be addressed along with any mental health issues that may have arisen from years of "isolation in a crowd."

What About Resistance?

After all these things to think about, parents may finally agree on what to say, when to say it and who to say it to! When you share these ideas with others, some people may be uncomfortable with it or even resist. Teachers, administrators or adult caregivers may think it is a bad idea! They have not done it before. They are afraid of what others will think. They are living with the backlash of the "labeling" controversy.

They may not see the benefit of telling others. They may have concerns about confidentiality and legal issues.

Ironically this may be due to the fact that some team members or staff do not have enough information! Teams will have to find a way to clarify things and work out any obstacles. One idea is to find staff and professionals who have been successful and have them explain to their colleagues. Continue to dialogue and educate and discuss until the team is in agreement.

A Case Example from Barbara

Parents certainly have the right not to disclose information about their child. One father said to me, "If my daughter knew that her classmates had talked about her 'behind her back,' she would be devastated." He simply refused, and as of this writing, I do not think that his daughter's classmates know anything about her special needs and special gifts. It was his right to do that and I will not second-guess him. I left the door open with him so that we could discuss the issue again in the future. I was careful not to let this turn into a "right or wrong" type of discussion. In that way, he could come back to me later to talk more about it without feeling like he had given in to me or lost some kind of battle. I accept that he has his reasons for his decisions and respect his right to choose what he thinks is best for his daughter.

Parents and staff will need to think carefully about whether or not to inform the child or adult that the discussion will or has taken place. This decision relates closely to how much the child or adult knows about his diagnosis and what it means. It does not make sense to create an information gap by telling others what the child or adult knows nothing about. This is another decision that can be carefully discussed with the full team until an acceptable plan is in place.

Telling the Child or Teen about ASD

One of the most difficult decisions a parent faces is deciding whether to explain the diagnosis to the child or teen. Parents worry:

- My child doesn't know she is different. She will only know that she is different if I tell her.

- If my child knows that he has a disorder, he will have poor self-esteem and think there is something wrong with him.

- If he feels he is different, he will feel singled out or set apart.

- My child may take it really hard and get very upset.

- My child could get "stuck" on this and not be able to move off the thought.

- My child has lived to this age without knowing, why tell her now?

These are all legitimate and thoughtful concerns based on how well parents know and understand the child. How much the child is told and how it is explained can make a significant difference. The individual will need time to understand, believe and accept, just like anyone else. Suggestions are made below about how to talk to your son or daughter using "chats."

Knowing when to tell the child or teen may be hard. Kids with ASD tend not to ask many questions that would let you know they are ready. You will have to watch for signs that the young person is becoming aware. For example, a child may ask, "Why does my sister always get invited to birthday parties, and I don't?" Sometimes a particular situation, such as being victimized or getting in serious trouble, makes it clear that she needs to know and it is time to start talking. If a crisis is the event that lets you know that the child needs information, wait until everyone recovers before you talk about ASD.

Need for Self-awareness and Self-advocacy

There are two other good reasons to begin to explain ASD to the person even if he is still a child. The ultimate goal for people with ASD is to live the most independent life possible. They need to be prepared to live successfully, have meaningful work, friends and fun things to do in the community. When students leave school and prepare to transition to adult life, a goal like this one is usually included on the transition plan: The individual will be able to explain his disability to others, identify when he needs help and ask for help when he needs it. These may be essential skills for a successful life!

Self-awareness is having a sense of identity that includes understanding how a person is affected by his disability. **Self-advocacy** is a skill in which a person is aware of a need, states the need and asks for help. These two things are considered keys to success and independence for adults with disabilities and perhaps for us all.

Can we expect to meet the goals of self-awareness and self-advocacy if we do not know about them? Neither can we expect them to be met if we do not bring up the subject of ASD or disabilities to the affected person. It is logical to meet the goals of self-awareness and self-advocacy by helping the person understand himself and explain himself to others.

Rather than wait for the day that the goal finally appears on the transition plan, information can be shared with the individual over time. The words chosen to model and teach should be matched to the person's age and ability to understand. Step by step, build on the essential information that a person needs to know and share. Don't wait: goals of self-awareness and self-advocacy can be written into a person's individual plan today for a person of any age.

Many students have been in special education classes for years, but no one has told them why. Some adults live in group homes, but no one has ever explained why. It can come as a great shock to find out why in some sudden, unplanned way. It doesn't have to happen like that!

Should I Talk to the Child or Adult with ASD Even if She Does Not Seem to Understand What I am Talking About?

Think of all the things that people with ASD "hear" about themselves across their lifetimes. It can start very early, usually when a parent or doctor discusses what is "wrong" with her, in front of her, during a diagnostic workup. It continues in school as teachers, students and others notice and mention differences that they have observed. Sometimes, unfortunately, people with ASD overhear themselves called "dumb" or a "retard" or other disparaging terms.

In our opinion, the *least dangerous assumption* is all of that negative information goes into the person's brain and is stored and retrieved *in some way*. The individual with ASD may come to think of themselves as not achieving, not being successful, or being dumb, bad, defective or unworthy.

When an individual cannot talk to us about what they are thinking and feeling, people begin to act as though the individual is **not** thinking or feeling. We disagree. We suggest that carefully thought out, positive explanations be provided to everyone with ASD even if they are deemed unable to understand. The worst that could happen is that the individual may be able to think and feel the positive things that we have told her.

It could be important to talk to the individual using themes such as "special learning differences" and "you are a good person" and "people like you" and " I know it is hard for you, but your dad and I know you are trying very hard." These themes may become a source of comfort and strength for the individual with ASD. It is hard to imagine that this type of talking could do harm to anyone.

An Example from Emily

Our Family's Way to Tell the Child, Teen or Adult.

When Tom was diagnosed, our family was in crisis. So many bad things were happening at school that it was a relief to have a diagnosis that made sense. My husband and I thought it was important for Tom to know, but we were very worried about what his reaction would be. We worried that hearing the news would be too stressful or make him feel bad about himself. He was 13 years old at the time.

I decided to talk to Tom to give him the initial information. He had two responses. First, he held his head and cried, and said, "My brain is broken and it can't be fixed." In the same conversation, he said, "You know, this explains a lot of things." Slowly, over months, we built on that conversation, one small piece of information at a time.

Barbara also explained things to Tom. Sometimes he was negative or upset. Usually he calmed down and took some time to think about what he was hearing. At one point, we heard him say, "Well you know, Albert Einstein and Thomas Jefferson and I all have problems in social situations." (We had told him that historians believe both Einstein and Jefferson were possibly people with ASD.)

Tom is now 19. Recently, we asked Tom how he thinks parents could tell their family member that he has ASD. Here is what he said:

- Pick a quiet time when there are no particular problems.

- Make sure you have his attention.

- Build him up.

- Remind him about things from the past that happened and explain about it. Tell him how it fits into a pattern.

- Tell him that the pattern has a name, and he is not the only one.

Expanding on those thoughts, these ideas evolved into having several "chats" with the child, teen or adult to help him learn about his disorder. As we know from living with special children, it is important to break things into pieces. Sharing small amounts of information at a time builds meaning and can help avoid overload. When each piece is understood, we can build to the whole. Giving the information in a gradual way can be effective because it relates to how our children learn and understand.

There are several advantages to using "the chats." Firstly, parents or staff model calm objectivity, speaking of facts. This helps children to understand that their parents accept and understand them. It helps them to accept and understand themselves.

If something is not understood during one chat, parents or staff can spend time clarifying and checking for understanding before going to the next step. Difficulties may include that the child or adult gets "stuck" on one part of the message and is not able to move on for a while. This can be part of the special processing needs of people with ASD.

Parents and staff can use language that the child can also use in thinking and speaking, such as "some things are hard for me," or "I am really strong in some areas, but other things are harder for me." The words the parents and staff use are like tapes playing in the child's or adult's head that she will reply many times. If they are loving, accepting and non-judgmental words, the child or adult can feel and internalize those positive things.

Thirdly, parents and staff can approach the fact that the child or adult has a disorder as a "difference." It is a difference that is only one part of who the person is. It helps the individual to know that in many ways he is just like everyone else. Parents can reassure the child or adult that things will turn out OK.

The "Chats"

(Presented here as for children, can be adapted for teens or adults)

Consult with your team or other people you trust to decide if this is a good approach to use with your child. The sample information presented here may be appropriate for verbal children or adults or high-functioning individuals. The words and information can be adapted based on the age and developmental stage of the child or adult.

If the child is young, or just beginning to be aware, you may want to continuously give chats 1-5 on a regular basis even if the individual does not appear to understand or be "listening." As the level of understanding grows, chats 6, 7 and 8 can be introduced.

Chat 1.

You are wonderful. You have many great things going for you. Lots of people think you are good and nice. I love you and will always be here for you.

Chat 2.

You are really good at certain things, (name a few). How does that make you feel? It's a good feeling to be able to do things. It is a good thing to have as many talents as you do.

Chat 3.

Some things are hard for you, (name one or two). How does that make you feel? Everybody has a hard time with some things, but they are still good people. Having a problem is just one part of who a person is; it is not everything about them. It is a good idea to get help for the things that are hard from someone who cares about you.

Chat 4.

You are really good at some things and other things are hard for you. You are not the only one who is like that. Other kids are just like you. It is not their fault that some things are hard. That just how they were born. No one is mad at them. They are OK. You are OK too.

Chat 5.

You will need some help with the things that are hard for you. You will have (name something such as speech therapy or a social skills group). We want you to have this, so the hard things will get easier for you. The people who give you the services and teach you care about you and want to help.

Chat 6.

Other people find some things easy and some things hard, like you. You have a very good brain, but sometimes it works differently. There is even a name for this. Do you want to know what it is called? Some famous people have this. Some say Einstein had it. You are going to be successful and have a good life too. (But you may not be as famous as Einstein!)

Chat 7.

It will take some time to get used to all these ideas. I am here to talk about it and answer all your questions. We have plenty of time.

Chat 8.

When something is hard for you, you need to let other people know. You can tell them how to help you. You can say, "it is too loud for me in here," or "please talk slower." It is OK to use words to tell people what you are feeling and what you need. If they understand, they will want to help.

Parent and Professional Collaboration for Sharing Information

Figuring out what to say and how to say it may hard for parents who are experiencing these challenges for the first time. Many teachers and professionals in the school or adult service delivery system have known many individuals with ASD in their years of experience. Many professionals have had training in working with people with ASD. They may know about a variety of ways to share information. These professionals can be a wonderful resource to parents. Staff may have excellent input and suggestions to help parents decide how to proceed.

Staff can help parents connect with parents with more experience who have been in the same situation. If you know a parent who is willing to be a resource to others, helping people connect can be as easy as asking a "new" parent, "Do you want me to give your telephone number to Mrs. Jones and ask her to call you?"

Sometimes staff will be responsible for informing an individual that they have ASD. The information in this section of our book can be adapted for that situation. Staff should be sure to always have a signed release form from the parent or legal guardian when they are preparing to inform an individual about any diagnostic information.

Many districts or local areas have an Inclusion Specialist. His job is to help students with disabilities be successful in their educational environment. This can include helping the student or supporting staff or classmates in including the individual. The Inclusion Specialist can meet with the family to come up with a plan for sharing information. The Inclusion Specialist can make presentations to the class. The Inclusion Specialist can also make a presentation to staff. Sharing information about ASD, without referring to a specific child, can increase the general level of understanding among staff.

Other school or district personnel may be skillful in educating others. Those with the most knowledge or experience are logical choices. Or, someone who has less experience, but is willing to work with the family, may be responsive and effective. Professionals who know the child well, such as the classroom teacher, the speech and language pathologist, the school psychologist, a counselor, an occupational therapist, the adapted physical education teacher or a behaviorist can consult with the family to make a plan to share information. They can also make presentations to the peers or to staff.

Another thing that professionals and staff can do is "give the words" to use in thinking and talking about some of the features of ASD. Staff can model the words for the benefit of the individual who can use the phrases for self-awareness and self-advocacy. Similar phrases can be used to make sense of what peers are seeing. Peers, classmates or housemates of the person with ASD can make these phrases and ideas part of what they say and think everyday. Here are some examples:

- Sometimes the noise in here is just too much for (me)/(James).

- (I'm)/(he's) still learning to _____.

- Please speak slower so (I)/(Jenny) can understand.

- I am (she is) learning to do better at_____.

- It's better to show me what you want me to do, than to tell me/It's better to show her what you want her to do than to tell her.

- (I learn) Pete learns the best if you will make a list for (me) him.

- Rachel is such a great speller! Why don't you ask her to help you?

All staff and professionals, both in the school and adult services settings, also have the opportunity to be role models. Whether or not a person's disability is explained to others, the behavior and attitude of staff reinforces how to respect and include the person. "You are being watched," Barbara tells professionals who attend her presentations. Remember that actions speak louder than words to many pairs of eyes and ears. You teach without telling everyday.

There are times when teachers, other professionals, and adult caregivers feel conflicted about the issue of talking about a person's disability. Here are some situations that staff may find difficult:

- The parents want to share information and you are not comfortable with it.

- The parents do not want to tell and you can see that lack of information or misinformation is causing problems.

- You are not sure how to handle intrusive questions or comments others make.

- You are not sure about the issues of confidentiality.

- You would like to have permission to share certain information in specific situations.

These issues can be brought up and discussed in private with the parents or in a team meeting depending on the circumstances. It may be helpful to parents when staff describe specific situations that demonstrate the need or reason to share information that parents may not be aware of.

Therese's Letter

Here is an excerpt from a letter written to Barbara from a woman named Therese. Barbara was part of the support team for Therese's son, George, starting in fourth grade. It is an excellent example of parent-professional collaboration and an inspiring story about children and the power of information. (Therese and George are happy to have their real names used, because they are proud of how hard they have worked and how far they have come!)

Dear Barbara,

Since you are the one who inspired me to share information about ASD with George's classmates, I want to fill you in and let know how things are going. The good news is George is doing better at his middle school than he ever has done in school!

You know that starting in third grade, the kids treated George like he was from another planet. He was not ever part of the group. They really had no idea how to help him fit in. George walked the perimeter of the playground at lunch and recited stories to himself. It was really sad.

You inspired me to do something when you reminded me that there were a few kids who would always be helpful to George without instruction. I thought the others might simply need to know what to do, but may not know how to ask. So I worked with Ann, the Speech and Language Pathologist, to decide "what to tell" George's classmates. When Ann and I went into the class, it was awkward at first. The kids were brutally honest after the first few minutes, and we clarified many things for them.

We defined what autism is, and what it means. We came up with some ideas, and we asked the kids to give us ideas for ways to help especially with unstructured social time. Us talking to them helped most of the kids realize that George couldn't help the things he said and did. They also felt good about helping him. We asked if they thought us coming to talk about ways to help George was a good idea and they all said, "yes!"

As you know, George needs to eat lunch in a quiet place and he was usually alone. We asked the kids if they wanted to have lunch with George. So many of them wanted to, we had to start making reservations for them after that day!! When one of the boys invited George to his Halloween Party, he made George's invitation with a schedule on it so that George would know what was going to happen at the party.

Ann and I went into the class each year including this year in the middle school. The kids were really receptive and many of them who had seen George crying on the first days of school told us that they were glad we came, because they had come to the wrong conclusions about George. I told them we needed their input because George doesn't seem to think about what his peers are doing. We asked the kids to tell us what kinds of things they think and talk about so that we can teach George the same kinds of things. The kids were so attentive and respectful, and it was just a great experience. They gave us great ideas about new videos and things that might help George be more able to have conversations about topics such as sports, college football, baseball, etc.

Mary, the SLP is the best!! With her direction and script writing, we made several instructional videos for George and plan to make many more. The students are involved in this, and everyone has a great time doing it. The best thing is that George learns so much from this, and because the kids are in the video, he really feels like they are special people to him. Some of the best comments and ideas came from the kids we would least expect to make such observations, so this can and should be a win-win situation for all of the students. I truly believe they think of it this way!

George ends each school year with a pizza party for all of his classmates. I order up enough pizzas to feed about 70 kids!! It is the social event of the year, I am told. George hands out invitations, and it is just a great fun time. Even with all of those people in one room, he handles it very well. The kids know that this is George's "Thank You!" to them, and they really love it. They all know that George cannot handle being in a noisy room and are all very quiet during this time, so the teachers love it. George has had a birthday party each year and this year's was the best! The kids totally understand that he needs to sit away from them when he eats, and it is ok with them. George went to another girl's party and some of the same people were there. He was just like a regular kid!!

The kids were just fantastic, and I am so proud of all of them. What a great bunch of people they are. I try to let their parents know, because most of the time, they have no clue how special their own kids are in this way. Many of the kids, who are so supportive of George, just do what they do and don't think much about it being special. These are the people who will help our kids when they are adults. We must support and recognize them!!!

They most certainly are special people. My experience with Franklin and the teachers there have given me the ability to look to George's future knowing that he will succeed in his life, and he will be OK. That my friend, is something that every parent of a child with autism needs to experience.

Therese

Emily's Approach to Talking to Typical Children about Kids with ASD

Here is a sample explanation to use or adapt to help increase the awareness of the peer group. This sample would be geared to fourth grade or older. These are the main points I like to make in explaining ASD you can adapt. It can also be used with neighbors, cousins, or siblings.

"Sometimes there is a lot of confusion about disabilities. People have ideas that may not be true. Do you think that people who cannot see have better hearing than you do? Well, that is an example of a myth that is not true. Many misconceptions get in the way of understanding other people."

"Sometimes it is easy to see that a person has a disability. We notice that a person uses a wheelchair or has a guide dog. But some disabilities are invisible. That means that the person looks like everyone else. Yet, a difference makes things harder for them, and can be truly challenging, everyday."

"Maybe you have heard of autism. There are many ideas associated with autism, but some of them are not true. It is important for us to understand what autism is and what it is not. Autism is a developmental disability. That means that a person is born with the disorder and it is expected to last the whole lifetime."

Here are some things to know about autism:

- Some people call autism a "spectrum disorder." This means that not all people who have autism seem the same.

- People use the term "ASD" for Autism Spectrum Disorders as an easier way to explain that people with autism may be very different from one another.

- Some people with ASD never speak, while other people with autism talk very well.

- Most people with ASD find it easy to learn some things and very hard to learn other things. Some people with ASD learn quickly. Other people with ASD need to be taught something many times and in special ways. People with ASD may be "gifted" in some areas and may learn more about some topics than the adults know!

- Most people with ASD are very nice, but they have a hard time learning how to make friends. It is hard for them to learn social rules. Children with autism might need help learning how to play or to join in a game, or talk with their friends.

- Some people with autism are very sensitive to things like noise or touch that don't bother most of us.

- Many things can help people with autism.

"Maybe you have heard about the movie "Rain Man." The character in the movie has autism. He cannot function on his own, although he has some great abilities. That is what most people think of when they hear the word "autism." But that is just one way a person with autism can be. Some people with Autism Spectrum Disorders are very smart and are able to achieve remarkable things in the areas they like to concentrate on like math, science, computers or art."

"At the same time, they may have a hard time learning how to make friends or socialize. They might have trouble when they try to be friendly or join in a game. They might say or do things that are different from most children and may confuse you until you understand more about them. They may be sensitive to noise, light or touch.

"People who have autism and function pretty well are said to have high-functioning autism or have Asperger's syndrome. Some people think that Albert Einstein and Thomas Jefferson may have had Asperger's syndrome. Some people think that many very successful computer geniuses may have a form of autism. There is hope for people with autism to be very successful."

"What do you think it might feel like to have ASD? People who have it tell us that everyday things can be very confusing for them. Picture yourself at a party with important people from a foreign country. Would you know what to say and do at the right time? Would you understand the signals and messages people were trying to send you if you did not speak their language? Not understanding the communication and not knowing what to do to fit in might make you feel very stressed. You might make some mistakes and feel embarrassed."

"For many people with ASD, everyday life can be confusing and stressful like being in a foreign place. Of course our friends with ASD speak our language and live in our culture. But many parts of social communication are hard for them. Differences in the way they learn and process information makes things that are easy for you, very hard for them." They can also feel sad and alone if they are left out in class and on the playground.

"That is why kids with Autism Spectrum Disorders get special education. Teachers in special education know how to teach and help boys and girls with ASD understand social situations better. They work on communication. They work on making friends. They work on the academics they are good at and get help with the school subjects that are hard for them."

"A disability like ASD is just one part of a person. Apart from their disability, boys and girls with ASD have a lot in common with you. They are more like you than you may think. They may like video games, TV shows, and movies, roller coasters, or skateboarding just like some of you do. They like to go places and have fun. They can be very nice to know and can be good friends to you."

"It is important to help kids with Autism Spectrum Disorders be included at school and feel like they belong. There are things you can do to help. One of the best things you can do to help is to get to know them and be friendly to them. You can introduce them to your other friends and include them in your plans. You can ask adults for help so that things go well and everyone is comfortable. If you see someone teasing or being mean to a person with ASD, tell the person being mean to stop or get some help quickly from an adult."

"By being a friend to your classmates with ASD, you will be making a difference in the lives of others. You will learn to understand and accept people who are different from you. You will show other people, who might have some mistaken ideas that boys and girls with ASD are nice to know and can be good friends. When you do activities with friends with ASD, you show that they belong at school and can help other people get to know them. You can be a bridge to more friends and social activities for students with ASD. And you will have a lot of fun doing it."

Barbara's Approach to Talking to Typical Children About Children with ASD

When I talk to students, I always ask the faculty to stay in the room. I want them to know what is said, how it is said and how to describe things in a person-friendly way. I write three columns on the board:

What it's called	What it means	How we help

I usually begin by talking about blindness. Blindness is something that most people can understand, even five year olds! We talk about what blindness could be called (vision impairment, low vision, etc.). We talk about words that might be used to describe a person who is blind and decide as a group whether or not we "like" those words (like "blind as a bat").

We talk about what it means to be blind. Depending on the age of the group, I generate discussion about things that are important to them. For example, for younger students we talk about what it would be like if you could not see the words in the book or see the cars coming on the street. For older students, I ask them to think about what it would mean if you could not watch a movie or drive a car. In any case, as we talk about what it means, I clarify any misconceptions, remove any myths and model appropriate language use.

Then we talk about how we can help the individual who cannot see. Smaller children will suggest reading to them or holding their hands to cross the street. (At this point, I always model appropriate sighted guide techniques. Be sure to learn them yourself!) Older students talk about how the individual who is blind could have a Seeing Eye dog, a cane or a special computer that could talk to them.

Throughout the whole discussion, I remind the students that children who are blind didn't do anything wrong to get that way and neither did the parents. I talk about how much people who are blind (like my husband Ed) add to our world with their kindness, listening and thinking skills, hard work and sense of humor. Then I encourage the students to talk about anyone in their families or social life that is blind or has visual impairment. While they talk, I listen for valuable points to focus on such as: this person contributes to others, is sensitive, has feelings, cares what others think about him, is trying very hard to do a good job, enjoys what other people enjoys and is more like us than unlike us.

If I have lots of time, I will lead a similar discussion about deafness: What it's called, What it means and How we help.

Then I write "special learning differences" or "special learning needs" in the column of "What it's called." I generate a discussion about learning differences. We talk about dyslexia and what that means to a student who is trying to learn to read.

Next, I bring up the topic of autism or ASD. I describe autism to the younger children as a good child who is trying hard to make friends, but who has a hard time knowing how to play with other children. I talk about the verbal and non-verbal differences and some of the unusual behavior the children may have observed in schoolmates with autism. In the "What it means" column, we describe the impact that autism has, for example that some children with autism can't talk at all, some talk too much and some talk about things that we do not understand.

We talk about autism as a difference in how the brain works. Sometimes we spend time talking about how the brain controls so much of what we do and how it would be if certain "parts" of our brains didn't work as well as we wanted them to. We discuss issues of playing with the younger children and issues of social relationships with the older children. I give them examples of children with autism who know a lot or can do "cool" things that are beyond what the typical children can do.

We spend time talking about how lonely you would be if you wanted to have friends, but did not know how. We talk about being left out. With older students, I teach the word "ostracize" so that they can understand this as a social phenomenon which happens to many people or groups considered "different." We discuss issues of bullying and victimization and how children with autism have less self-defense skills than other people do, even though they are very smart in other ways.

We talk about the fact that everyone can learn new things, and that children with autism will learn to communicate (maybe in some special ways), will learn to be a good friend and how to play and will have a good life and be a good grown up in our community or wherever they go.

Then we get to my favorite part and talk about "How we help." By this point the students are generally revved up and thinking of many creative and friendly things to do. One five-year-old said to us, " Well you could just be nice to a person with autism and that would make her feel really happy." One third-grader said, "I guess a person with autism would really appreciate it if I played ball with him on the playground." One first-grader said, " Why, we could all eat lunch together!"

At the end of the discussion for that day, I let the children know that it is ok to quietly ask an adult questions about another student if they are trying to understand and be friends with that student. I let them know that it is OK to tell teachers if they see anyone being mean to a person with a special learning need.

Sometimes, at some point in the discussion, the students have thought of a specific child who seems to have the features in the "What it Means column." I try to be ready for this by talking to parents and staff in advance and planning what to say and describe if the group brings up a specific child. If it is likely that a child with autism will be identified by the class that day, I usually arrange the talk for a time when that child is not present, just in case. That way, with parental permission gained in advance, I can divert the discussion from a more general one to a more specific one and help the students understand and appreciate the gifts and talents of their classmate with ASD.

If the child with autism is not identified or brought up by the children that day, I can arrange to give another talk on another day specifically about that child. My preference is to do a general discussion with all students in the school, class by class, at the beginning of the year and follow up with additional discussions in classrooms where students are in contact with a child with ASD.

We hope that these two examples of different approaches to talking to students provide you with some ideas that you can adapt for specific situations and individuals with autism supported in schools and agencies everywhere. So get talking!

CHAPTER 9: SUMMARY

- Sharing information about ASD can be a sensitive issue and a matter of personal choice. Ideas have been presented to help decide what to share, with whom and how.

- Preconceived notions and generalizations surround autism, even today. Sharing information will help increase understanding and help dispel bias and prejudice.

- Information can have a big impact for many people, and may help them think differently, feel differently and act differently through understanding and acceptance.

- Providing information sometimes causes a negative reaction. Some people may avoid you and your family because they are not ready to deal with the situation.

- When isolation occurs, families need to call friends and relatives, invite them back into the family's life and tell them that everyone can learn about ASD together.

- It is up to parents, guardians or the adult with ASD to decide if, when and how to share the diagnostic information with other people including the individual himself.

- We have suggested using language, words, terms or descriptions that are appropriate and comfortable to explain what the diagnosis means. The idea is to help others understand and explain what the diagnosis means.

- It may be unrealistic to think that because no one knows why the child or adult is different, that no one knows that he is different! People (even very young children) notice differences and draw their own conclusions. If you want them to draw the right conclusions, empower them with information and explanation.

- Using the correct "label" to begin to understand a person's needs and sharing this information may be useful, efficient and prevent misunderstanding and wasted time.

- Think about who needs to know based on the daily activities and routines the person follows. The "Circle of Friends" model may be helpful for this. Consider whether you wish to only describe the patterns of ability and need or use a diagnostic term.

- Ask, "What will help the person to understand?" Or, "What does the person need to know?" Make sense of what people see and discuss how ASD affects the person.

- Methods, materials and considerations for sharing information are shared in this chapter including sample letters and sample presentations for typical peers at school.

- One of the difficult decisions a parent faces is deciding when to explain the diagnosis to the child or teen. Watch for signs that the young person is becoming aware and wants to know more. The individual will need time to understand, believe and accept, just like anyone else. Breaking the information into "chats" over time may be a good approach to the situation.

- **Self-awareness** is having a sense of identity that includes understanding how a person is affected by his disability. **Self-advocacy** is a skill in which a person is aware of a need, states the need and asks for help. These are keys to success and independence for adults with disabilities. A person with ASD will need information to help himself.

- We suggest that positive explanations be provided to everyone with ASD over time, even if they are deemed "unable" to understand. Model appropriate words to use in thinking and talking about features of ASD.

- Professionals and staff may have excellent suggestions to help parents decide how to proceed and may know about a variety of ways to share information. Experienced parents may be willing to offer guidance and advice.

REFERENCES

Church, Catharine Critz, Ph.D., CPNP, and Coplan, James, M.D. "The High Functioning Autistic Experience: Birth to Preteen Years." Journal of Pediatric Healthcare, Volume 9, Number 1, pp. 23-29.

RESOURCES

Free booklet explaining Autism, Publication Number 97-4023 from the National Institute of Mental Health; copies mailed to any individual at no charge. Information and Inquiries Branch 5600 Fishers Lane, Room 7C-02, MSC 8030 Bethesda, MD 20892-8030 phone 301.443.4513; FAX 301-443-4279 Print online version from website at http://www.nimh.gov.

Autism Society of America booklets, *Shaping our Futures* (for educators, $2), and *Growing Up Together*, (for students, $1). For sale to members. Call 1-800-3AUTISM, extension 104, to order.

Autism Society of America, *Public Awareness of Autism in the Schools Project.* Contact at 1-800-3AUTISM, ext. 104

Amenta, Charles A. III. (1992). *Russell is Extra Special: A Book About Autism for Children.* Magination.

Brown, Tricia, and Fran Ortiz. (1995) *Someone Special, Just Like You.* Owlet Books. (For reading ages 4-8, about kids with disabilities, in general.)

Gagnon, Elisa. (1999) *This is Asperger's Syndrome.* Shawnee Mission, KS: Autism Asperger Publishing Company. (Reading ages 6-12).

Lears, Laurie, Judith Mathews, Editor. (1998) *Ian's Walk: A Story About Autism.* Albert Whitman and Co. (Reading ages 4-8).

Rogers, Fred and Jim Judkis. (2000). *Extraordinary Friends (Let's Talk About It).* Puffin (For reading ages 4-8, about kids with disabilities, in general).

McGuire, Arlene and Sheila Bailey. (2000) *Special People, Special Ways.* Arlington, TX: Future Horizons.

Miller, Nancy. (1999) *Nobody's Perfect, Everybody's Different.* Paul H. Brookes Publishing Company.

Schnurr, Rosina G., and Strachan. (1999) *Asperger's Huh? A Child's Perspective.* Shawnee Mission, KS: Autism Asperger Publishing Company.

Simmons, Karen L. (1997). *Little RainMan: Autism Through the Eyes of A Child.* Arlington TX: Future Horizons, Inc. (Also available in Spanish).

Werlin, Nancy. (1994). *Are You Alone on Purpose?* Fawcett Books

VIDEOS

Here are a few of the selections available from the Indiana Institute on Disability and Community, phone 812-855-6508, or www.iidc.indiana.edu/~cedir/autism.html

- *Autism: Being Friends.* 8-minute video recording, for young children. 1991.

- *Autism: Learning to Live.* Focus on children and young adults in the community. 1990.

- *Out of the Darkness: The Jeff Matney Story.* 12-minute video recording.

- *Finding Out What Works: Creating Environments Where All Can Learn.* Strategies for Inclusion and Success at School; for teachers and staff; includes what peers need to know.

A few selections from the Attainment Company, 1.800.327.4269, or www.attainmentcompany.com

- *Autism Spectrum Disorders.* A comprehensive view of autism from professionals.

- *Straight Talk About Autism.* Interviews with kids with autism and their parents. 41 minutes.

• *Asperger's Syndrome.* Video for staff and parents.

UCLA Family Support Community Program. Thank You For Trusting Me: A Three-Video Series about Accepting Difference and Including Everyone. Available through Special Needs Project, 1-800-333-6867 or www.specialneeds.com. Includes autism and Asperger's Syndrome. For use at home and in the classroom.

Circle of Friends: Developing friendships for children with challenging needs. Portage, WI: The Portage Project, CESA5. 18-minute videotape about a boy with autism included in a regular education class.
See www.coe.missouri.edu/~mocise/library/circle.htm.

CHAPTER 10

THEORIES OF CAUSE IN AUTISM SPECTRUM DISORDERS

One of the goals in writing this book is to objectively present information that parents and professionals "need to know" to be well informed. We are two "regular" people, like most people who have children with ASD or who teach and work with individuals with ASD and their families. We know that scientific theories and language can sound confusing and how hard it is to make sense of it all. In this chapter, technical topics are discussed in a way every reader can understand. For "just the basics," read the first few paragraphs in a section. Reading the entire section will provide more details for those inquiring minds who want to know.

What you will learn in this chapter:

- Theories about the causes of ASD.

- Areas being researched and studied.

- How the development and function of the brain relates to autism.

- Questions to ask about proposed cures and treatments.

- How to help promote research and progress.

What is the Cause of Autism Spectrum Disorders?

"What are the theories about the causes of autism and Autism Spectrum Disorders?" is a more accurate question. Many important theories are actively being researched. At this time, no conclusive scientific evidence has proven any particular theory. In the cases of most individuals who have autism, no cause or causes have been identified.

It is possible that there may be more than one cause or a combination of causes. Stephen Edelson, Ph.D., of the Center for the Study of Autism, writes, "Although there is no known unique cause of autism, there is growing evidence that autism can be caused by a variety of problems."[14]

However, it is agreed that an Autism Spectrum Disorder is not mental illness and has no psychological cause. Previous beliefs that autism is caused by the "Refrigerator Mother" or "poor parenting" have been proven untrue.[15]

Looking At the Science

Research in autism is complex. A great deal has been written about it, but it is certainly not easy material to read! At the same time, parents and professionals want to be aware of current thinking. For that reason, we have summarized some of the theories and research related to cause (also called etiology).

We have tried to use straightforward language, quotations from experts and examples to illustrate important points. In simplifying the language or explanations, there is no intention to minimize the complexity of the issues involved in autism research.

Readers are encouraged to "go to the source" for more detailed explanations or information. The materials used to prepare this chapter and references are listed at the end of the chapter. For in-depth analysis, please refer to these and other sources such as:

• Articles and studies written by researchers.

• Critiques and analysis of research by experts and authorities.

- Bibliographies of research projects.

- Websites of interest.

- Organizations that fund and advocate for research.

Sometimes the difficult language of science may sound harsh. Scientists use words that are accurate and precise, but may shock readers who do not have a background in science. Be prepared to see phrases like "insult to the brain," "damage to the central nervous system," "abnormal development," and autism as "mental illness," which are part of the scientific jargon. Looking at cells under the microscope, or even smaller components of life, the efficient language of science sometimes does not reflect that scientists are actually studying and describing people!

The majority of studies to date have used the diagnosis or criteria of "autism" for selection of participants or collection of samples or data. This chapter discusses the research and theories about "autism," because such a great proportion of the research has dealt with "autism."

The results of studies on autism are scientifically valid only about autism. However, from a common sense point-of-view, it may be useful to think that what is being learned about autism (also called Autistic Disorder) may apply to or shed light on Asperger Syndrome (AS), Pervasive Developmental Disorders (PDD), and Pervasive Developmental Disorders Not Otherwise Specified (PDD-NOS).

New information may help explain how the disorders in the autism spectrum are related to one another, while the causes of autism are being researched. Research may discover whether the Autism Spectrum Disorders are actually separate disorders with different causes, or one disorder along a spectrum of severity or intensity.

Research on causes of autism may compare with studying the causes of cancer. Observations, personal accounts and analysis of data lead scientists to form theories about what the causes could be. Systematic study then confirms some theories as more information becomes available. Continued research rules out theories that are not valid. The study of cancer has shown that there are many types of cancer, with different causes. Some people have a higher risk of developing cancer than others. The role of family inheritance and the genetics of cancer are still being investigated.

Similar methods and approaches are being used to look at autism. Scientific study and research are ongoing—building on what is known or learned. Some findings are "generally accepted," but many have not been proven conclusively. The study of autism will continue to change as new information is taken into account. Theories can be expanded, revised or discarded as more is learned and shared in many fields of science.

Become a Savvy Reader

People with a child, student or client with ASD may find themselves with an unexpected need or desire to understand the facts, science and research about autism. For most people, biology and other high school science that did not seem important in daily life may suddenly become relevant and interesting.

As parents and professionals deepen their understanding about autism and stay informed, they will want to be "savvy" readers of autism studies. Logic and critical thinking come into play as readers analyze factual reports and conflicting arguments and points of view. Readers will need healthy skepticism and critical reading skills to identify flawed or false reasoning presented as facts or truth.

You may remember learning about the theory of "spontaneous generation." When maggots were seen on rotten meat one day, and had not been there a short time before, scientists devised the theory that rotting meat "spontaneously generates" maggots. Even though the idea went against logic and most people's view of reality, some kind of an explanation was demanded and this absurd notion was believed for centuries.

Francesco Redi challenged the theory in 1668 using "controls" to test his hypothesis of where the maggots came from. He exposed some meat to air, while other meat was sealed in a jar. He proved the connection between meat exposed to air and flies that lay eggs that hatch into little creatures. Many people thought his work was inconclusive. Introduction of the microscope confused the issue, because even more "spontaneous" creatures were seen in the meat. Finally, in 1859, Louis Pasteur built upon the ideas of several scientists who preceded him, designed an excellent experiment and disproved, without a doubt, the theory of spontaneous generation.[16]

As much as we want to demand answers about autism, we must resist the urge to "believe" things that defy logic. Tremendous advances are constantly being made in science and technology, yet we may have to be patient while current beliefs, ideas and theories are put to the test, and extraordinary new facts continue to be revealed.

Of course, the average reader will not be expert enough to know if a study is flawed or a conclusion not supported. Fortunately, research in scientific fields is held to high standards and open to objective criticism from other scientists (called peer-review). A project, study or conclusion that cannot be defended will now be discredited more quickly than in the past.

Challenges to Researchers

Researchers follow protocols and design studies carefully in order to create a defensible project that produces valid conclusions. Researchers are aware of the many difficulties and variables that can affect or invalidate a study. In addition, one study is usually not enough to support a conclusion, and multiple studies need to produce the same result. Many different scientists and researchers all over the world are working on projects, trying to share information and are working to answer complex questions about autism, including the cause or causes of the disorder. An awareness of the pitfalls facing researchers may help readers become more careful consumers of information.

Here are some of the challenges and difficulties researchers may face in their studies that make it difficult to come to a definitive conclusion about the causes of autism:

- Small numbers of participants in studies or small amounts of samples studied.

- Conflicting findings; for example, increased brain mass in some people with autism, smaller brain mass in others.

- Inconsistent findings or a wide range of results in studies.

- Determining whether a discovery is an "incidental finding" or a significant finding.

- Difficulty in interpreting data.

- Variations in findings among participants: "nothing" seems true for "every" participant in a study; "some, but not all" applies to much work in autism.

- Difficulty linking "a finding" to a cause.

- Problems with validity of scientific method; weakness or errors in study designs.

- Problems matching the "control group" for age, gender and IQ, to make accurate comparisons about findings in people with autism and those without autism.

- Problems of bias or conflict of interest.

- The "placebo effect" in which participants report improvement, because they are receiving a treatment and expect to improve.

- Variation in identification or diagnosis among study participants.

- Difficulty comparing one study to another.

- Difficulty "replicating" findings: getting the same result using the same method at another time or place.

- Difficulty sharing information among researchers.

- Lack of funding or resources.

Who and What are Being Studied Where?

In different parts of the world, and even within different parts of the same country, people may use the same terms, but attach different meanings to them. The variation in use of terms and diagnostic criteria in different places can be an obstacle in collaboration between researchers. It affects which individuals are selected to be included in a study and results in difficulty comparing the conclusions of one study to another. For example, one study may be designed to include individuals with "High-Functioning Autism." The study may include or exclude people diagnosed with Asperger syndrome depending on the scientific belief and custom in that place and time. Because researchers must interpret criteria and whether the criteria fit the people being studied, there may be room for other interpretations, and researchers in other places may disagree or apply them differently.

Another example is that researchers who organized "older" studies selected participants using criteria for autistic disorder from the DSM-III (the third addition of the Diagnostic and Statistical Manual). "Newer" studies may select participants using the criteria from the DSM-IV, (the fourth edition of that manual) which are different. In such cases, researchers ask whether they can compare the results of "old" and "new" studies. When the DSM-V comes out, will the criteria for ASD be so different as to affect the selection of study participants and comparison of results?

Outstanding experts around the world are working with people with ASD and studying the disorder. No one person or organization coordinates the various projects. The resulting lack of standardization, conflicting beliefs and inconsistent duplication are an unfortunate consequence common to many fields of science. Many national and international groups are forming to encourage collaboration on research projects. One example is the International Molecular Genetic Study of Autism Consortium with scientists from many nations.

In response to the need to coordinate efforts and share information in the United States, the National Institutes of Health (NIH) established the Collaborative Program of Excellence in Autism, (CPEA). The CPEA coordinates projects and shares information between private researchers, university researchers, government agencies and the public. The National Institute of Health, part of the federal government's primary agency for biomedical and behavioral research, will provide autism research grants totaling more than $50 million dollars in 2002.[17] Grants for research create opportunities for progress relating not just to finding the cause of autism, but also to effective interventions and treatments.[18]

In 1997, the NIH also formed its own Autism Coordinating Committee (NIH/ACC), and a program to "create a nationwide network of major autism research centers." Studies to Advance Autism Research and Treatment, STAART centers, are being established in various parts of the United States to bring together expertise and resources and share the results with the public.

Private individuals and organizations have taken the initiative to lobby for more government support and public and private funding of autism research. Individuals and groups have sponsored research, established tissue banks and databases and helped families to become aware of and involved in research opportunities.

Occurrence of Autism

Epidemiological studies examine the total number of births in the general population in a year and the number of those individuals diagnosed with a disorder. The data for the year 2000 suggest that autism occurs in 1 in 500 births.Approximately 4 out of 5 of those affected are male.[19] In 1998, the Centers for Disease Control and Prevention began "surveillance" to measure the prevalence of autism, and find out how many people have autism.[20]

Measuring changes in the number of cases reported over time is another way of looking at the incidence of ASD. The number of individuals diagnosed and reported with Autism Spectrum Disorders is increasing throughout the United States, and in other countries. For example, in California, the number of people with autism being served in the Regional Center and developmental center systems more than doubled for the period 1987 to 1998.

Reports like the one in California cause great concern for many reasons. One reason is that it makes clear to people in all fifty states that there is no national system in place to actually count and keep track of the number of cases of autism and ASD. New legislation was introduced in 2002 to have a national system to determine and keep track of how many people in the United States have autism and ASD.

Dramatic increases in the number of people diagnosed and served such as those seen in California, are being investigated to determine to what degree autistic disorder is actually on the rise. People want to know whether there is more autism or if other factors have an effect in finding more cases. This includes examining to what degree the increase in cases reported in California and elsewhere is partly due to factors such as:

- **Changes in the diagnostic criteria**, such as including persons with average or above average intelligence who were not previously considered to have autism.

- **Better screening and referral** by pediatricians. There may be some relationship to the current trend of diagnosing children at an earlier age.

- **More public awareness** to help both parents and teachers recognize the signs of the disorder and seek treatment.

- **Environmental factors** in specific geographical areas.[21]

- **Misdiagnosis**: people who had a different diagnosis, such as mental retardation or emotional disturbance, getting a more accurate or dual diagnosis and being "counted" as a person with autism; and the possibility that a diagnosis of autism is given to people who don't have it.

Many professionals studying the incidence of ASD say that the factors mentioned above do not fully explain the ever-growing numbers of new cases. The California report comments, "The number of persons entering the system far exceeds the expected number determined by traditional incidence rates." The increase in the number of cases of autism spectrum disorders is so dramatic that it is called by some an "autism epidemic."[22] As the number of cases rises, public awareness is increasing. As a result, there has been increased political pressure to fund more research and determination to get some answers.

Questions That Need Answers

Much of the research and studies done by government agencies, private and public foundations and universities in the United States and in other countries focus on autism as a neurological disorder. This can be stated as "differences in the brain and central nervous system cause a person to have autism." Major questions explored in past, current and future projects are:

- What exactly are the differences in the form or function in the central nervous systems of people with autism?

- What causes the differences?

- What stages of typical development are different than what is expected?

- What influence does genetics, family history and disease have?

- What elements of the environment may cause damage?

- Do people have autism for different reasons?

The Medical Model

A widely held view is that autism (and ASD) arise from damage to the central nervous system. B.J. Freeman, Ph.D., of the University of California, Los Angeles, describes the "Medical Model" of autism:

"Autism is a heterogeneous syndrome with multiple etiologies. Currently, the view is that some factors or combinations of factors act through one or more mechanisms to produce a final common pathway of CNS [central nervous system] insult that results in the behavioral syndrome of autism."[23]

In simpler language, this means that autism may be caused in different ways in different individuals. The features of autism are viewed as the result of the damage to the central nervous system which includes the brain and spinal cord. Damage to the central nervous system may occur in different ways or for different reasons. People with autism have similarities and differences; autism is a disorder that can appear "differently." People with autism do not have every possible characteristic in common, or to the same degree, yet they still all have autism.

Most people can understand various types of visual impairment. Like the disorders of the autism spectrum, vision loss can involve a spectrum of impairment from mild to severe. Thinking about what we know about visual impairment is a good analogy for understanding the approaches to finding the cause or causes of autism. A person can be blind or visually impaired because he:

- Was born with no vision or low vision.

- Had a disease of the eye or a disease of the nerves of the eyes.

- Had an accident involving the eye or the nerves of the eyes.

- Had injury to the brain, like a stroke or an accident.

- Had an illness that resulted in visual impairment, such as diabetes.

- Lost vision due to the aging process.

- Had a chemical, toxin or foreign substance damage the eyes or optic nerves.

- Is blind for no physical reason, but for a psychological reason.

Different people have different degrees of visual impairment for different reasons. There are many credible explanations of when, why and how visual impairment occurs. Scientists in a variety of fields have explored the genetic risks and environmental factors that make a person susceptible to visual impairment.

It appears much more difficult to uncover the causes of a developmental disorder, such as autism, than a physical disorder like visual impairment. This is due to the complexity studying the development of the brain and central nervous system.

The "mechanisms," or biological factors responsible in causing autistic disorder have not yet been identified, but possibilities are being considered in a variety of projects. Various researchers work from the point of view that Autism Spectrum Disorders:

- Are present from birth and have a genetic component.

- Are caused by trauma or disease during pregnancy, birth or early childhood.

- Can occur after birth, due to environmental factors such as disease or toxins.

- Are "triggered" by an environmental factor in genetically predisposed people.[24]

In the case of Autism Spectrum Disorders, scientists are looking at individual circumstances, data and evidence to determine when, why and how autism "happens." The following sections summarize research in autism and various explanations of:

- What is known about autism from a variety of fields of science.

- Theories about the timing of the developmental differences.

- Considerations of possible damaging "agents" or "insults."

The Genetic Component

A genetic theory suggests that autism occurs in a child because of transmitted "information" contained in the deoxyribonucleic acid (DNA) inherited from the parents. DNA is genetic material inherited in the form of genes and chromosomes. Each child inherits half of her genetic information from the father and half from the mother. DNA is the blueprint of the individual that determines the traits and characteristics of an individual's development. Inherited DNA can influence or determine everything about a person's physical and mental makeup, from eye color to intelligence.

Genetic studies often focus on the occurrence of autism in twins. This is because it is thought that identical twins should have the exact same genetic information.[25] If autism were purely genetic, then logic predicts that 100% of identical twins should both have autism. This is called **concordance**.

One twin study put the concordance at 60% for identical twins both diagnosed with "autism." The percentage rose to 92% when the comparison was broadened to include the twin pairs having autism in some form.[26] Another study concluded that 95.7% of identical twins in the study both had autism in some form.[27/28] The incidence in autism in identical twins is remarkably higher than the incidence in fraternal twins.[29]

A recent study included families with two siblings (brothers or sisters) with autism. Only 166 sibling pairs enrolled. Of the 166 pairs, 30 were twin pairs. Researchers consider this "a remarkably high, statistically significant number."[30] While population statistics would lead them to expect several twin pairs, they did not expect to find so many twins with autism in a sample of 166 families.

The link between genetic makeup and incidence of autism in other family members is being explored. Data suggests, "In families with one autistic child, the risk of having a second child with the disorder is approximately five percent, or one in 20, which is greater than the risk for the general population."[31] The risk of having a second child with autism in families where one person has an autism diagnosis has also been described as 45-90 times greater than the risk to the general population.[32] Many more families today are having more than one child diagnosed on the autism spectrum than in the past. Families that have more than one family member with autism are being asked to participate in studies to find out if this is due to genetic causes or something else, such as environmental factors.

Another situation that suggests a genetic link in families is called **shadowing**. In some families where one person is diagnosed with autism, it is often noted that another family member, who might not be diagnosed with autism, may have some traits or characteristics that are part of the autism spectrum. This is called having "shadow characteristics" and may be an indicator of a genetic link.

Detailed studies of DNA and chromosomal variations are under way. It is generally agreed that there is no one gene for autism; no single gene has been identified that causes autism. Instead, the genetic factor is thought to involve a combination or interaction of multiple genes. The way in which genes that cause autism are inherited, or passed on through families is also thought to be complex and is currently unknown.[33]

Here is a brief summary of a few of the avenues pursued in genetic studies. New findings and repeated findings may provide clues in the search for the genetic underpinnings of autism. Specific findings give researchers direction in forming theories and using scientific methods to test their theories. "Small" findings, or findings that are true for individuals or small numbers of study participants must be tested to see if they hold true for a large group of people.

- **Identifying specific genes**. Five or six genes have been identified that may be related to the inheritance of autism, helping scientists "to narrow down the search to specific genes and the functions they control."[34] "Candidate genes" such as HOXA1, WNT2, and ATP10C have been considered, and current studies are intended to confirm or deny their role.[35/36] Researchers estimate that as many as 15 genes may be involved.[37]

- **Looking for "marker" genes**. Some gene differences may not cause autism but may signal that a person is likely to have autism. Scientists are searching for **marker genes** that indicate susceptibility. For example, the association of the reelin gene with autism is being investigated.

- **Narrowing down the chromosomes involved**. Genes on particular chromosomes have been identified for susceptibility to autism. Researchers are currently focusing on five particular chromosomes: 2, 3, 7, 15 and X.[38]

- **Looking at differences in chromosomes**. Specific chromosomal abnormalities in people with autism are being identified. Investigation is underway to see whether an irregularity in the order of chromosomal material, called "**sequence variants**" has bearing on the development of autism.

- **Looking at "extra" genetic material**. An extra marker chromosome, or area of **duplication** on the 15q11-q13 chromosome region, has been found in about 1% of people studied with autism.[39] Investigation is being done to see how **polymorphisms**, or repeated patterns in genes, may be significant.

- **Identifying "missing" genetic material.** Researchers identified a chromosome with "deleted segments of DNA" in a boy with autism. The 1,000 building blocks of DNA missing from the 15th chromosome may lead to investigation of whether the same material is missing in others with autism. If so, researchers want to know what affect the material has on development.[40/41/42]

- **Finding a link to existing genetic disorders.** Researchers have found evidence of a link between autism and particular single-gene disorders. Scientists know that some of the following disorders may also cause autism in a small number of individuals, perhaps 10 to 15% of those affected.[43] However, how these conditions lead to the development of autism is not known.[44] The genetic disorders include:

  — Aarskog Syndrome

  — Cornelia de Lange Syndrome

  — Down Syndrome

  — Rett Disorder

  — Fragile X Syndrome

  — Neurofibromatosis, Type 1

  — Phenylketonuria (PKU)

  — Tuberous Sclerosis

  — Hypomelanosis of Ito

  — Joubert Syndrome

  — Lujan-Fryns Syndrome

  — Moebius Syndrome

  — Neurofibromatosis

  — Williams' Syndrome

— Sotos Syndrome

— Smith-Lemli-Opitz Syndromes

— Tourette Syndrome

In an article about genetic research, Ghaziddin and Burmeister summarize the situation with the comment, "The list of chromosomes associated with autism is long; however, the extent to which any of the reported abnormalities bear a specific relationship with autism is unclear."[45] Many current studies are testing hypotheses about the involvement of specific genes and chromosomes and how genetic factors affect development.

Researchers are looking at specific types of genetic errors, such as duplications, deletions, or sequence variations in some people with autism and comparing these to others who have autism. Just as importantly, they make comparisons to people who do not have autism. Further studies are being conducted to prove whether specific theories and associations are correct.

Genetic research is promising because it is believed that if a genetic cause is identified, there is a greater chance of finding a cure. Future understanding of the complex genetic components of Autism Spectrum Disorders may make it possible to develop genetic counseling for family members. Some people hope that someday progress in genetics can lead to a genetic test for autism, gene therapies, prevention or even an eventual cure.

Genetic research is an "extremely high" research priority of the National Institute of Mental Health[46] Universities in the U.S. and other countries, along with other private and public agencies, are actively pursing the genetic link. The Brain Molecular Anatomy Project (BMAP) is under development to share information about brain development and gene activation starting with the brain of the mouse. Information will be available on the Internet at http://www.resgen.com/products/BMAP.php3.

The Human Genome Project is a public and private project to "map" the entire DNA in the human body using computers. During the year 2000, all the millions of DNA strands and their components were successfully identified. Progress being made in the Human Genome Project may provide important information to researchers in the field of autism in the not-too-distant future.

A huge government-authorized project in Iceland managed by deCODE Genetics follows both genetics, and the history of thousands of families over eleven centuries, in a huge and controversial database of medical and genealogical information. This project has already mapped a gene linked to Parkinson's disease, a degenerative disease of the nervous system.[47] There is the possibility that deCODE's project could also shed light on the discovery of the genetic component of autism.

Neurology: Understanding the Brain and Central Nervous System

Scientists who study brain development suggest that the brain and nervous system of a person with an autism spectrum disorder does not develop typically. This results in differences in the size or structure and, therefore, the functioning, of different areas of the brain. It is agreed that differences in brain and central nervous function can result in differences in thinking, learning and processing information. Many neurologists believe that the characteristics and behaviors of Autism Spectrum Disorders are the results of these differences.

The National Institute of Mental Health offers this clear explanation of typical brain growth and development:

- The brain of a fetus develops throughout pregnancy. Starting out with a few cells, the cells grow and divide until the brain contains billions of specialized cells, called **neurons** ... cells find their way to a specific area of the brain and take on special functions.

- Once in place, each neuron sends out long fibers that connect with other neurons. In this way, lines of communication are established between various areas of the brain and between the brain and the rest of the body.

- As each neuron receives a signal it releases chemicals called **neurotransmitters** which pass the signal to the next neuron. By birth, the brain has evolved into a complex organ with several distinct regions and subregions, each with a precise set of functions and responsibilities.

- Brain development does not stop at birth. The brain continues to change during the first few years of life as new neurotransmitters become activated and additional lines of communication are established. Neural networks are forming and creating a foundation for processing language, emotions, and thought.[48] New information confirms that the brain continues to grow, or remain "plastic" through the teenage years and even into adulthood.[49]

The reasons and the ways the brain develops differently in people with ASD are being examined. Professor Anthony Monaco of the Autism Consortium comments, "Currently there is no consensus amongst researchers about what is actually going wrong in the brain when a child develops autism."[50] Dr. Nancy Minshew, a Child Neurologist, summarizes a popular theory of the causative links between each level of development as follows:

10.1 AUTISM: COMPONENTS OF CAUSE

Abnormalities in Genetic Code for Brain Development

⬇

Abnormal Mechanisms of Brain Development

⬇

Structural and Functional Abnormalities of the Brain

⬇

Cognitive and Neurologic Abnormalities

⬇

Behavioral Syndrome [Autism][51]

Neurologists continue to study the brain and central nervous system to understand specific differences in the process of development, form and function in autism. Understanding these differences helps to identify and learn about the impairments in thinking, understanding, processing information, relating and communicating experienced by individuals with ASD.

Anatomy of the Brain

Problems that interfere with normal brain development affect the ability to coordinate sensory information, thoughts, feelings and actions. Even to people who are not scientists, the puzzle of autism and the symptoms associated with it appear to make some sense when looked at in light of brain function. Some of the regions of the brain that appear to be affected by autism and the things those regions are believed to regulate are described below. This information is adapted from materials from the National Institutes of Health.[52]

- **Limbic system:** The brain's center of emotion, mood, pain and pleasure. Responsible for the body's response to emotion and "affects" the expression of emotion. Regulates self-preservation, fear and rage.

- **Hippocampus:** Part of the limbic system affecting memory processing, and knowledge acquired by analysis.

- **Amygdala:** Part of the brain that regulates social and emotional response and behavior, mood, feeling and instinct. Affects sensory modalities and generalizing information from one setting to another; works with the hippocampus. Tied to the sense of smell.

- **Cerebrum:** Involved in problem solving, planning, understanding the behavior of others, and controlling impulses. The frontal lobes of the cerebrum are thought to be the seat of empathy, sympathy, and "mentalizing," or understanding the mental processes of others, all elements basic to socialization.[53]

- **Cerebellum:** Structure of the brain responsible for the "highest levels of behavioral organization and integration" and "complex cognitive processes."[54] This includes complex voluntary movement involving timing, coordination, balance and proprioception. Affects muscles used in speaking, language planning, speech, memory, sequencing, predicting, problem solving, learning and attention. This part of the brain "interacts" with other parts of the brain in a "feedback" system. It "continuously processes input from cerebral motor cortex, brain stem nuclei and sensory receptors."[55]

- **Corpus Callosum:** The area that passes information from one side (hemisphere) of the brain to the other.

Researchers have discovered physical differences in size, form or function of several parts of the brain in some people with autism.[56/57] Some findings have been discovered using post-mortem dissection (autopsy after death). Functional Magnetic Resonance Imaging (FMRI) is a technology that creates images of the brain of a living person either at rest, or patterns of energy while the brain is "working."

Studies are also under way to explain how different brain regions interact, and the interaction of brain and body in processing sensory input. These studies include the use of Positron Emission Tomography (PET), a technology that allows observation of the chemical activity in the brain while it is processing information. PET images show different colors that correspond to subtle temperature changes as the brain thinks. Single Photon Emission Computed Tomography (SPECT), is another sensitive technology that can measure activation of various regions of the brain in response to stimulation.

Research in brain form and function appears promising and is expanding. At this time, many results are preliminary and not conclusive. Important challenges in brain-based research are to have large enough sample studies, consistent findings, independent verification or replication of findings and controlled comparison to the brains of people who do not have autism. Other important goals are to establish a cause-and-effect relationship and to understand if or how a genetic component causes the brain differences.

Biochemistry of the Brain

Brain differences in people with autism may not be limited to size or form of the regions of the brain. The chemistry of the brain may be affected. This would involve "abnormalities in neural circuitry," the physical aspects of the process of sending and receiving messages between nerve cells of the brain and the central nervous system. Brain chemistry problems may affect how different regions of the brain communicate with one another and how the right side of the brain communicates with the left side of the brain.

People with ASD often have "processing problems" that may be related to their brain chemistry. Links with an electrical "circuitry" of the brain in autism is suspected because of the incidence of epileptic seizures that occur in an estimated 20 to 30% of people with autism.[58] Many people with autism are also reported to have abnormal electroencephalograms (EEGs).[59]

The circuitry problems may affect the ability to think about and understand social interactions and social cues.[60] Sensory over-stimulation and hypersensitivity may be related to biochemical aspects of the brain. "Biochemical research is showing that people with autism literally become overwhelmed by sensory input."[61]

Neurotransmitters are the "chemical messengers" responsible for passing nerve impulses in the brain and nervous system. Differences in the levels of two neurotransmitters, serotonin and dopamine, have been found in people with autism. It is possible that this difference may be related to the distortion of sensations that accompanies autism. Altered levels of the neurotransmitters epinephrine and norepinephrine have been found in subjects with autism.[62]

Some studies have discovered a reduced amount of a particular neurotransmitter, the Purkinje Neuron. The Purkinje Neuron "communicates" with the cerebellar nuclei, and affects attention, intentional motor behavior, emotional behavior and sensory systems. The Purkinje Neuron affects the activity of other neurotransmitters. People with autism may have 60 to 90% fewer Purkinje cells than people who do not have autism.[63]

Besides differences in the amounts of particular neurotransmitters, a difference in the size and density of neurons has been discovered in the brains of some people with ASD. Physical differences in nerve cells include smaller nerve fibers, fewer "branches" on the neurons, and increased cell-packing density.[64] Another difference that has been found is that the myelin sheath, or protective coating on neurons, may be compromised in individuals with autism. These findings may account for problems "sending information" in the brain.

A recent study using computerized imaging has defined differences in the brain at the cellular level. The study looked at "minicolumns" in the brain that can be compared to the computer chips in a computer. "Minicolumnar abnormalities" found in the frontal and temporal lobes of the brain showed that "cells were more numerous, smaller, less compact and had less neuropil space in the periphery" than control subjects who do not have autism.[65]

The excess of minicolumns could cause people with autism to "receive more signals" and be "overpowered by the amount of information coming into the brain." Findings like this one are exciting to scientists and to others who hope every day for breakthroughs. At the same time, new findings raise new questions and open avenues for research.[66/67]

Using a variety of methods and technology, Dr. Eric Courchesne and his colleagues have developed a theory that autism is related to unusual brain growth patterns. They draw the conclusion: "Abnormal regulation of brain growth in autism results in early overgrowth followed by abnormally slowed growth."[68]

There is evidence that the brains of people with autism have too many neurons and that the brains of people with autism do not shed off unneeded neurons as others do. As a result of having more neurons, people with autism may have greater brain mass. They may have unusual or inefficient neural pathways in the brain that affect thinking and processing of information and affect how different regions of the brain respond and interact.[69]

The theory of overgrowth of the brain in autism may be supported by the surprising findings of another scientist, Dr. Karin Nelson. With colleagues in a project of the

National Institutes of Health, the California Birth Defects Monitoring Program, and the M.I.N.D. Institute, Nelson and colleagues analyzed the umbilical cord blood samples of babies born in part of California in the 1980's, who were later diagnosed with autism or mental retardation. The researchers checked the blood samples for the presence of proteins that affect nerve growth and connection in the brain. Dr. Nelson found "strikingly higher levels of four substances crucial in nervous system development in children with autism." The proteins were not overabundant in the control group of children who did not later develop autism or mental retardation.[70/71]

The presence of the proteins may potentially be a "marker" to identify if a child is at risk for autism or mental retardation. The findings suggest that the biology of autism may be similar to that of mental retardation in a way that was not recognized before. It was not clear from the research whether the overabundant proteins were a cause or an effect of autism.

Some people interpret these findings to mean that children who will develop autism may be disposed to do so from birth. The link between overabundance of brain growth proteins and overgrowth of the brain is implied. The study presents many possibilities and will have to be put to the test, confirmed and expanded. Perhaps in the future, a screening tool can be designed using the protein markers. [72]

While neuronal and biochemical differences in the brain are documented, one of the main questions is what causes the differences. A related question is whether the neurological differences cause the disorder of autism or whether autism causes the neurological differences to occur. There is general agreement that continued study of the brain and genetics are crucial in understanding the nature and cause of Autism Spectrum Disorders.

Embryology and Autism

Embryologists are scientists who study human development before birth. Some recent findings in their field may shed new light on the timing of the problem that may cause typical development to go off course and result in ASD. Dr. Patricia M. Rodier, and her colleagues, have evidence that leads them to believe that in many cases, if not all, the problem in development occurs between *days* 20 and 24 of the pregnancy when the brain and nervous systems are just beginning to develop.

This timing is very, very early in the pregnancy when most women would not even know that they were pregnant. This early "damage" may affect development of specific nerves at that time and have secondary effects. This means that the early damage may affect the form or function of different parts of the brain in later stages of development. The team believes, but have not yet proven, that these problems may be related to variations in the gene HOXA1.[73]

Eric Courchesne, and other researchers, have documented differences in the anatomy of various areas of the brain. Courchesne theorizes that the fifth week of pregnancy may be a "window of vulnerability for autism," because the neurons of the specific affected areas are thought to be generated at the fifth week of gestation.[74]

Research and analysis by Christopher Gilberg, of the University of Goteburg, Sweden and Mary Coleman, of the Georgetown School of Medicine, examines the timing of an "insult" to the fetus to explain the difference in brain function in people with autism. Their idea is that the first trimester (three months) of pregnancy proceeds normally. This is when the parts of the body and facial features are being formed. This is thought to explain why so many children with autism are physically perfect and attractive.

The studies of Gilberg and Coleman lead them to conclude that something happens to the fetus in the second trimester that causes damage to the central nervous system. Gilberg and Coleman conclude that malformations of the cerebral cortex found in some high-functioning persons with autism and Asperger Syndrome are "due to errors, misplacements and failures of neuronal migration" that may occur in the second trimester of pregnancy when the brain is growing and developing. Normal development may be interfered with by "different noxious agents," such as "viruses, trauma, genetically triggered metabolic failure ... etc." The damaging agent may be disease, environmental or genetic. However, it is not clear how the agent causes the damage.[75]

The findings of Rodier, Courchesne, Gilberg and Coleman may not conflict. Rodier's theory of early damage followed by later affects may be consistent with the patterns of development in fifth week theorized by Courchesne and in the second trimester as described by Gilberg and Coleman. Continued study of brain differences in people with autism, and their link to the development of the embryo and fetus, may result in a definitive conclusion.

Obstetrics: Risk Factors Before, During, and After Birth

A relationship has been identified between particular events in pregnancy and birth that result in a higher risk of autism. Examples are complications like bleeding or infection in the mother or lack of oxygen to the child at birth.

However, these same events happen to many other people and do not cause autism. Why does it happen in some cases and not others? Bryna Siegel, Ph.D., of the University of California-San Francisco explains:

"A generally accepted view is that pregnancy risks that occur to a somehow vulnerable fetus may combine to produce autism. Vulnerability may be something like the presence of an abnormal gene or the lack of a particular antigen to fight off a certain type of infection the fetus might be subject to."[76]

Fetal alcohol syndrome, use of medications known to harm the fetus, infections such as rubella, herpes simplex, HIV, and cytomegalovirus have been studied as possible "toxic or noxious agents" that may result in autism when there is also genetic predisposition of the fetus.[77/78] These things may increase the risk of autism occurring, but a definite link to cause is not established. This is, in part, because of the fact that many children have been exposed to the same risk factors, but do not have autism.

In a study of 287 pregnancies that resulted in the birth of a child with autism, no single factor that occurred before, during or after the birth was discovered to be the cause. Freeman concludes, "It is now well recognized that no single pre-, peri-, or neonatal factor can account for all cases of autism and that any event that causes damage to the CNS [Central Nervous System] may also produce autism."[79]

Epidemiology: The Study of Diseases

Encephalitis, infantile spasms, toxoplasmosis and cytomegalic inclusion disease have been known to occur in children who later are diagnosed with autism. The question is whether the diseases caused autism in the affected persons. Some scientists believe that diseases such as these may cause autism by causing damage to the central nervous system. Of course, similar to the diseases of pregnancy, not every person who has encephalitis, infantile spasms, toxoplasmosis or cytomegalic inclusion develops autism. Scientists ask whether a genetic predisposition is involved and look for any other explanation of the differences among individuals.

The study of diseases not directly related to the cause of autism may be important in making progress in autism research. What scientists learn about the brain and the body from studying one disease may prove relevant and revealing to the study of other disorders. One example is the study of multiple sclerosis (MS). Myelin, the covering of the nerve fibers of the brain and the spine, is affected in MS. People with MS have been found to lack a protein that creates myelin. Stem cell research is being done to see whether someday myelin can be repaired or regenerated in people with MS.[80] The studies and progress made in this and other areas may prove of great importance to the study of ASD.

Biomedical and Environmental Theories

Many scientists suspect that problems after birth may give rise to autism. Because the brain continues to grow and develop after birth, the infant or young child may be vulnerable to noxious agents, toxins or trauma to the central nervous system that may cause ASD. Biomedical and environmental theories include possible causes of autism after birth such as autoimmunity, toxic poisoning, damage from vaccination and nutritional theories.

Biomedical and environmental theories belong in an informed and balanced discussion of the subject of cause. These theories are worth considering both for any scientific merit and because of the great variation found among people with autism. It is reasonable to think that with all the differences among people with autism, in personal development, biology and the manifestation of the disorder, there may be more than one cause, or different causes, in different people.

However, some of the biomedical and environmental theories of cause are controversial. While some people may think that there is evidence to support a theory, others find the evidence unconvincing or incomplete. Consequently, there are strong opinions in the scientific community for and against some theories. Parents and other individuals will have definite opinions about these topics!

For informational purposes, a brief discussion of biomedical and environmental theories is presented here with suggestions of other resources for in-depth understanding. We encourage readers to refer to the original sources, other authorities, and trusted medical experts for more information.

One informative resource is *Autism: An Overview and Theories on its Cause*, an internet website with topics including enzymes, hormones, amino acids, vaccinations, immune problems, allergy, nutrition and absorption, viruses and more. (This section alone prints out to about 47 pages). It also explains treatments such as chelation of heavy metals, etc. and resources for more information. http: www.healing-arts.org/children/autism-overview.htm.

What Makes a Theory Controversial?

The results of research projects are usually published in journals to be held to a standard of "peer review." This allows work to be scrutinized by scientists in the field in a type of quality review process. However, sometimes criticism or disagreement arises when research is published. As a result of the peer review process, some theories about the cause of ASD are debated or considered controversial because:

- Research results are inconclusive or inconsistent.

- Different studies looking at the same subject area have conflicting outcomes.

- An association is suggested, but no link, or cause and effect, can be proven.

- Findings of one study cannot be independently reproduced.

- The scientific method used in a study is questioned.

- Claims related to cause may be based on the experiences of a very small group of people.

- A concern or feature is looked at in children with autism, but not compared to typical children who may or may not have the same feature.

- There is not enough information to either prove or disprove a theory: this is called an "**inconclusive correlation**."

- It has been shown that a theory has limited scientific validity, but people continue to believe that it is true.

- There is a question of "biological plausibility," if or when a theory is not consistent with what is known about the functioning of the human body.[81]

- A researcher is viewed as biased when he has a vested interest in a particular outcome or works for a company or organization that does.

When faced with inconclusive or contradictory information, jumping to conclusions can be very risky. The problem with accepting an unproven theory is the potential to do harm. It may be dangerous to act on a belief that may turn out to be unfounded. It is important for parents and professionals to be critical and objective in evaluating information about causes and cures and to separate what is known and proven from what is suspected or supposed.

At the same time, there is risk in completely ignoring or discounting controversial theories until more is known. Many times in medicine and science, personal accounts, popular notions and public observations have given direction to the scientific community. One example would be suspecting and then proving that toxins in drinking water were causing illness and disease in some communities.

It is appropriate to keep an open mind, look at the facts, objectively question, explore cause-and-effect relationship and to consider all the possibilities. It is then up to the scientific community to collect evidence to prove whether a theory is valid or not.

Many projects have been done or are under way. The University of California-Davis, the M.I.N.D. Institute and the National Institute of Environmental Health Sciences are beginning a $9 million research project to specifically study the role of the environment in autism. The goal is to identify any harmful environmental substances in order to limit exposure and prevent damage. A case-controlled study of 2,000 children will be conducted, along with research projects in the immune and nervous systems.[82]

Autoimmunity

Immunity involves how the body fights disease and other foreign substances that do not belong in the body. The simplest definition of autoimmunity is the body "resisting itself." The rejection of a transplanted organ is an example of an autoimmune response. In the case of autoimmunity, the body harms healthy cells that actually belong causing dysfunction and other problems. Type 1 diabetes, multiple sclerosis and systemic lupus are autoimmune disorders that affect individual organs or the entire body.[83] The situation with regards to autism can be summarized as follows:

"Some researchers feel that autism is actually an autoimmune reaction to viruses or vaccines that are seen in genetically pre-disposed children. However, there have been no validated studies to prove this theory although there have been links documented ..."[84]

This complex subject and any link to autism are currently being researched. V.K. Singh, and his colleagues, found in a study of 33 children with autism that 19 of the children had brain auto-antibodies to myelin basic protein (anti-MBP) and auto-antibodies to neuron-axon filament protein (anti-NAFP). This means that antibodies were present in 58% of the children studied that could cause their bodies to "fight" their good brain proteins as if they were a disease. The antibodies may hinder the development of the nerve fibers in the brain specifically the myelin covering and axons (or branches) of the brain cells. This would affect the normal function of nerve impulse transmission.[85]

The relationship between antibodies to brain proteins and autism is not clear. It is not understood how or why children with autism may develop "inappropriate immune responses" to brain protein.[86]   Could it be a reaction to an overabundance of brain growth proteins at birth?[87]   Research will continue because of the belief that auto-immunity may be a critical factor in the cause of autism.

Viruses and the Measles Virus

A follow-up study by Singh was designed to determine if a virus such as measles or herpes could cause the heightened level of autoimmunity. The research team reports that their study is the first to support the hypothesis that "a virus-induced autoimmune response may play a causal role in autism."[88]

An opposing view is expressed by the American Academy of Pediatrics, which states,

> *"Even if measles virus were consistently shown to be present in intestinal specimens of children, this would not conclusively indicate that measles causes autism. It is possible that the measles virus persists in the intestines of children with autism, i.e., the measles virus in the intestine is a side effect of autism not a cause. In addition, to implicate measles virus as a cause of autism, it would be important to show that measles virus is not present in the bowel of healthy children who are of the same age as the autistic children and at the same vaccination status. Also, there is no scientific evidence to show how intestinal inflammation with measles virus would cause the chronic neurological and behavioral difficulties seen with autism."*[89]

The role of immunizations in causing autoimmunity in autism is being considered. Few studies have been done and no study has proven any link at present. One theory explores the possibility that vaccination may cause an autoimmune response in some children through the mechanism of "molecular mimicry." Molecular mimicry may result in the stimulation of harmful immune responses through a "trigger effect."[90]

The Immunization Safety Review Committee has reviewed the association between autoimmunity and vaccination and the biological mechanism of molecular mimicry and immunization. The committee concludes that no evidence exists to support such an association and that the mechanisms must be considered theoretical only. Their executive summary states,

> *"In the absence of experimental or human evidence regarding molecular mimicry or mercury-induced modification of any vaccine component to create an antigenic epitope capable of cross-reaction with self epitopes as a mechanism by which multiple immunizations under the U.S. immunization schedule could possibly influence an individual's risk of autoimmunity, the committee concludes that these mechanisms are only theoretical. The committee concludes that there is weak evidence for bystander activation, alone or in concert with self epitopes, as a mechanism by which multiple immunizations under the U.S. infant immunization schedule could possibly influence an individual's risk of autoimmunity."[91]* (For a full explanation, refer to the report.)

Mumps, Measles, and Rubella Vaccine (MMR)

Parents and professionals have heard about the possibility of a cause-and-effect relationship between the Mumps, Measles and Rubella Immunization and symptoms or diagnosis of autism in children. Some people believe that the MMR vaccination, a component of it, the timing of it, or the continued presence of viral material from the shots, is responsible for the occurrence of autism in their child or children. They consider that autism is an "immunotoxicological injury" to an otherwise normal child.

In a fact sheet, the United States Department of Health and Human Services states,

> *"Recently there has been attention focused on the theory that autistic behaviors in children seemed to occur or to worsen shortly after vaccination. At the current time, no conclusive data indicate that any vaccine increases the risk of developing autism or any other behavior disorder. Nonetheless, given the level of concern among parents and others regarding vaccines and autism, the CDC is committed to investigating this issue to the fullest extent possible using the best scientific methods available."[92]*

The possibility of a connection with immunization was suggested by Dr. Andrew Wakefield and his colleagues. Based on the incidence of autism in twelve children in London, it was hypothesized that the MMR vaccination caused bowel problems. Related nutrient absorption problems, in turn, were believed to cause autism.[93]

The Medical Research Council (MRC) in the United Kingdom assembled a panel of experts to evaluate data based on several hundred cases relating the Mumps, Measles, and Rubella (MMR) Immunization and the link to autism. The panel concluded that there was no evidence of the MMR vaccine causing autism. No cause for concern was found with the safety of the MMR Immunization.[94] Professor John Walker-Smith, the senior author of Wakefield's work, has publicly supported the safety of the MMR.[95]

In the United States, National Academy of Sciences' Institute of Medicine (IOM), formed the Immunization Safety Review Commission in fall of 2000. After examining scientific studies regarding the MMR vaccine, the committee reported, "there is no basis for implicating the MMR vaccine as a potential cause of Autism Spectrum Disorders." The IOM recommended further study to see if the MMR could be a risk factor in rare cases.[96]

A panel of experts of the American Academy of Pediatrics concluded, "The available evidence does not support the hypothesis that MMR vaccine causes autism or associated disorders or Inflammatory Bowel Disease [IBD]. The American Academy of Pediatrics recommends that immunizations be given according to schedule."[97]

Some scientists believe that there is a "**temporal relationship**" between the MMR vaccine and the onset of the characteristics of ASD. This means that they occur at about the same time. Because no cause-and-effect relationship has been established in any recent studies and investigations, the timing of the MMR and the onset of symptoms of autism are scientifically considered a coincidence.[98]

Many people do not accept this explanation. They feel sure that immunizations have harmed their children or patients. In some places, a "backlash" against the MMR vaccine is occurring. While the government and most scientists say the benefits of vaccination greatly outweigh the risks, some people are refusing to vaccinate their children with the MMR vaccine for Mumps, Measles and Rubella, because they are not confident that it is safe, or they fear that it could cause ASD.

Some medical experts fear that the actions of people who choose not to immunize their children may put the health of the public at risk. For reasons such as these[99]:

- Unvaccinated children are at risk of getting the mumps, measles and rubella and potentially serious side effects of the diseases. By the summer of 2000, deaths in children due to mumps, measles or rubella were reported in Ireland in unvaccinated children. Prior to this time, those diseases no longer threatened children's lives due to the "success" of the vaccine.

- Diseases such as mumps, measles and rubella are often "imported" from places where immunization rates are poor. While this has always happened, it was not a threat to a population that was well vaccinated. Since the diseases are contagious, unvaccinated children are at risk for an outbreak and spread of the diseases.

- Exposure of pregnant women to unvaccinated children who become ill with mumps, measles or rubella increases the risk of birth defects in unborn children. It is ironic that getting rubella while the baby is in the womb is thought to be a cause of autism in some cases,[100] yet exposure of pregnant women to rubella is preventable by safe levels of immunization.

It is crucial not to "jump to conclusions" and create panic about immunizations. Parents who are concerned should discuss the matter with their child's pediatrician or other medical experts. Parents can bring up and discuss the option of giving the Measles, Mumps and Rubella inoculations separately, although there are arguments against that option. Parents and doctors should discuss the Center for Disease Control recommendation that, "children who are moderately or severely ill at the time the shot is scheduled should usually wait until they recover before getting the MMR vaccine."[101]

New information may help parents and doctors feel more comfortable about the MMR Immunization. A large study in Denmark, published in the New England Journal of Medicine, November 2002, looked at the occurrence of autism in 440,655 children who were immunized with the MMR. Researchers compared that rate to the rate of autism in about 96,000 children who had not been immunized. The result was that the occurrence of autism was not higher in the children who had the MMR; the rate was acutally slightly higher in the children who had not been immunized. Their conclusion is, "This study provides strong evidence against the hypothesis that MMR vaccination causes autism."[102]

If the study is considered scientifically sound, it may help put the MMR controversy to rest. It will be important to get consistent results in other studies. If the study is found to be flawed, or if future studies cannot support the conclusions of the Danish study, the uncertainty will continue.

Heavy Metals

A similarity in immune, sensory, neurological, motor and behavior factors between ASD and mercury poisoning has been documented in studies. Some scientists think it is possible that:

- The symptoms of ASD may be caused by, or may actually be, mercury poisoning.

- Some exposure to mercury is from thimerosol, a preservative used in some vaccines for infants and children.

- Adverse effects of exposure to mercury occur only in some children predisposed by genetic and non-genetic factors that are not identified.[103]

A study done by the Health Research Institute and Pfeiffer Treatment Center of Naperville, Illinois, reported in November 2001, found "metal metabolism disorders of unusually high incidence and severity." They discovered that 499 of the 503 children studied with PDD, autism or Asperger Syndrome were missing a protein called metallothionein, MT. MT is used by the body to bind to toxic metals and wash them out of the body. William Walsh, senior scientist in the study, thinks that children who lack MT can develop an Autism Spectrum Disorder before age 3 because the child cannot excrete toxic metals such as mercury, and they cause damage to the brain and gut.[104]

Like any study with significant findings, the scientific validity of this study would have to be intact. The results would have to be replicated, that is, find similar results in other studies. The levels of MT may need to be compared with children who do not have autism. The results would then be interpreted to find the significance related to the cause and treatment of ASD.

The next question raised by this study is how young children would be exposed to mercury. Some question if it is in fish that contains high levels of methylmercury, either consumed by pregnant women, or small children. The possibility is being investigated.

Another potential source, called ethylmercury, was identified in thimerasol, a preservative used in the Diptheria-Tetanus-Pertussis (DPT) immunization, the hepatitis B shot, and the Hib vaccine (Haemophilus Influenza Type B).

Critics argue that the level of thimerasol used in the vaccines would be too low to cause a problem. Others believe that the amount of mercury in the preservative is clearly intolerable. As often happens in the study of autism, the question of why some children who are exposed to the same risk, such as the same amount of fish or the same amount of thimerasol, do not develop autism, while others do. The Institute of Medicine of the National Academies of Science concludes, "Current scientific evidence neither proves nor disproves a link between the mercury-containing preservative thimerosol and neurodevelopmental disorders in children."[105] This is an example of "inclusive correlation": the case is not made and the case is not disproved."

In the meantime, until science is conclusive one way or the other, it is prudent to limit the amount of certain kinds of fish eaten by pregnant women and small children, and recently the U.S. government issued a warning about this. Importantly, parents can request that only thimerosol-free immunizations be given to their children. The National Academies of Science recommends that existing supplies of vaccines containing thimerosol should not be used if an alternative is available.[106] This option should be discussed with the family's medical professional, usually the child's pediatrician. Immunizations produced in the future in the United States will no longer contain thimerasol because of these concerns.

Diet, Nutrition, and Digestion

Through the observation and experience of parents and medical professionals, some propose that ASD may be caused due to problems related to diet, such as digestion and absorption of nutrients or the inability to break down proteins in foods. More professionals are becoming interested in this possibility and research is being conducted, seeking scientific evidence and answers to support observation and beliefs. As with other possible theories of cause, there is not yet enough scientific evidence to confirm dietary or digestive causes of ASD. Dietary issues could not be considered to be the cause of autism and related disorders in all cases.

Some parents who use special diets or supplements report improvements in the features of ASD in their children. While improvements in behavior may result from dietary changes, including avoidance of some foods and supplementing with vitamins, glyconutrients or fatty acids, critics assert that this does not prove a cause-and-effect relationship between diet and autism. They believe that modifications to the diet may be a useful therapy in some cases, but are not a cure for the disorder.

It is up to parents and professionals to assess current information and make informed choices. For a detailed discussion of research and studies related to these topics, please refer to the suggested reading. Here is a brief summary of some of the topics related to diet, nutrition and digestion that parents and professionals may want to know more about:

- **Digestion and absorption.** Some medical professionals link the symptoms of autism to a lack of specific nutrients in the body, such as particular vitamins or certain fatty acids. Others think that poor nutrition is caused by difficulty absorbing vitamins, minerals and nutrients. This may be caused by enzyme deficiency or inhibition, problems with the intestines, such as inflammation or problems at the cellular level. The result in such cases is thought to be compromised functioning of the body, from the cellular level, to the immune system, to the functioning of the central nervous system and other health problems.[107]

Doctors who use nutritional approaches may order laboratory blood tests to assess the current nutritional levels of a person with autism. They may prescribe a specific dietary supplement to be given in a controlled manner. They will follow up with parent reports of improvement or worsening of symptoms.[108] However, methods can vary significantly from one practitioner to another, and some suggest there has been limited formal scientific study of the effectiveness of such treatments.[109]

- **Yeast/Antibiotics.** The overuse of antibiotics changes the natural balance of "flora" in the intestines. The imbalance, called **intestinal dysbiosis**, enables yeast and fungus to dominate and cause problems including "leaky gut."

- **"Leaky gut" in autism.** Increased permeability of the intestinal wall allows protein peptides and/or metabolites to pass into the bloodstream and pass through "the blood-brain barrier." "Once in the brain, these molecules can cause neurological problems by interfering with the neurotransmitters and the chemical and electrical functioning of the brain."[110]

- **Gluten and Casein.** Gluten is wheat and other plant proteins; casein is dairy protein. One theory is that children with autism are not able to completely break down these proteins in food. As a result, the proteins leak into the gut, undigested as molecules with opiod-like properties."[111] This causes a toxic effect, intensifying the neuroregulatory role of natural opioid peptides and disrupting the normal functioning of the central nervous system.[112] Perception, cognition, emotions, mood and behavior are thought to be affected. Several researchers are pursuing the "opioid excess" theory.[113]

Other research is aimed at trying to determine what digestive enzyme is lacking in children with autism that would contribute to poor breakdown of gluten and casein proteins. The benefit of adding digestive enzymes remains to be adequately researched.

A gluten-and-casein-free diet is intended to remove foods containing those proteins in order to reestablish optimal functioning of the central nervous system and reduce the symptoms of autism. There has been no conclusive scientific study to support its effectiveness. However, many parent testimonials have been positive.[114]

Environmental Toxins and Pollutants

Two trends have led people to suspect a link between environmental factors such as toxins pesticides and pollutants and ASD. One is the rise in the number of reported cases of autism in general. It is natural to ask, "What are we doing differently?" or, "What has changed recently in the environment?" that could be responsible for the rise.

The second trend is identifying particular places with a concentration of people with ASD. Patterns have emerged in certain towns and geographic areas with a greater reported incidence of autism than in other places. Together, these issues raise questions about what toxins or environmental substances in those areas may be triggering or causing more autism.

Brick Township, New Jersey had dramatic rises in the number of people diagnosed with autism, measured as a percentage of the population. Study and investigation was done to determine if there was an environmental factor related to causing autism. However, no toxin or pollutant was identified as the cause of autism. Other studies continue to examine the correlation between environmental factors and autism.[115]

People continue to ask why one area would have more reported cases of autism or more people receiving autism-related services than another place. It is worth questioning, observing and investigating any substantial risk posed to a particular community.

Other "coincidental" reasons for concentration or clustering of people with autism need to be considered and ruled out. Here are some situations to take into account:

- **A socioeconomic difference** may cause parents to be more educated or proactive in seeking help for their children.

- **Families "cluster" where services are known to be good** when their children have ASD; this would mean that families come from different places with their children not that the autism occurs in a specific place.

- Health and educational professionals in some localities are better at **screening and diagnosis** than professionals in other places; this may mean that more people are diagnosed.

- People who may be genetically predisposed to have children with autism may **cluster in a certain geographical area** because of their line of work, such as computers or aeroscience. One example sometimes mentioned, including by people who live there, is the Silicon Valley in California.[116]

Looking more closely at the subject of toxins and pollutants, it is important to remember that environmental studies have shown the many ways toxic chemicals affect our water and air and plant and animal life. What more fragile and vulnerable life form is there than a developing fetus or young child? Yet the connection between the toxic chemicals used in the United States each year, and increases in disorders such as autism, has not been studied in a comprehensive way until recently.

A multidisciplinary research project at the M.I.N.D. Institute at the University of California-Davis, announced in October 2001, will "study the possible role that environmental contaminants, such as pesticides, polychlorinated biphenyls (bcps) and heavy metals play in the development of autism." The study will involve 700 children with autism, matched to "control" children who do not have autism, in the first-ever "epidemiological case-controlled study." Research projects will explore how environmental exposure to contaminants could affect or alter the development of a young child; one study will examine effects of toxins specifically on the amagdala, the part of the brain thought to affect social behavior. Another study will look at the amount of toxins in the bloodstreams of children with autism compared to children who do not have autism. In addition to identifying substances that cause harm, other outcomes may include ways of preventing exposure and developing treatments for those harmed by exposure. Funding for this project from U.C.-Davis and the M.I.N.D. Institute will be supplemented by a grant from the National Institute of Environmental Health Services.[117]

Is There a Cure?

There is, at present, as much diversity of opinion regarding possible cures, as there are theories about cause. There is currently no widely accepted, scientifically proven "cure" for autism or ASD. Finding a cure is closely linked and dependent on understanding the causes of the disorder.

Scientists, parents and professionals are very anxious to find a cure. It is often the source of hope that keeps families going. The idea of a cure for Autism Spectrum Disorders can be emotionally charged. It is tempting to jump on the bandwagon of the latest trend. However, it is important to consider the safety and appropriateness of proposed cures for a person with ASD. Careful analysis of options may help avoid the heartbreak of false hope. These are complex issues, and parents and medical experts should work together to make informed choices.

There are claims of cures, based on the experiences of individuals and families, supported by personal testimonials. Proponents of some treatments claim that they lead to "recovery." However, the evidence to support these claims may be limited, particularly when they are based on a small number of subjects.

Some improvements in the behaviors of very young children are called "cures." The claim of a cure may be premature. At the age of 6 or 7, it may be too soon to measure if difficulties that typically appear at a later age will be present or not. These include cognitive deficits in higher-level thinking and learning skills and the ability to communicate with and relate to peers.

Although there is currently no proven cure, much can be done to support individuals with ASD and improve their progress, functioning, and education. Such options are considered treatments to address the characteristics of ASD, rather than cures. It is important to stay hopeful and optimistic, and there is good reason to be positive. Treatments can be very effective, especially when they are individualized to the specific needs of the person with ASD in all areas of need.

As with proposed cures, there are diverse opinions about treatments! Some are widely accepted, some are novel, and some are controversial.

Evaluating Proposed Cures or Treatments

In evaluating the sometimes confusing or conflicting information about "cures" or treatments, these key questions and any other specific questions you have must have satisfactory answers:

1. Is the treatment proven safe, for short-term effects, long-term effects and side effects? Are there longitudinal studies (over a long period) which document the effects throughout the lifespan? Have there been studies on animals (in the case of a drug or supplement to be given to the individual) that show that this substance or practice will not do any harm?

2. Is there valid scientific evidence to support the effectiveness of the treatment? Is the research methodology strong and consistent? Have the results of the study of the treatment been duplicated by other people?

3. How "independent" are the people who propose a treatment? Are the researchers biased for the method? Are the proponents making money "selling" the treatment? Do they get a financial gain for getting people to try the treatment? Does a company or agency that would profit or benefit fund their research?

4. Are there valid arguments or scientific evidence to dispute the safety or effectiveness of the treatment?

5. What do the opponents of the treatment or proposed cure say? Have you carefully considered information both for and against it? Can the proponents of the treatment put you in touch with people who have used it, some of whom had success and some of whom didn't?

6. Is the person providing the treatment licensed and/or certified? Is the treatment legal or within the law?

7.   Does the treatment produce permanent or temporary results?

8.   Does the treatment result in the alleviation of the disorder or in a lessening of symptoms? Can it possibly make anything worse? Could it cause allergic reactions?

9.   Is the course of treatment tolerable to the person? Will it be hard to endure, painful or stressful?

10. Are the costs of the treatment, in time or money, tolerable to the family? Could the treatment completely preoccupy the family and cause an imbalance in family life or financial disaster?

11. Is the treatment consistent with the person's individual needs? Is it in line with what others, the same age or developmental stage, would be expected to do?

12. What will the effects be, on the individual and on the family, if the cure is not successful? How will the family react if the treatment does not work and their hopes are dashed and their time, money or other valuable resources gone?

Cooperative Empowerment

Every reader can learn what can be done now to support a person with ASD whether it is your family member, a person in your care or you. Parents are often determined to do all they can to help the individual with ASD, themselves and the family. Professionals can share that determination to do everything possible to become well informed, cooperative and supportive of the individual and the family. Adults with autism have a personal perspective to share and can give a voice to important issues. Each person doing what he can to help contributes to the best possible outcome.

It is important to continue to hope for a proven cure in the future and support those who work towards it. Here are four important ways that everyone can help make progress towards understanding causes and finding cures for Autism Spectrum Disorders.

1. Join an advocacy organization that is working to promote public awareness and funding for research, such as the Autism Society of America (ASA) and Cure Autism Now (CAN). These organizations and others publish newsletters and have websites to help you learn more.

2. Contact your government representatives and ask them to support legislation to create and sustain research funding. Express your support, and ask your elected officials to continue funding the "Centers of Excellence" in Autism. Encourage others to do the same. The more support that is expressed the better. The "Autism Caucus" has been formed in Congress, and several members of Congress who have family members with ASD are a voice for the rest of us. Share your stories, concerns and needs with elected officials.

3. Learn about research studies that are under way. Many universities and private researchers are recruiting participants, and you may consider whether any of them are suitable to your family. The National Institutes of Heath website, ClinicalTrials.gov, lists studies that are enrolling participants. Or, you may be interested in CAN's Autism Genetic Resource Exchange (AGRE), that seeks genetic data from families who have more than one family member with autism. The Autism Society of America (ASA) Tissue Donation program is seeking brain donation after death, of people with and without autism, for research scientific studies of brain form and function.

4. Stay informed about current trends and issues in autism. Become an avid reader or spend time with people who are well-read. The Internet is full of information, that you can access for free at a public library, if you do not have access at home. Remember to be objective and be a critical thinker!

CHAPTER 10 SUMMARY

- Theories about the causes of autism and Autism Spectrum Disorders are actively being researched. So far, no conclusive evidence has proven any particular theory.

- It is likely that there is more than one cause or a combination of causes.

- Autism Spectrum Disorder is not mental illness and has no psychological cause. It is not caused by a "refrigerator Mother" or "poor parenting."

- We have summarized some of the theories and research related to cause; readers are encouraged to "go to the source" for more in-depth explanations or information.

- Researchers may discover whether the Autism Spectrum Disorders are separate disorders with different causes or one disorder along a spectrum of severity.

- The variation in use of terms and diagnostic criteria in different places can be an obstacle in collaboration between researchers.

- In the "medical model," autism is viewed as a neurological disorder, meaning that differences in the brain and central nervous system cause a person to have autism.

- The "mechanisms," or biological factors responsible in causing the disorder have not been identified, but studies try to determine when, why and how autism "happens."

- A genetic theory suggests that autism occurs in a child because of transmitted "information" in the genes and chromosomes (DNA) inherited from the parents. Studies examine the involvement of specific genes and chromosomes, and how genetic factors affect development and specific genetic errors that could relate to autism.

- Neurologists continue to study the brain and central nervous system to understand differences in the development, form and function of people with autism.

- Difference in the chemistry of the brain in autism may involve "neural circuitry" and physical aspects of the process of sending and receiving messages between nerve cells of the brain and the central nervous system. "Processing problems" may also be related to brain chemistry.

- Embryologists, who study human development before birth, are exploring how, when and why typical development may go off course and result in ASD.

- Particular events in pregnancy and birth can result in a higher risk of autism, although many children have been exposed to the same risk factors and do not have autism, and are trying to account for the number of cases.

- Epidemiologists are looking for a causal effect between known diseases and autism and are trying to account for the number of cases.

- Biomedical and environmental theories include possible causes of autism after birth such as autoimmunity, toxic poisoning, damage from vaccinations and nutritional theories.

- There is at present as much diversity of opinion regarding possible cures as there are theories about cause. There is currently no widely accepted, scientifically proven "cure" for autism or ASD. Finding a cure is closely linked to and dependent upon finding the causes of the disorder.

- It is important to continue to hope and work for a proven cure in the future. Everyone can help make progress by joining an advocacy organization, contacting congressional and state representatives, asking them to support and fund research. Families can participate in research studies, if feasible. Everyone can stay informed and be objective.

Resources

Ackerman, Lowell Ph.D. *Nutritional Intervention in Autism* 1997.

Adams, James, Ph.D. and McGinnis, Woody, M.D. *Vitamins, Minerals and Autism.* The Advocate Volume 34, No. 4, Fourth Edition 2001.

American Academy of Pediatrics. *IOM Report on Vaccines Should Reassure Parents; Children Should be Vaccinated.* News Release: October 1, 2001.

American Academy of Pediatrics Media Resource Team. *Just the Facts ... MMR Vaccine and Autism.* 2002. http://www.aap.org/mrt/factsmv.htm

Autism Genetics Cooperative. *Genetics Overview.* 2001. http://www.exploringautism.org/genetics/index.htm

Autism Genetics Cooperative. *What is Autism: Genetic Conditions Associated with Autistic Disorder.* http://www.exploringautism.org/autism/evaluation.htm

Bailey A, LeCouteur A., Gottesman I, Bolton P., Sminoff E., Yuzda E., Rutter M. *Autism as a Strongly Genetic Disorder: Evidence from a British Twin Study. Psychol Med,* 1995 Jan; 25(1): 63-77.

Bauman, Margaret and Kemper, Thomas, Editors. *Neuroanatomic Observations of the Brain in Autism. In, The Neurobiology of Autism.* Baltimore: Johns Hopkins Press, 1994.

Bernard, S., Enayati A., Redwood L., Roger H., Binstock, T. *Autism: A Novel Form of Mercury Poisoning. Medical Hypotheses,* 2001. April 56(4):462-71.

Blakeslee Sandra, *New Theories Help Explain Mysteries of Autism. The New York Times,* December 28, 1999. *Science Times,* pages 1 and 4.

Blakeslee Sandra. *A Decade of Discovery Yields a Shock About the Brain. New York Times,* January 4, 2000.

Boyar, F. et al. University of Florida College of Medicine, Gainesville and Greenwood Genetic Center, Greenwood S.C., etc. *A family with grand-maternally derived interstitial duplication of proximal 15q.* 2001.

California Health and Human Services Agency, Department of Developmental Services, *Changes in the Population of Persons with Autism and Pervasive Developmental Disorders in California's Developmental Services System: 1987 through 1998, A Report to the Legislature, March 1, 1999.* Sacramento CA: California Health and Human Services Agency, 1999.

Casanova MF, Buxhoeveden DP, Switala AE, Roy E. *Minicolumnar Pathology in Autism. Neurology* 2002 Feb 12; 58(3):428-32.

Centers for Disease Control and Prevention. *Autism Among Children,* 2000 at http://www.cdc.gov/nceh/programs/cddh/dd/ddautism.htm.

Centers for Disease Control and Prevention, *Inflammatory Bowel Disease (IBD) and Vaccines: Questions and Answers.* November 2000. http://www.cdc.gov/nip/vacsafe/concerns/autism/ibd.htm.

Cook, Edwin H. Jr. *Genetics of Autism, Mental Retardation and Developmental Disabilities Research Reviews,* Volume 4, Issue 2, 1998, Pages 113-120. (Special Autism Issue).

Courchesne, Eric. *Brainstem, Cerebellar and Limbic Neuroanatomical Abnormalities in Autism. Current Opinions in Neurobiology,* 1997. Apr; 7(2): 269-78; Corrections in 1997 Aug; 7(4): 568

Courchesne, Eric et al. *Unusual Brain Growth Patterns in Early Life in Patients with Autistic Disorder: an MRI Study. Neurology,* 2001. July 24; 57(2): 245-54.

Courchesne, Eric. Presentation at the Autism Society of Los Angeles, Pasadena, CA April 2001.

DeMyer M.K., Pontius W, Norton J.A., Barton S., Allen J., Steele R. *Parental practices and innate activity in normal, autistic, and brain-damaged infants. Journal of Childhood Schizophrenia* 1972; 2: 49-66.

Edelson Stephen M., Ph.D. *Overview of Autism*. Center for the Study of Autism, Salem Oregon. Found on the website: http://www.autism.org/overview.html.

Fombonne, Eric. *Ask the Editor*. Journal of Autism and Developmental Disorders, Volume 29, Number 4, August 1999, pp. 359-60.

Freeman, B.J. Ph.D. *The Syndrome of Autism: Update and guidelines for diagnosis*. Infants and Young Children, 1993: 6(2): 1-11.

Freeman B.J. *Autism and Pervasive Developmental Disorders* 20th Annual Review, American Academy of Child and Adolescent Psychiatry. Presented at Beverly Hills, CA June 1995.

Ghaziuddin Mohammad and Burmeister Margit. *Deletion of chromosome 2 q37 and Autism: A Distinct Subtype?* Journal of Autism and Developmental Disorders, June 1999; Volume 29, Number 3.

Gilberg Christopher, and Coleman Mary. *The Biology of the Autistic Syndromes--2nd Edition*. Clinics in Developmental Medicine No. 126; Mac Keith Press, 1992. Distributed in New York by Cambridge University Press.

Greenberg DA, Hodge SE, Sowinski J., Nicoll D. *Excess of twins among affected sibling pairs with autism: implications for the etiology of autism*. American Journal of Human Genetics, 2001 Nov; 69(5): 1062-7.

Halsey, Neal A, Hyman, Susan L, and the Conference Writing Panel. *Measles-Mumps-Rubella Vaccine and Autistic Spectrum Disorder: Report from the New Challenges in Childhood Immunizations*. Conference Convened in Oakbrook, Illinois June 12-13, 2000. http://www.aap.org/mrt/mmrv.htm

Huff, Ron Ph. D, *California Reports an Increase in Children With Autism*. California Pediatrician, Fall 1999.

Immunization Safety Review Committee. *Multiple Immunizations and Immune Dysfunction: Executive Summary* 2002.

Kallen, Ronald J. M.D. *What is Autism?* 1999.
http://www.autismbiomed.org/whatis.htm

Kelly, Marguerite. *Family Almanac*. Washington Post, November 1, 2001,
postnet.com 12-20-01.

Knights, Edwin M, M.D. *Mining Genealogy for Genomics*. Family Chronicle,
Volume 6, Number 4, March April 2002 pp. 25-26

Lewis, Lisa S. *An Experimental Intervention for Autism: Understanding and
Implementing a Gluten & Casein Free Diet*. 1194, 1997.
http://www.princeton.edu/~serge/11/gfoaj.html

London, Eric M.D., Johnson, Catherine Ph.D., Editor. *Two Candidate Genes for
Autism Identified in NAAR-Funded Research Projects. Narrative, Number 7,
Spring 2001*. http://www.naar.org/naarative7/candidategenes.htm

McGinnis, Woody, M.D. *Fatty Acids and Autism*. The Advocate Volume 34, No.
4 Fourth Edition 2001.

Mehl-Medrona, Lewis. *Effective Therapies for Autism and Other Developmental
Disorders*. Autism/Asperger's Digest Magazine, 2000.

Minshew, Nancy J. M.D. *Autism as a Disorder of Complex Information
Processing and Underdevelopment of Neocortical Systems*. The Handbook of
Neuropsychology, Volume 6, published by Elsevier Health Sciences, Reprint
Edition 1994.

McKinney, Merritt. *Brain Abnormalities Identified in Autistic Brains*. Reuters
Health, Feb 11, 2002.

National Academies. *Link Between Neurodevelopmental Disorders and
Thimerosol Remains Unclear*. Press Release, October 1, 2001

National Academies. *Infant Immunizations Not Shown to be Harmful to
Children's Immune Systems*. Press Release Feb 20, 2002.
http://www4.nationalacademies.org/news.nsf/isbn/030908381?OpenDocument

National Institute of Child Health and Human Development. *A missing piece of a chromosome could be tied to autism.* October 2001. http://www.nichd.nih.gov/publications/pubs/autism/factsheets/sub4.htm

National Institutes of Health, *Blood Markers Associated with Autism and Mental Retardation.* Press Release, April 25, 2001. http://www.nih.gov/news/pr/apr2001/ninds-25.htm;

National Institutes of Health, *NIH Funds $3.9 Million In New Grants For Autism Research.* Press Release, October 2001.

National Institutes of Health, *Reports from Special Environmental Health Issue Explore Links to Autoimmune Diseases-Diabetes, Lupus, Multiple Sclerosis and Arthritis.* Sept 1999. http://www.nih.gov/news/pr/sept99/niehs-28.htm

National Institute of Mental Health. *Autism Research at the National Institute of Mental Health: Fact Sheet.* Updated August 2001. http://www.nimh.nih.gov/publicat/autismresfact.cfm.

National Institute of Mental Health, *Brain Gene Implicated in Autism.* Press release May 17, 2001.

National Institute of Neurological Disorders and Stroke, and the National Institutes of Health. *Autism Fact Sheet* May 1999 http: www.mhsource.com/hy/autism.html.

Article by Nelson in the May 2001 Annals of Neurology. Nelson, K.B.; Grether, J.K.; Croen, L.A.; Dambrosia, J.M.; Dickens, B.F.; Jelliffe, L.L. Hansen, R.L.; Phillips, T.M. *Neuropeptides and Neurtrophins in Neonatal Blood of Children with Autism or Mental Retardation.* Annals of Neurology, May 2001, Vol 49(5), 597-606

Neuwirth, Sharon M.Ed., Autism. National Institute Mental Health. NIH Publication Number 97-4023, September 1997.

Pisani, David and Powell, Ellen. *Diagnostic Breakthrough in Autism and Mental Retardation Reported.* March of Dimes. May 3, 2000. At http://www.feat.org/scripts/wa.exe?A2=ind0005A&L=FEATNEWS&P=R1179

Recer, Paul. "Stem Cells May Restore Neurons." Associated Press, June 8, 1999.

Richard, Gail J. Ph.D., CCC-SLP. *Educational Strategies Address Pragmatic and Behavior Deficits in Autism,* by Sherry Fox, reprinted from Way/SAC News, Fall 1994.

Ritvo, ER, Freeman, BJ, Mason-Brothers A, Mo A, Ritvo AM. *Concordance for the syndrome of autism in 40 pairs of afflicted twins.* American Journal of Psychiatry 1985 Jan; 142 (1) 74-7.

Rodier, Patricia M. *Early Origins of Autism: New Research into the Causes of this Baffling Disorder Focusing on Genes That Control the Development of the Brain.* Scientific American, February 2000.

Shattock, Paul and Savery, Dawn. *Autism as A Metabolic Disorder,* 1997. Urinary Profiles of People with Autism: Possible Implications and Relevance to other Disorders. Paper Presented at the Durham Conference 1996. http://osiris.sunderland.ac.uk/autism/pshdur 96.

Satcher, David, Surgeon General of the United States. *Mental Health A Report From the Surgeon General,* December 13, 1999. http://www.surgeongeneral.gov/library/mentalhealth/chapter3/sec6.html#autism

Shoenfeld Y, and Aron-Maor A. *Vaccination and Autoimmunity- 'Vaccinosis:' A Dangerous Liaison?* Journal of Autoimmunity, 2000 Feb; 14(1): 1-10.

Siegel, Bryna. *The World of the Autistic Child Understanding and Treating Autistic Spectrum Disorders.* Oxford University Press, 1996.

Singh V.K., Warren R.P., Odell J.D., Warren W.L., Cole P. *Antibodies to myelin basic protein in children with autistic behavior.* Brain Behavior and Immunity, 1993 Mar; 7(1): 97-103.

Singh, VK, Lin SX, Yang VC. *Serological Association of Measles Virus and Human Herpesvirus-6 with Brain Autoantibodies in Autism.* Clinical Immunology and Immunopathology, 1998 Oct; 89 (1): 105-8.

Smith M., Filipek P.A., Wu C., Bocian M., Hakim S., Modahl C and Spence M.A. *Analysis of a 1-megabase deletion i9n 15q22-q23 in an autistic patient: identification of candidate genes for autism and of homologous DNA segments in 15q22-q23 and 15q11-q13.* American Journal of Medical Genetics (Neuropsychiatric Genetics), 96:765-770, 2000.

Smith, Richard. *The Discomfort of Patient Power.* BMJ Volume 324 2 March 2002 Editorial, pages 497-498.

Stuss, Donald, Gallup, Gordon G., Jr., Alexander, Michael P. *Frontal Lobes are Necessary for 'Theory of Mind.'* Brain [Journal] Vol 124, No. 2 279-286, February 2001.

Trottier G., Srivastava L., Walker C.D., *Etiology of Infantile Autism: A Review of Recent Advances in Genetic and Neurobiological Research.* Journal of Psychiatry and Neuroscience, 1999 March; 24(2): 95-6.

United States Department of Health and Human Services. *HHS on the Forefront of Autism Research* HHS Fact Sheet, November 16, 2001 http://www.hhs.gov/news/press/2001pres/01fsautism.html.

University of California Davis. *New $9 million Center at UC Davis to Study Role of Environment on Autism.* Sacramento CA: Press Release, October 21, 2001.

University of California Irvine, Press release, *Chromosome Deletions in Autistic Patient Point to Possible Genetic Links to Autism.* December 1, 2000. At http://www.newswise.com/articles/2000/12/AUTISM.UCI.html.

Walker-Smith, John. Letter in the Lancet. Volume 359, Number 9307, 23 February 2002. http://www.thelancet.com/journal/vol359/iss9307/full/llan.359.9307.correspondence.20101.1.

Reading and Websites

- Try the free *Schaefer Autism Report* (formerly the FEAT Newsletter) that finds reports on autism and related topics in the media, including research journals, on a daily basis. Provides, links or refers readers to the full article or report. Also offers calendar, reader postings and archives to search. Enroll at website http://home.sprynet.com/~schafer.

- Medline Plus: Abstracts of articles from national and international scientific journals. Searchable by subject, etc. No charge to view abstracts; actual articles can be ordered.

- National Library of Medicine: Pub Med; http://www.ncbi.nlm.nih.gov/entrez/query. Works like Medline Plus, offering free abstracts and full articles for a fee.

- Autism Society of America Online Newsletter. Complete the form at www.autism-society.org

Information about Immunizations

- U.S. Department of Health and Human Services Centers for Disease Control and Prevention.

- National Immunization Program Vaccine Information Statement; MMR (12/16/98) 42 U.S.C. 300aa-26 Phone1-800-232-2522. Website: http://www.cdc.gov/nip.

- The National Network for Immunization Information http://www.immunizationinfo.org/features/index.cfm?ID=34

- Vaccine Adverse Event Reporting System (VAERS)   1-800-822-7967

- The National Vaccine Injury Compensation Program   1-800-338-2382 http://www.hrsa.dhhs.gov/bhpr/vicp

Diet

- Lewis, Lisa S. "Special Diets for Special Kids Understanding and Implementing a Gluten and Casein Free Diet to Aid in the Treatment of Autism and Related Developmental Disorders." Arlington, TX: Future Horizons, 1998.

- Gluten Solution Foods, 1999. www.glutensolutions.com

Organizations and Contacts

[These are some that the authors are aware of, have contacted or belong to; there may be many, many more where you live. We do not wish to offend anyone by being left off the list! If you are part of a great research and advocacy organization, write and let us know for the next update of this book!]

- Association for Science in Autism Treatment (ASAT), South Hills Medical Building, Suite 201, 575 Coal Valley Road Jefferson Hills, PA 15025 Phone: 412-469-7600 Website: http://autism-treatment.org

- Autism Research Institute ARI, 4182 Adams Avenue San Diego CA 92116 FAX 619-563-6840 Website: http://www.autismresearchinstitute.com.

- Autism Society of America 7910 Woodmont Avenue, Suite 650, Bethesda, MD 20814, Phone 800-328-8476, or 1-800-3AUTISM.
Website: http://www.autism-society.org

- Center for the Study of Autism, P.O. Box 4538 Salem OR 97005 Phone/FAX 503-363-9110 Website: http://www.autism.org.

- Cure Autism Now Foundation (CAN), 5225 Wilshire Blvd., Los Angeles, CA 90036, Phone 323-549-0500 1.888.8AUTISM
Website: http://www.canfoundation.org

- Defeat Autism Now (DAN)

- The Doug Flutie, Jr. Foundation for Autism P.O. Box 767, 233 Cochituate Rd., 2nd floor, Framingham MA 01701 Phone 1-866-3AUTISM (toll free in the U.S.) 508-270-855 Fax 508-270-6868 Affiliated with WebED at http://www.WebED.com/autism, for online autism courses.

- Families for Early Autism Treatment. (FEAT)http://www.feat.org

- Future Horizons, Inc. http://FutureHorizons-autism.com

- MIND Institute: Medical Investigation of Neurodevelopmental Disorders at the University of California, Davis http://www.mindinstitute.ucdmc.ucdavis.edu

- National Alliance for Autism Research, 414 Wall Street, Research Park Princeton, NJ 08540 Phone 888-777-NAAR or 609-430-9160 Website: http://www.naar.org

- Website on genetic information: http://www.exploringautism.org

- National Autism Hotline C/O Autism Services Center, P.O. Box 507, 605 Ninth Street, Prichard Building Huntington, West Virginia 25710-0507 304-525-8014

- National Institute of Mental Health 5600 Fishers Lane, Room 7C-02, MSC8030 Bethesda, Maryland 20892-8030; Phone 301.443.4513 http://www.nimh.nih.gov. Request or download the booklet, Autism, free of charge NIH publication 97-4023.

- National Institute of Child Health and Human Development Building 31, Room 2A32, Bethesda, Maryland 20892-2350, Phone 301.496.5133.

- National Institute of Neurological Disorders and Stroke (NINDS)Office of Scientific and Health Reports, P.O. Box 5801, Bethesda, Maryland 20824 Phone 301-496-5751 or 800-352-9424.

ENDNOTES

[1]Rasking, M.H., Goldberg, R.J.; Higgens, E.L. &Herman, K.L. (2003). Life success for children with learning disabilities: A parent guide. Pasadena, CA: Frostig Center. Available online http://www.frostig.org/LDsuccess

[2]Klin, Volkmar and Sparrow, *Asperger's Syndrome*, 1999.

[3]Reprinted with Permission from the Diagnostic and Statistical Manual of Mental Disorders, 4th Edition, Text Revision ©2000, American Psychiatric Association.

[4]Reprinted with Permission from the Diagnostic and Statistical Manual of Mental Disorders, 4th Edition, Text Revision ©2000, American Psychiatric Association.

[5]Reprinted with Permission from the Diagnostic and Statistical Manual of Mental Disorders, 4th Edition, Text Revision ©2000, American Psychiatric Association.

[6]Donnelly and Smith, 1996.

[7]Klin, Volkmar and Sparrow, 1999 p.430, *Asperger's Syndrome*

[8]The National Attention Deficit Disorder Association. "Guiding Principals for the Diagnosis and Treatment of Attention Deficit Hyperactivity Disorder." 2000. Found on the organization website at http://www.add.org/gp98.htm.

[9]Reprinted with Permission from the Diagnostic and Statistical Manual of Mental Disorders, 4th Edition, Text Revision ©2000, American Psychiatric Association.

[10]COPAA, The Council of Parent Advocates and Attorneys "Child Find Requirements Under IDEA" http://www.copaa.net/

[11]IDEA Law, Subpart B 300.125, Regulations from the Federal Register" Child find." Once source to read this part of IDEA is http://www.ideapractices.org/law/regulations/searchregs/300subpartB/Bsec300.125.php

[12]Waterman, National Information Center for Children and Youth with Disabilities.

[13]Letter from the William S. Hart Union School District to Parents, October, 2002.

[14]"Overview of Autism" copyright Stephen M. Edelson, Ph.D., Center for the Study of Autism, Salem Oregon. Found on the website: http://www.autism.org/overview.html

[15]DeMyer MK, Pontius W, Norton JA, Barton S, Allen J, Steele R. "Parental practices and innate activity in normal, autistic, and brain-damaged infants. Journal of Childhood Schizophrenia 1972; 2: 49-66

[16]Russell Levine and Chris Evers; "The Slow Death of Spontaneous Generation (1668-1859) by the National Health Museum, Access Excellence; http://www.accessexcellence.org/AB/BC/Spontaneous_Generation.html

[17]National Institutes of Health, "NIH Funds $3.9 Million In New Grants For Autism Research." Press Release, October 2001.

[18]National Institute of Mental Health. "Autism Research at the National Institute of Mental Health: Fact Sheet." Updated August 2001. http://www.nimh.nih.gov/publicat/autismresfact.cfm

[19]Centers for Disease Control and Prevention "Autism Among Children," as of March 2000 at http://www.cdc.gov/nceh/programs/cddh/dd/ddautism.htm

[20]United States Department of Health and Human Services. "HHS on the Forefront of Autism Research." November 16, 2001 http://www.os.dhhs.gov/news/press/2001pres/01fsautism.html

[21]Huff, Ron Ph. D, "California Reports an Increase in Children With Autism." California Pediatrician, Fall 1999.

[22]California Health and Human Services Agency, Department of Developmental Services "Changes in the Population of Persons with Autism and Pervasive Developmental Disorders in California's Developmental Services System: 1987

through 1998 A Report to the Legislature, March 1, 1999." Sacramento CA: California Health and Human Services Agency, 1999.

[23]B.J. Freeman "Autism and Pervasive Developmental Disorders" 20th Annual Review, American Academy of Child and Adolescent Psychiatry. Presented at Beverly Hills, CA June 22, 1995.

[24]Trottier G, Srivastava L, Walker CD. "Etiology of Infantile Autism: A Review of Recent Advances in Genetic and Neurobiological Research." In The Journal of Psychiatry and Neuroscience 1999 March; 24(2): 95-6.

[25]Perhaps identical twins do not have the exact same DNA. Identical twins have different fingerprints and irises of the eye; can these differences be explained as some genetic difference?

[26]Bailey A, LeCouteur A, Gottesman I, Bolton P., Sminoff E., Yuzda E., Rutter M. "Autism as a Strongly Genetic Disorder: Evidence from a British Twin Study. Psychol Med 1995 Jan; 25 (1): 63-77.

[27]Ritvo, ER, Freeman, BJ, Mason-Brothers A, Mo A, Ritvo AM. "Concordance for the syndrome of autism in 40 pairs of afflicted twins." American Journal of Psychiatry 1985 Jan; 142 (1) 74-7.

[28]"A look at the genetics of autism." http://www.dna.com
Also, B.J. Freeman "Autism and Pervasive Developmental Disorders" (20th Annual Review, American Academy of Child and Adolescent Psychiatry.) Presented at Beverly Hills, CA June 22, 1995.

[29]Cook, Edwin H. Jr. "Genetics of Autism" in Mental Retardation and Developmental Disabilities Research Reviews, Volume 4, Issue 2, 1998, Pages 113-120. (Special Autism Issue).

[30]Greenberg DA, Hodge SE, Sowinski J., Nicoll D. "Excess of twins among affected sibling pairs with autism: implications for the etiology of autism." American Journal of Human Genetics 2001 Nov;69 (5): 1062-7.

[31]"Autism Fact Sheet" http: www.mhsource.com/hy/autism.html May 1999 from information provided by the National Institute of Neurological Disorders and Stroke, and the National Institutes of Health.

[32]Cook

[33]Kallen, Ronald J, M.D. What is Autism? 1999. http://www.autism-biomed.org/whatis.htm

[34]Monko 2001

[35]National Institutes of Health December 2000, in Teratology) (NIMH, May 2001 described in the American Journal of Medical Genetics, May 2001, American Journal of Medical Genetics, 2002, etc.

[36]National Institutes of Mental Health, "Brain Gene Implicated in Autism." Press release May 17, 2001.

[37]London, Eric M.D., Johnson, Catherine Ph.D., editor. "Two Candidate Genes for Autism Identified in NAAR-Funded Research Projects. Narrative, Number 7, Spring 2001. http;//www.naar.org/naarative7/candidategenes.htm

[38]Autism Genetics Cooperative. Genetics Overview.2001. http://www.exploringautism.org/genetics/index.htm

[39]Boyar, F. et al. University of Florida College of Medicine, Gainesville. "A family with grand-maternally derived interstitial duplication of proximal 15q."2001.

[40]M.Smith, P.A. Filipek, C. Wu et al. "Analysis of a 1-megabase deletion in 15q22-q23 in an autistic patient: identification of candidate genes for autism..." American Journal of Medical Genetics (Neuropsychiatric Genetics) 96:765-770, 2000.

[41]National Institute of Child Health and Human Development. "A Missing Piece of a Chromosome Could Be Tied to Autism." October 2001

[42]University of California Irvine. "Chromosome Deletions in Autistic Patient Point to Possible Genetic Links to Autism. December 2000.

[43] Gilberg and Coleman, The Biology of the Autistic Syndromes. Second Edition. New York: Cambridge University Press, 1992.

[44]"A Look at the Genetics of Autism." http://www.dna.com

[45]Mohammad Ghaziuddin and Margit Burmeister "Deletion of chromosome 2 q37 and Autism: A Distinct Subtype?" In Journal of Autism and Developmental Disorders, June 1999; Volume 29, Number 3.

[46]National Institute of Mental Health, 1998.

[47]Knights, Edwin M. M.D. "Mining Genealogy for Genomics." Family Chronicle, Volume 6, Number 4, March April 2002 PP 25-26

[48]National Institute of Mental Health/National Insitutes of Health. Autism. Publication Number 97-4023, September 1997. P.22.

[49]Blakeslee Sandra. "A Decade of Discovery Yields a Shock About the Brain." New York Times, January 4, 2000.

[50]Monaco

[51]Nancy J. Minshew, M.D. "Autism as a Disorder of Complex Information Processing and Underdevelopment of Neocortical Systems." The Handbook of Neuropsychology, Volume 6, published by Elsevier Health Sciences, Reprint Edition 1994.

[52]Sharon Neuwirth, M.Ed.,
National Institute Mental Health. NIH Publication Number 97-4023, September 1997, page 23.

[53]Stuss, Donald, Gallup, Gordon G., Jr., Alexander, Michael P. "Frontal Lobes are Necessary for 'Theory of Mind.'" Brain [Journal] Vol 124, No. 2 279-286, February 2001

[54]The Neurobiology of Autism, edited by Margaret L. Bauman, M.D., and Thomas L. Kemper, M.D. Baltimore: Johns Hopkins University Press, 1996

[55]The Neurobiology of Autism, edited by Margaret L. Bauman, M.D., and Thomas L. Kemper, M.D. Baltimore: Johns Hopkins University Press, 1996

[56]Courchesne, Eric. "Brainstem, Cerebellar, and Limbic Neuroanatomical Abnormalities in Autism." Current Opinions in Neurobiology 1997 Aut; 7(4): 269-78

[57]For example, a recent study has documented that some sub regions of the corpus Callosum are smaller in twenty-two individuals with autism, compared to the twenty-two individuals in the control group. The size difference is consistent with frontal lobe dysfunction that is seen in autism. October 2000. Department of Psychiatry, Western Psychiatric Institute and Clinic, University of Pittsburgh School of Medicine, Pittsburgh, PA 15213

[58]"Autism Fact Sheet." www.mhsource.com/hy/autism.html May 1999 from information provided by the National Institute of Neurological Disorders and Stroke, and the National Institutes of Health.

[59]Trottier G, Srivastava L, Walker CD. "Etiology of Infantile Autism: A Review of Recent Advances in Genetic and Neurobiological Research." In The Journal of Psychiatry and Neuroscience 1999 March; 24(2): 95-6.

[60]David Satcher, Surgeon General of the United States. "Mental Health A Report From the Surgeon General" December 1999. Reprinted on the website http://www.surgeongeneral.gov/library/mentalhealth/chapter3/sec6.html#autism

[61]Gail J. Richard, Ph.D., CCC-SLP in "Educational Strategies Address Pragmatic and Behavior Deficits in Autism" by Sherry Fox, reprinted from Way/SAC News, Fall 1994

[62]Sharon Neuwirth, M.Ed., Autism. National Institute Mental Health. NIH Publication Number 97-4023, September 1997, p.25

[63]"New Theories Help Explain Mysteries of Autism" by Sandra Blakeslee. The New York Times, Tuesday December 28, 1999; detail from the graphic by Steve Duenes.

[64]Bauman, Margaret and Kemper, Thomas, Editors. "Neuroanatomic Observations of the Brain in Autism." In The Neurobiology of Autism. Baltimore: Johns Hopkins Press, 1994.

[65]Casanova MF, Buxhoeveden DP, Switala AE, Roy E. "Minicolumnar Pathology in Autism." Neurology 2002 Feb 12; 58(3): 428-32.

[66]McKinney, Merritt. "Brain Abnormalities Identified in Autistic Brains." Reuters Health, Feb 11, 2002.

[67]Casanova MF, Buxhoeveden DP, Switala AE, Roy E. "Minicolumnar Pathology in Autism." Neurology 2002 Feb 12; 58(3): 428-32.

[68]Courchesne, Eric et al. "Unusual brain growth patterns in early life in patients with autistic disorder: an MRI study." Neurology 2001 July 24; 57(2): 245-54.

[69]Courchesne, Eric. Presentation at the Autism Society of Los Angeles, Pasadena, CA April 2001.

[70]Pisani, David and Powell, Ellen. "Diagnostic Breakthrough in Autism and Mental Retardation Reported." March of Dimes. May 3, 2000. At http://www.feat.org/scripts/wa.exe?A2=ind0005A&L=FEATNEWS&P=R1179

[71]National Institutes of Health, "Blood Markers Associated with Autism and Mental Retardation." Press Release, April 25, 2001. http://www.nih.gov/news/pr/apr2001/ninds-25.htm;

[72]Article by Nelson in the May 2001 Annals of Neurology.

[73]Early Origins of Autism New Research into the causes of this baffling disorder if focusing on genes that control the development of the Patricia M. Rodier, Scientific American, February 2000; pp 56-63.

[74]Courchesne, Eric. "Brainstem, Cerebellar and Limbic Neuroanatomical Abnormalities in Autism." Current Opinions in Neurobiology 1997 Apr; 7(2): 269-78; Corrections in 1997 Aug; 7(4): 568.

[75]The Biology of the Autistic Syndromes--2nd Edition by Christopher Gilberg, and Mary Coleman (Clinics in Developmental Medicine No. 126; Mac Keith Press 1992. Distributed New York by Cambridge University Press). pp 304-5.

[76]Siegel, Bryna. The World of the Autistic Child Understanding and Treating Autistic Spectrum Disorders. Oxford University Press, 1996. Page 93.

[77]David Satcher, Surgeon General of the United States. "Mental Health A Report From the Surgeon General" December 1999. Reprinted on the website http://www.surgeongeneral.gov/library/mentalhealth/chapter3/sec6.html#autism

[78]Christopher Gilberg and Mary Coleman, The Biology of the Autistic Syndromes, p.219.

[79]Freeman, B.J. Ph.D. "The Syndrome of Autism: Update and guidelines for diagnosis." Inf Young Children 1993: 6(2): 1-11.

[80]Recer, Paul. "Stem Cells May Restore Neurons." Associated Press, June 8, 1999.

[81]Immunization Safety Review Committee. "Multiple Immunizations and Immune Dysfunction: "Executive Summary" 2002.

[82]University of California Davis. "New $9 million Center at UC Davis to Study Role of Environment on Autism." Sacramento CA: Press Release, October 21, 2001.

[83]National Institutes of Health, "Reports from Special Environmental Health Issue Explore Links to Autoimmune Diseases-Diabetes, Lupus, Multiple Sclerosis and Arthritis. Sept 1999. http://www.nih.gov/news/pr/sept99/niehs-28.htm

[84]Ackerman, Lowell Ph.D. "Nutritional Intervention in Autism" 1997

[85]Singh VK, Warren RP, Odell JD, Warren WL, Cole P. "Antibodies to myelin basic protein in children with autistic behavior." Brain Behavior Immune 1993 Mar; 7(1): 97-103

[86]Mehl-Madrona, Lewis M.D., Ph.D., "The Autoimmune Theories" Center for Complementary Medicine. From the website at http://www.healing-arts.org/children. (Technical language).

[87]Iland, Emily. March 9, 2002. A non-scientist's logical synthesis of expert opinion. If there is an overabundance of specific brain proteins at birth, does the body react as if the proteins were a disease? Does the body eventually create antibodies to fight the protein, setting off an autoimmune response, and resulting in the observed elevated levels of auto-antibodies to myelin and brain protein? Is this not consistent with Courchesne's theory of overgrowth of the brain, first caused by too much brain protein, like a disease running its course, and then abnormally slow development by the time the auto-antibodies are produced and the body "stops" the growth. Does the autoimmune response take over and continues to attack and degrade brain proteins and myelin?

[88]Singh, VK, Lin SX, Yang VC. "Serological Association of Measles Virus and Human Herpesvirus-6 with Brain Autoantibodies in Autism." Clinical Immunology and Immunopathology 1998 Oct; 89 (1): 105-8

[89]American Academy of Pediatrics Media Resource Team. "Just the Facts...MMR Vaccine and Autism."http://www.aap.org/mrt/factsmv.htm 2002.

[90](Shoenfeld Y and Aron-Maor A. 2000). Vaccination and Autoimmunity See Page 419

[91]Immunization Safety Review Committee. "Multiple Immunizations and Immune Dysfunction: "Executive Summary" 2002.

[92]United States Department of Health and Human Services. "HHS on the Forefront of Autism Research." November 16, 2001 http://www.os.dhhs.gov/news/press/2001pres/01fsautism.html

[93]Eric Fombonne, Ask the Editor, in Journal of Autism and Developmental Disorders, Volume 29, Number 4, August 1999, pp 359-50.

[94]Charles G. Prober, M.D. "Evidence Shows Genetics, Not MMR Vaccine, Determines Autism." American Academy of Pediatrics News, December 1999. Autism Biomedical Information Network. http://www.autism-biomed.org/aapnews1.htm.

[95]Walker-Smith, John. Letter in the Lancet. Volume 359, Number 9307, 23 February 2002.
http://www.thelancet.com/journal/vol359/iss9307/full/llan.359.9307.correspondence.20101.1 (Pediatrics 2001).

[96]Immunization Safety Review Committee. "Multiple Immunizations and Immune Dysfunction: "Executive Summary" 2002.

[97]American Academy of Pediatrics. "News Release: IOM Report on Vaccines Should Reassure Parents; Children Should be Vaccinated." October 1, 2001.

[98](Fombonne 1999).

[99]Smith, Richard. "The Discomfort of Patient Power." BMJ Volume 324 2 March 2002 Editorial, pages 497-498.

[100]" Halsey, Neal A, Hyman, Susan L, and the Conference Writing Panel. Measles-Mumps-Rubella Vaccine and Autistic Spectrum Disorder: Report from the New Challenges in Childhood Immunizations Conference Convened in Oakbrook, Illinois June 12-13, 2000." http://www.aap.org/mrt/mmrv.htm

[101]Measles Mumps and Rubella Vaccines, What You Need to Know. Vaccine Information Statement, MMR (12/16/98) 42 U.S. C. 300aa-26. Centers for Disease Control. U.S. Department of Health and Human Services.

[102]Meldgaard Madsen, Kreesten; Hviid ,Anders;Vestergaard, Mogens; Schendel, Diana; Wohlfahrt, Jan; Thorsen, Poul; Olsen, Jorn; Melbye, Mads. "A Population-Based Study of Measles, Mumps and Rubella Vaccine and Autism.." The New England Journal of Medicine Volume 347, Number 19 , pp.1477-1482. November 7, 2002.

103Bernard, S., Enayati A., Redwood L., Roger H., Binstock, T. "Autism: A Novel Form of Mercury Poisoning." Medical Hypotheses 2001. April 56(4): 462-71.

104Kelly, Marguerite. "Family Almanac." Washington Post, November 1, 2001, postnet.com 12-20-01. National Academies of Sciences "Link Between Neurodevelopmental Disorders and Thimerosol Remains Unclear." Press Release, October 1, 2001.

105National Academies of Sciences "Link Between Neurodevelopmental Disorders and Thimerosol Remains Unclear." Press Release, October 1, 2001.

106

107Adams, James, Ph. D. and McGinnis, Woody, M.D. "Vitamins, Minerals and Autism." The Advocate Volume 34, No. 4 Fourth Edition 2001.

108Rimland

109McGinnis, Woody, M.D. "Fatty Acids and Autism." The Advocate Volume 34, No. 4 Fourth Edition 2001.

110Wobus, J.M. "Autism FAQ: Theories and Causes" http://web.syr.edu/~jmwobus/autism/autismfaq-theo.html

111Mehl-Medrona, Lewis. "Effective Therapies for Autism and Other Developmental Disorders." Autism/Asperger's Digest Magazine, 2000.

112Lewis, Lisa S. Ph. D. "The Scoop on Dairy & Grains" The Advocate Volume 34, No. 4 Fourth Edition 2001.

113Shattock, Paul and Savery, Dawn. "Autism as A Metabolic Disorder" 1997.

114Lewis, Lisa S. "An Experimental Intervention for Autism: Understanding and Implementing and Gluten & Casein Free Diet. 1997.

115Center for Disease Control and Prevention. "Prevalence of Autism in Brick Township, New Jersey, 1998 Community Report." April 2000.

[116]Steve Silberman"The Geek Syndrome." Wired Magazine, December 2001.

[117]University of California Davis Health System. " New $9 million Center at UC Davis to Study Role of the Environment in Autism." October 2001.

INDEX

A

B

C

D

E

H

I

J/K

L

M

N

O

Q

R

S

T

U